THE INTELLECTUAL ORIGINS OF AMERICAN SLAVERY

The Intellectual Origins *of* American Slavery

English Ideas in the Early Modern Atlantic World

JOHN SAMUEL HARPHAM

Harvard University Press
CAMBRIDGE, MASSACHUSETTS · LONDON, ENGLAND · 2025

Printed in the United States of America
Second printing

EU GPSR Authorised Representative LOGOS EUROPE,
9 rue Nicolas Poussin, 17000, LA ROCHELLE, France
E-mail: Contact@logoseurope.eu

Library of Congress Cataloging-in-Publication Data
Names: Harpham, John Samuel, author.
Title: The intellectual origins of American slavery : English ideas in the early modern Atlantic world / John Samuel Harpham.
Description: Cambridge, Massachusetts ; London, England : Harvard University Press, 2025. | Includes bibliographical references and index.
Identifiers: LCCN 2025000594 (print) | LCCN 2025000595 (ebook) | ISBN 9780674278370 (cloth) | ISBN 9780674301917 (epub) | ISBN 9780674301924 (pdf)
Subjects: LCSH: Slavery—Philosophy—History. | Slavery—United States—History. | Transatlantic slave trade—History. | Race—Philosophy—History. | Slavery—Economic aspects —History. | Slave traders—England—History.
Classification: LCC HT867 .H26 2025 (print) | LCC HT867 (ebook) | DDC 306.3/6201—dc23/eng/20250331
LC record available at https://lccn.loc.gov/2025000594
LC ebook record available at https://lccn.loc.gov/2025000595

To my mother and my father, with love

CONTENTS

THE INTELLECTUAL ORIGINS OF AMERICAN SLAVERY

Prologue

THIS BOOK has been personal for me. I was born and raised in New Orleans, Louisiana, the center of the antebellum domestic slave trade. Until I moved to Cambridge, Massachusetts, for graduate school, I had never lived outside of the American South. As an undergraduate, I studied European intellectual history and, in graduate school, pursued what was at the time a standard education in the history of political ideas. In part as a result, when it came time to start my career as a scholar, I did not know much about the history of slavery. This seemed wrong to me: I sensed that the texts in which I had been immersed did not fully explain the nation in which I lived. And so I set out to learn what I could about the history and memory of American slavery.

Over time, I realized that at the root of my interest in slavery was an effort to answer a question. I wanted to know how what we now consider perhaps the most terrible wrong in the history of the nation came to be seen not only as necessary or profitable but as right from a moral point of view. And I was haunted, too, by the need to answer a more direct question. I needed to know what moral account I would have given of myself if I had been raised where I was raised but had been born two hundred years before. The list of southerners from that time who were convinced that slavery was an evil was too short to ease a troubled mind.

At first I framed my research as a response to these paired lines of inquiry. My topic was the antebellum proslavery argument from 1831 to 1860. The more I learned about this awful chapter in American intellectual history, however, the clearer it became that I needed to find a new project. As I waded through the shifting definitions, endless digressions, and misquoted authorities in the texts that had been presented in defense of slavery, I could not help but suspect that these were all so many tactics used to cover up truths that their authors must have known but were powerfully motivated to conceal. These authors had developed a body of thought in which thought was not at the heart. At the least, I came to the conclusion that a project could only go so far if the author held its subjects in contempt.

There was one aspect of the American proslavery argument that did prompt me to further inquiry. That was the surprise expressed by a number of antebellum writers that they would need to defend the practice of slavery at all, since it seemed to them to be an ancient tradition handed down from the remote past. I started to follow their often inexact references back in time to explore the history of slavery in Western culture.

As I studied the cultural background against which American slavery began, I found that my attention was drawn to origins in general. I realized that in order to understand how American slavery began, I would have to understand the English culture from which in some complex sense it had developed. I studied how English authors had tended to account for the first appearance of slavery in the world, what they described as the most common routes into slavery, and what they believed to have caused certain critical shifts in the practice of slavery over time. I read all I could about the Caribbean colonies that were the earliest slave societies in the English Atlantic world. And my attention was drawn from there back to Africa, where the English had sailed to purchase so many of the persons whom they then pressed into service in their colonies across the ocean. I read the narratives that described how persons in Africa were sold along the western coast to merchants from Europe, and I worked to trace the lives of such persons back to the moments at which they had been enslaved.

The texts that I searched out in order to understand these issues came from what we now tend to treat as an array of different genres. They were travel narratives and descriptions of the world, atlases and maps, manuals for travelers and official correspondence, law codes and guides for global commerce, medical manuals and scientific inquiries, popular sermons and theological treatises, biblical genealogies and etymological dictionaries, histories of the world and compendia of classical wisdom, works of drama and literature, poems and serial periodicals, and philosophical reflections on politics and more.

In this period, when research was still a form of exploration, my method was simple. Since for the most part I worked backward in time, I would follow the notes and references in a text back to their sources and then work from those sources back to theirs. In scholarship on the context of ideas in which American slavery began, there was a small set of texts and characters and events that had come to be seen as essential. But the area that I had started to explore was much vaster and more complex. That small set of events and characters and texts was surrounded by many more of each one, and I came to believe that one could only make sense of them all if one attempted to make sense of them together. It became clear that I would need to expand the sources upon which I drew for the narrative that I now started to imagine. Of course all of the standard sources would appear. But they would be treated as no more important than they had been at the time. Perhaps their role in my account would be as the sources that most fully absorbed and also reflected the contexts around them. And at a certain point I realized that what I had found was not simply a collection of sources and texts but an entire context within which these cohered.

The first feature of this context that stood out to me was that I was now concerned with a much earlier period in time than I had ever expected to be the case. The focus of my account was the period from 1550 to 1700. To be sure, I worried about the familiar problem with the search for the origins of historical events. I was aware that to some extent it might be an illusion to think that these did not in each case extend without end into the past. As a matter of fact, one essential theme of my work as it developed was the intimate relationship between the ideas of the period that was my focus and those that had preceded it. I wanted to define the terms of this relationship with precision. Above all, I wanted to know to what extent the ideas that English authors had about freedom and slavery were drawn from those that they took to have been current across the cultures of the ancient world. I was fascinated with the deep cultural roots of early-modern ideas.

That said, since the book would have to begin at some point, there was good reason to start an account of the origins of American slavery in the middle of the sixteenth century. It was around this time that the peoples of Africa became much more an object of interest in England than they ever had been before. By far the most detailed accounts of Africa ever to become well known in England started to circulate in a series of books that were printed both in Latin and in English. The first printed map of Africa that was based upon the reports of modern travelers came out around this time as well. The regular English commerce with the western coast of Africa started in 1553. In 1554, on the return from the second English voyage to the region that was then known as Guinea, the crew took with them either four or five persons—on this point, the record is unclear—whom they referred to as slaves. Already the English trade in enslaved persons from Africa can be said to have begun.

It was around this time, too, that English authors came to articulate the conviction that theirs was a nation that was dedicated to freedom. The distinctive English tension so much remarked upon later in the eighteenth century—that a nation that plumed itself upon its own special relation to liberty would be so eager to hold and trade some persons as slaves—can also be dated to this period.

To be sure, the regular English commerce in enslaved persons from Africa was not established until the middle of the seventeenth century. The first English American colonies had been founded in the first decades of the century, and the first Africans who were taken there and forced to labor arrived in Bermuda in 1616 and in Virginia in 1619. The remote island that was to become the most important colonial possession in the seventeenth-century English Atlantic world, Barbados, was settled in the next decade. Only in the period after the planters discovered that Barbados would support the cultivation of sugar did ships from England start to send a more or less continual stream of enslaved persons from Africa to the colonies across the ocean.

What happened next happened fast. By the close of the seventeenth century, English colonies that stretched in a greater Caribbean orbit from Barbados to the Leeward Islands to Jamaica to Carolina to Virginia were no longer societies in which slaves happened to appear. They were ones that were founded upon slavery as an institution. And to this extent, slavery was the foundation of the new English Atlantic world.

What was more, back across the ocean, the position of Africa in the English Atlantic world had shifted as well. In the final decade of the century, for the first time, the total value of the persons came to exceed the total value of the gold that English merchants received in trade on the western coast. At the same time, the most acute observers in England became aware of the extent to which the rapid development of the Caribbean colonies had come to depend upon the commerce that supplied them with enslaved laborers from Africa.

Indeed, it was Africa that was so much at the center of English discourse about slavery in the seventeenth century. And this was the second feature that stood out to me about the context with which my work was now concerned: America was peripheral to the context of ideas in which American slavery began.

As a matter of fact, little was known across the English Atlantic world about slavery as it had developed in the colonies. Until around the end of the seventeenth century, England had received an immense amount of sugar but almost no reports from the slave societies in the Caribbean. The small number of visitors who had traveled there from abroad had been taken aback at what they had seen. It was a "*mystery of Iniquity*" that he had come across on Barbados, recalled one traveler to the island in 1680, and he promised that his report would be the first one in which it would be "laid open to the view of the World" what had happened there.[1]

A novel form of life had been established almost at once. In its brutality, in its stark divisions on racial lines, and in its relentless pursuit of profit, the world of the slave colonies seemed not to resemble any the English had encountered so far. For their part, the planters had produced the most minimal written records. They tended not to reflect too much upon the moral character of their actions. They were desperate to establish and maintain control. Regardless—and in this respect the planters were not alone—they appear to have assumed that the legitimacy of slavery in America was founded upon a certain received view about the sources of slavery in Africa.

The central site of moral reflection, in other words, was not the institution of slavery in America. Still, at the close of the seventeenth century, English authors had only started to imagine what might be said in its defense. No rich fabric of myth and association had as yet been pulled over the facts of American slavery. No ancient tradition had been enlisted upon its behalf. No aspect of their national past had prepared the English to embrace the societies that they had created in the Caribbean. These hardly seemed to be societies in the traditional sense at all. Their population could not reproduce itself: the people, both free and enslaved, died too fast.

Nevertheless, the slave colonies were in the middle of a period of rapid development, and attention fixed upon the source of their growth. It was the slave trade, more than slavery as such, that English observers in this period believed they needed to explain. In order to do so, they looked back toward its point of departure. Here was a part of the world in which the customs of enslavement appeared to have developed in a manner the English were more prepared to accept.

The focus of this book is English perceptions of Africa. The attitudes and actions of the English with respect to the establishment of slavery in America are treated in detail. In some form or another, America appears in each one of the chapters after the first. However, the balance of the material in this book resembles the balance of the material that is available from the time, in that both are focused less upon the New World than the Old.

The sources that English observers of Africa had before them were neither rare nor novel. From around the turn of the seventeenth century, readers in England had started to receive an immense amount of information about the peoples of Africa. This information had come to them both from the accounts of English travelers and from those that were the work of a number of authors from abroad. These accounts were published in short popular works as well as books that ran into the thousands of folio pages. These books often came out in several editions. They were embellished with woodcut images and maps. Their most important reports were distilled and then became common topics for reflection. In short, in the seventeenth century, Africa was perceived to be a well-known part of the world.

In turn, two features stood out to me about these English perceptions of Africa. The first one of these was that authors from England would so clearly have depicted the ordered character of African life. Indeed, the models upon which such authors drew for their accounts were the same ones that they had before them to describe the standard structure of human life in general. The political units into which they divided the continent were the region, the empire, and the kingdom or nation. Within the nations of Africa, English authors elaborated upon the routine practices of agriculture, commerce, and war. The people were seen to be ranked at points upon a graded social spectrum, which ran from laborers, merchants, and farmers up through nobles, judges, and monarchs. In antebellum America, the authors of the proslavery argument were interested above all to set themselves over and against the native peoples of Africa. In contrast, English authors from the seventeenth century had represented African peoples for the most part as conventional.

Nowhere was the conventional character of African peoples more vividly rendered than in maps. In addition to the written texts of the seventeenth century, the maps from the time are a source of insight into English attitudes.

Well into the second half of the sixteenth century, most maps of Africa that were available in England were drawn from a model of the continent that had first been described in the classical world. As the cartographers of the early-modern period came into their own practice, they produced an elaborate new model of the continent. The popular seventeenth-century maps of Africa were lined on their top and bottom borders with views of its towns and portraits of its rulers and on their side edges with figures of the peoples from its various regions. In such works the names of ports and cities were engraved inward from the outline of the coasts. At points the print was so dense that the names of cities were drawn outward, too, like whiskers over the water. Thin lines that swooped and swirled over the land marked the borders between regions. Tiny castles were used to denote the locations of nations. These spread on riverine routes toward remote inland empires that for the most part no European had seen. Beyond the reach of their experience, observers tended to assume that the familiar forms of African life extended without end into the interior.

The second feature that stood out to me about the works of English observers in this period was, in a word, how modern these works themselves often appeared. No doubt their authors were impressed with this as well. They were eager to announce the dramatic shift in culture on the basis of which the seventeenth century is now seen to be the pivotal period in the early-modern era.

The observers of Africa in this period were well aware that what was now believed to be known about the continent far surpassed the little information that had been available to observers from the classical world. They dismissed the conviction on the part of classical authors that the extreme heat in Africa rendered human life all but impossible. They rejected as well the rumors that had circulated in classical culture about the weird, half-human forms of life that alone were able to survive within the Torrid Zone. In turn, early-modern English authors also cast doubt upon a popular method of biblical interpretation that had been relied upon to understand the origins and character of African peoples. English authors often observed that at this point it would be futile to attempt to trace peoples in the present back to persons in the Bible. And in part as a result, one would never be able to fasten upon some event in the sacred text as the cause of some particular feature of African life.

The studies of Africa that came out in this period were advertised as ones drawn from the experience of travelers who had been there. Even for areas that no European traveler had seen, accounts of Africa maintained that the people more or less resembled those with whom Europeans had been in regular contact. These accounts were received into a European public that was keen for the most current information. They were annotated and edited, compared with one another, and credited or discredited on the basis of whether or not they seemed to be true. When more information was wanted about one issue or another, detailed lists of questions were sent out for which future travelers were expected to collect the answers. This was the period that marked the rise of modern natural science, and the study of Africa developed in the context and indeed in the spirit of that broad cultural enterprise. Observers from this period were confident that more was known about Africa now than in the past and that more would soon be known than was in the present.

As my research led me further back in time, in other words, it led me into a context that appeared less unusual than the one with which my research had at first been concerned. To be sure, the strangeness of intellectual life in early-modern England was never far from my mind. The very material features of the texts through which I was able to encounter it—their thick gilded linen pages, the acid odor of their cured leather covers—could not fail to impress upon me the distance that stood between me and the persons who were the subjects of my work. The feature of their world that I had set out to explain was the ease with which they had accepted that slavery was one of the forms that human relations could legitimately assume. As I went about this task, I had the sense of following an unrecognizable idea as it made its way through minds that were more or less recognizable to me.

This was an unnerving impression, for of course the subjects of my work were the people who were responsible for the development of American slavery. Some of them had traded iron bars and cowrie shells and woolen cloth and colored beads in return for persons on the western coast of Africa. Some of them had sailed across the Middle Passage in ships from which enslaved Africans would leap overboard and hold themselves underwater until they drowned in the Atlantic. Others had worked to establish and maintain systems of slave labor that were the purest form of human cruelty, and still others had funded and overseen the development of those systems.

All of these people seemed to be aware that they would benefit from the development of American slavery. However, almost none of them complained, as antebellum southerners so often did, that they had had no choice but to take part in the institution. And they did it anyway.

As I turned these facts over and over in my head, a line from Joseph Conrad's *Heart of Darkness* came to mind. For the most part, I had not found the novel to be a useful source of insight into European representations of Africa from the precolonial era. The term "dark continent" was an invention of the nineteenth century, and the famous image that appears at the start of the book, of a massive blankness at the center of a map of Africa, would have surprised anyone who was familiar with the full and intricately detailed maps of the continent that were current throughout the seventeenth century in England. At least at one moment, though, Conrad brought to the surface a theme that I had seen as it had started to emerge in much earlier materials.

Toward the middle of the novel, as Marlow steers his steamboat up the Congo River, he turns to the shore and considers how absolutely foreign the whole scene is to him. "The earth seemed unearthly," he recalls, "and the men were—No, they were not inhuman. Well, you know, that was the worst of it—this suspicion of their not being inhuman." At an earlier point in my research, the flash of recognition that follows the hyphenated pause in the first sentence here had seemed to recall English attitudes from the early-modern era, when the human status of the peoples of Africa had served as the point of departure in descriptions of the continent. Now I had come to suspect that this remark held within it another dimension. The subjects of my work did not at all appear inhuman to me. As Marlow might have said, that was the worst of it.[2]

After years of work, I had found myself in a familiar position: at once fascinated and horrified by the suspicion of my "remote kinship," in Marlow's phrase, with the authors of the evils of the past. And yet over time, my view of the past had changed. The paradox of the way in which I had come to see the history of slavery was that I was less able to detach myself from the writers of early-modern England than from those who had struggled to preserve a social world amid whose ruins I had been raised. The writers who contributed to the antebellum American proslavery argument had been liars. They had trumpeted the rightness of an institution whose wrongness must have been apparent, not least because in the decades before southerners started to assert that slavery was a positive good they had acknowledged that it was an evil, if a necessary one, they said.

In contrast, early-modern English authors had made no extravagant efforts to defend the practice of slavery. They held that slavery was in some cases legitimate. But they were aware as well that to be enslaved was a terrible misfortune. They reported upon the sorrow and dread that spread among the peoples of Africa as they were loaded into ships along the western coast. No English observer from this time expressed a hint of surprise when, again and again, the slaves in the Caribbean rose in rebellion against their masters. This was what was expected. To state a complex matter in simple terms, the moral failure in early-modern English culture was not to have said that what was wrong was right. It was to have accepted what never should have been accepted.

This kind of moral failure might be more common than we would like to imagine. As my research into the intellectual origins of American slavery has neared its end, I have imagined a scholar who is born and raised some four hundred years in the future. I wonder what will appear to this earnest inquirer as the most terrible crimes of the culture in which I lived. I do have some ideas. Among them would be our failure to ensure that the abolition of slavery meant full freedom for the people who had been enslaved. That said, the point of the exercise is to realize that I do not know how the distant future will reflect back upon the present. The subjects of my work do not at all appear inhuman to me. As I would myself be understood, so I have tried to understand them.

❧

Before we proceed, a word about the relationship between ideas and interests—and in particular, economic interests. I have come to the work on this book with a deep interest in this relationship but without an established sense of how it must work. It does not appear to me that one should have such a sense. The relationship between ideas and interests is the product of historical development. It has shifted from time to time and from place to place. In any one historical context, it will best be understood in the course of a close examination of the available evidence. That is what I have tried to do in this book.

To state an obvious point, the origins of American slavery were not only intellectual. Both ideas and interests were at work. In the early decades of English settlement in America, the labor force in the colonies was composed of servants from Britain and a smaller number of African and Native American persons who were enslaved. The difference between them was perhaps not so much one of treatment as one of juridical status: servants were indentured to serve for a limited term, whereas the status of slaves was permanent and heritable. Around the middle of the seventeenth century, the supply of servants from Britain who would travel to the crucial Caribbean colonies started to decline. At the same time, with the introduction of sugar as a staple crop, the demand for labor, which was always acute in the early colonies, underwent a rapid increase.

For the most part, the men who confronted this situation were narrow-minded men. As planters and overseers, merchants and seamen, colonial and metropolitan officials, advocates and investors, these men understood that the rate of return for investment in slaves was higher than for servants. And they were also well aware that there was what seemed to be an infinite supply of slaves on the western coast of Africa. In or around 1640, the English African slave trade began and soon entered a period of acceleration that continued more or less into the nineteenth century. In turn, in the colonies, the transition from servant to slave labor swept in a jagged northward curve from Barbados to Virginia.

This sequence of events—rendered here in the simplest possible form—is now one of the most well-known in American history. Generations of historians have described it in careful detail. Close attention has been paid to the local contexts in which versions of these events took place. Broad accounts have been put forward in order to connect these various local contexts within narratives of tremendous scope and ambition. Revisions have followed upon revisions. And over time, our sense of the origins of American slavery has been refined in the period since scholarship on slavery moved toward the center of the historical profession in the United States in the decades after the Second World War.[3]

All the same, one theme has remained consistent over the course of this period. That is the economic focus of studies in the field. Historians have tended to treat the development of American slavery as a simple function of material interests, an almost automatic response made to new conditions of supply and demand. The narrow focus of scholars in the field has reflected the narrow-mindedness of most of the historical actors whom these scholars have worked to understand.[4]

In contrast, in this book I have worked to develop a much broader account. There is no doubt that it has seemed to be a mark in favor of the economic approach that most of the persons who participated in the construction of slave systems in the English Atlantic world never made an effort to explain their actions in terms of moral or political or philosophical ideas. This fact has seemed to indicate to many scholars that no such ideas were present at the origins of American slavery. But, of course, that is not necessarily what this fact means. It could also mean that the architects of the institution believed their actions did not need to be explained, because they fit well within a cultural consensus about the parameters of what it was possible to do.

Now, to make a statement of this kind is to move outward from the economic in the examination of historical events. It is to speak not so much about the calculation of material interests as about the terms themselves that are involved in that calculation. It is to work to understand, in this case, not so much the reasons for the transition from servitude to slavery in the early-modern English Atlantic world as the reasons for which slavery was available as an option—that is, the reasons for which slavery was understood to be a status about which narrow-minded men could make calculations. Economics alone cannot provide us with an account of these reasons.

Indeed, at this point, we have arrived in the realm of ideas. The idea that slavery is never acceptable is now so familiar that we can sometimes overlook how recent it is. Ideas about slavery permeated early-modern English culture. And at their most basic level, these ideas were seen to be a matter of common consensus. They were part of the basic structure of social and political thought. In this book, I have treated the ideas about slavery that were current across early-modern English culture as a kind of pattern or model, one to which the practices of slavery at the time could be compared. Over the course of the period that I have examined, the practices of slavery in the English Atlantic world were seen to fit this model. Already, however, toward the end of the seventeenth century, the tension between practices and models, interests and ideas, had become almost impossible to ignore.

There is a standard point to be made in response to an account of this kind. It is that the premise is mistaken. Even if ideas do at times appear to have an effect on the course of historical events, ideas themselves have no independent existence. The social and political ideas that circulate within a historical context are an expression of the material conditions of life that obtain within that context. This is one of the main tenets of the analytical method known as historical materialism, which can trace its roots back to Karl Marx. Marx held that the material conditions of life, in particular the conditions of production, form the economic structure of a society. This structure in turn produces the institutions and ideas that will tend to support and sustain it. These form what Marx called the superstructure. It is no coincidence when ideas fit the interests of those who control the conditions of production. These ideas are best understood as their interests transmuted into another form.

Marx had a term for ideas of this kind. He called them ideological. In the time since Marx wrote, this term has been used in a number of different contexts and for a number of different purposes. There has never been consensus about what it means. But at least in its classic Marxist formulation, the one from which all the later formulations are derived, it is used to refer to ideas that are created and determined by a particular mode of production. And it is with this sense of the term in mind that I have avoided it in the title of this book. I have chosen another term, "intellectual," in order to indicate that the book deals with ideas but has not decided from the start whether and to what extent and in what sense these ideas can be said to be ideological.

As a matter of fact, the relationship between ideas and interests in this book cannot easily be explained on the standard Marxist model. Above all, there is one reason for this. It is that the set of ideas and perceptions from which American slavery first drew support was in place before the institution was established in the English Atlantic world.

At least in part in order to make this point, I have paid close attention to the order of the events that this book describes. The narrative starts almost a full century before the start of the regular English African slave trade and the establishment of the earliest English slave colonies. It shows that the news of these events was slow to reach many observers back in the metropole. Only in the decade of the 1660s did these events become at all well known. Only in the final decade of the century did it become clear how profitable the slave colonies had become. Only at this point could the case be made that slavery as a mode of production had become part of what Marx would have called the economic structure of English society. And still, at this point, no one seems to have anticipated how much more important slavery was to become to the rise of the British Empire in the decades that followed.

All the while, the ideas about slavery that were current in English culture remained more or less the same. These ideas were not created and determined by the development of slavery as a mode of production across the English Atlantic world. But they did seem to be consistent with this development. And what was more, they worked to direct and to channel attention. They prepared English observers to take the keenest interest in certain aspects of the practice of slavery and almost none in certain others. In their sheer persistence over time, and indeed also in their association with ideas about slavery from the ancient past, these ideas had another effect.

They served to mask some of the radical innovations that were at work in the Caribbean colonies. If pressed, an Englishman could respond that slavery as it had been established there was little more than a new instance of an old pattern.

This book represents an effort to put the history of ideas into close contact with the history of slavery. It aims, in particular, to understand the role of ideas in the development of slavery in the early-modern English Atlantic world. It does not claim that ideas were the cause or motive of this development. Economic interests are more than sufficient to account for the transition from servitude to slavery as the dominant form of labor in the seventeenth-century Caribbean colonies. Nevertheless, this book does propose and work to establish that ideas were a condition of this momentous event. They helped to make it possible. The awful and almost incredible fact is that the architects of American slavery believed that what they did was legitimate as well as profitable. What follows here is an inquiry into how this could have been the case.

❧

There is precedent in the field for an intervention like the one this book proposes to make. It is the precedent set in the work of the late historian David Brion Davis. What I aim to do here is to some extent similar to what Davis was able to accomplish. In his monumental *Problem of Slavery* series, which came out in three volumes between 1966 and 2014, Davis helped to move ideas toward the center of scholarship on the antislavery movement in the Anglo-American Atlantic world.

When Davis started work on the first volume in his series, the field he would soon help to transform was unconvinced of the central role of ideas. The dominant account of the antislavery movement at this time was a book titled *Capitalism and Slavery,* which was the work of the West Indian historian and politician Eric Williams. Williams had come from a generation of scholars who were determined to expose the hidden motives beneath what had often been believed to be disinterested actions. His premises and methods were drawn from Marx. Williams held that the sudden rise of the antislavery movement toward the end of the eighteenth century in Britain was a direct response to economic forces. The old slave system had entered a period of terminal decline. With the rise of a new form of industrial capitalism, slavery was now an impediment to growth. It was in the interest of the capitalists that slavery be abolished—and so it was. The humanitarian rhetoric that had been presented in support of this action was little more than a cover for motives so bare and self-interested that it would have been an embarrassment to put them before the public.[5]

In contrast, the more that Davis read in the records of the antislavery movement, the more he was convinced that it would need to be seen from a much broader perspective. The insight that most animated the movement was not that the slave system in the British Empire was in terminal decline. It was that slavery as such presented a genuine moral problem. Over the course of the eighteenth century, Davis observed, more and more men and women across the Atlantic world started to see "the full horror of a social evil to which mankind had been blind for centuries." This dramatic shift in moral perception was the real point of departure from which to understand the antislavery movement. And shifts in moral perception tended to work more slowly than ones in economic affairs. They drew upon patterns and traditions that were as old and deep as the cultures they aimed to transform.[6]

The book that developed from such reflections was titled *The Problem of Slavery in Western Culture.* Davis intended it to serve as an introduction to a history of the antislavery movement. What he needed now was to produce an account that would show how the ideas he had presented in such rich and vivid detail became effective in action and informed a social movement that led to direct and forceful political reforms. That was what he did in the second volume in his series, *The Problem of Slavery in the Age of Revolution,* which was published in 1975. In the final volume, *The Problem of Slavery in the Age of Emancipation,* Davis traced an evolution in the methods of the antislavery movement that helped to produce an ultimate resolution to the problem of human bondage.[7]

Even before it reached its conclusion, the *Problem of Slavery* series had assumed the status of a foundational text in scholarship on the antislavery movement. Its success has been due to a number of different factors. There is no doubt that one reason scholars have so often accepted the account that Davis put forward of the noneconomic sources of the movement to abolish the slave system in the British Atlantic world is that what Williams had said about its decline was later shown to be incorrect in essential respects. As a matter of fact, the slave system was viable and profitable up until the moment when it came under sustained popular attack. For all its manifest brilliance, *Capitalism and Slavery* had presented much too simple an account of the economic context for the rise of the antislavery movement.[8]

Perhaps the most important factor in the success of the series to which Davis devoted much of his career was that he was so well able to adapt his approach over time. He had been trained as a cultural historian, and he had put his expertise in this discipline on full display in *The Problem of Slavery in Western Culture.* But as he considered the transition between his first and second volumes, he realized that he would need to become much more aware of the function of ideas in structures of economic and political power. At times, in *The Problem of Slavery in the Age of Revolution,* what he said about this issue could sound almost as if it had come from Williams. He said that even as the contributors to the antislavery cause had been sincere in their moral commitments, these commitments reflected the needs and values of the ascendant industrial capitalist class that included at least some of the reformers. The kind of layered description of interests and ideas that Davis produced on the basis of this observation has since become the standard in scholarship on the antislavery movement. Perhaps the best recent example is the work of Christopher Brown, whose *Moral Capital* has considered the complex effects of American independence upon the course of British abolitionism.[9]

The relationship between interests and ideas in the establishment of American slavery was different from what it was in the movement to abolish the institution. As Davis observed, the antislavery movement at once reflected and acted upon a radical departure from the ideas of the past. In contrast, at least at first, the slave systems in the American colonies were seen to draw upon patterns that had been set down over the course of millennia. And as we have also seen, ideas were never the motive or cause that drove forward the development of these slave systems. Unlike in the antislavery movement, the role of ideas in the establishment of American slavery was little more than as a condition for decisions made on the basis of the purest form of self-interest.

That said, what Davis showed was that interests and ideas needed to be understood in the closest association with each other, and that is as true about the start as it was about the formal end of slavery in America. In one final respect, too, the work of Davis has inspired my own. I have planned this book as the first of three volumes in a series that would examine the ideas associated with the origins and development of American slavery. This series would run in parallel to the *Problem of Slavery* series but would also intersect with it at countless points, since, as Davis insisted time and again, slavery and antislavery helped to shape each other. In the next volume, I plan to cover the continuities and points of dramatic rupture in discourse about slavery across the eighteenth-century British Atlantic world. And in the final volume, I intend to return to the place where my research began and to describe the shape of the debates about slavery in the antebellum United States. Insofar as it is ever possible to envision the future course of one's research, this is how mine looks to me.

As I write these sentences, I am humbled by the scale of the task that is before me. I wish that I could ask Davis for his advice about how to approach the work ahead. I never had the chance to meet him before his death in 2019, but his books have never left my desk as I have written my own. Over time, I have come to feel almost as if I know him. Such was the level of his commitment to his craft, the moral and intellectual seriousness with which he approached it, that he seemed to put a whole human self onto the page. At the same time, as much as I have tried to learn from him, I am well aware that I will never be the scholar that he was.

As Davis would have been the first to admit, his books left much unsaid. Moreover, scholarship in the related fields of slavery and antislavery has made considerable advances in the time since he wrote. In the first volume in his series, Davis remarked that the period before the eighteenth century was marked by a certain kind of blindness with respect to the moral issues that were at stake in the idea and the practice of human bondage. This is the period to which we now turn, in an effort to provide some insight into the intellectual origins of American slavery.

❧

Now, one final note about method. This book is a work of intellectual history, but it cannot be considered a complete intellectual history of slavery in the early-modern English Atlantic world. In particular, it cannot be considered a contribution to the vast and important field of studies in what has come to be known as the Black Atlantic. Almost all of the authors whose texts are described in what follows here were white. In part this fact reflects the focus of this book as a description of English attitudes. In the next volume in the series that I have planned, the works of the famous Afro-British leaders in the early antislavery movement will move much more toward the center of the narrative. Readers who want to know more about the experiences and ideas of Black persons who were faced with enslavement in the British Atlantic world should refer to the field that has developed over the course of several decades in the studies of scholars from Paul Gilroy to Orlando Patterson, Hilary Beckles to Stephanie Smallwood, Vincent Brown to Jennifer Morgan, and dozens more.[10]

Moreover, this book also cannot be considered a contribution to the field of African history. To be sure, the book has placed Africa and Africans in a complex active role at the center of the history of slavery in the Atlantic world. In so doing, I have drawn upon decades of detailed and sophisticated scholarship in the field of African studies, which has aimed to do the same. Many of the sources that I have used—from travel narratives to maps to atlases to company records—are ones that historians of Africa in this period have also used. Indeed, these sources might well be more familiar to historians of Africa than to most scholars who are concerned with the origins of American slavery. I have worked to produce an account of these sources that is in essential respects consistent with what historians of Africa have said about them. All the same, I have turned to these documents as sources of insight into English attitudes and not as ones that reflected the actual facts of African life. At root, this book is concerned with English attitudes: it is no more and no less than an account of the intellectual origins of American slavery.[11]

As a work of intellectual history, there are real limits to the scope of this account. I would like to be clear about these limits before we proceed. In what follows here, I have for the most part relied upon documents that appeared in print. (This means, for example, that I have made limited use of the voluminous unpublished records of the royal companies that controlled English commerce with Africa in this period—even as I have often consulted and cited the works of the scholars of these companies and studied at least some of these records in the useful modern editions in which some of them have been collected.) Perhaps most of the authors of these documents can be said to have occupied the social role of intellectuals, and one should never assume that the opinions of intellectuals can stand in for the opinions of a complex and diverse cultural whole.[12]

When I state that this book is a work of intellectual history, however, I do not mean that it is concerned with intellectuals alone. Rather, what I mean is that it is concerned with ideas. Within the broad field of early-modern English print culture, I have placed inquiries far and wide. I have never restricted my research on the basis of the genre of the document that was next on my list to read. I have drawn upon all of the materials that it seemed most important to include. My aim has been to produce as complete an account as possible of the ideas that formed the context for the development of American slavery. Even as this book has continued to expand over time, I have always been convinced that it really should cover much more than it does. At each point, I have done as much as I could in the time and space that I had.

As a work that is concerned with ideas, rather than with intellectuals alone, this book moves back and forth between multiple levels of discourse. The most important material that appears here is the material on Africa. This is the fullest and most detailed description of early-modern English perceptions of Africa that has ever appeared in print. From at least the turn of the seventeenth century, the accounts of Africa that were current in English culture were themselves composed, or were at the least drawn from, the reports of persons who had been there. For the most part, these persons were not intellectuals: they were medical doctors and priests and, above all, merchants and seamen of various kinds. The reports of these travelers rarely made it into print in an unedited form. They were abbreviated and supplemented, evaluated and compared, translated and retranslated, and in the process no doubt altered by the more learned observers back in

Europe who put these firsthand accounts into public circulation. But these accounts remained the basis for English attitudes about Africa. Their authors were considered authorities in virtue of their experience. The discourse that developed from what they said they had seen was one that took place on multiple levels. Ideas moved between authors of different kinds of social position and experience.

Over the course of the early-modern period, Africa was not often the topic of broad public interest and discussion in England. It was never as present across the standard forms of popular culture—from the theater to the pulpit and from the pamphlet to the newspaper—as it would become over the course of the eighteenth century. The accounts of the continent circulated within a somewhat limited set of interested observers.

Even so, I have worked to establish that Africa was an important site of early-modern English attention. And the accounts of the continent from this period arrived in a culture that was prepared to receive them in a particular manner. Common ideas in English culture had no doubt informed the descriptions of Africa that were written around this time, and in turn these ideas contributed to the context in which these descriptions were received.

As much space as I have devoted in this book to early-modern English descriptions of Africa, then, I have also set out in detail the cultural context in which these descriptions were written and discussed. What I have said about this context is much less original, from the point of view of established scholarship, than the claims I have made about how Africa was perceived. Indeed, it would not be incorrect to observe that my method in this book has been to connect certain well-known currents of early-modern English culture to less familiar discussions of Africa and Africans.

In this respect, one current of early-modern culture in particular has been important. That is the one that I have termed the Roman tradition of slavery. In the period when reports from Africa started to filter back into England, English culture was saturated in ideas about slavery and freedom that had their roots deep in the ancient world. The clearest expression of these ideas was to be found in the standard texts of Roman law. But it was often the case that Roman law served to summarize and condone customs that were common across the ancient Mediterranean world; and indeed, the provisions for slavery that were laid out in the Bible fit within the structure set down in the legal treatises of the Roman Empire.

In early-modern culture, the reception and development of the Roman tradition took multiple forms. Roman ideas spread across genres and into popular as well as elite culture. They became the basis for a common consensus about what slavery was and where it came from. With respect to these essential issues, Roman law had set down a simple structure. It had offered a model that could be worked with and filled out. In early-modern England, the Roman model informed the treatments of slavery in works of drama, history, and literature. Treatises on the English common law adapted Roman accounts of slavery in order to define the sources and character of human subjection. Sometimes English authors drew upon a kind of shorthand form of these Roman accounts. Sometimes they reproduced certain features of the Roman model but appear to have been unaware of where it came from. As Roman ideas spread and developed across English culture, they sometimes came to lose their association with the culture of the ancient world. They could seem to express the common sense of all cultures about a common institution in human life.

There was one more area of early-modern culture in which the reception of Roman ideas about slavery took place in full awareness of where they had come from. That was in the philosophical discourse about politics that flourished across Europe and in particular in England. The famous political philosophers from the period worked more or less within the standard structure of Roman law. They aimed to translate the basic terms of Roman law into a distinctive modern discourse of political rights. In the process, these authors produced the most profound reflections from the early-modern period upon the principles and methods of the Roman model. They turned out theories of freedom and slavery that were at home in the modern world. These are the theories to which we now turn—as we start to assess the ideas about slavery that would have been available in the period when the English started to make ideas into brutal realities.

CHAPTER 1

From Freedom to Slavery

In early-modern Europe, two traditions of slavery survived from the culture of the classical world. The first one of these traditions was drawn from the *Politics* of Aristotle, which held that some persons were fitted by nature to be ruled as slaves no matter their status in fact. The second was derived from the legal treatises of the Roman Empire, which maintained that all persons were free by nature but that some persons might be made slaves as a result of accident or misfortune.

In early-modern English culture, as the influence of Aristotle declined, the theory of natural slavery was most often rejected. But the Roman account of slavery was received and was refashioned in works of drama, history, and literature and, above all, in texts on the common law and the classic early theories of natural rights.

In recent decades, historians who have aimed to describe the context of ideas from which slavery in America first drew support have rooted their accounts in the development of racial prejudice toward the native peoples of Africa. In turn, scholars of racial attitudes have suggested that these might be relied upon in order to explain the origins of American slavery.[1] Nevertheless, in the early-modern era, when slavery in the English Atlantic world began, the modern concept of race had not yet been developed and the most important idea of slavery in England was a fundamentally Roman one that was premised upon the natural freedom of all humankind. These facts point toward a different account of the intellectual origins of American slavery, one in which a certain conception of slavery was understood to arise from a certain conception of freedom.

Indeed, it was precisely the transition from freedom to slavery that most interested English authors from this era. To be sure, the classical discussions of slavery they had before them were varied and dense. On the one hand, Aristotle, in both his *Politics* and his *Ethics,* had set out to describe slavery as a distinct kind of relation between persons. It was different from the relations between equals that characterized the political life in a state. It was carried on within the household, according to a set of principles that were all its own. There was a science of the slave, Aristotle explained, and there was a science of the master. In his treatment of slavery, he was thus concerned with such matters as the kinds of bodies that slaves ought to possess, the sorts of tasks that they should be made to perform, and the particular brand of virtue in which they had to be instructed—as well as with the manner in which masters ought to converse with their slaves, the methods they should use in order to punish them, and the extent to which masters and slaves could ever be said to be friends.

The treatment of slavery in Roman law was even more complex. For early-modern authors the essence of Roman law was preserved within what had come to be known as the *Corpus Juris Civilis,* a series of texts that had been compiled under the emperor Justinian in the sixth century CE. The largest and most important one of these was the *Digest,* which was half again as long as the Bible and composed of statutes, decisions, and commentaries that had been selected from the past half millennium of jurisprudence. As in the other texts of the *Corpus Juris,* there was no separate law of slavery in the *Digest.* Its authors tended to work at the level of the particular rather than general, and had come upon slavery for the most part only in the course of their efforts to articulate rules for the many areas of the law in which slaves happened to appear. They had elaborated, for example, upon the ceremony in which ownership of a slave was transferred from one master to another and the defects in the slave for which the seller could be held liable, the circumstances in which a slave could act as the agent of a master and the delicts of the slave that the master might need to redress, the methods by which slaves could acquire property in some form and the formal process by which slaves could be manumitted.[2]

Almost as a rule, such issues did not hold the attention of the readers of Roman law in early-modern England. Neither did the subtle science of slave and master that Aristotle had described. Each had been produced through reflection upon the complex needs of a society that was founded upon slavery. But by the early-modern period, as we will see below, the English believed that theirs had long been a nation in which all persons were free. In part as a result, their interest in slavery was far narrower than that of their classical sources. They rarely considered slavery as an institution or as the basis for a certain kind of social, political, and economic order.

In this respect the main authors of the proslavery argument in antebellum America absorbed the lessons of classical culture more fully than had their much more learned early-modern predecessors. They drew succor from their impression that the glory of Greece and the grandeur of Rome had rested upon the institution of slavery. Slavery had come to seem to them as the deep source of the values, the traditions, and even the taste in art and literature that marked the American South as peculiar in the modern industrial world. In the famous phrase, it was the cornerstone of the new nation that, upon secession, they set out to establish.[3]

No such ambitions animated the works of the authors who will appear in the course of this chapter. They understood slavery as a form of personal status rather than as the basis for a way of life. They referred less often to slavery as such than to slaves, and in particular, they were interested in a single feature in the lives of such persons, which was the source or origin of their condition. These authors did also reflect upon the extent of the power that masters held over slaves and even the circumstances in which slaves could resist or escape, but they did so because they believed that these matters were related to the origin of slavery. This was the central point around which early-modern English discourse revolved. Slavery appeared here as the aftermath of an event—the calamitous occasion in which free persons were enslaved.

In this context the power of Roman law, and in turn the challenge of Aristotle, was that each had put forward an account of the proper source of slavery.

❧

There have been few historical introductions to ideas of slavery, but one of these did appear in one of the great works of modern scholarship: *The Problem of Slavery in Western Culture,* by David Brion Davis, which was published in 1966. Here Davis aimed to explain the rise of the antislavery movement in the second half of the eighteenth century. His claim was that the antislavery movement had developed out of certain novel currents in European culture rather than as a response to some shift in the character of slavery. In fact, he believed that throughout history, from the ancient to the modern world, from region to region, and in the works of philosophers from Aristotle to John Locke, "the hard core of slavery was much the same." The core of slavery was not its physical cruelty or economic exploitation: these were factors that had varied across space and time. The core of slavery was "the underlying conception of man as a conveyable possession." Thus the problem that slavery had forever posed was that it consisted in "the ultimately impossible attempt to define and treat men as objects." This attempt had always been the cause of tension and conflict in Western culture until at last the antislavery movement announced its ultimate failure.[4]

According to Davis, then, there was at root one ancient conception of slavery that had been passed down to the modern world. As a matter of fact, however, there were two. The authors of early-modern Europe were aware that there had been a debate about slavery between classical authors. They knew that to set themselves within the tradition of slavery that could be traced back to Roman law would in some sense be to set themselves against the tradition whose earliest and most powerful statement was to be found in the corpus of Aristotle. The present chapter is an account of the early-modern discourse that developed around this position. It was a discourse defined by the attempt to draw the slavery of some persons out of the natural freedom of them all.

By contrast, Aristotle had held that both freedom and slavery inhered in the natural order. Throughout the universe, he argued in his *Politics,* wherever there was a whole that was composed of parts, "a distinction between the ruling and the subject element comes to light." The soul ruled the body in each animate creature, and humans ruled animals among the forms of animate life. The same tiered scheme held true among humans, because "from the hour of their birth," Aristotle famously asserted, "some are marked out for subjection, others for rule."[5]

The persons marked out for subjection were those whom Aristotle said were slaves: they were human, to be sure, but formed that part of humankind whose proper role was to serve. In this sense they resembled beasts of burden and could be used, in the manner of any tool or instrument, as the mere extension of the will of their masters. For this reason Aristotle on occasion suggested that slaves were more part of their masters than they were a distinct part of humankind. They were able to participate in reason, he allowed, but only insofar as they were able to apprehend the reason of their masters rather than to exercise it for themselves.

Aristotle once referred to a slave as "he who can be, and therefore is, another's"—and here was his theory captured in a phrase. The status of a slave did not depend upon any act or agreement. It was a matter of his settled position in the order of nature. A slave by nature was always a slave regardless of his actual status: he could be a slave, and therefore he was one. To enslave such a person was only to direct him toward the end for which he had been made. Aristotle did observe that some persons who were enslaved in the present may not have been slaves by nature and noted as well that entire peoples who had not been enslaved—for example, "the natives of Asia" and "barbarians" in general—were intended by nature to be slaves. But these facts seem to have troubled him less than scholars who have hoped to recover some critical intent in his theory have realized. Aristotle aimed not so much to critique or even to defend the practice of slavery as to define slavery as a certain kind of rule, one that was appropriate for a certain kind of person.[6]

Aristotle presented this account as an effort to refute the opinion of unnamed other authors that the rule of a master over slaves was "contrary to nature" and founded instead upon convention alone. This was the premise from which discussion of slavery in Roman law began. In the *Institutes* of Justinian, which was written as an introduction to the other texts of the *Corpus Juris,* slavery was introduced with the note that it was "contrary to the law of nature." "By the law of nature," according to the authors of the *Institutes,* "all men were initially born free."[7] The opponents of Aristotle had argued that because slavery had not been established by nature, it could not be just. In a similar manner, Aristotle held that slavery was natural in order to be able to maintain that for some persons it was just, or as he also put it, "both expedient and right."[8] That said, in Roman law, the natural freedom of all men was not taken to mean that men might never rightly be enslaved. Nature had in a sense not settled that issue. And the law of nature was only one of the sources of law that were recognized in Roman legal texts.

In fact, the critical fault line in Roman law ran between the law of nature and what the jurists called the law of nations. According to Ulpian, a third-century jurist from whom about one-third of the *Digest* was drawn, the law of nature described the principles that nature had instilled in all animals. It was composed of the most basic elements of animate life, such as the union between male and female and the rearing of children, and could be observed in the behavior of "land animals, sea animals, and the birds as well," Ulpian said. Since each animal was understood to be free and equal with respect to every other, slavery was not present in the order that nature had established.[9]

By contrast, the law of nations was the product of human invention and composed of the customs "which all human peoples observe," Ulpian explained. Not all of the jurists drew such a sharp distinction between the law of nature and the law of nations. For example, Gaius, whose second-century textbook had become the model for Justinian's *Institutes,* said that the law of nations itself was "the law which natural reason makes for all mankind," and as a result, the law of nature had little independent role in his work. Even for Ulpian, and in the *Digest* in general, these two sources of law were said to be in conflict on one particular issue. That issue was slavery.[10]

For nature may have made men as free and equal as animals, but the human world had soon begun to come apart in a manner that the animal world never had. Property was made private, land was divided, and nations were formed. Wars between these nations had been contested, and in war a custom had become so common as to be legitimate under the law of nations: that captives were enslaved and that children born to enslaved mothers were held as slaves as well. Slavery, Ulpian concluded, thus "came in by the *ius gentium,*" or law of nations. These were the two most important sources of slavery in Roman law, as indeed they were in the Roman world at large and had been in classical Greece at the time of Aristotle. There was only one other source of slavery that was accepted as legitimate in the texts of the *Corpus Juris:* enslavement under the civil law, which included all rules that were particular to Rome, for persons who had been convicted of certain crimes. In short, slavery arose in Roman law as the result of history rather than nature, as a fact of modern life rather than a timeless feature of the universe.[11]

After the fall of the Western Empire, in the fifth century, the influence of Roman law declined across much of its former territory. Toward the end of the eleventh century, however, a revival began in the universities of continental Europe, and by the close of the sixteenth century a number of states had adopted the texts of the *Corpus Juris* as the basis for legal doctrine and practice. During this time the Roman law often came to be referred to as the civil law: as the civil law had been at Rome, the Roman law was now considered to be the particular set of rules that had been enacted across much of Europe.

This reception of Roman law has long been said never to have reached the shores of England. The common-law tradition has seemed to generations of scholars to have developed in an insular manner through the slow accretion of unwritten custom from "time out of mind," in the favored phrase of early-modern English jurists. And of course the civil law never entered the common law by means of the sudden adoption of a foreign code. Its influence was more subtle. Over time, as authors in England started to gather together the laws and customs of the country, they found that, homegrown though these were, they had tended to flourish within a formal order that was more or less universal. And such authors found, in addition, that this order was the one that had been set down in the legal treatises of the Roman Empire.[12]

The earliest treatise that aimed to compile the laws and customs of England was the one that appeared under the title of *Bracton,* the name of its supposed author, around the middle of the thirteenth century. The structure of this text was for the most part borrowed from that of the texts of the *Corpus Juris,* or at least from the thorough glosses upon them that recently had become available from southern Europe. The sources of law were divided here into the law of nature, the law of nations, and the civil law, which for Bracton was the common law of England. By the law of nature, according to Bracton, all persons were born free and thus slavery was "an institution of the *ius gentium,* by which, contrary to nature," one person was subjected to the dominion of another. When this happened, Bracton noted, the natural freedom of the slave was not denied or disavowed: it was merely obscured, as if it were behind a cloud.[13]

By the time of Bracton, slavery had more or less disappeared across England, and he made no effort to assert that there were any persons whose exact status corresponded to that of the slaves in the era of Justinian. That said, Bracton also repeated the maxim of the civil law that all persons were either free or enslaved—there was no status that was in between. He observed that there was in England a class of dependent peasants known as villeins who labored upon lands owned by their lords. He was well aware that villeins could assert themselves before the law in a manner that slaves in Rome had never been able to do. Nevertheless, he often used the terms in Law Latin for villein, *nativus* and *villanus,* interchangeably with the term for slave, *servus,* and Bracton assumed as a matter of course that the Roman account of the origin of slavery could also describe the beginning of villeinage.[14]

In turn, for other authors in the era of Bracton, the beginning of villeinage could best be described from within the Roman account of the origin of slavery. The treatise known as *Britton,* which came into use toward the end of the thirteenth century, was the work of one such author. Britton had hoped to render the whole of the common law in a more practical form than Bracton had done. He was less familiar than his predecessor with the tradition of the civil law, and to a great extent composed his text as a gloss upon Bracton. The chapter that he included in his text on villeinage, for example, was written in this manner.

There were free persons, Britton said, and then there were villeins, and each villein was as much a villein as all of the others. There had been no villeins by the law of nature, because according to this law "all men were entirely free." And yet long ago the number of men had started to increase. They took for their own use goods that before had been held in common. They set boundaries around their lands, erected buildings next to one another, and around these formed villages and cities. Kingdoms and nations were soon established, and battles between them broke out throughout the world. It was in this context, according to Britton, "by the constitution of nations, and not by the law of nature," that villeinage had begun. For it had been agreed that whenever one man had overcome another man in war, the defeated man and his entire line were enslaved to the victor, who for his part could do with them "whatsoever he would."[15]

Britton never doubted that, in the course of this account, he had traced the origin of a current institution. Even in his era, though, villeinage was in decline across England, and by the second half of the sixteenth century it had all but disappeared. Their perception of this development was one source of the acute sense among authors in the late Tudor era that England was a nation uniquely dedicated to freedom. The Roman account of the origin of slavery remained a standard point of reference in this period, but for the most part only as a description of the start of an institution that had now come to an end.[16]

This was how the matter appeared to Sir Thomas Smith, the humanist scholar and diplomat whose report upon the legal and political order of England, titled *De republica Anglorum,* was published in 1583. Smith started from the familiar point that the government of England was a commonwealth in the sense that it was an association of free persons for the sake of their common benefit. A slave could take no part in an association of this kind, Smith explained. He drew upon Aristotle when he noted that a slave was considered as the instrument of their master, whose own benefit was regarded as the sole object of the relation between them.[17]

Later on in his text, Smith ran through the different ranks of free persons in the commonwealth of England, and again, at the end of this list, he noted that there were no bondmen or slaves to be found among them. This had not always been the case, Smith admitted, as there used to be villeins. The status of such persons had recalled that of the slaves who lived among the Romans. The slaves who appeared throughout the *Digest* were captives taken in war and children born to slave mothers, Smith continued. Like them, the villeins in England had been bought and sold in the manner of other goods, but they were treated with far more gentleness and moderation than the bondmen in Rome. Above all, Smith was pleased to report that in all his life he had never heard of any villein who lived within the realm.[18]

In spite of his broad classical education, then, Smith hoped to demonstrate how far English custom had moved from ancient precedent. Around the turn of the seventeenth century, however, a new movement for legal reform took shape in England. The ambition of its principal authors was more similar to that of Bracton than Smith, and it was Bracton to whom their writings constantly referred. At times these authors said that their aim was to do no more than remind their readers of the multiple points of practical agreement between the common law and the civil law. But more often they said that they were determined to make clear that the dense sprawl of common-law custom still was set within the formal order of the civil law. This was an ambition that could be traced back to Bracton, but that of course had its origins much further in the past, as it recalled the reform that Justinian had brought to the laws of the Roman Empire.[19]

After the text of the same title that had served to introduce the others of the *Corpus Juris,* the central text of the movement for legal reform in England was titled the *Institutes.* This was the work of John Cowell, who, as Smith had done, served as Regius Professor of Civil Law at Cambridge from 1594 until his death in 1611. Like Bracton, Cowell composed his work in Latin, and the structure he gave it was taken from Roman law as well. He divided the sources of law into the law of nature, the law of nations, and the civil law, which in England was referred to as the common law. He said that the status of all persons was either free or enslaved, and moreover, when a person was enslaved under the law of nations, either as a captive in war or as a child born to an enslaved mother, their natural freedom never entirely disappeared, "albeit it may be under a cloud."[20]

In his *Institutes,* which came out in 1605, Cowell was careful to observe that in the present there were no persons in England whose status was the same as that of slaves in the era of Justinian. For this reason, he added, a number of the old Roman rules for the sale and punishment of slaves were now out of date. Even so, unlike Smith, Cowell did not put forward an account of the special English dedication to freedom. And elsewhere in his works, the presence of slavery in the civil law came to suggest that it must have a parallel in the common law. In his popular 1607 dictionary for legal terms, *The Interpreter,* Cowell stated that the term *Villein* was used to mean "in our common lawe a bondman, or as much as *Servus* among the Civilians."[21]

In his own *Institutes,* which appeared in 1628, Edward Coke agreed that *villein* was the term in the common law used to refer to "hee which the Civilians call *servus.*" *Villeinage* was defined as "the service of a bondman," he continued, and it had arisen deep in the past through the "constitutions of Nations." At first men had lived under the natural law alone, and held in common the fruits of the earth. And yet in time the number of men had multiplied. They had made into private possessions those things that before had been shared by all. Nations had divided the land, and wars between them were the result. Soon it was agreed that each man who was taken in battle as well as "all that should come of him" would remain forever bound to the man who had taken him. The latter man might keep the former man and compel him to serve but also was permitted, Coke said, "to give or to sell, or to kill" him at will.[22]

Coke did not present this account as one that had been adapted from the texts of the civil law. His comment that *villein* was the common-law term for a person who in the civil law was called *servus* was a rare instance in which he noted a point upon which the common law and the civil law happened to agree. In fact, in the early Stuart era, Coke was the foremost opponent of the movement to fit the laws of England within the order that was set down in the legal treatises of the Roman Empire. His *Institutes* was composed in part as a response to that of Cowell. The text was a vast and scattered commentary upon a commentary upon medieval land law. Its form attested to the long and insular process by which the common law had been refined over time. The sources upon which he drew were almost all English in origin, and this was the case throughout his treatment of villeinage, where above all he relied upon Bracton and Britton.[23]

Coke seems hardly to have been aware that the narrative that such authors had told about the beginning of villeinage was little more than a gloss upon the Roman account of the origin of slavery. In this respect his work is a measure of the influence of Roman legal ideas in England. By the time he wrote, Coke was able to tell the Roman account of the origin of slavery on the basis of English sources alone.

❧

The discourse of the common law was thus one channel through which the Roman account of slavery passed into early-modern English culture. In this discourse, the Roman law was relied upon in order to explain the origin of slavery in two senses: on the one hand, English authors drew upon Roman texts in order to describe the first appearance of slavery in the world, and on the other hand, such authors turned here in order to define the context in which particular persons were reduced to that condition. English authors found that, for both of these purposes, the Roman legal tradition had located the origin of slavery in war. In war, they learned, the natural freedom of all persons did not prevent the enslavement of some of them.

To be sure, it was not only in their encounter with legal texts that readers in England learned that war had been the origin of slavery in the classical world. The works of history and literature that they had before them attested as well to what had been a common theme in classical culture.

In fact, in the first scene in Western literature, *The Iliad* started in a dispute over the possession of a captive taken in war, and in *The Odyssey,* when at last the hero returned to his former home, he met an aged slave whom his father had purchased from the men who sacked the city of his birth. The most famous chronicles of war from classical Athens, those of Herodotus and Thucydides, treated slavery as the routine fate for members of the defeated side in a conflict: it often happened in these accounts that once the men were slaughtered, the women and children were made slaves. The unnamed opponents of Aristotle were also aware that slavery arose as a status assigned to captives in war, since this was the convention upon which they said the institution was founded. Even Aristotle allowed that war could be waged for the purpose of enslaving the enemy, so long as they were slaves by nature.[24]

Although no Roman author endorsed the doctrine of natural slavery as a cause for war, many authors whose works were well known in early-modern England accepted that slavery was often a result of war. The historians of the late Republic and early Empire, for example, from Diodorus to Livy and Plutarch to Tacitus, all told of the immense influx of slaves into Rome from the wars of expansion in this period. In addition, they reported that recent captives from abroad had banded together to start the major slave revolts from this time. Such authors noted that the struggle against Roman forces was understood from Germany to Britain as an effort to escape the enslavement that would follow upon defeat, and they came to think that when a Roman general chose not to enslave a defeated nation this was a special act of mercy. By the time of Justinian, in the sixth century, the compilers of the

Corpus Juris were so sure that slavery came from war that they included this among the customs that all peoples observed.[25]

In early-modern England, even as this custom was no longer observed, the association between war and slavery survived from the culture of the classical world. The works of history and literature in which this custom was described were printed in popular Latin and vernacular editions. The themes and lessons from these works were distilled in learned commentaries and compendia of ancient wisdom. These made clear that it was the warfare of the ancient world that had produced its ultimate form of subjection. Indeed, in the early-modern period the most subtle treatments of the origin of slavery were the work of authors who were concerned not so much with the particular laws and customs of England as with the laws and customs of war.[26]

The first of these authors was Alberico Gentili, whose treatise on the law of war was printed in 1598. Gentili was a Protestant exile from Italy who had arrived in England in 1580 and served as Regius Professor of Civil Law at Oxford from 1587 until his death in 1608. During this time, he was a central figure in the revival of the civil law in England. It was as a scholar of the civil law that he approached the issue of war. His fundamental aim was to establish that there was a law of war and that in turn it was to be found in the texts of the *Corpus Juris*. The problem he faced was that these texts had devoted almost no attention to war: they were more interested in the private relations between persons than in the public law of the state, much less in the laws that would obtain in the relations between states. Gentili stated that war was a public contest of arms. And then he set out to turn what he understood to be the principles of Roman private law into the basis for a novel doctrine of the law of war.[27]

According to Gentili, the most basic principles of Roman law were set down in the law of nature, and these principles were simple: one should not harm another, for example, one should give every person their due, and one should acknowledge a certain kinship with all persons. Of course, it so happened that states as well as persons on occasion came to violate these principles, and on such occasions other states could declare war in response. In so doing, these states might break the peace that existed by nature, since Gentili insisted that there was no conflict in the order that nature had established. And yet he also asserted that war could be in accord with nature, when it was waged in order to enforce the natural law. The same was the case for slavery. Slavery was "contrary to nature," Gentili said, "and yet at the same time in accord with nature." Gentili accepted the Roman notion of the natural freedom of all humankind. But he noted that humans were not made so free by nature that they could never be enslaved. He had learned from the Roman legal tradition that this was what tended to happen to the members of a nation that had been defeated in war and their descendants. The enslavement of such persons was in a sense both natural and normal.[28]

In his treatment of slavery, Gentili thus aimed to resolve the conflict in the Roman legal tradition between the law of nature and the law of nations. As a matter of fact, this was a more general feature of his work. The law of nature was the basis for his doctrine of the law of war, but he held that the only method by which the law of nature could come to be known was through close attention to the law of nations. He drew from the *Institutes* of the classical jurist Gaius the insight that the law of nations itself could be seen as "the law which natural reason has established among all human beings." In truth, the principles that Gentili attributed to the law of nature had for the most part appeared in Roman legal texts as ones that belonged instead to the law of nations. This included the further principle that one could use force to defend oneself from harm, upon which Gentili said the right to make war ultimately was founded.[29]

Gentili believed that this principle could be used to support a broad array of acts of war. He argued that a state could make war not only against another state that had attacked it but also against another state that might well be expected to attack, against one that had attacked any other state, and against one that could be said to have violated any of the laws of nature. Gentili did to some extent hope to restrain the common cruelty of war. He insisted that prisoners captured in war should be enslaved rather than killed and that slaves should be well fed and dressed and treated with a minimal measure of respect. Nevertheless, in most respects the effect of his work on the law of war was to stretch the law of nature so far that it came to cover the permissive customs of the law of nations.[30]

That at least was the opinion that the Dutchman Hugo Grotius held of the work of Gentili. In the decades after *The Law of War* came out in print, the major treatment of that issue was Grotius's masterpiece, *The Law of War and Peace,* which first appeared in Latin in 1625 and had been printed in English in two separate editions by the end of the century. Grotius set out to place the law of war upon a more certain basis than he said Gentili or any other author had been able to do. The cause of the confusion on the part of his predecessors was that none had made a clear distinction between the law of nature and the law of nations. Grotius believed that the law of nature could be discovered and stated on its own terms. The immense task that he set for himself was to build a complete system of law up from the law of nature alone.[31]

According to Grotius, the law of nature was of a different kind from the version of natural law that had been put forward in the texts of the *Corpus Juris.* It was present only in humans, rather than in all animate creatures, since it had to be discovered by means of the faculty of reason that only humans possessed. In turn, it was to be stated not so much in terms of the principles that ordered human life as in terms of the rights that humans possessed. The fundamental natural right was that of self-preservation, Grotius said, and this entailed the additional right of each human to use force in order to defend oneself against harm and to seek out and appropriate those things that were useful for living.[32]

The system of natural law that Grotius developed was thus far more concerned with the preservation of life than it was with liberty as such. Indeed, he asserted that when these two values were found to conflict, a person had the right to renounce the latter in an effort to secure the former. It was in the context of this insight that Grotius introduced a discussion of slavery into his work. What he said was that a desperate person might engage himself as a slave to a master in return for what he needed to survive and, moreover, that an entire people might agree to do the same when they found themselves "upon the Brink of Ruin" with "no other Means to save themselves." It was also as an exercise of the natural right of self-preservation that Grotius understood the right to punish a violent offender with force and even, for "he who has deserved to lose his Liberty," enslavement.[33]

These were the first two sources of slavery that Grotius treated in *The Law of War and Peace*. Slavery here stemmed from some particular action, either as the result of some agreement or in consequence of some crime, and at least in principle it was a status that applied only to the subjects of that act, even if Grotius did also allow that parents might sell their children into slavery on the basis of "mere Necessity" when they could find no other means to keep them alive. Since slavery in these cases arose from the natural right of each person to preserve his own life, masters were required to maintain the health of their slaves and could only put them to death when they were found to have committed some crime that merited this punishment.[34]

At the same time, however, Grotius was also aware that there was one more source of slavery, one that was not so carefully confined within the bounds of natural right. This was the method of enslavement set down in the Roman doctrine of the law of nations. In the third and final section of his work, in the course of his discussion of lawful conduct in and after the conclusion of war, Grotius observed that the law of nations allowed for the enslavement of "all Persons whatsoever" who were captured in war and "their Posterity for ever," whether or not they had taken part in the conflict. Under the law of nations, Grotius continued, the power of the master was "infinite," so that there was "nothing that the Lord may not do to his Slave."[35]

Scholars in recent decades have tended to assume that this doctrine of slavery was the one that Grotius himself endorsed. But he said no more than that it had long described the common custom of the world. In several late chapters on moderation in war, he urged that what he called "the extravagant Licence of War" in this respect be restricted upon the basis of natural right. "I must now reflect," he wrote, "and take away from those that make War almost all the Rights, which I may seem to have granted them; which yet in Reality I have not." He argued that upon a correct interpretation of the law of war, nations must not exert against their enemies the full measure of cruelty that the law of nations allowed. They must take captives only in wars that were just, in the sense that they were fought in order to assert some natural right; they must take as captives only those persons who themselves had taken part in the conflict; and they must exercise the power of life and death only over those captives who had committed some capital offense.[36]

Grotius in essence proposed that slavery in the context of war be made as much as possible to resemble slavery in peace, and the ambivalent effect of his work was to so limit the practice of slavery that in each case it would happen under the cover of natural right.

That said, even as he wove around his account of slavery a discourse of rights that Roman jurists had never had in mind, Grotius preserved the basic structure of the Roman tradition. The story of his early intellectual career was to a great extent that of his gradual rejection of the Aristotelian culture in which he had been educated, and by the time he wrote *The Law of War and Peace,* Grotius was prepared to make his final break from Aristotle. Here he denounced what he termed the "Tyranny" of the Philosopher in European culture, and his treatment of slavery reflected this broader aversion. He declared that there was "no Man by Nature Slave to another." Each person was born free to the extent that each was in full possession of certain natural rights. And yet he also accepted that it was a consequence of living with these rights that certain persons would come to lose them. This was what he meant when he said that it was "not repugnant to natural Justice, that Men should become Slaves by a human Fact." As he went on to elaborate upon the circumstances in which this might take place, Grotius reproduced the movement in the Roman tradition from freedom to slavery.[37]

At the same time, however, in *The Law of War and Peace* Grotius also founded a new tradition. He himself was well aware of the novelty of his work, and from the period when it appeared until well into the next century, many readers across Europe shared in his assessment. He seemed to have been "the first who broke the Ice" after the long scholastic winter, in the phrase of his French translator Jean Barbeyrac, with a system of morals that was based upon the rights expressed in natural law. The major authors who followed him worked to alter certain parts of that system or focused their attention upon certain parts of it more than upon others, but all understood themselves as heirs to a tradition that started with Grotius.[38]

Among authors in England, the most important early reader of Grotius was Thomas Hobbes, and the system that Hobbes developed was in its basic aspect the same as that of Grotius. At Oxford in the first decade of the seventeenth century, Hobbes too had received a traditional Aristotelian education, even if he may also have attended lectures by Gentili. But throughout his mature political works, he dismissed as little more than a mark of pride the idea, which he attributed to Aristotle, "that some Men are by Nature worthy to Govern, and others by Nature ought to serve." He held that all persons possessed the fundamental natural right to preserve their own lives and to decide for themselves the means that would be required for that end. And as Grotius had also done, Hobbes concluded that the sole source of government was the decision of persons to confer the exercise of that right upon it.[39]

Perhaps the most original aspect of the system that Hobbes developed was his rich and vivid description of the condition of persons who lived in the absence of government. This was what he called "the condition of meer Nature," and it was none other than a state of war. What made life in such a state so famously insecure, on Hobbes's account, was that persons here were so equal: each person could harm every other, all could hope to achieve their own ends, and every one had the right to do what they believed they must do in order to survive.[40]

By the time he wrote, toward the middle of the century, Hobbes could have drawn upon any number of sources for his account of the natural freedom and equality of persons. This was a rare point of consensus in the pamphlet literature of the English Civil War. As John Milton observed in 1650, "No man who knows ought, can be so stupid to deny that all men naturally were borne free." For his part, Milton held that on this point nature set a standard from which human action could not depart. The natural freedom of all mankind must be taken to mean that no men could agree to be enslaved. And since the power of an absolute monarch was as much as that of a master, Milton concluded that no people could agree to be governed by one without what he said would be an impermissible "violation of thir natural birthright."[41]

Even those authors who wrote in defense of the royalist cause in the context of the Civil War tended to accept what Milton had said about the natural freedom of all mankind. What such authors denied was that nature here set a limit upon the consequences of human action. Their most common argument was the one that they understood to have come from Grotius: that a people had the unlimited right to place themselves under the government of an absolute monarch. Such authors may have "bravely vindicated the right of kings in most points," in the opinion of Sir Robert Filmer. "Yet all of them," Filmer went on, "when they come to the argument drawn from the natural liberty and equality of mankind, do with one consent admit it for a truth unquestionable." Filmer was the foremost English opponent of this argument. And yet in the course of his own patriarchal defense of the royalist cause, even he never ventured to assert that the subjects of a king could be considered his slaves by nature.[42]

For sources upon which to draw for his account of the natural freedom and equality of mankind, Hobbes also could have turned to the civil law tradition in which he was well versed. In the library in which he worked for most of his career, Hobbes had before him an edition of the complete texts of the *Corpus Juris.* This library also held the first edition in English of Aristotle's *Politics,* which had been published in 1598. In this text the modern editor had laid aside the opinion of the author that "some are naturally bondslaves, others naturally freemen," the conviction of the "Romane Civill lawyers" that slavery was "contrary to nature" and had instead been "brought in by the law of Nations." Hobbes was familiar in addition with the complex reception of Roman law in the works of English authors from Bracton to Coke to Richard Zouche, the foremost midcentury scholar of the civil law. In the pattern of authors in this tradition, once Hobbes had stated that all persons were by nature free and equal, he set out to develop an account that would explain how some persons came to be enslaved.[43]

Over the course of his career, the structure of Hobbes's account remained the same. And yet between its three main statements—*The Elements of Law,* which was completed in 1640; *On the Citizen,* which was first printed in 1642; and *Leviathan,* which was published in 1651—the meanings that he attached to freedom and slavery changed dramatically.

To begin, *The Elements of Law* was the most forceful defense of the absolute power of government that Hobbes ever composed. He held that the natural right was unlimited in the sense that it could be surrendered without reserve, and he stated that as a matter of fact to leave the state of nature and form a civil society was to agree to do just this. There were two contexts in which such an agreement could be made. The first was the mutual consent of each member not to resist the central power that they thus established.

The second was conquest, and here the agreement took the form of a "Covenant from him that is overcome, not to resist him that overcometh." No matter how it arose, the power of a sovereign was as absolute as that of a master. In turn, the "losse of Liberty" on the part of a subject was of the same extent as for what Hobbes called a servant. Only a "Servant taken in the Wars" who had not made an agreement not to resist his captor and was "kept bound in natural Bonds, as Chaines and the like, or in prison" was the kind of servant who "ordinarily and without Passion, is called a *Slave*." "The *Romanes* had no such distinct name" as slave and servant, Hobbes noted. They had "comprehended all under the Name of *Servus*." For the distinction between them was no more than that slaves stood at the furthest possible point down a long line of subjection.[44]

The Elements of Law was concerned with subjection more than freedom. But by the time Hobbes composed *On the Citizen*—in which he revised his earlier work and translated it into Latin—he had developed a powerful new account of freedom, one that entailed a new account of slavery. He still defined the natural right as that of each person to preserve their own life and to judge for themselves the means that were required for that end. Now, however, he held that persons did not need to surrender this right entirely in order to enter into a civil society. In fact, what he called "civil *liberty*" consisted in the right each person retained, against all forms of sovereign power, of "doing all he can and trying every move that is necessary to protect his life and health." Liberty as such was "simply the *absence of obstacles to motion*." Because only captives in war who were held and forced to labor "in prison, workhouses, or bonds" were unable to direct the movements of their bodies so as to protect their lives, only these persons were not free. The Romans had even had a name for them, Hobbes now recalled. They were called *ergastuli* in Latin, as distinct from the more general term *servi*. Whereas in *The Elements of Law* the essential fact of civil society was the loss of freedom on the part of each subject, in *On the Citizen* freedom had become the almost universal condition of civil life.[45]

This was the central transition in the effort that Hobbes made to define slavery and freedom over the course of his career. In its discussion of these issues, *Leviathan* did little more than sharpen the arguments and clarify the terms that had appeared before in *On the Citizen*. On the one hand,

Hobbes was now even more careful to establish that the right of nature could not be surrendered in civil society. What he called "the Liberty of a Subject" was the right that each person possessed to do whatever they pleased that the government did not prohibit. Liberty as such, Hobbes continued, should be understood to mean simply the absence of "externall Impediments of motion," as distinct from the internal inability of a body to move.[46]

On the other hand, in *Leviathan,* Hobbes settled upon a word in English that could be used to describe the status of persons who were not free. In the lexicon of *The Elements of Law,* slaves, servants, and even subjects alike lacked freedom. In *On the Citizen,* the term *servus* was often used to refer to both servants, who were free, and slaves, who were not. In *Leviathan,* Hobbes at last made clear that when a captive in war made a covenant with their captor, "after such Covenant made, the Vanquished is a SERVANT." But until that point, in the period when this person was "kept in prison, or bonds," and so was unable to move on their own or act on their desires, then they alone—of all the characters who moved across the political world of Hobbes's articulation—were not free. They fell into the special class of such persons as were "Commonly called Slaves."[47]

After Grotius, then, Hobbes marked a return to a more purely classical treatment of slavery. Grotius had presented a complex account of the sources of slavery, which for him included self-sale, crime, and war. By contrast, Hobbes followed the doctrine of the law of nations as this had been set down in the legal treatises of the Roman Empire when he held that war was the only context in which slavery might arise and even, by the time he came to write *On the Citizen,* the only context in which a person could lose their freedom. Hobbes also adhered to the law of nations in that, unlike Grotius, he made no efforts to restrict the practice of slavery in war. He placed no limits upon who could be taken as a slave in war, never required that such a war be just in any sense at all, and seemed to accept as a matter of course that the children of enslaved mothers would inherit their status.[48]

Both Grotius and Hobbes started from the distinctive modern premise that persons possessed the natural right to preserve their own lives. Grotius had made this right into the sole basis for his account of the legitimate sources of slavery. Hobbes treated it as the basis for the covenant between master and servant, both of whom thus aimed to ensure their own protection. He did hold that the natural right continued in full effect in the relation between master and slave. Because no agreement had been made between them, they were in a state of nature with respect to each other: each could attack the other at any time. In the course of his discussions of the origin of slavery, though, Hobbes spoke of it more or less in the terms in which it had appeared in the law of nations—that is, as a matter of discretion rather than rights. Slavery arose from the decision of the captive not to submit and, in response, the choice of the victor to keep him in chains until, as Hobbes put it in *Leviathan,* he "shall consider what to do with him."[49]

For Hobbes, the essence of slavery was thus the refusal of consent on the part of the captive in war. By contrast, according to Grotius, slavery and consent were bound up with one another, since one might consent to sell oneself to a master and, even in the context of crime or war, Grotius observed, persons who violated the rights of others had in a sense consented to their slavery as punishment because they must have known that what they did was wrong.[50]

In the several decades after *Leviathan* appeared in print, the most famous author in the tradition of Grotius and Hobbes was the German scholar Samuel Pufendorf. His major work, *The Law of Nature and Nations,* came out in Latin in 1672 and in an English edition in 1703. Here he started from the familiar premise that the belief, which was "derived from the Ancient *Greeks,* of *some Mens being Slaves by Nature*" would need to be set aside. All persons were by nature free and equal with respect to one another, and each person had the natural right to do what they believed they must in order to survive. To this extent, as Jean Barbeyrac later observed, Pufendorf "pursu'd the Genius and Method of *Grotius.*" As had Grotius, Pufendorf insisted that persons entered civil society not only to secure their rights but also to satisfy their natural desire to live in close association with others. That said, the real foundation in the system that he developed was consent—in other words, the conviction that the sole source of legitimate authority was an agreement initiated by the subject. More so even than Grotius, Pufendorf made consent the basis for his account of slavery.[51]

In fact, according to Pufendorf, slavery had its origin in consent rather than in war. "In the early Ages of the World," he explained, as social forms started to emerge, women and men contracted in marriage, children promised obedience to their parents, and peoples asked for the government of rulers. Then at a certain point, "as Men began to quit their primitive Plainness and Simplicity," some of the poor agreed to serve the rich as slaves for life in return for food and shelter. Under the doctrine of the law of nations, slavery arose as the social world started to unravel in war. But Pufendorf understood the rise of slavery as part of the massive process in which people first knit themselves together in states. He did allow that "in succeeding times, when Wars grew more frequent in the World," the number of slaves increased and their treatment became far more "hard and grievous." Nevertheless, he held that the power of a victor over a captive was no more than a continuation forward in time of the right to kill an enemy in war. Pufendorf was well aware of the departure this marked from Hobbes when he said that a captive assumed the status of a slave only when this person consented to serve his captor in return for "the Security of his Life."[52]

The English editions of *The Law of Nature and Nations* and the abridgement of the text, which came out in Latin in 1673 and in English in 1691, tended to record a distinction between slaves and servants: the former had consented to their status in the aftermath of war, whereas the latter had done so in peace. Pufendorf had used the term *servi* in both cases and reported that he was unable to find a basis in natural law for this distinction. Unlike Hobbes in *On the Citizen*—which was the work of Hobbes that Pufendorf, like most readers on the Continent, considered to be definitive—Pufendorf never proposed that either kind of *servus* was free. What he said was that because *servi* both in war and in peace had put themselves under the authority of another person forever in order to secure their mutual benefit, both were involved in varieties of the same condition. Both had consented to slavery.

❧

In the final decades of the seventeenth century, the principal author in the tradition that now ran from Grotius to Pufendorf was John Locke. In contrast to both of these earlier authors, Locke did not present himself so much as an opponent of Aristotle. The scholastic education that he had received at Oxford toward the middle of the century appears to have left little impression upon his mature political thought. He presented his major political work, *The Two Treatises of Government,* which was printed in 1690, rather as a response to the work of the royalist Sir Robert Filmer, whose *Patriarcha* had been written in the context of the debates about the nature of royal power in the first half of the century but had not appeared in print until 1680, when it was enlisted in support of an unaltered line of succession in the context of the Exclusion Crisis.

Filmer had never maintained that any persons were natural slaves in the sense that Aristotle had described. That said, he was at pains to deny that any persons were naturally free. All persons were born under the absolute power of a father, he observed. The power of monarchs was in turn derived from this original paternal power, which could be traced back to Adam, and the one power was as absolute as the other. In particular, in his *Second Treatise* Locke aimed to establish that all persons were by nature born free and equal with respect to each other. Each person possessed the fundamental natural right to act in such a manner as to preserve themselves as well as all humankind. The proper source of political authority was the agreement of persons to confer upon it the exercise of this right.[53]

Up until this point, Locke worked more or less within the natural rights tradition as it had been developed in the works of Grotius and Pufendorf. Indeed, he once recommended their major works as the two most important books that had been written about the nature and origin of political society. After this point, however, Locke departed dramatically from the natural rights tradition as he had found it.[54]

Both Grotius and Pufendorf had accepted that one legitimate use to which the right of nature could be put was for a person to enslave themselves to a master. Of course, both authors had believed that in this case the master was bound to preserve the life of the slave, who in all likelihood would not have been able to do so on their own. But Locke held that the real essence of slavery, in all cases, was a power so absolute as to include an unlimited authority to take the life of the slave at will. It was in the context of this particular conception of slavery that Locke so often said that Filmer—an advocate for the absolute and arbitrary power of monarchs who had never imagined that this would mean he was an advocate for slavery—was "*an Ad-*

vocate for Slavery." It was also in this context that Locke concluded that no person could consent to be enslaved.[55]

Scholars in recent decades have tended to treat as the basis for this conclusion the point that Locke made that the natural right came from a prior natural law, which said that each person was "*bound to preserve himself.*" And yet this had been a common premise in the works of authors who had said that a person could indeed enslave himself to a master. To be sure, it was present in the works of Grotius and Pufendorf, and it was present as well in a book written by a close friend of Locke whose name was James Tyrrell. In *Patriarcha non Monarcha,* which came out in 1681 as his own response to the work of Filmer, Tyrrell put forward what was a more or less conventional system of natural rights. He maintained that a person could only be enslaved as a result of his capture in war or his own agreement. In either case, Tyrrell explained, his master had to provide him with "all the necessaries of life." If his master attacked him with force, then he could defend himself. If his master did not give him what he needed to survive, then he could "run away from his Master, and set himself at liberty if he can."[56]

Locke rejected the version of slavery that he had come upon in the works of such authors, and the basis for his conclusion that no person could consent to be enslaved was his unusual conviction that to do so was in a sense to invite death. Grotius and Pufendorf had offered as evidence that persons could enslave themselves the example of the Hebrew law as this was described in the Bible. Locke responded that among the "*Jews,* as well as other Nations," persons were allowed to sell themselves into "*Drudgery*" in the service of a master but "*not to Slavery.*" The difference was that such persons never ceded to another person the perfect control over whether they lived or died. This alone was what it meant to be enslaved.[57]

Unlike Grotius and Pufendorf, then, Locke held that no person could consent to be enslaved. Moreover, in contrast to Filmer, Locke believed that all persons were born free. Locke followed the doctrine of the law of nations when he maintained that there was only one route into slavery and it started in war. Hobbes also had followed this doctrine. But in a manner that even Hobbes had not done, Locke made an elaborate attempt to explain the enslavement of persons in war in the terms of his system of natural rights. In the course of this attempt, the natural rights in which freedom was said to consist became the means by which some free persons came to be slaves.

When two persons were found in a state of nature, Locke explained, each one was bound in their mutual relations by the natural law. This law had two parts: the first one was that each person was bound to preserve his own life, but the second one was that each person was bound "*to preserve the rest of Mankind.*" When one person attacked the other person with force, he had thus broken the second part of the natural law. He may well not have made a direct attempt upon the life of his victim. He may only have tried to get him "into his Absolute Power"—or in other words, Locke said, as he slipped into the first-person perspective of the victim, to "make me a Slave." This made no difference to Locke. After all, he had held that to be made a slave was to lose control over whether one lived or died. This was a serious offense, and Locke did not hesitate to assert that it could be punished in kind. The offender in this case had, "by his fault, forfeited his own Life, by some Act that deserves Death." In turn, "he, to whom he has forfeited it," Locke continued, "may (when he has him in his Power) delay to take it, and make use of him to his own Service, and he does him no Injury by it."[58]

The man who enforced the natural law here acted upon the right that it entailed: to do what one believed one must in order to preserve oneself as well as the rest of mankind. The power that he now held was more or less the reverse of the one that his aggressor had tried to acquire over him. It was the power both to take the life of another person and also to delay this act for as long as one wished. Like Hobbes, who drew the term from the ancient Greek word Δεσποτης, Locke called this "*Despotical Power.*" It was the power of a master over a slave when this had been acquired in accord with natural right. And it was the same as the power of a conqueror over the persons who were captured in a just war. As a matter of fact, Locke said, to attempt to gain absolute power over another person was to create a miniature "*State of War*" with them. Wars between nations thus resembled war between persons—and slavery was none other than this "*State of War continued.*" At the moment when a person who held despotical power agreed to protect the life of his subject in return for his obedience, this state of war was at last at an end. The person who had been enslaved resumed his life as a free man.[59]

Locke had narrowed down to war the contexts in which a person could be enslaved. He had made clear that only in a just war, which was waged as punishment for a violation of natural law, could anyone at all be enslaved. In a late chapter on conquest in the *Second Treatise,* Locke added that even in a just war between nations only certain persons could be taken as slaves. The conqueror in such a war could acquire despotical power over the lives of "those, who have actually assisted, concurr'd, or consented to that unjust Force, that is used against him." The conqueror could acquire no such power over his allies, the members of the defeated nation who had not helped to attack him, or the wives and children even of those who had done so.[60]

Locke was well aware that to limit the sources of slavery in war ran "quite contrary to the practice of the World." He had in this respect restrained, on the basis of natural law, the practice of slavery under the law of nations. But in another respect, Locke had come to embrace the most brutal version of slavery ever recorded in the Roman legal tradition.

In the law of nations as this was set down in the texts of the *Corpus Juris,* slavery had started in war. In fact, the term for slave, *servus,* was said to have come from the term for preserve, *servare,* as in the custom by which generals had preserved and then sold their prisoners when they might otherwise have killed them. That said, slavery presented to such persons an uncertain grant of life, because in the law of nations, masters had held what was called an unlimited "power of life or death" over their slaves. In a series of statutes enacted over the course of the Empire, this power was gradually restrained in the Roman civil law. Still, the old account of the origin of slavery was never far from the minds of even the most sophisticated of the Roman jurists. In one of the final statements in the *Digest,* Ulpian said that he and his colleagues had continued to "compare slavery closely with death."[61]

In the early-modern era, this close association between slavery and death survived from the legal treatises of the Roman Empire. The authors from this era knew these works well enough to have studied the restraints that had been placed upon the power of masters over their slaves by the time of Justinian. For their part, Bracton and Britton had remarked upon these measures with approval. Around the turn of the seventeenth century, so did scholars as different from one another as Smith, Cowell, and Coke. Of all the scholars from this period in England, perhaps none was as learned in the principles of the law of nations as Gentili. He did urge that persons enslaved in war be treated with a minimal measure of respect, but he also knew all too well that appeals of this kind were often disregarded. He started the chapter about this matter in his work with the remark that "slavery is all but death."[62]

In the natural rights discourse that would develop in England over the course of the seventeenth century, the most important political concern was seen as the preservation of human life; and the continued interest in slavery in this discourse was no doubt due in part to the perception that it was the human status closest to death. At the same time, however, there was also in the works of the authors who contributed to this discourse a persistent refrain that as a matter of right even the life of a slave should be protected. No matter the circumstances in which they had been reduced to their present status, the slave was by nature free and equal to every other person. As Pufendorf insisted, a master could not be allowed "to extinguish all Marks of primitive Equality in a Slave." In the treatment of such a person, he concluded, one could never "forget that this Servant is a *Man*."[63]

This was one point that Locke never insisted upon in his discussion of the treatment of slaves in the *Second Treatise*. In fact, time and again, he said that slavery was so distinct from the lawful and consensual relations that were appropriate to a political society that it was a form of authority more proper to beasts than to men.[64]

Locke's doctrine of natural freedom and his system of natural rights had led him to narrow down the sources of slavery to their finest possible point. They had also seemed to him to condone, not as the common practice of the world but precisely as right, the barest form of domination ever conceived in the Roman tradition.

Since around the middle of the twentieth century, historians have wondered what the discourse of slavery in early-modern England really was about, and in recent decades it has become common to assert that the ideas of slavery in this period were developed in some sense with the contemporary practice of slavery in mind. Scholars of John Locke in particular have maintained that the account of slavery in his principal political works was composed in order to defend, or on the other hand to attack, the practice of slavery across the English Atlantic world. To be sure, one of the aims of this book is to demonstrate that there is more evidence to support claims of this kind than many of the scholars who have made them seem to have imagined.[65]

That said, for the modern reader, perhaps the most striking aspect of the ideas about slavery that have been described here is their abstraction—that is, the extent to which they seem not to have an object in the real historical world. In the course of his own discussion of such ideas in *The Problem of Slavery in Western Culture,* David Brion Davis paused to remark upon this aspect of them. As one read more and more of the early-modern treatises on slavery, Davis reported, one came to sense that "it was as if the learned volumes of law and statecraft had been produced in a different world from that which contained the Negro captives awaiting shipment at Elmina Castle, the disease and sickening stench of the slave ships, and the regimented labor of colonial plantations." This chapter has aimed to describe the terms and themes and tensions within what Davis termed this "different world."[66]

As Davis well understood, the discourse of slavery in the early-modern period had become to some extent an insular system. The authors who contributed to it worked within a context that they believed to have been set by the works of other authors like themselves more than any trend or event to which these works might have been written as responses. Bracton had borrowed from the works of such medieval glossators as Accursius and Azo; Britton had in turn glossed Bracton; and Coke, in the course of his own commentary upon the treatise of Littleton, more or less followed Britton. Grotius aimed to improve upon the treatise of Gentili; Hobbes built upon the system that Grotius had laid down; Pufendorf had immersed himself in the study of Grotius and Hobbes; and for all his famous involvement in Atlantic slavery, when Locke wrote about slavery in the *Second Treatise,* he addressed himself above all to Grotius, Hobbes, Pufendorf, Filmer, and Tyrrell. All of these authors had set themselves against the authority of Aristotle. And all of them set themselves within a tradition whose origins were to be found in complex legal texts that had been produced in ancient Rome. Slavery passed back and forth between their many works in the manner of an idea that was in a sense just an idea.

Insofar as the authors who have appeared in this chapter believed that there was a context in which the idea of slavery was made real, they found this context not so much in the modern as in the ancient world. The texts of the *Corpus Juris* could, of course, be mined not only for certain fertile concepts but as a fund of information about the world that they had been intended to govern. For information of this kind, early-modern authors turned in addition to the works of the poets and historians, playwrights and orators, that were the stable points of reference in learned culture. References to such works filled the books that have been discussed here, in the form of marginal annotations and parenthetical citations, indented quotations and footnotes. By such means the authors of these books could be seen to illustrate and test their ideas about slavery against what was known about the institution across the ancient world and in particular in Greece and Rome. They might have given to their readers the impression that slavery was a concept that endured but a practice whose time had passed.

This was not the case.

And yet at the same time it must be said that in the early-modern period the English knew very little about the practice of slavery in their colonies across the ocean. By the end of the seventeenth century, they had only started to come to terms with the character of the slave systems that had been established over there. Reports from what were then the most important slave colonies in the English Atlantic world—Barbados and Jamaica—were not printed and widely read until the final three decades of the century. The travelers who had written them had been shocked at what they had seen on these remote islands. No ancient tradition seemed to sanction it. Among English authors, perhaps only Locke had imagined such cruelty. The Caribbean colonists themselves were desperate to establish and maintain their control. They had only just started to seek out the kinds of ideas that might make their actions appear to be legitimate.

In the early-modern Atlantic world, there was another context in which the English had studied the practice of slavery. This was in Africa—where from the second half of the sixteenth century, English readers had received a stream of detailed information. They had learned about nations and empires whose own customs seemed to resemble those laid out in the Roman legal tradition. The texts in which these customs were described had shown little interest in the particular positions that slaves tended to hold across the range of African life. Their attention was drawn rather toward the point around which discussion of slavery had always revolved in the long Roman tradition. It was most of all the sources of slavery that interested English observers of Africa in the early-modern era. They wanted to know by what means persons were enslaved there and whether this was done in a manner that one could come to accept.

CHAPTER 2

English Freedom in a World of Slaves

THE ENGLISH did not at once come to accept that they would trade in enslaved persons from Africa. The first voyage from England arrived on the western coast of Africa in 1530, and within a quarter of a century, English merchants had established regular commerce with the region that was then known as Guinea. In the decades that followed, the goods that English merchants hoped to receive from the peoples whom they met along the shore were pepper, ivory, redwood, wax, and most of all gold. Not until perhaps as late as 1640 did the regular English commerce in persons from Africa begin.

The English had been late to arrive on the western coast of Africa. By the middle of the sixteenth century, merchants from Portugal had traded there for more than a century. The English were also late to enter into the trans-atlantic trade in enslaved African persons. English observers were well aware of both of these facts, and scholars have often remarked upon them. Even so, the period between these events has not often been examined in close detail. But it is essential to an account of the origins and development of African slavery in the English Atlantic world. Its role in this account is in the contrast that it presents with the period that followed. To describe the thoughts and actions of the English in the period when for the most part they did not trade in slaves is to recover an entire complex of assumptions and associations that had to be altered or cast aside when the English came to accept that that was exactly what they would do.[1]

For what stands out most to the modern observer about the period when the English did not trade in slaves is that they perceived this fact to be so central to their conception of themselves as a nation. To be sure, this never led them to conclude that slavery as such was an absolute evil. Their culture was saturated in what was described in Chapter 1 as a broad Roman tradition of slavery. Within this tradition, all persons were believed to be free with respect to the natural order. Slavery arose, through accident and misfortune, most often for persons who were taken captive in war. The code that covered the rise of slavery in Roman legal texts was known as the law of nations. This was said to be composed of the customs that all human peoples observed, and English authors in the early-modern period were aware that, in the ancient texts that they still took to be authoritative on matters of law and politics, slavery was considered to be more or less universal.

Chapter 1 also described the natural rights discourse that developed across early-modern Europe. This was the discourse in which the characteristic movement within the Roman tradition from freedom to slavery was explained in the clearest and fullest detail. The authors who contributed to this discourse, from Grotius to Locke, hoped to set down accounts of the origins and character of political authority that could be accepted as true in absolute terms. They started from what they took to be the most minimal possible premises and worked toward conclusions upon which they believed all persons would be able to agree. In so doing, these authors said that their model in philosophical method was mathematics, another science that did not depend for its validity upon any particular facts. Slavery appeared in their works at once as an abstract idea, one that was almost without an object in the real historical world, and as a feature of the essential order in political life.

In early-modern English culture, however, even as the Roman tradition of slavery was received and refashioned, another, more particular development also took place. From the second half of the sixteenth century, English authors came to articulate the conviction that theirs was a nation dedicated to freedom. The context for this conviction was shaped in part by the end of villeinage, which over time had declined to the point that most observers concluded that no villeins remained within the realm. The presence of villeinage had been the fact that indicated to such medieval authorities on the common law as Britton and Bracton that the status of slaves in Rome had a parallel within the present social order of England. In turn, the disappearance of villeinage was the event that led many authors to conclude that now all the people of England could be said to be free.[2]

In the decades that followed, moreover, many English authors drew from this one a further conclusion. They said that the free status of the people of England reflected some deep fact about the character of the nation. The most important accounts of the history of the nation that were written in this time, such as those of Holinshed and Camden, did not hesitate to admit that several times in the distant past it had been conquered, and its people enslaved, by foreign powers. This was what the Romans had done, of course—and it was also what the Normans had done in the eleventh century. That said, the theme upon which such accounts tended to dwell was that each time the inhabitants of the island had mounted fierce resistance against the enemies that had threatened them with the yoke of subjection. In such events the real features of the national character had been formed. The descriptions of England from this time affirmed that the people were strong in body and brave in spirit. These were the features of people who were determined to be free.[3]

In turn, according to Sir Thomas Smith, this was as much as to state that the people of England were the proper members of a commonwealth. For a commonwealth, explained Smith in his own description of the nation, *De republica Anglorum,* which was printed in 1583, was an association of free persons for their common benefit. A slave could not take part in an association of this kind, and Smith noted that the disappearance of villeinage in England meant that now none of the persons here could be said to be enslaved. The "nature of our nation," he declared, "is free, stout, haulte, prodigall of life and bloud." "Servitude and servile torment & punishment it will not abide." Over the course of his account, Smith considered slavery within the same particular context as the people whom he described. It was a matter of the account of the nature of the nation that he wished to affirm.[4]

In the final quarter of the sixteenth century, the most sophisticated version of this approach to the matter of slavery was the work of the French lawyer and philosopher Jean Bodin. His principal work had first appeared in French in 1576 and came out in an English edition in 1606. The title that it received here was *The Six Bookes of a Commonweale.* As did Smith, Bodin started his work with an effort to define its central term. Unlike Smith, he never held that there could be no slaves within a commonwealth. The most original aspect of his system, in the history of political philosophy, was the doctrine that a commonwealth must be under the rule of a sovereign, whose power was absolute. He noted that of course it would be the decision of the sovereign whether to allow slaves within the realm. But he himself had also reflected upon this issue, and he had concluded that slavery was ruinous to a well-ordered state.[5]

Before he arrived at this conclusion, Bodin had considered the arguments that had been presented in defense of slavery in Western culture. He reported that these could be divided into two distinct positions. The first was the one presented in the works of Aristotle, who had held that "the servitude of slaves is of right naturall," for the reason that whereas some persons were made "to command and governe," others were "naturally made to serve and obey." The second of these positions was the one associated with the classical Roman jurists, who held that slavery was "directly contrarie unto nature" and rightfully arose instead as a punishment for crime and as a status that was assigned to prisoners in war.[6]

Bodin cast doubt upon both of these positions. On the one hand, he was concerned that the common custom of the world seemed so often to reverse the ideal relation of slave and master that Aristotle had defined. He allowed that perhaps it would be just for a strong but foolish man to have to serve one who was feeble but wise. "But for wise men to serve fools, men of understanding to serve the ignorant, and the good to serve the bad; what can bee more contrarie unto nature?" he inquired. On the other hand, Bodin wondered whether the enslavement of prisoners who might otherwise have been killed was as merciful an act as authors from the Roman legal tradition had sometimes assumed. If the enslaved person was then subjected to a brutal regime of perpetual labor for the profit of their master, then death might well have been for them the more merciful fate.[7]

Bodin was a more subtle critic of the two main classical traditions of slavery than any English author in the early-modern era. Nevertheless, what was most important to him was to some extent different from what was most important to them. He was interested not so much in the reasons that might be presented for the enslavement of certain persons as in the effect of slavery upon the order of a state. He had read more than enough in the history of the ancient world to have learned from "the examples of so many worlds of years" about the "rebellions, servile warres, conspiracies eversions and chaunges to have happened unto Commonweals by slaves." The proverb that warned, "*So many slaves, so many enemies in a mans house,*" had proven to be correct, and what was true in the context of the household had also been shown to be the case at the level of the commonwealth.[8]

Bodin was thus pleased to report that since the twelfth century there had been no slaves within the commonwealth of France. And he also remarked with approval upon another, more recent event. A Genoese merchant had arrived in Toulouse with his slave. This slave had sued for his freedom, and the magistrates of the city had granted his suit, on the basis of the principle that "the slaves of strangers so soone as they set their foot within Fraunce become franke & free." As it happened, a similar case had been decided in England around this same time. In 1569, the Court of Star Chamber had freed a slave who had been brought into the country from abroad. "*England* was too pure an Air for Slaves to breath in," the Court resolved. This case was not reported in print, but it was known to William Harrison, who soon referred to it in the description of the nation that he composed as an introduction to Holinshed's popular *Chronicles.* The case was a point of national pride for Harrison. He said that it would have been an "iniurie to nature to make or suffer them to be bond, whome she in hir woonted course dooth product and bring foorth free." The freedom of the English could be seen to reflect and preserve the natural freedom of all humankind.[9]

In the second half of the sixteenth century, a popular consensus thus developed in England that the people of the nation stood in some special relation to freedom. They did not allow slaves within the borders of the realm. And what was more, it was often said that such was the extent of their commitment to freedom that the people of England would not make slaves of the persons they encountered in the wide world abroad.

❧

In this period the most vivid and immediate context in which the English came to articulate their special commitment to freedom was international rather than local. It was framed within the contrast that they aimed to establish between the character of their own nation and that of their principal rival and opponent in Europe—which was Spain.

In the terms of this broad contrast, the commitment of the English to freedom was set in opposition to the determination of the Spanish to enslave. Around the same time that English authors became aware that slavery had ended in their corner of the world, English observers also learned that it now flourished far to the south on the Iberian Peninsula.

In fact, from the second half of the fifteenth century, merchants from Portugal had carried on a regular commerce in persons from the western coast of Africa. Most of these persons were taken back to Lisbon, and some in turn were sold into coastal cities in Spain. Over the course of the sixteenth century, African slaves composed around one-tenth of the total population in Seville. One Spanish author remarked that, as a result, the city had come to resemble "a giant chessboard containing an equal number of white and black chessmen." The development of African slavery as an institution in Spain made an impression as well upon observers from elsewhere. One of these was Jean Bodin. Bodin was concerned that in recent times it was the absence of slavery in France that had come to seem unusual. More and more he believed "the whole world is full of Slaves" and, even in Europe, slavery had started to spread. He noted that the Genoese merchant who had come to Toulouse with his slave had purchased this person in Spain. There it was the case that "now whole droves of slaves are sold and that openly," Bodin said, and lamented that such persons were treated "as if they were beasts."[10]

In England, the concerns about Spain in this period were even more acute. English observers worried that they themselves would soon become in some sense enslaved to their enemies. To be sure, over the entire course of the sixteenth century, Spain remained much the richest and most powerful nation in Europe. In the first half of the sixteenth century, as the Habsburg monarch Charles V was elected to rule over the Holy Roman Empire and the colonies in both the East and West Indies continued to expand, the Spanish Empire became the first in the world to be described as one upon which the sun never set. Toward the end of his life, Charles abdicated much of his European empire. But when his son and successor Philip II acceded to the throne in Portugal, in 1580, the event seemed to herald the return of the universal aspiration of Spain. Philip adopted and embraced a title that had earlier been accepted more reluctantly by his father. He was denominated the *dominus totius orbis*—that is, lord of all the world.[11]

Indeed, in England in this period there seemed to be no limit upon Spanish ambition. In 1585, in the first year of a period of conflict that was to last for the next two decades, the privateer and sea commander Francis Drake raided the Spanish West Indian town of Santo Domingo. When he entered the house of the colonial governor, Drake ascended a staircase and found himself in a gallery. There was a large shield mounted upon the wall. Painted on this shield was the Spanish coat of arms and, underneath it, a terrestrial globe. A horse was painted over the globe, reared up on its hind legs as if to leap, and in its mouth it gripped a scroll. The scroll was inscribed with a legend that, in the decades that followed, English observers would often reproduce as a true statement of the real scope of Spanish aims. The legend read, NON SUFFICIT ORBIS: the world is not enough.[12]

Three years after Drake came upon this scene, the full imperial ambition of Spain seemed to have turned toward England. This was the year of the famous first Armada crisis, and it so happened that Thomas Hobbes was born in this year. He later reflected, perhaps so as to explain the source of his distinctive account of the tense relations between persons in the absence of a sovereign power to enforce order between them, that in 1588 "My Mother Dear / Did bring forth Twins at once, both Me, and Fear." As the dreaded Armada prepared to sail northward from the Bay of Biscay, the Tudor monarch Elizabeth I issued an order in which she warned that its intention was "utterly to overthrow our most happy estate and this flourishing commonweal." The Spanish would subject the free people of England to "the proud, servile, and slavish government of foreigners." Under such a regime the English would become "subjects and slaves to aliens and strangers."[13]

In this period the English had before them at least one example of the character of Spanish imperial rule. This was in America, where in some areas for almost a century the Spanish had worked to bring the native peoples under their control. As English observers first learned about the actions of the Spanish on the other side of the Atlantic, they did not at once conclude that the Spanish had reduced the peoples who lived there to the status of slaves. As a matter of fact, to Richard Eden, the author and editor of the first books about America to be printed in English, close to the opposite seemed to be the case.

The two books on America that Eden composed both came out in the brief interval around the middle of the sixteenth century when an alliance had been established between Spain and England. The Catholic monarch Mary Tudor had acceded to the throne in 1553 and soon married Philip II. In this context, Eden was eager to extol the virtues of Spanish monarchs, and this he did in the extended Preface to the most important of his books on America, the *Decades of the Newe Worlde,* which was for the most part translated from Spanish and Italian sources and appeared in 1555. Eden was aware of the fabulous wealth and immortal fame that had accrued to the Spanish Crown from the exploration that it had overseen in the New World. But he maintained that the Indians had benefitted even more. He had heard it said that the Spanish had come to "use theym as bondemen and tributaries, where before they were free." He responded that their present condition was "much rather to be desired then theyr former libertie." And insofar as the Spanish had started to instruct them in the Word of God, even the subjection of the Indians was better seen as a new form of spiritual freedom.[14]

According to Eden, Spain had set an example in America that his own nation would do well to follow. There was still so much land over there that so far even the Spanish had not explored. "Stoope Englande stoope," Eden advised, "and learne to knowe thy lorde and master." Soon after Eden delivered this advice, expressions of submission toward Spain all but disappeared from English culture. In 1558, Elizabeth inherited the crown and carried on with the work of the Reformation. Through the close of the century, the tension with Spain continued to increase, and it was one feature of this cultural shift that in England the most popular book on the Spanish enterprise in America was the one that had been most critical of it. This book had first been published in Seville in 1552, as the *Brevísima Relación de la destrucción de las Indias.* When it appeared in an English edition in 1583, as *The Spanish Colonie,* the title had been altered so as to ensure that it was clear who had been the cause of the destruction of the Indies.[15]

The author of this book was a Dominican friar named Bartholomé de Las Casas, who had lived much of his life in the Spanish colonies in America and reported that he had seen at least some of the events that he described. The title of his book captured its one essential theme, and what Las Casas meant when he said that the Indies had been destroyed was, in bare and simple terms, that the native peoples there had almost all been murdered. Over the course of his account, Las Casas moved from region to region across the New World, and at each point he made a record of the methods that the Spanish had used to complete their slaughter. They had starved the Indians and tortured them, thrown them into pits and fed them to dogs, drowned them in the ocean and burned them alive, hacked them to pieces and worked them to death. Always Las Casas tracked the numbers of people whom the Spanish had killed. Gradually he built toward the conclusion that, in the short time since the arrival of Columbus, and "only for getting wealth and riches," the Spanish had "slaine and destroyed 20. millions of soules."[16]

It was an indelible document. Across the nations of Europe, the book was read and remarked upon, perhaps nowhere more so than in England. Here it was often accepted as the most accurate account of the actions of the Spanish in America. It was also the only work from Las Casas ever to become well known outside of Spain. And yet the *Brevísima Relación* was to some extent unlike the rest of his immense literary output. For most of his life, which came to an end in 1566, Las Casas was less concerned with the sheer spectacle of Spanish cruelty. He was involved instead in a learned dispute about the nature and basis of Spanish rule over the native peoples of America.

No doubt the most dramatic occasion in the course of this dispute was the formal debate that was held in Valladolid in 1550 and 1551. At the height of the Spanish Empire, and in part in response to the insistence of Las Casas, Charles summoned a panel of select members chosen from the religious orders and royal councils to decide a question that had been considered in Spain almost from the moment of the discovery of the New World. At issue in Valladolid was no less than whether the conquest of the Indies could be understood to be just. Las Casas would assert that it could not; his opponent, the court official and humanist scholar Juan Ginés de Sepúlveda, would hold that it could.[17]

The argument that Sepúlveda put forward in defense of this position would already have been a familiar one in Spain. The structure of his account was drawn from the *Politics* of Aristotle. What he said was that the Indians came under the definition of persons whom nature intended to be slaves. When persons of this kind encountered persons whom nature had marked out to be masters, then the one was bound to submit to the rule of the other. In the event that they resisted, as it was observed that some of the Indians had done when the Spanish first came upon them, then a war was just that would compel them to submit. On an incredible scale, the conquest of the Indies was a war of this kind.[18]

Las Casas worked within the Aristotelian structure of the argument that Sepúlveda had put forward. What he denied was that the Indians had been found to be natural slaves. On the contrary, prior to the arrival of the Spanish, they had made for themselves the kind of stable and ordered communities that on their own fulfilled the needs and possibilities of human life as Aristotle had understood them. The conquest of the Indies was not founded upon the order of nature. In turn, the submission of the Indians came under the other sort of slavery that Aristotle had defined. It was conventional, which meant that it came from the common custom wherein the losers in war were made to serve the winners. It was founded upon force alone.

It must be said that the record of the debate in Valladolid never passed into English culture in full. The best account of it that appears to have been available in the Elizabethan era was one that was included in the English edition of the *Brevísima Relación*. Here, at the end of the text, the editor printed a short report upon the exchange between Las Casas and Sepúlveda. This started with the claim from Sepúlveda that the conquest of the Indies was just, for the reason that the Indians were "bound to submitte them selves to the Spaniards government, as the foolishe to the wise." There followed the response from Las Casas that Spanish rule over the Indians was "wicked and tyrannous."[19]

In this period there was one more complete record that was available in England from the long dispute in Spain about the nature and basis of Spanish rule over the Indians. This was the work of the foremost theologian at the great center of Spanish intellectual life in the sixteenth century, the University of Salamanca. The lectures that Francisco de Vitoria composed on the affairs of the Indies were delivered in 1539 and published widely in Latin in the second half of the century. The question that he considered here was more or less the same one that would be at issue in Valladolid. What Vitoria wanted to know was by what right the Indians had been brought under Spanish rule.

In order to answer this question, Vitoria assessed in order each one of the arguments that had been put forward in order to defend what the Spanish had done. Like Las Casas, Vitoria was a member of the Dominican order, and he reported in private that he had been shocked to learn about the violence that had been used in the recent conquest of Peru. That said, in his lectures Vitoria stated his concern in the terms of a certain academic discourse in which Las Casas had never been trained. Vitoria was the leader in a movement that has come to be known as the Second Scholastic, which aimed at a revival of Thomism. As had Aquinas, Vitoria worked to incorporate within a single complex scheme the categories and objectives of Aristotle, the doctrine of the Church, and the principles of natural law.

The first argument that Vitoria assessed in defense of the conquest of the Indies was the Aristotelian one to which Las Casas would respond at Valladolid. It worked in the same circular manner: if the Indians were slaves as a matter of nature, then of course the Spanish could enslave them. This was what Vitoria meant when he said that this argument held that since "the barbarians were slaves, the Spaniards could appropriate them." Vitoria dismissed this claim in short order. The Indians had established "some order in their affairs," he noted, and he went on to list the elements of civic life on the Aristotelian model that the Indians had been found to possess. People whose rational character found expression in families, laws, cities, and commerce had to be considered the natural masters of their own affairs.[20]

The second claim that Vitoria examined was always understood to be the principal one that could be relied upon in support of Spanish dominion in the New World. This was the claim provided by the Bulls of Donation that the Pope issued upon the return of Columbus from his first voyage to the Indies. These had declared the rulers of Spain to be lords of all the peoples who were to be found on the other side of the ocean. It was an awesome grant of power, and Vitoria denied it because he held that the Pope had never possessed this power such that he would be able to make a grant of it.

His authority did not extend over the secular concerns of political communities.[21]

Over the course of his lectures about the conquest of the Indies, as Vitoria examined reason after reason that had been presented in its defense, he came to conclude that in truth none of them could authorize what the Spanish had done. All the same, if this was the case, then perhaps "*the whole Indian expedition and trade would cease,*" and this in turn would be "to the great loss of the Spaniards." It would be "intolerable," he said. Vitoria appeared at this point to accept the actions of his countrymen abroad, even as he declined to defend them on principle. He was one of the first intellectuals in Europe to respond in this manner to reports about novel forms of domination that had been established in America. He was far from the last.[22]

As it happened, in the decades that followed, the closest reader of Vitoria in England believed that he had been able to locate a principle that would support the Spanish conquest of the Indies. Alberico Gentili modeled much of his own treatise about *The Law of War* upon the lectures that Vitoria had delivered about that same matter. As a scholar of the civil law who was an important figure in the revival of the discipline in England, Gentili relied upon a basic scheme that was simpler than the one the Salamanca theologian had worked to develop. Gentili hoped to establish that the law of war could be constructed from the law of nature alone—even if, as we have seen in Chapter 1, the most distinctive feature of his account of the law of nature was that he was convinced that it could only come to be known from the study of the law of nations and that both were best expressed in the legal treatises of the Roman Empire.[23]

In *The Law of War,* Gentili thus aimed to produce a complete treatment of the field. But time and again, in the course of this work, he returned to consider what he understood to be the war that the Spanish had made upon the Indians. It was one of the most important modern cases that he used to test and illustrate his ideas. To a certain point, he did follow what Vitoria had said; as a matter of fact, the lectures of Vitoria were the main source he cited for insight into the dispute in Spain over the affairs of the Indies.

As had Vitoria, Gentili dismissed the argument that the conquest of the Indies was authorized by the natural slavery of the Indians. The natural slave status of a people would have to be seen as a reason to make war in order to enslave them, and Gentili was careful to maintain the premise set down in the texts of Roman law that peace was the rule in the order that nature had established. In addition, Gentili drew upon Vitoria in his rejection of the claim that the war upon the Indians was justified by the mere fact that they were not Christian or would not at once accept the faith. The Romans had never made war for such a cause, Gentili observed; regardless, the true faith could be accepted on the basis of free choice alone.[24]

One other principle of natural law that Gentili had come across in the *Corpus Juris* was that there was a natural association or kinship of the human race. Of course, each person was entitled to use force in order to defend themselves from harm, but moreover, each state could make war in order to defend the common interest of all persons in the enforcement of natural law.

According to Gentili, the Spanish conquest of the Indies could best be understood as a war of this kind. The Indians had "practised abominable lewdness even with beasts," he said, and they "ate human flesh, slaying men for that purpose." These were old themes in Spanish accounts of the peoples of America: Gentili could well have found them in the works of Richard Eden. Bestiality and cannibalism were clear violations of nature. For his part, Vitoria had doubted that such acts could have furnished a just cause for the actions of the Spanish in America. There were sinners all over the world, he noted. To attack some of them would often amount to aggression against peoples who were not Christian due to the mere fact of their unbelief. Gentili disagreed. He maintained that the Spanish had punished the Indians on behalf of all humankind.[25]

This was an uncommon position. It was a rare author in Elizabethan England who would defend what the Spanish had done to the Indians. To be sure, in the case of Gentili, this defense stemmed in part from another position he held that was aggressively opposed to Spain. He was a member of the circle around the Earl of Essex in the final decade of the century that urged the bolder prosecution of the conflict. *The Law of War* was dedicated to Essex. The bellicose posture that Gentili developed in this work did lead him to support the actions of the Spanish in America, but it was intended, as Gentili did not hesitate to admit, to lead England to take action against its own enemies abroad.[26]

In this period the more common position than that of Gentili was the one assumed by the English observer who was best informed about the actions of the Spanish in America. This was a scholar and editor named Richard Haklyut who served as chaplain to the ambassador to Paris. In 1584 he presented to the Queen a report in which he stated what he understood to be the most complete case that could be made in support of the expansion of English enterprise in America. Here Hakluyt elaborated upon what he believed to be the "greate necessitie and manifolde commodyties" that would attend upon this endeavor. But it was quite clear to him that first he would have to press the English claim to a share in the promise of America against the Spanish claim to complete dominion there.[27]

It was for this reason that Hakluyt devoted much the longest chapter in his report to an answer to the Bulls of Donation. He described in detail the circumstances in which these had been granted and said they were invalid for reasons that recalled those Vitoria had provided for the same purpose. Hakluyt more or less accepted the control that Spain had established in America south of the Tropic of Cancer. His focus was the vast tract of land that stretched northward from Florida. Not so much as a single Spanish town had been built there. Any one of the nations of Europe could move in.[28]

What was more, according to Hakluyt, the English did have a special claim over the northern portion of America. There was a rich history of English exploration there. He then went on to produce an extended account whose principal events would soon become stable points of reference in the literature on America. There was the supposed westward journey of the medieval Welsh prince Madoc, and there were the voyages of the Bristol navigators John and his son Sebastian Cabot to the far northern mainland that started in 1496. In 1583, Humphrey Gilbert sailed to Newfoundland under letters patent that would have him claim it on behalf of the Crown. In the next year, after Gilbert's death at sea, Walter Raleigh received from the Queen a charter of his own to settle in a more temperate place that came to be known as Virginia. Raleigh asked Hakluyt to write in support of this project, and the 1584 report was his response.[29]

For the Queen and her circle of advisors, the real purpose of westward expansion at this point was to weaken the Spanish Empire. The gold and silver that Spain received from the mines that it controlled in America were what had enabled "the insatiable Spaniardes," in Hakluyt's phrase, to pursue their imperial ambition in Europe. At the same time, the settlement of the English in America would at a minimum stop the spread of Spanish power and could even be used to disrupt the operation of the Spanish West Indian system.

In this context, Hakluyt devoted rather little attention to the particular form that the settlement of the English in America would take. And he had only started to imagine the kinds of relations that the English settlers might enter into with the native peoples there. What did seem certain to him was that they would welcome the newcomers in their lands. As soon as the English arrived, Hakluyt said, the peoples of America would "crye oute unto us their nexte neighboures to comme and helpe them." One reason for this warm reception would be that the Americans had been so mistreated by the Spanish. In a chapter in which he described the "proude and bluddy governemente of the Spaniarde," Hakluyt reproduced and reflected upon the famous work of Las Casas. The Spanish had established a cruel and tyrannical regime over the Indians. The English promised to set them free.[30]

As it happened, the first expedition that Hakluyt expected to carry this promise across the ocean met there with little success. In 1585, Raleigh sent a fleet of ships to settle an island named Roanoke. Within three years, the ships that could have supplied them with much needed relief were ordered to remain at home to defend against the Armada. In 1590, Roanoke was found to have been abandoned. Through the close of the Elizabethan period, the naval resources of the nation were consumed by the sea war with Spain.

When James VI of Scotland succeeded to the English throne, in 1603, as James I, he was determined to end the Spanish conflict. Soon the peace that followed the agreement of a treaty with Spain, in 1604, came to be seen as a chance to renew and extend the Virginia enterprise. James chartered a London company for this purpose, and in 1606 the company sent a fleet across the ocean that entered Chesapeake Bay and settled along an inland river at a place they named Jamestown.

Back in London, as the new settlement at Virginia suffered from famine and disease, the company met to discuss what might be said about it. It was proposed that some text be written and distributed that would explain "y[e] Justice of y[e] action." This text would have two aims. The first one of these would be to demonstrate the English claim to dominion in Virginia "comparatively to be as good as y[e] Spaniards." This was understood to be a simple task, since none of the members of the company seems to have been inclined to respect the Papal Bulls. That said, the second aim in a defense of Virginia was seen as more difficult to accomplish. It would be to show the English title to the land "absolutely to be good agaynst y[e] Naturall people" who lived there.

One member of the company noted that the Spanish had never been able to establish their own title to the West Indies in this manner. When their explorers had first come upon it, their authors were unprepared. They were forced "to resolve roundly upon y[e] worst way" to defend their dominion, so as not to have none. They had decided that it would be best to draw upon a doctrine that they already knew well and to "prosecute y[e] Indians as Barbar's, and therby Naturally slaves." According to this member of the Virginia company, after half a century of bloodshed in the name of the Philosopher, the Spanish Crown had at last been dissuaded from "that severe and unJust course." Nevertheless, in the decades that followed, the further reasons that had been presented in support of Spanish dominion in the Indies—from the Bulls of Donation to the Indians' supposed violations of natural law to the effort to introduce Christian religion—had also failed to persuade. In order to settle the justice of their action in Virginia, the English would have to pursue another course.[31]

At first the Virginia company decided not to issue a statement on their own behalf. They were concerned that to do so might draw attention to their project. This in turn would enrage the Spanish and inconvenience the King, who was anxious to maintain what seemed to be a tenuous peace. In 1609, however, with the colony upon the brink of ruin, a decision was reached to attempt to save it. The company was restructured; a new charter was issued; and as part of this broader effort, a promotional campaign was initiated whose aim was to enlist public support for the Virginia enterprise.

The theme that was most prominent in this initial campaign for Virginia was one that had been present from the earliest English promotional tracts about America. This was the claim that expansion in America was authorized by the intention of the English to convert the native peoples to Christian religion. In this respect, as in others, the Spanish supplied a negative example. The Bulls of Donation had granted dominion in the New World for the express purpose of the advancement of the Kingdom of God. Rather than win the Indians to the faith by peaceful means, the Spanish had murdered and mistreated them. In contrast, English authors hoped that the success of their own efforts at conversion would demonstrate what they took to be the superiority of their Protestant faith. The advancement of the glory of England would follow upon the advancement of the glory of God.

Indeed, in the rhetoric of the time, the religious purpose of the American enterprise was often said to come before whatever temporal purposes there might have been. For his part, Hakluyt had presented the purpose of westward expansion in this manner. In his 1584 report the first chapter was devoted to the argument that settlement in Virginia promised to contribute "greately for th'inlargemente of the gospell of Christe." It was in part because the Indians wished to hear the Gospel that Hakluyt was certain they would welcome the English settlers who came to live in their lands. The royal charter for Virginia from 1606 had stated a similar aim. James commended the desire that the company had expressed "in propagating of Christian religion to suche people as yet live in darkenesse." This same desire was expressed time and again in the texts that were written in support of Virginia from 1609, as almost all of these were delivered in the form of sermons.[32]

All the same, when it came down to it in Virginia, the stated aim of the company to spread the Word never extended to include the real intention to do so. No substantial plans for the conversion of the native peoples were ever made, and efforts in this vein were soon all but abandoned.

In this period the actual interest of most of the participants in the Virginia enterprise was in commerce rather than conversion. Their attention was directed toward the kinds of goods that they hoped the Indians might want to trade more than toward the state of their immortal souls. In this context the settlement at Virginia was often imagined as a simple outpost for exchange. It would on occasion serve as a base for privateer operations in the West Indies, but most of all it would be a site where merchants from England could become accustomed to meet their local counterparts and sell bonnets, kettles, and some of the plentiful stock of English wool in return for hides, spices, and sassafras—as well as the emeralds, silver, and gold that at this point observers still anticipated were to be found within the northern American mainland.

In early-modern discourse, customs of this kind carried with them their own proper justification. And this in turn came from the law of nations as this was recorded in the texts of the *Corpus Juris*. Within the arc of development that the law of nations described, after property was made private and nations were formed, but before war and slavery came into the world, commerce had been established. By this means, as the resources and abilities of the people in one part of the world were seen to complement the needs and desires of those in another, networks of trade became the practical expression of the kinship or likeness of all humankind—which was, of course, what made it possible for there to be a common law of nations in the first place.[33]

No doubt both Vitoria and Gentili had accepted the protection that was thus afforded to commerce under the law of nations. Nevertheless, both authors were also well aware that the Spanish had done much more in the Indies than trade. In contrast in this period, a certain number of English authors did believe that their intention to trade and their promise to introduce Christian religion could almost on their own be relied upon to support the actions of their countrymen in America. To be sure, the most important author of this kind was none other than Hakluyt, but one more such author was George Peckham, whose 1583 *True Reporte* on the Newfoundland expedition of Humphrey Gilbert included a brief but learned defense of the English enterprise in America that was twice reprinted before the end of the century.[34]

As travelers from England continued to settle in America, however, and more and more of them crossed the ocean over time, many authors came to conclude that they would need to explain the English project in America as more than a religious mission or a mere commercial enterprise. Above all, what they intended to do there was to find a new place to live. Even their religious and commercial aims would be almost impossible to accomplish if they were unable to do this. They would have to "plant" themselves in

America, was what they often said. And in order to defend this particular action, English authors would have to draw upon a resource that was suited for the purpose.

Again, that resource was the Roman legal tradition. However, it was not the law of nations that would best support the intention of the English to plant in America. It was the law of nature as this was recorded in the standard texts of the *Corpus Juris*. In the sections of these texts that described the proper methods by which things came to be the property of persons, one method was said to be as old as the natural order. This was the method by which things that belonged to no one came to belong to someone. Wild beasts, birds, and fish were the examples that the jurists provided—and what they said was that these became the property of the first person who took them into their possession. At one point land came up in connection with this principle. The jurists said no more than that if a new island arose in the sea, it would belong to the first person who took it.[35]

In the early years of contact, English observers do not appear to have realized what this principle from Roman law might have to do with their project in America. The northern mainland was not a new island in the sea: there were people who had lived there before the English arrived. That said, from the start, the travelers who went over to America were startled at how few native people there did seem to be there. Even Virginia was much less populous than the southern mainland was reported to have been when the Spanish had first arrived. And more than this, what stood out was how immense the New World was. In truth, it was the land even more than the people that arrested the attention of the English observers of America.

At times some authors did express concern that when the English went to plant themselves in America they would dispossess the native peoples of their land. What such authors said in response was that the planters had no such intention. There was more than enough room over there. It became a common theme in English discourse about America that the native peoples only lived in small parts of the continent. Their settlements, as neat and well-ordered as these were at least on occasion admitted to be, appeared almost as islands of habitation within the wide circuit of open space. The planters would set down near them but would be sure to keep themselves to land that to that point had been vacant.

The term that was often used to refer to land of this kind in America was that it was "waste" land. And English observers did share the sense that there had been some terrible failure to make use of the incredible natural resources of the New World. The very purpose of the land had been neglected. The most powerful text that English authors had at hand in order to develop this conviction was the Bible. For in the Book of Genesis, God instructed Adam and Eve to be fruitful and multiply and to fill the earth and subdue it. Later, after the Flood, He said much the same to Noah and his sons. Indeed, the clearest statement of the consequences that would follow from the failure to use the land in America came in a sermon that the poet John Donne preached before the members of the Virginia company late in the fateful year of 1622.

Here Donne worked to distill the essence of an argument that by this time was well known in the literature on America. The purpose of the earth, he explained, was to meet the needs of the creatures to whom God had granted dominion over it. In turn, in order to own any portion of the earth, one would have to use it for the end for which it was made and turn it to the benefit of mankind. One would have to settle it and cultivate it—in a word, plant it with crops as well as men. In the case that one failed to do this, as Donne and other authors believed the native peoples in Virginia had, then one lived on the land and moved over it but could not be said to possess it. Virginia thus resembled the new island in the sea that Roman law books had discussed. It was a thing that belonged to no one. The English could take it all.[36]

In early English discourse on Virginia, the several arguments that were presented in support of the colonial enterprise there were rarely seen to pull apart from one another. The tension that there might have been between them was not often remarked upon. One might have wondered, for example, whether one would be able to instruct in the Christian religion people with whom above all one wanted only to trade. In turn, one might have asked how it would be possible to establish profitable commercial relations with people whose relation to the land on which they lived was as minimal as that of "heardes of Deare in a Forrest," in the phrase of one author.[37]

Even so, for the most part, English authors treated the claims that had been made in support of the Virginia enterprise as ones that tended to complement one another. For their part, the Virginia company had treated such claims in this manner. Even in the period when they had declined to issue a statement in public, they expressed satisfaction in private that there were "inducinge and Convenient arguments" that could be made on their behalf and that these could be derived from several sources of authority. There were arguments from "God, and Nature, and Nations" that were all on their side, according to the company.[38]

Perhaps the most important feature that these arguments seemed to have in common was that they fit within a vision of the English enterprise in America as one that in essence would be peaceful. For in this period, almost all observers from England were in agreement that what their countrymen did to the people in America should not be so cruel as what the Spanish had done. In a word, it should not have the character of a conquest. But at the same time, most English observers were also able to envision that at some point in the course of their relations with the Indians the colonists would have to resort to force.

Each one of the arguments that was used in order to defend the involvement of the English in Virginia entailed a particular account of the manner in which the Indians would have to respond to them. The English would sail across the ocean in order to preach or trade or plant, and when they arrived, the Indians would convert or trade or allow the newcomers to settle upon the land. In each case, as English authors made clear, if the Indians refused to act in accord with the plan that had been made for them, then they would have denied to the colonists what they had had a right to expect. At this point the character of the relations between them would change.

Of course, English authors had at hand a word to define the kind of action that they could pursue if their lawful endeavor in Virginia met with a hostile response, and this word was war. The Latin phrase one author used to state the principle upon which such an action would rest was *vim vi repellere*. It was a principle as old and familiar as the common law of nations, in which persons were allowed to use violence in order to defend themselves from the same.[39]

Under the law of nations, there was no limit to what could be done in the course of a war, and English observers of Virginia were well aware of this point. They noted that if the Indians came to attack them, the English could make them convert and compel them to trade and take over control of the land. They could appropriate all of their possessions, as a matter of fact, because in war all that the defeated side had had became the property of the victor. This was even true of persons. As early a promoter of peaceful English enterprise in America as George Peckham had also warned that the native peoples there would do well to know that, under the law of nations, "such as should fortune to be taken in warre, should be servauntes or slaves."[40]

For a time, peace rather than war did seem to the colonists to be the rule in Virginia. Then, one morning in March 1622, that changed. In the period that preceded this date, the area of English settlement had expanded, as the rich potential of tobacco spurred the spread of new plantations along the rivers that cut across the Tidewater. In the process the Indians were pushed farther and farther back from the coast. They had come to live in "dayly feare," in the phrase of one later English account, that soon the planters would dispossess them of their former lands altogether. In an effort to avert this outcome, they struck at settlements on the James River and killed 347 of the colonists.[41]

When news of the event reached London, it came almost at once to be referred to as a "massacre." It was "a *Flood,* a *Flood* of *bloud*" that rushed in upon Virginia, according to Donne. Even so, in the period that followed, as would befit the biblical allusion that Donne had made, a note of optimism can be detected in the reactions of those who now rushed to the defense of the colonial enterprise in Virginia. The King supplied a gift of arms, and the company called for war. The official account that the company put out explained that in the end the massacre would prove to be a benefit. Above all, this was because "our hands which before were tied with gentlenesse and fair usage" in relations with the Indians were now instead "set at liberty."[42]

"By right of Warre, and law of Nations," the official account went on, the colonists could now exercise violence of a kind that earlier observers had only been able to imagine. They could set the native rulers against one another and divide and overcome them in turn; they could chase the Indians down on horses and have their mastiffs seize them; they could beat them back ever farther into the interior; and in short, they could pursue the destruction of the Indians, as the company observed in a letter to the colonists, to the point of "rooting them out for being longer a people uppon the face of the Earth."[43]

Statements of this kind could have appeared to invite comparison to the actions of the Spanish in America. To such an observer of events as Samuel Purchas, this would have been rather unwelcome. Purchas was an editor and author who had risen to become a rector in the Church of England in London. Just before news of the massacre in Virginia reached home, in 1622, he had been admitted as a member of the company. In 1624, as he reflected upon the recent bloodshed on the James River, he composed a discourse, titled "Virginias Verger" and published in 1625, which was from this period the most learned defense of the English response.[44]

As much as any observer from this time, Purchas was well read in the literature on the European involvement in America. He had prepared the second English edition of the *Brevísima Relación* of Las Casas, as well as a translation of the Papal Bull of Donation. In an extended comment upon this text, he had drawn upon the lectures of Vitoria in order to refute the claim that the Pope had the kind of power in temporal affairs that would have enabled him to issue it. Indeed, the assertion of papal dominion was above all what troubled Purchas about the Spanish discourse on America. As had Hakluyt, he more or less accepted the control that Spain had long since established over the southern portion of the continent. As it was for Hakluyt, the site of his obsession on that side of the Atlantic was Virginia.[45]

Here Purchas put forward what would have been at least in form a familiar account of the legitimate basis for the English enterprise. He worked within the terms of the Roman legal tradition and embroidered these with lessons and examples chosen from the Old and New Testaments. He urged the colonists to work for the conversion of the Indians, even if he had also started to doubt that this could ever be accomplished. The two more important claims upon which he rested his account were the right that came from the law of nature to possess and plant in vacant places on the earth and, in turn, the right of commerce that was protected under the law of nations.

According to Purchas, these claims had supported the efforts of the English to trade and settle in Virginia. However, neither one would have entitled the colonists to attack the native peoples or drive them from what parts of the land they themselves could claim to have settled. That was what the "late barbarous Massacre" had done. In the aftermath of this event the colonists could add to the rights upon which they based their actions in Virginia the ones that were seen to attend upon a "iust invasion and conquest." The actions of the Indians had exposed them to "the severitie of the Law of Nations." They had forfeited their lives and all of their possessions. They had made "both them and their Countrey wholly *English*," was what Purchas said.[46]

That said, not even Purchas imagined that Virginia would at once become "wholly *English*," in his phrase. At least for a time some of the Indians would have a role within the new social order that the colonists would establish. At the same time that they pursued their campaign for the destruction of the Indians and forced them into retreat from what would now be the English sphere, the colonists would also spare some of the persons whom they captured and use them for their own ends. Once "the extirpation of the more dangerous" of the Indians was accomplished, Purchas explained, then there would be commodities to be "raised out of the servilenesse and serviceablenesse of the rest."[47]

As it happened, in the course of their own conquest in the Indies, the Spanish were said to have acted upon a similar plan. This was one of the main themes that ran across the works of Las Casas. In his *Brevísima Relación*, between indelible scenes of the destruction of the Indians, there were reports of episodes in which some of them had been enslaved.

As a matter of fact, it was the standard practice of the conquistadores, according to Las Casas, when they arrived in each region of the New World, to demand that the people submit to the Spanish Crown. If they refused, then the conquistadores would either murder them at once or put them to work as slaves. In the end it was all more or less the same. The work that the Indians were forced to perform, as miners or farmers or divers for pearls, was so arduous that it soon killed them. This too seemed to serve the ultimate aim of the Spanish with respect to the Indians—which was "to eradicate and abolishe them from off the face of the earth," Las Casas said.[48]

To Las Casas, the brutal character of slavery in the Indies was further proof that the practice here did not conform to the model that Aristotle had had in mind. The Philosopher had insisted that for a person whom nature had intended to be a slave, the rule of a natural master would be "not only necessary, but expedient." Indeed, Aristotle understood the relation between them to be one of such mutual dependence that in a sense the death of the one would mark the end of the other, because, as he observed, "if the slave perish, the rule of the master perishes with him." In contrast, in America, slavery had become another route to death. It was a method to draw some profit from the Indians in the course of their ultimate replacement with their masters from Europe.[49]

For decades the English had maintained that their own actions in America would not resemble those of their Spanish rivals, but now they had arrived at a similar point. To be sure, they had come here upon a different route. Authors from England had never held that a distinction in nature entitled their countrymen to rule the native peoples in America as masters over slaves. On the contrary, it had been a standard theme in English discourse that their aim would be to deliver to the Indians the "libertie & freedomme" that they so desired from Spanish rule, as Richard Hakluyt had written in 1584. What had happened since then was that the English believed that they had been harmed—and that this harm entitled them to redress of the most complete and serious kind. They would make the Indians serve them as slaves until such time as the English would uproot them from the face of the earth.[50]

The actions of the English in America would thus come to resemble the worst that had ever been said about the actions of the Spanish. And in this context at least one observer believed that it would be appropriate to defend the one in the same terms as were known to have been used in order to defend the other.

John Bonoeil was a French horticulturalist who worked for the Virginia company. In 1622, in the immediate aftermath of the massacre, Bonoeil published a pamphlet about how to raise silkworms and plant vineyards that was to be distributed to each household in the colonial settlement. In the final section of his book, he included advice on other issues, and one of these was the relation of the colonists to the Indians. "I utterly disclaime them," he wrote of the latter. The best course of action would be to vanquish them, for they were "an unprofitable burthen onely of the earth." All the same, if they were allowed to live for some time, then the Indians should be treated as some of the persons Aristotle had said were "naturally borne slaves," who were in need of others whom nature had made to "direct them aright, to governe and command." Bonoeil believed the colonists were persons of this kind.[51]

The colonial experience had been the occasion for a shift in the national character. When it had started, the English understood themselves to be threatened with enslavement from the Spanish. Now it was at least possible to believe that no less than nature had made them masters in the New World.

Nevertheless, it was also possible in this period to overlook the hard-won lessons of Virginia. There the colonists had started a war upon the Indians that would continue on and off for the next decade. But back in the metropole the political situation made it difficult to appreciate the extent to which the actions of the English in America conformed to a model that the Spanish had first set down. Indeed, the political situation in this period recalled that of the Elizabethan era. In an effort to secure and extend the peace that he had made with Spain, James had pursued a marriage between his son and successor, the prince Charles, and the daughter of the Spanish monarch Philip III. When this effort ended in disaster, in 1623, the alliance that James had worked for years to maintain came under popular attack. Soon after Charles's accession to the throne, in 1625, he moved to reopen the war with Spain.[52]

In this context, the most important case for war was the one that came from the most prominent statesman of his era. Francis Bacon had come of age under Elizabeth as a favorite of the Earl of Essex, and he had condemned the Spanish cruelties toward the Indians in the standard terms of the time. Under James he rose to become the lord chancellor of the realm but was never reconciled to the alliance that James had established. To the end he opposed what was known as the Spanish Match. Upon the occasion of its failure, Bacon composed and presented to Charles a text in which he laid out what he understood to be the complete case for what would be a war "for our *Prince,* our *Nation,* all that we have."[53]

The central consideration in this text was the familiar source of Elizabethan dread: the Spanish ambition for universal dominion. According to Bacon, it was this ambition, as well as the constant aggression it called forth, that furnished England with a just cause for war. Here he drew upon a doctrine that held the mere fear of an imminent attack could be met with the same violent response as an actual one. It was a doctrine from Roman law that he cited with the Latin phrase *justus metus*. Bacon could have come across this doctrine in Gentili, whose work he knew well, but he himself was also educated in the discipline. He had been the central figure in the movement for legal reform that had aimed to fit the laws and customs of England within the formal order of the civil law. Now Bacon turned to the civil law in order to press the case for war in Europe.[54]

Indeed, this European context was the one in which Bacon drew upon the resources of the civil law in order to press the case for war. He was not one of the English observers who enlisted the law of nations in support of the campaign of destruction that took place in Virginia in response to the massacre in 1622. To be sure, he would have been well aware of the colonial enterprise. When a new charter was issued, in 1609, he had been named to the royal council for the Virginia company. A number of his close associates were members of the company. One of these was Hobbes, who was admitted the month after Purchas, in June 1622.[55]

Around this time, however, Bacon's attention was directed toward the conflict that he anticipated would come with Spain. Here what he wanted was to draw the contrast between the two nations in the starkest possible terms. In advance of his death, in 1626, he did have one last word on the recent events in Virginia. But what he said was subtle. In the final edition of his *Essayes,* he added a new one, titled "Of Plantations." "I like a *Plantation* in a Pure Soile," he explained, "that is, where People are not *Displanted,* to the end, to *Plant* in Others. For else, it is rather an Extirpation, then a *Plantation.*" As he would have known, this was now the character of the English enterprise in America as much as it had been that of the Spanish one.[56]

Still, at this point the shift that had happened in America had not happened in Africa. Here the turn toward a system of slavery on an immense scale was still in the future. In this context, the old themes in English discourse remained more or less intact. The cruel actions of the Iberian powers were contrasted with the intention of the English to deal on peaceful terms with the peoples whom they encountered across the Atlantic world.

In this period, Africa was never as much a site of English dreams and ambitions as America. No promises were ever made to the effect that the English would come and help the peoples of Africa or free them from tyrannical rule. At the same time, a broad aversion to the behavior of their Iberian rivals did lead a certain number of Englishmen to condemn the practices of enslavement that the Iberians were well known to have established.

These condemnations of Iberian practices can be read in turn as condemnations of later English ones. As in America, Englishmen soon moved to embrace the business of slavery in Africa after a period in which at least some had said that they were opposed to it. They adopted many of the practices that they had associated with their enemies. At the close of the seventeenth century, England had established an African slave trade that nourished an Atlantic slave empire of its own.

But all this happened over a short span of time. Back in the first quarter of the seventeenth century, it had barely been imagined. What follows in this chapter is a focused description of English encounters with Africans across the Atlantic world in the period that preceded the regular English African slave trade. The aim is to produce a prehistory of the slave trade, so as to throw into sharper relief the more familiar period that followed.

The encounters between Englishmen and Africans from this earlier period are different in character from the ordered procedures that were developed in order to facilitate the transatlantic commerce in bound and captive persons. Often these encounters take place on an intimate scale. Their violence is vivid and immediate. The intense mutual interest that animates them can be seen to reflect the sense that both sides were vulnerable to attack and both hoped to benefit from their relations with each other.

The most important printed source from the first decades of regular contact between Africans and Englishmen was a text that was the work of Richard Hakluyt. In the time after he delivered his 1584 report to the Queen, Hakluyt had continued to work on the project of overseas expansion that

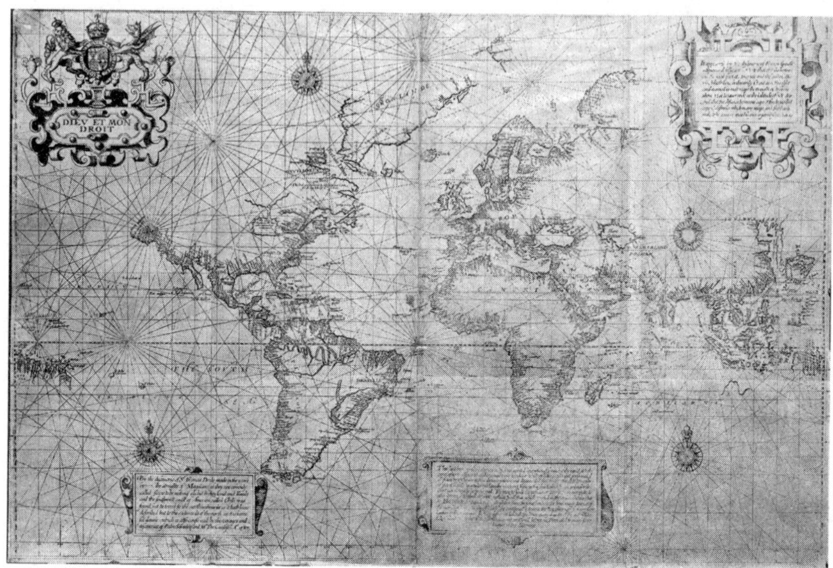

FIG. 2.1 Richard Hakluyt's focus upon commerce as the proper form of English overseas enterprise is reflected in the world map included in the second edition of his collection of travel narratives. The world this map describes is for the most part a maritime one: the coasts and islands are labeled in fine and dense print, while the continental interiors are left almost unmarked. According to many Elizabethan observers, the sea would be the site of English commerce abroad and thus the true route to England's arrival on the world stage.

Credit: Edward Wright, "A True Hydrographical Description of So Much of the World as Hath Beene Hetherto Discovered and Is Come to Our Knowledge," in Richard Hakluyt, *The Principal Navigations, Voyages, Traffiques and Discoveries of the English Nation,* 3 vols. (London, 1599–1600), vol. 1, before title page. STC 12626a (B): Houghton Library, Harvard University.

had come to define his career. He gathered as much evidence as he could find to demonstrate that England had become a power on the world stage and printed what he found in a collection of travel narratives that came out in 1589 and in a revised and much expanded second edition in 1599–1600 under the title *The Principal Navigations, Voyages, Traffiques and Discoveries of the English Nation* (see Figure 2.1).

The focus of the documents collected in this text was America, the central site of Hakluyt's overseas obsession. But by the time of the second edition of his *Principal Navigations,* Hakluyt had also collected more than two dozen accounts of English travel to the western coast of Africa. These accounts reflect the vision of overseas enterprise that was developed with so much care and attention in the writings about Virginia from this era. The adversaries they depict are the Iberian powers upon whose Atlantic empires the English aim to intercede. The exclusive interest of the authors of these documents is commerce, and the commercial relations they describe are for the most part peaceful and profitable.

A more ominous event appeared in the account of the second English voyage to the western coast of Africa, which was conducted in 1554. Hakluyt published this account in his collection, but it had first appeared in print in 1555 when Richard Eden included it in a short section on Africa near the end of his *Decades of the Newe Worlde*. In truth, Eden had written this account, which he seems to have composed on the basis of reports from the captain of the voyage: a man from a prominent family of merchants whose name was John Lok.[57]

The Lok voyage returned home with a cargo of gold, ivory, and pepper. According to Eden, the crew also had with them a number of persons he referred as "certeyne blacke slaves." Eden did not make clear how many of these there were. In his account of the next English voyage to Guinea, in 1555, William Towerson said that he met an African man near the main Portuguese outpost in the region, a fortress from the fifteenth century known as Mina, who told him that the English had taken five men home with them in the previous year. When Towerson came to a town named Shamma, just to the west of Mina, however, Towerson said the Lok crew had taken four men from there rather than five (see Figure 2.2).[58]

When the Towerson crew arrived at Shamma, they found the local people were "bent against us," in his phrase. They lured the crew ashore with the promise of trade and then shot at them. Eden had never described the circumstances under which Lok had taken the persons he referred to as slaves. Now Towerson said that Lok had taken them "perforce" and "with their gold, and all that they had about them." This event had even caused the local people to become "friendes with the *Portingals,* whom before they hated." Towerson was aware that he would need to explain what had happened. The man he met near Mina had come aboard his ship, "and as soone as he came, he demanded, why we had not brought againe their men, which the last yeere we tooke away."[59]

FIG. 2.2 This Ortelius map of Africa remained the standard one in use in England through the close of the Elizabethan era. As such, it can be used as a guide to references in this chapter to locations on the western coast of Africa. Ortelius labeled as "Guinea" the thin stretch of coast to the south and east of Sierra Leone, but English observers also used this title to refer to the entire coastal region that ran from the Senegal River in the northwest to the Bight of Biafra in the southeast.

Credit: Detail from "Africae Tabula Nova," in Abraham Ortelius, *Theatre de l'univers, contenant les cartes de tout le monde* (Antwerp, 1581), after fol. 4. MO 1.1581 pf*: Harvard Map Collection, Harvard University.

What Towerson said in response to this question was that the men whom Lok had taken were still in England. They were there to learn English and then would return home in order "to be a helpe to Englishmen in this Countrey." This does appear to have been the case, and it was perhaps the first instance of what would become a common practice in the decades that followed. In the time before the English started to build commercial outposts of their own in Guinea, a number of merchants brought local men home with them in order to prepare them to serve as intermediaries for trade. When Towerson returned to Guinea in 1556, he had with him two of the men whom Lok had taken. One of these men was named George, and Towerson described the manner in which he facilitated the purchase of gold at towns on the coast. When Towerson arrived back at Shamma, he presented the local men he had with him, and "the men of the towne wept for ioy." They asked George where two other men, named Anthony and Binny, were. He responded that they were still in England and would return on the next voyage. Towerson told the ruler of the town that there was no need to fear the Portuguese: from this point forward, the English would protect them.[60]

In interactions of this kind, Englishmen on the western coast of Africa were forced to work within a practical context that differed from the one that would later come to define the slave trade. To break with custom was to face a swift reprisal. To venture ashore without permission was to risk a violent response. At some towns on the coast, the two sides would make an exchange of persons, referred to as "pledges," in order to ensure fair and peaceful trade. The ratios varied from place to place. Sometimes an English merchant would provide one pledge and receive two in return. Sometimes one African was delivered as a pledge in return for one Englishman. At a town on the coast near Cape Verde, in 1566, the merchant George Fenner found that the people used an unusual ratio. He recalled that they had been "content to deliver 3. of their *Negros* for 5. of our men." He had accepted their offer. Centuries passed before this ratio was enshrined in law, in reverse, as an expression of the comparative worth of Black and white persons.[61]

In this period, Englishmen in Guinea also had before them the example of another approach to relations with the people who lived there, and this was the example of the Portuguese. The man whom Towerson met near Mina told him that "the Portingals were bad men." They made the native people "slaves, if they could take them, and would put yrons upon their legges." As a matter of fact, the man said, they had done this to him. He had only just made his escape from Mina. When Towerson told him that the men Lok had taken would soon be returned, he did so in an effort to assure his interlocutor that those men had not been taken in the same sense as the Portuguese had taken him.[62]

In Africa, Portugal rather than Spain was England's Iberian rival. In 1455, after a series of expeditions farther and farther down the western coast, the Pope had issued a Bull in which he granted dominion to the rulers of Portugal over all the lands and peoples to the south of Cape Bojador. The Bulls of Donation that established Spanish dominion across the New World had been careful not to unsettle any prior arrangements in the Old. In 1494, the Treaty of Tordesillas confirmed this rough division of the Atlantic sphere. By the time English merchants such as Lok and Towerson started to arrive in Guinea, merchants from Portugal had traded for persons there for more than a century. Most of these persons were taken back to Europe, but tens of thousands of them had been carried across the Atlantic. It was Portugal that controlled the trade that supplied the Spanish American empire with African slaves.[63]

More so than in America, where to this point Englishmen had been all but excluded from areas under Spanish control, the English merchants in Africa had studied their Iberian counterparts. The African materials in the Hakluyt collections were filled with information about them. Much of this information came from the reports of local African officials, who were asked to describe where the Portuguese were and what they intended. Most often when English and Portuguese travelers came into contact in Guinea, what happened was that they shot at each other from a distance. And yet on occasion a closer relation developed between them. On the route home from Cape Verde, the Fenner crew had five Africans aboard with them. The exchange of pledges on the coast had been a ruse. The Africans escaped almost at once. In the skirmish that ensued, two members of the English crew were taken prisoner and the five Africans seem to have been abducted in response. When Fenner came across a Portuguese ship, he sold these persons to the captain for several chests filled with sugar. In interactions of this kind, Englishmen in Guinea insinuated themselves into the Iberian trade in African persons. They did this almost without comment, and perhaps without reflection, upon what they had done.[64]

The notorious career of the sea captain John Hawkins has to be understood within this Iberian Atlantic context. Hawkins would have been familiar with the western coast of Africa from his father William, who had touched down to trade there several times on the route to Brazil. But Hawkins also stressed that he drew inspiration from the example of the Iberian empires. In the Spanish Canary Islands, he later recalled, he had heard "that *Negroes* were very good marchandise in *Hispaniola,* and that store of *Negroes* might easily be had upon the coast of *Guinea.*" In shorthand form, this was the agenda for his three transatlantic voyages in the 1560s, each of which moved from Plymouth to Cape Verde to Guinea and on to Spanish America.[65]

On the Guinea coast at Sierra Leone, the Hawkins crews attempted the kind of open slave raids that at this point even the Portuguese had all but abandoned. They pursued and captured as many native persons as they could find. When Hawkins and his men came upon deserted towns, they noted the intricate arrangement of their streets and houses and burned them to the ground. They shot their harquebusiers at persons who were too far off to catch by other means. The natives shot back with bows and arrows dipped in poison. In one such encounter, Hawkins lost seven of his men and made off with ten Africans. Later he and his crew narrowly escaped what would have been a disastrous ambush. On his final voyage to Guinea, in 1568, Hawkins made an alliance with a local ruler and led an armed assault on a fortified town. He took as many of the prisoners as his allies would allow.[66]

In the Roman tradition, slavery was seen to be one of the possible consequences of war. In contrast, Hawkins never hesitated to state that slavery was the purpose of his violent actions in Guinea. In the account of his first voyage to the area, he reported that the persons he took from there had come into "his possession, partly by the sword, and partly by other meanes." The unpublished official records attesting to his methods indicate that at least some of the persons whom Hawkins acquired in Guinea were obtained in the course of peaceful commerce with local Portuguese merchants. In his own public statements, Hawkins made only the most veiled references to such events. He referred to the Africans he loaded onto his ships as his "praye."[67]

All told, Hawkins carried more than one thousand Africans across the ocean to sell to the colonists in Spanish America. In the process, he completed the common circuit of the slave trade in the Iberian Atlantic world. At the same time, his real aim was to challenge the Iberian empires—to plunder and profit at the margins of their control. This fact was not lost upon the Spanish Crown. In 1568, the colonial viceroy of Mexico ordered a massive attack on the Hawkins fleet near Vera Cruz. Most of his ships and crew were lost. Hawkins barely made it back home. Around one hundred of his men were left to fend for themselves on the Spanish Main.

In the aftermath of this defeat, the English African slave trade did not resume; in fact, as the Queen worked to avoid an escalation of the conflict with Spain, English trade with Africa soon all but came to a halt. In the final decades of the century, no more than a dozen or so English voyages touched down on the Guinea coast. They traded for pepper and ivory as well as hides and palm oil. Not until the King made peace with Spain, in 1604, did the Guinea trade start to accelerate. A small number of voyages stopped at Sierra Leone on the route to the East Indies, and a direct trade from England was established for wax from the Senegal River region and for redwood from Sierra Leone.[68]

In 1618, James chartered the first English company with an exclusive right to trade in West Africa. Its official aim was to find the gold mines that were believed to be at some point inland from the coast, and the company sponsored three unsuccessful voyages down the Gambia River for this purpose. The captain of the third voyage was a merchant named Richard Jobson, whose narrative of his experience came out in 1623 as the first book about Africa that was the work of an English author. Jobson recalled that far down the river he had met an African merchant who offered to sell him three women as slaves. Jobson declined the offer. The merchant observed that slaves were "earnestly desired" by the Portuguese traders who had long since established themselves on the river. Jobson told him, in reference to the Portuguese, that "they were another kinde of people different from us."[69]

When Jobson delivered this response, the English African slave trade had been all but dormant for half a century. In the same period, Iberian traders had carried almost half a million enslaved Africans across the Atlantic Ocean. From at least the time of Hawkins, English travelers in Guinea had been aware that slaves from there were "caried continually to the *West Indies,*" in the phrase of one merchant who had been down the Gambia in 1591. Off the Guinea coast, English ships often encountered Portuguese caravels that were loaded with dozens and even hundreds of Africans. On the coastal island of São Tomé, Englishmen witnessed the forms of slave labor that had been developed for the cultivation of the oldest sugar plantations in the Atlantic world. By the start of the seventeenth century, the center of the Iberian African slave trade had moved south from Guinea to the western central coast. The Englishmen who found themselves down there reported that a "world of slaves" were sent to the Americas on an annual basis, in the phrase of one well-informed observer.[70]

Of course, it did not escape the notice of such observers that no parallel English practices had been established in Africa. In 1631, the African company formed in 1618 was reorganized under a new charter with a view to advance the search for precious metals as far as the Gold Coast. In all likelihood, no English ship had sailed from Guinea with more than perhaps five persons held as slaves since the final voyage of John Hawkins.

In recent decades, historians of this period have tended to obscure the clear contrast between English and Iberian participation in the African slave trade. They have preferred to treat the early-modern Atlantic world instead as a fluid system in which practices, persons, and ideas moved smoothly back and forth. What happened in the Atlantic world had much more to do with the particular features of an interconnected maritime context than with the hostile postures of nations in Europe. National narratives developed at home were found to be out of place at sea, where pragmatism and adaptation were the rule.

In the context of this orientation toward the early-modern Atlantic world, a number of historians have asserted that the English adopted Iberian practices of slavery more or less as they came across them. "From them they learned to accept African slavery as a matter of course," Robin Blackburn has explained. "The Portuguese and Spanish had set an example that could be followed," according to Philip Morgan. Almost as soon as they determined to claim a place for themselves in the Atlantic world that to that point had been dominated by the Iberian nations, this was what the English had done.[71]

In the early-modern period, however, tension and conflict were as much the rule in relations between England and the Iberian nations as were imitation and exchange. Indeed, at least through the time of Richard Jobson, most observers of Africa would have been well aware of the difference between English and Iberian practices of slavery.

In America, this difference was even more pronounced. The small number of Englishmen who traveled to the Spanish American colonies did so as pirates and privateers. They attacked at the outskirts of societies that depended more upon enslaved African labor than would any of the English American colonies until around the middle of the seventeenth century. They observed that the Spanish had put African slaves to work in the pearl fisheries off the coast of Venezuela, in the cattle farms on Cuba, in the silver mines in Mexico, and in the shipyards at Vera Cruz. Most members of the final Hawkins crew who were left behind here in 1568 were soon taken prisoner by the Spanish. Some of these men were then put to work as the overseers of African slaves in the Mexican silver mines. Later on they insisted that they had treated the Africans better than the Spanish had treated them. But at the same time, they had never made an effort to set these persons free.[72]

In such situations, Englishmen more or less assimilated themselves into the system of African slavery in Spanish America. To be sure, this was what Hawkins himself had tried to do, and it was also what a number of privateers did in the course of the sea war in the final decades of Elizabeth's reign. Across the Caribbean in this period, English sea captains often seized the African slaves aboard Spanish ships in order to ransom them back to their former owners or sell them at port towns. In this respect as in others, these Englishmen followed the famous example of Francis Drake. In the course of his raid on Santo Domingo and then on Cartagena in 1585, Drake had taken hundreds of Africans aboard with him. He could well have sold them off at Spanish ports as his fleet sailed north for the new English settlement at Roanoke. Perhaps he planned to put them to work for the desperate settlers there. Drake never mentioned what he did with these Africans. By the time his fleet sailed for England, they had disappeared from the historical record.[73]

In the first decades of the seventeenth century, as the peace with Spain opened new channels of communication and commerce, Englishmen in the Caribbean would sometimes purchase enslaved Africans from Spanish colonists. But no rule was without an exception in the unstable circumstances of the Atlantic world. A number of Englishmen continued the old Elizabethan campaign of plunder against their Iberian rivals. On occasion these men would sell the Africans they seized from Spanish or Portuguese ships to settlers in the new English colonies. This was the manner in which most of the Africans who arrived on Bermuda came there in this period. It was also the manner in which the first Africans arrived in Virginia in 1619. They came aboard a pair of English privateers that had intercepted a Portuguese slave ship on the well-traveled route from Angola to Vera Cruz.[74]

In cases such as these, Englishmen in the Americas at once defied their Iberian rivals and seemed to confirm the status of Africans as slaves. In other cases, however, the English found that their efforts to undermine the Spanish American empire allowed them to find common cause with the Africans whom the Spanish had pressed into their service. This was the backdrop for the celebrated alliance that formed between English privateers and the escaped former slaves, known as *cimarrones,* who also had claimed a place for themselves at the margins of Spanish control.

The first Englishman to enlist the *cimarrones* in a conflict with the Spanish Empire was none other than Drake. Drake had commanded a ship on the final transatlantic voyage of John Hawkins, but when he returned to the Caribbean in 1572, he discovered that a new approach to African peoples could help him accomplish his ultimate anti-Spanish aim. He and his African allies ambushed and pillaged the Spanish silver train as it moved overland in Panama. It was the first spectacular success of his career. Spanish authorities soon launched a war of reprisal against the *cimarrones* that ended their brief period of cooperation with the English. Even so, Drake never forgot the old alliance. As late as the disastrous expedition to Panama in 1595 in which both Drake and Hawkins lost their lives, he held out hope that the alliance could be revived.

No doubt this had been "a marriage of convenience," in the phrase of one historian. To Englishmen such as Drake, the *cimarrones* were the enemies of their enemies. Of course, the reverse was also true. And yet the combination between them drew upon a popular sense in English culture of the particular place of the nation in the Atlantic world. It was a nation that was as much able to find common cause with the victims of Spanish oppression as with the Spanish themselves. A brief account of Drake's exploits with the *cimarrones* appeared in both editions of the Hakluyt collection. But the full narrative of their association first came out in print in 1626, in the rush of anti-Spanish sentiment that followed upon the failure of the Spanish Match. Well into the seventeenth century, colonial promoters continued to urge their countrymen abroad to enlist the *cimarrones* in their cause. The failure of such efforts across the Atlantic had not dimmed the hopes that attached to them in some circles back in the metropole.[75]

In the view of the authors who placed their faith in it, an alliance between Englishmen and *cimarrones* would be founded upon the same basis as the alliance that English observers had hoped could be established with the native peoples in America. In America, both Indians and Africans were victims of "the proude and bluddy governemente of the Spaniarde." This was the phrase of Richard Hakluyt, and Hakluyt himself drew the parallel. In the 1584 report in which he condemned the Spanish treatment of the Indians, he also drew attention to what he called their "barbarous and savage endeles cruelties" toward the Africans whom they had carried to America and held there as slaves. It was the cruel treatment they had received that had provoked some of these persons to escape into the mountain redoubts from which the *cimarrones* now planned and executed their attacks upon the Spanish Empire.[76]

In turn, England's promise to the Africans in Spanish America would recall the one that authors such as Hakluyt had held out to the Indians. It was no less than to set them free. Whereas the Spanish Empire was founded upon oppression, Englishmen in America would offer freedom to the peoples they proposed to rule. And perhaps they could offer more than this. In November 1585, Drake and his crew were stationed on the Cape Verde Islands in preparation for their raid on Santo Domingo. They had with them an African man who was to serve as their guide. Drake spoke to the man and "promised this *Nigro* that if wee coulde take the Spaniarde that the *Nigro* was before slave unto, that then the Spaniarde shoulde bee slave unto the *Nigro*."[77]

This would be a dramatic reversal. In the meantime, a number of Englishmen whose imaginations were less vivid than Drake's found that at the least they could offer a sensitive appraisal of the condition of the Africans who suffered under Spanish rule. They commented upon the "poore naked *Negroes*" who were sold to Spanish colonists on Puerto Rico, upon the little rags that such persons sometimes received to cover themselves aboard the caravels that took them across the Atlantic, and upon the tricks that Portuguese traders in Angola would use in an effort to convince the native people that what was to meet them on the other side of the ocean was not so awful as they often suspected. In such moments, English observers found that a broad aversion to the behavior of their Iberian rivals could prompt them to expressions of concern for "the poore Nigrite their slave," in the phrase of one sermon delivered in York in 1597.[78]

In comments scattered across the wide field of early-modern English culture, some observers even seemed to propose that the actions of the Iberians in the Atlantic world had laid bare a problem with slavery as such. It was an "unnatural merchandise" that had been established to transport enslaved Africans to the Americas, wrote one colonial promoter in a pamphlet in 1624. Indeed, such authors focused their attention in particular on one feature of the Atlantic slave system. The commerce in persons, these authors said, was a violation of the proper order in human affairs.[79]

Of the Englishmen in this period who were known to have carried on a commerce in persons, John Hawkins was no doubt the most famous. And as a matter of fact, his later reputation reflected a sense of unease about his actions in this respect. Hakluyt printed the accounts of Hawkins's three transatlantic voyages in both editions of his collection. But he placed them in the sections of these texts that were concerned with travel to America. Here was where Hawkins had earned the enduring admiration of the English public, as one of a generation of sea captains who had defied the Spanish Empire abroad and at the same time resisted its incursions close to home. In contrast, what Hawkins and his crews had done in Africa was almost never mentioned in the decades that followed. When their participation in the African slave trade was remarked upon, it was at least sometimes condemned. One author who did so was the historian William Camden, whose 1615 *Annales* was the most detailed chronicle of events in Tudor England. Camden noted that in the 1560s, Hawkins used to sail to the Gulf of Mexico to trade "Negro slaves, of whom the *English* then made ordinary sale, having learn'd it of the *Spaniards;* but I know not," Camden reflected, "with what honour they might so doe."[80]

This was a subtle position. Authors such as Camden never reflected upon the slave trade in an abstract or philosophical context. They considered it in the context of the same particular discourse that we have worked to describe over the course of this chapter. It was an occasion to draw the contrast ever sharper between the character of their own nation and that of their Iberian rivals. In the terms that Camden would have used, to draw attention to the dishonorable practices of the Iberians was to affirm the national honor of England.

It was as a matter of national character, too, that the merchant Richard Jobson had accounted for his refusal to trade in slaves on the Gambia River. After he had observed that the Portuguese merchants who participated in this trade were a different kind of people from Englishmen like himself, Jobson explained to his local African counterpart that "we were a people, who did not deale in any such commodities, neither did wee buy or sell one another, or any that had our owne shapes." Jobson was not the only Englishman abroad in this period who advertised his commitment to this principle. As it happened, in India in 1617, Thomas Roe had done much the same. Roe had come to India as the first English ambassador to the Mughal Empire after a short time as a privateer in Spanish South America. He recalled that on one occasion the Emperor had offered to sell him three persons who had been sold to him as prisoners from the wars across the Arabian Sea in Ethiopia. Roe had declined the offer. "I answered," he explained, as he seemed to speak at once for himself and for the nation whose interests he represented, that "I could not buy men as Slaves, as others did." In the end, as an act of charity, Roe did buy these persons—and then at once he "freed the Slaves."[81]

Interactions such as these reflected an entire context of custom and opinion. Still, on the eve of their entrance into the transatlantic trade in African slaves, Englishmen such as Roe and Jobson plumed themselves upon their nation's special commitment to freedom.

Over the course of the seventeenth century, it became more difficult for Englishmen to cast themselves as the liberators of peoples across the Atlantic world. Indeed, as the slave trade accelerated, not even the most vocal critics of its conduct seemed to recall that at least some Englishmen had once said they were opposed to it. So decisive was this shift that one could assume there must have been some transformation in ideas about slavery. But as we have established, the basic structure of ideas about slavery remained more or less intact over the course of the early-modern period in English culture. Rather, what had shifted was the part of this structure upon which English observers focused their attention.

In the Roman tradition, slaves had always been understood to be persons who were owned. They were items of property, which could be traded from person to person and from place to place. Many of the rules that dealt with slaves in Roman law were ones that defined the procedures to be followed in transactions of this kind. The trade in slaves was the feature of slavery that English observers focused upon when they said that it was unnatural to treat a person in the manner of a common possession and complained, in the phrase of one treatise on commerce in 1601, about the Iberian merchants who in recent times were seen to "have made marchandise of mens soules."[82]

At the same time, however, as we have also seen, the status of the slave as an item of property had never been the central point around which discourse revolved in the Roman tradition. That was a prior point in the sequence of slavery—the one in which naturally free persons were enslaved.

In the initial period of their contact with the peoples who lived on the western coast of Africa, Englishmen had almost never remarked upon this feature of slavery. The sources of slavery in African life had not been a point of interest, either in their own observations or in their reports about the actions of the Portuguese. The blunt force of the raids that Hawkins led in Guinea bespeaks an almost total inattention to the routine customs of enslavement as these had developed across the continent. In the accounts of Africa that started to circulate around the turn of the seventeenth century, however, this was the issue that moved toward the center of informed discourse in England.

In turn, as English observers learned more and more about the sources of slavery in Africa, they started to think differently about the role of Europeans in the transatlantic trade in African slaves. When they had had their attention upon the fact of the slave trade as such, they had been well able to see that this was an act for which Europeans were responsible. In contrast, as they turned to consider the sources of slavery, it occurred to them that the slave trade had its roots back within the interior of a continent over which none of the powers of Europe, least of all England, had any real control. As the English made their entrance into the regular African slave trade, it was with this passive attitude that they did so.

The attitude of the English with respect to their own participation in the slave trade was all the more remarkable for the fact that this developed over such a short span of time. From the time of their arrival on the island, in 1627, the settlers on Barbados had had with them a small number of African slaves. As in the other English American colonies in this period, these persons had in all likelihood been seized from Spanish or Portuguese ships in the Caribbean. As elsewhere in English America, too, the settlers on Barbados at first tried their hand at the cultivation of tobacco. Soon after the introduction of sugar, however, that crop became the dominant one on the island, and in the course of this transition, the settlers turned more and more to Africans to perform the immense amount of labor required for the cultivation of sugar.[83]

From around 1640, ships sent from England had started to deliver to the port towns on Barbados a small number of persons from the western coast of Africa. These persons had been made to labor on plantations that produced tobacco and cotton. But the sugar revolution drove a rapid acceleration of the English African slave trade. And in turn the acceleration of the slave trade drove the sugar revolution that was at work on Barbados. Soon it had become apparent that "Negroes" were "the life of this place," as one visitor to the island observed in 1645. Such was the value of their labor in the process of production, according to this visitor, that the more Negroes whom the planters were able to "buie, the better able are they to buye," for in a short period, "they will earne (with God's blessing) as much as they cost."[84]

From as soon as 1660, African slaves outnumbered English colonists on Barbados, and that remote island toward the southeastern corner of the Caribbean arc was the richest colonial settlement in English America. Even so, at this point, the slave trade represented no more than a small fraction of English commerce on the western coast of Africa. By 1660, the charter for the African company formed in 1631 had almost run out. The charter that Charles II issued to form a new royal company did not mention a commerce in slaves. The Crown's principal interest was in "discovering the golden mines" that it was still believed there were to be found on the Gambia River. When the charter of the company was revised and reissued in 1663, this became the first such document to mention "negro slaves" as one of the commodities that English merchants were expected to purchase in Guinea.[85]

In 1663, the new African company promised the colonial governor of the Caribbean islands to deliver for sale "a constant supply of Negro-servants." Indeed, in this period the regular annual volume of the English African slave trade started to approach that of the old Iberian commerce in African slaves. The acceleration of the English African slave trade in this period was made possible by an earlier shift in approach to commerce on the Guinea coast. From the sixteenth century, English merchants in Guinea had for the most part carried on a ship-based trade, in which they came and went without any permanent establishment on land. From the 1630s, however, the former African company had sponsored the construction of a series of forts and factories on the coast. In this, the company had followed the example of the Portuguese, whose factories and castles had served for well over a century as the locus of European commerce in much of the region. The English outposts in Guinea were minimal structures. But they promoted a more regular and efficient flow of trade—and soon became centers of the trade in slaves.[86]

In the second half of the decade, the Second Anglo-Dutch War caused the collapse of the African company that had been established in 1663. In 1672, Charles incorporated a new company, the Royal African Company, under a charter that granted to its members an exclusive right to trade on the western coast for a term of no less than one thousand years. The Royal African Company was never able to exclude unauthorized or "separate" traders from the Guinea trade. Even in combination, the persons they supplied seem never to have kept pace with colonial demand for slaves. All the same, in the final quarter of the century, more than a quarter of a million Africans were delivered into the American colonies.[87]

Almost all of these Africans arrived in the Caribbean colonies. The labor that they were forced to perform turned the sugar islands—first Barbados and then Jamaica and the Leeward Islands—into the jewels of the new English Atlantic empire. From as soon as the 1690s, informed observers in the metropole were aware of how important the sugar islands had become. There was no other area of overseas commerce so profitable to the nation "as that we manage to *Africa* and our own Plantations in *America,*" observed one merchant in a popular pamphlet. This author was well aware that the most important commodities that passed from Africa to English America were the persons sent there to labor. He advised that the commerce in such persons be opened fully to the separate traders, so as to allow for its volume to increase. The benefit would be substantial, as "these are the Hands whereby our Plantations are improved." "The hands Employ'd in the Collonies," explained another merchant, in a 1690 account of the rise of the English Caribbean, were the most profitable persons in all the realm, "as well to the ends of Consumption and Delight, as for Increasing the Wealth, Power, and Glory of the Nation."[88]

At this point, England was far from the only nation whose power and wealth, delight and consumption, drew upon the system of African slavery in America. The same was the case for Portugal and Spain, even as both of their Atlantic empires had now entered a period of decline. Merchants from the Netherlands had inserted themselves into every area of the Atlantic slave trade—and had even, for a period, taken over the slave trade to Spanish America—and France had established Caribbean sugar colonies of its own. In the classical law of nations, slavery had come to be accepted because it was a custom that all peoples could be seen to share. Now Englishmen could assure themselves that in their participation in the system of American slavery, they were not alone. Their nation was not so distinctive anymore. That time had passed.

CHAPTER 3

The English Image of Africa

BEFORE THE English African slave trade began in earnest, another, more gradual shift had taken place. Not only had demand for African slaves suddenly increased in the American colonies and supply of English servants declined, but in a broad sense the English image of Africa had been transformed. This transformation had started around the end of the sixteenth century. Its essential elements were present in the accounts of the continent that Richard Hakluyt published in his 1589 *Principall Navigations* and were also reflected in the several alterations that he made to the 1599–1600 second edition of the text. Nevertheless, in part because the materials on the areas to the south of the Senegal River that appeared in the Hakluyt collections were so limited, the shape and significance of the shift that they helped to initiate would not have been clear to many more than the most interested observers until the next famous collection of travel writings, the *Pilgrimes* of Samuel Purchas, came out in 1625.[1]

The subject of this chapter is the shift in English perceptions of Africa in the three-quarters of a century that ended around this date. From the middle of the sixteenth century, when regular contact with the western coast was established, observers from England most often founded their opinions of the continent upon the authority of classical texts. These had treated the peoples of Africa as exotic and almost inhuman forms of life—as, on the one hand, those people so inferior as to live in the manner of animals and, on the other hand, those so close to perfect as to resemble the gods.

As the English became more involved in Guinea, however, and reports from other European travelers circulated in England, opinions of Africa started to depend more upon what recently had been seen there. To this point, Purchas would boast that in his collection "the Worlds Rarities, are by a world of Eywitnesse Authors, Related to the World." To such authors as those whose accounts were printed in the *Pilgrimes,* what seemed most important about Africa was not how different it was but rather how familiar. The peoples there were human, and had for the most part formed stable social and political units that anyone who was acquainted with the nations of Europe could comprehend.

Perhaps even more than Europe, Africa contained a range of human customs. The peoples there were varied in almost every aspect of life in which observers from abroad took an interest. This impression of the variety of the continent was due at least in part to the manner in which it had come to be known. The travelers whose reports were read most often in England were almost all merchants of some kind. Their accounts took the form of ship's journals, which set down in order a record of the events that took place on each date, or topographical surveys, which ran across the features particular to each part of a defined area of the land. The educated scholars and clergymen, such as Hakluyt and Purchas, who compiled the works of the travelers or drew upon them for the several descriptions of the world that were written in this period were all but overwhelmed by the amount of information they had received in the chaos of what has come to be known as the Age of Discovery. Their books were storehouses of detail. They rarely paused to reflect upon the character of the whole whose parts they had labored to assemble.

In this respect, popular sources on Africa differed from those that were relied upon for information about the other area of English enterprise in the Atlantic world. The accounts of America that were current in early-modern England tended to have a far more definite structure. These accounts were produced in the context of the expansive colonial projects of the time. Over the course of the previous century, settlers from the Iberian nations had established themselves across the New World. They had asserted their right to rule over the native peoples and had worked to impose upon them the customs of civil behavior and the practice of Christian religion. What they wanted to know about the native peoples of America was above all whether and to what extent these peoples could be made to conform to what were held to be the tenets of European culture.

Around the turn of the seventeenth century, as the English planned and struggled to establish their own colonial settlement in Virginia, the sources that held their attention were those that they believed could help them determine whether the peoples who lived there could be brought within the bounds of the new social order that they hoped to create. To ask this was often to seek to decide whether the Americans were civil or savage, in the common contrast from the time. The accounts of the Spanish missionaries Las Casas and Acosta—which were premised upon a division of barbarians into three kinds, wherein the first was civil but not Christian, the second was civil to a certain extent, and the third was no more than savage—were only the most sophisticated efforts to reduce the variety of the New World by means of a system of cultural classification. The works of Léry on Brazil and Strachey on Virginia were lesser efforts of a similar kind.[2]

The accounts of Africa from this time were produced in a different cultural context. The aim of the European nations here was neither settlement nor conversion, other than in the western central kingdoms of Congo and Angola, where Portugal to some extent pursued both. Elsewhere the interest of the Europeans in Africa was the much more minimal one of commerce. Indeed, as the involvement of the English in the continent increased, commerce was almost the exclusive focus.

In the initial period of English commerce in Africa, merchants found that they were able to conduct their business on the western coast without any permanent presence on land. Over the course of the seventeenth century, the series of African companies that received their charters from the English state made it their mission to construct a network of factories and forts that extended across much of the Guinea littoral. At times, these nourished hopes of more extensive settlement. The charters that were issued to the African companies in 1660 and 1672 both authorized the establishment of "plantations" in Guinea and indicated that these would be useful if gold and silver were to be discovered and mined in the interior. Plans of this kind could have seemed to envision the application in Africa of the model for the extraction of precious metals that the Spanish had developed on such an immense scale in America. But in the seventeenth century, no such plans were put into effect. The rise of the British colonial enterprise in Africa was still far in the future. At no point in this period were there more than five hundred Englishmen in total in residence on the entire western coast (see Figure 3.1).[3]

In this context, English discourse about Africa lacked some of the depth of English discourse about America. The rich early-modern concepts of the civil and the savage were never as embedded within it. English authors did at times remark that African peoples were rude or courteous, wild or well-mannered, barbarous or savage or civil. But in each case the use of such terms was haphazard and their significance was far from clear. What English observers wanted to know about African peoples was not so much whether they were civil as such. It was whether they possessed the common features of civil life, such that they would be effective partners in trade. Around the turn of the seventeenth century, what had become clear was that they did.

Such a shift could at first seem to have worked against the development of the slave trade in the decades that followed, inasmuch as scholars have often maintained that the trade drew upon the impression that Africa was "beyond the pale of civilization," in the phrase of Winthrop Jordan, whose 1968 account, *White over Black: American Attitudes toward the Negro, 1550–1812,* remains the classic statement of this position.[4]

The truth was closer to the opposite. As English observers learned more and more about African peoples, they discovered in their practices of government, punishment, war, and commerce what before they had so conspicuously not possessed: a method to account for the sources of slavery, to explain in detail how free persons were made into slaves. By the middle of the seventeenth century, English traders were no longer concerned that they themselves or even Europeans in general had been the cause of slavery in Africa. The open slave raids of John Hawkins had long since fallen out of favor. The English had found that the sources of African slavery could be traced back into the continent and that these arose from the order and sophistication of African life.

To be sure, the effect of these findings upon the development of the English African slave trade, a material event of immense scope, is not the kind of inquiry that will admit of a definite answer. The conviction that animates the present study is that this event—if indeed the term is sufficient to describe a turn in the past whose consequences have been so profound—was not the effect of one cause but several, which overlapped and interacted

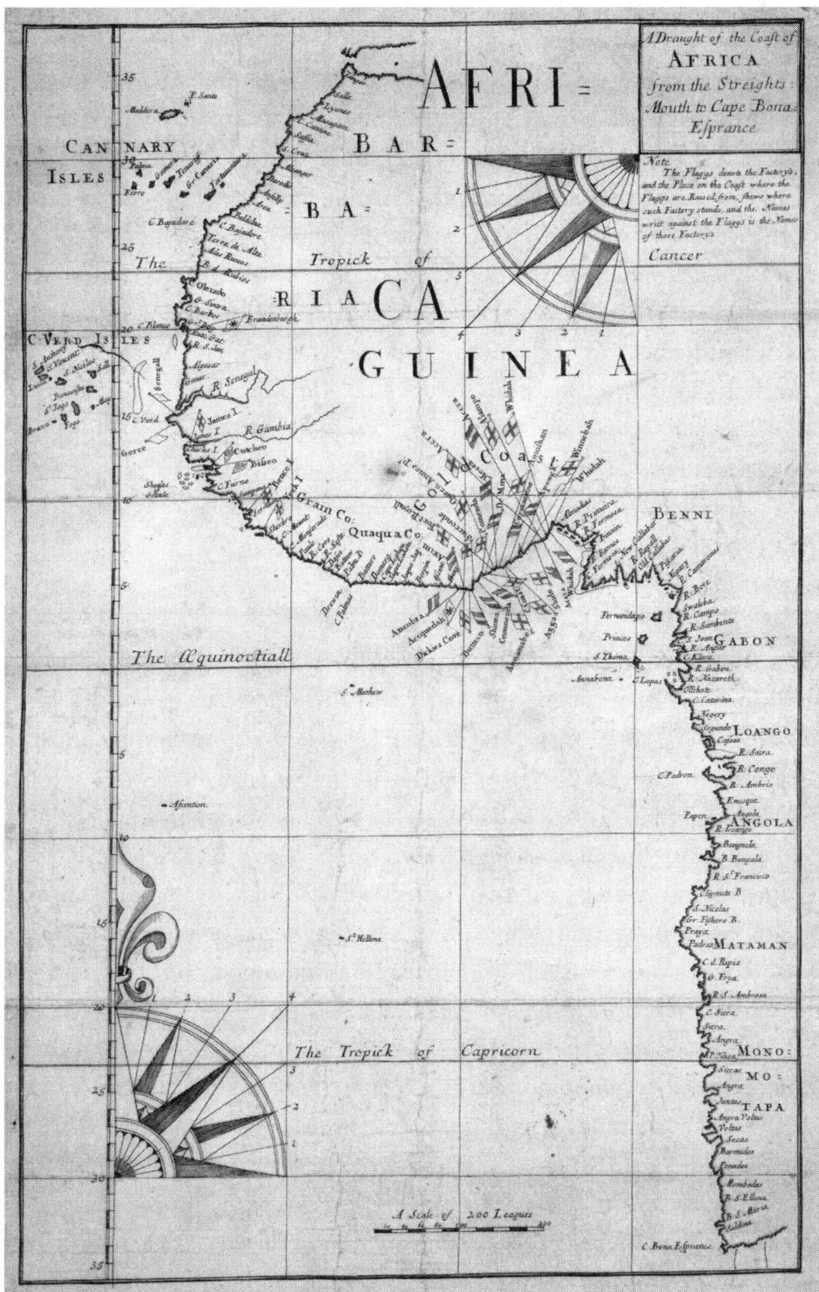

FIG. 3.1 This map records the network of European outposts on the western coast of Africa, with a particular focus on the Guinea coast. Almost all of the factories shown here are situated in the area known as the Gold Coast, where they are clustered on the shoreline. To the west of the Gold Coast, all of the factories in Guinea were built on coastal islands. This map thus attests to European interest in commerce in Africa rather than colonial settlement or colonial rule.

Credit: "A Draught of the Coast of Africa from the Streights Mouth to Cape Bona Esprance," Royal African Company map, 1663–1681. The National Archives, MPG1/221.

with one another. In this vein, perhaps we can speculate that the English entrance into the slave trade, in a transition that has so often been explained as a direct response to new conditions of supply and demand, had been prepared by a transition in thought that had been in the works for decades. At the least we should observe that as the sugar revolution swept across their Caribbean colonies, the English started almost at once to send enslaved persons there from the western coast of Africa without any discernible trace of guilt about what they were doing.

Perhaps a shift in their common perception of Africa had allowed the English to see the enslavement of Africans in a different moral light. The practice no longer appeared to violate their acute sense of national virtue. It hardly appeared to be a practice that could be attributed to them. All of their former concerns had vanished.

❧

The early English voyages to the western coast of Africa had set out from a nation whose image of the continent was still shaped by classical understanding. According to the classical geographers, the defining feature of Africa was its climate: it fell for the most part within what Aristotle termed the "Torrid Zone," the belt of land that ran along the Equator where the heat rendered human life impossible. The interior of Africa, reported the Roman compiler Julius Solinus, was a vast desert "broyled continually wyth unmeasurable heate of the parching sunne burning, hoter then any fire." Only beasts could survive in such an environment, the ancient authors believed, and in their descriptions, Africa teemed with a profusion of fearsome animals, from elephants to dragons to hyenas, crocodiles to lions to panthers, rhinoceroses to hippopotamuses to serpents. "*Affrick* swarmeth in such wise with Serpents," Solinus remarked. Because water was so scarce, these animals gathered around "the few places where springs are to be found," according to Aristotle, and mated here to produce novel hybrid species. It was as he reflected upon this distinctive setting that Aristotle introduced into Western culture the proverb that Africa "is always bringing forth something new."[5]

The scattered peoples who did live in Africa south of the populous northern coast were clustered just above the Torrid Zone, at the extreme edge of the habitable world, and shared as their only common attribute a certain strange point of deviance from the normal human form. The principal source of opinion in this respect was Pliny, whose first-century *Natural History* had enlarged upon the earlier work of Pomponius Mela, who had in turn drawn upon an earlier Greek tradition that stretched back to Herodotus. In Ethiopia, Pliny explained, there were men known as Troglodytes, who lived in caves below the ground and gnashed their teeth but could not speak; Cinamolgi, whose heads were those of dogs; bow-legged Himantopodes, who crept and slid over the earth on all fours; and Satyres, who were "scarce men," as Mela put it, "but rather halfe Beastes." The classical geographers were thus prepared to concede that some humans could survive in the African interior. What they denied was that these were men fully worthy of the name.[6]

In classical descriptions the deviance of Africans near the Torrid Zone was not only physical but also fundamentally cultural. They did not only look like beasts; in a sense they lived like beasts as well. Alongside the Himantopodes and Satyres in Ethiopia, continued Pliny, there were Anthropophagi, who fed on human flesh; Garamantes, who did not marry and held their women and children in common; Gamphasantes, who did not wear clothes and engaged in neither commerce nor war; Augylæ, who worshipped subterranean devils; and Ptœmphenæ, whose ruler was a dog.

The fantastical Plinian litany of central African peoples thus formed in composite a negative image of what human culture was imagined to be. They "are entirely savage and display the nature of a wild beast," wrote the first-century BCE Greek historian Diodorus Siculus of Ethiopians. They had developed "none of the practices of civilized life as these are found among the rest of mankind." The Ethiopians who were known as Atlantes were in particular, in the opinion of Solinus, "altogether void of manners meete for men." They neither dreamed nor assigned proper names to one another, and in a trope that appeared in a number of classical accounts, the Atlantes would curse "the sun at his rising, and curse him likwise at his going downe." "Because they are scorched wyth the heate of his burning beames," Solinus wrote, "they hate the God of light." The burning heat of the sun near the Torrid Zone often figured in classical culture as the cause of the primitive character of the peoples of Africa just as, in a scheme developed most thoroughly in Strabo's first-century *Geography,* the temperate climate of the Mediterranean world was seen to be the condition of its advanced civilizations. Far to the south, at the bottom border of the habitable world, even the most basic human customs were spectacularly absent.[7]

The classical image of Africa was also developed in cartography, where above all the second-century Alexandrian Ptolemy gave form and dimension to the writings of the geographers. Ptolemy divided the continent into three distinct regions, Egypt, Ethiopia, and Libya, where Libya covered the western area south of the northern coast and Ethiopia described both the eastern area south of Egypt and the immense tract of land below Libya. Ptolemy placed little emphasis upon the Torrid Zone as an absolute limit upon the reach of human life. In fact, in his guide to a map of the world, titled the *Geography,* he placed the kingdoms of Azania and Agisymba below the Equator. Even so, he was also aware that this territory remained for the most part unexplored and that reports of human life here, much less of civilization, were rare. He drew upon the Plinian geographical tradition for many of what he said were the names and locations of African peoples, from the Troglodytes to the Anthropophagi, from the Garamantes to the Ichthyophagi (or the fish-eaters). And so, even as he did not dwell upon the mythic horrors of the Torrid Zone, he in essence reproduced in cartography the image of Africa that he had found in the works of the geographers.[8]

By the time that the *Geography* of Ptolemy was rediscovered and translated into Latin, in 1406, the maps that appear to have been included in the original work had been lost. Their reconstruction became a central project of the Italian Renaissance, and in 1477 the *Geography* came out as the first atlas to appear in print. Four of its maps were ones of Africa that would become the models for most European maps of the continent until well into the next century.[9]

During this time, as reports of recent Portuguese expeditions filtered back through Europe, maps labeled *Africa Tabula Nova* started to appear that showed the full shape of the western and southern coasts as well as coastal nations that Pliny had never mentioned. Even in the most faithful sixteenth-century reproduction of Ptolemy's Africa (Figure 3.2), the cartographer Sebastian Münster observed that the land to the south of the twen-

FIG. 3.2 This map identifies the source of the Nile River as three lakes that flow from the "Montes Lunæ," or Mountains of the Moon. On this point, Münster departed from Ptolemy, the ancient authority upon whom he otherwise relied. Ptolemy had the Nile begin in two parallel lakes, and already in the "Nova Tabula" he included in his atlas, Münster reproduced this feature of the hydrographic system he had encountered in the works of the Alexandrian.

Credit: "Aphricæ Tabula IIII," in Sebastiani Munsteri, *Geographia universalis, vetus et nova, complectens Claudii Ptolemæi Alexandrini ennarrationis libros viii* (Basel, 1542; orig. pub. 1540), fol. 16. G1005 1545*: Harvard Map Collection, Harvard University.

tieth parallel below the Equator was "unknown to Ptolemy" rather than absolutely unknown. Nevertheless, such popular maps as those of Apian, Ruysch, Fries, Mercator, and Münster all came out in editions of the *Geography,* which were printed across Europe into the seventeenth century. In the distinctive style of the Renaissance, these cartographers worked to improve upon the ancient Alexandrian even as they relied upon him as an enduring source of authority.[10]

In the second half of the sixteenth century, the maps of Africa made on the model of Ptolemy began to be replaced by ones drawn from far more recent authorities. Even so, among written works available in England, the ancient image of Africa would continue to dominate almost until the end of the century. The works of Mela, Pliny, and Solinus were rendered in the vernacular, and the *Histories* of Herodotus and *Geography* of Strabo were widely read in Latin editions. Moreover, even the new surveys of the peoples of the world that came out in this period were deeply indebted to classical sources. The descriptions of Africa that appeared, for example, in William Prat's *Discription of the Contrey of Aphrique,* William Waterman's *Fardle of Facions,* William Cuningham's *Cosmographical Glasse,* André Thevet's *New Found Worlde,* and Stephen Bateman's *Batman uppon Bartholome* were for the most part composed as compendia of the works of classical authors and their later compilers, from Orosius and Isidore in Late Antiquity to the medieval Bartholomaeus Anglicus to the Renaissance *Cosmography* of Apian.[11]

Nowhere was this debt to classical authors more evident than in the narrative of the second English voyage to Guinea that was printed in Richard Eden's *Decades of the Newe Worlde* in 1555. Here, near the end of an account of routine navigation and trade that was based upon the reports of the sea captain John Lok, Eden himself inserted "a brefe description of Africa." The people there, he wrote, were "a people of beastly lyvynge, without a god, lawe, religion, or common welth, and so scorched and vexed with the heate of the soonne, that in many places they curse it when it ryseth," as in classical accounts the Atlantes had done. The heat was so intense that at times the people in Africa seemed to "live as it were in fornaces." They were nomads, Eden continued, who wandered "among many horrible wyldernesses and mountaynes replenisshed with dyvers kyndes of wylde and monstrous beastes and serpentes."

As had Ptolemy, Eden divided the landmass of Africa into Libya and the two parts of Ethiopia, though he did add that in western Libya and below eastern Ethiopia there were the recently discovered kingdoms of Guinea and Melinde. He listed the peoples who lived among those lands, and these were compiled from classical texts as well: the Troglodytes, Blemmyi, Anthropophagi, Satyres, Garamantes, and Ichthyophagi all appeared, as did more than a dozen other peoples named in Ptolemy. The authorities to whom Eden referred were classical scholars from Pliny to Diodorus to Gemma Frisius, who had edited the work of Apian.[12]

One source to whom Eden did not refer was Lok, who in the pages that preceded his "brefe description" had produced the most precise accounts of the shape and terrain of the Guinea coast and of the towns where his crew had stopped to trade. Toward the start of his narrative, Eden had praised Lok for taking care to note "as he founde and tryed all thynges not by coniecture, but by the arte of saylynge," on a voyage that had been "wel observed by art and experience." In his description of Africa, Eden did not attempt to refute or even add to what Lok had "founde and tryed." He ignored him. For Eden was aware that to produce an account of Africa as such was not to make a record of experience so much as summon conjectures from the classical past.[13]

The classical accounts of Africa were more complex than has been described here so far, however, and this complex character was reflected in Renaissance English culture. Classical authors had of course divided Africa below the northern coast into Libya and Ethiopia, but much more important in their minds had been the division of Ethiopia into its southern and eastern parts.

On the one hand, the inhabitants of southern Ethiopia resembled those of Libya in that both were understood to be "people of beastly lyvynge, without a god, lawe, religion, or common welth," according to Richard Eden, who thus captured the consensus of classical authors. Perhaps the most terrible creatures in the Plinian imagination, the Anthropophagi, were said to be found here. In contrast, the eastern part of Ethiopia, and in particular the area to the south of Egypt, was believed to be the site of an advanced civilization that centered on an island in the Nile River named Meroë. Münster recorded this belief with the placement of four red castles, at Meroë, Sabath, Dire, and Rapta, that stood out from vast expanses of unsettled land. Already in the Archaic period, Homer had spoken in the *Odyssey* about "th'Æthiops" who were "farre dissunderd in their seate; / (In two parts parted; at the Sunnes descent, / And underneath his golden Orient / The first and last of men)."[14]

Over the course of the next millennium, Greek and Roman authors would develop into a statement about culture as well as geography the insight that Ethiopia was to be seen not as one place but as two.[15]

Ethiopia had appeared in the *Odyssey* as the destination for an annual banquet of the gods, who feasted there with what Homer said were its "blameless" inhabitants. In time the perfection of the Ethiopians was taken up as a theme in Herodotus, who provided the first detailed account of their region in Western culture. The *Histories* thus recorded a contrast between the savage peoples of western Libya—who included the "dog-headed men and the headless that have their eyes in their breasts," Herodotus wrote, in phrases that would later capture the attention of Pliny—and the peoples of eastern Ethiopia, which was for Herodotus an earthly paradise. The land produced "great plenty of gold, and abundance of elephants, and all woodland trees, and ebony," he believed, and the people were "the tallest and fairest and longest-lived of all men."[16]

Into the next millennium, even as Diodorus and Strabo took up and elaborated upon Herodotus's negative opinion of the peoples of western Africa, they also confirmed his high regard for the eastern Ethiopians. "In general," Strabo explained, "the extremities of the inhabited world must needs be defective and inferior to the temperate part," and yet it so happened that these Ethiopians were neither. They had been the first men, according to Diodorus, as they had been generated out of the earth by the warmth of the African sun. They had been the first men taught to honor the gods, who in turn were said to find that the sacrifices the Ethiopians offered were "those which are the most pleasing to heaven." Their kings were subject to the laws and customs of the country, but were worshipped by their subjects as though they were divine. When they died, they were embalmed in gold coffins that were painted to recall their living features, in a practice that the Egyptians later adopted for their pharaohs. In the classical world the drama and fascination of Ethiopia thus consisted in the contrast that it accommodated between men who lived almost as beasts and those who appeared almost as gods.[17]

According to Greek historians from Herodotus to Diodorus, it was the gods that had protected the Ethiopians from foreign invasion. "For from all time," Diodorus wrote, "they have enjoyed a state of freedom and of peace one with another." Even as "many powerful rulers have made war upon them, not one of these has succeeded in his undertaking." But by the time of Strabo and Pliny, the area around Meroë had been laid waste. The Romans had done it, according to Strabo, while Pliny believed it had been the Egyptians. "At this day there is neither sticke nor stone to be found" from the cities that were "recorded in times past to have been in those parts," Pliny wrote. All that remained were "deserts and a vast wildernesse" and the bands of barely human creatures that dominated his account of Africa.[18]

In the centuries after Pliny wrote, however, reports of a great kingdom in Ethiopia never disappeared entirely from Western culture. These were shaped and sustained by the story told in the Old Testament and developed in Josephus about the Queen of Sheba, who had traveled from Ethiopia to Jerusalem "with great pompe, glorie, and riches," according to Josephus, in order to test the wisdom of King Solomon. In turn, in the New Testament, Philip was said to have baptized the eunuch of another Ethiopian queen. And in the works of such early Church historians as Sokrates and Rufinus, Matthew had gone to Meroë to preach the Gospel. In fact, in the fourth century, the kingdom of Aksum, in the area south and east of Meroë, had converted to Christianity; although this was not widely known in Europe in the centuries that followed, it did become one source of the view that arose in the eighth century and would come to prominence in the late Middle Ages that one of the three Magi who visited the newborn Jesus was a black African. For throughout this period the Church had well preserved the ecumenical belief recorded in the Psalms that "Ethiopia shall soon stretch out her hands to God."[19]

And so in the twelfth century, when a letter addressed to the emperor of Byzantium from a powerful Christian monarch named Prester John began to circulate in Europe, Pope Alexander III sent his response to Ethiopia. The letter had identified Prester John only as ruler of "the three Indies," a Far Eastern empire whose exact location and extent were not well known. During this period, and in fact until the fifteenth-century revival of Ptolemaic cartography, Ethiopia was often included as part of India rather than Africa, with the Nile and not the Red Sea given as the border between them. After the Pope's message received no response from Ethiopia, the search for Prester John carried on in Central Asia and as far east as China. The popular fourteenth-century *Travels* of Sir John Mandeville, for example, placed him near the kingdoms of Tartary and Cathay. He presided over "many good cities and good townes," according to Mandeville, in "a great land" where rivers ran out of Paradise through hills that were covered in crystal and gold.[20]

Mandeville's work was well known in England through the close of the sixteenth century, and his chapters on Prester John were even printed in the long Latin extract from the *Travels* that Hakluyt included in the first edition of his *Principall Navigations*. Hakluyt would leave Mandeville out of the second edition of his collection, however, and already in the period when the *Travels* was composed, belief in the Indian Prester John had started to wane and the legend had started to shift back to eastern Africa. Here classical accounts of Ethiopia's blameless men were revived and reconfigured to accommodate new rumors of a spectacular Christian dominion.[21]

The legend of Prester John, situated either in Asia or in Africa, has often been seen as the expression of a credulous medieval cast of mind that all but vanished from European culture with the rise of the Age of Discovery. But reports of an Ethiopian Prester John remained common all the way through the close of the sixteenth century and during this time betrayed little doubt as to the actual existence of their subject.[22]

The continued presence of Prester John in European culture is best seen in the maps of Africa that were in circulation in the second half of the sixteenth century. Already in the edition of the *Geography* that Münster put out in 1540, the *Africa Tabula Nova* had shown the royal seat of Prester John with a five-turret kingdom drawn among the branches of the Nile River to the south of Meroë (Figure 3.3). In the decades that followed, as the influence of Ptolemy declined, Meroë disappeared from most popular African maps. The new works of Hondius and Ortelius identified the center of eastern African civilization instead as the inland domain of the "*imperitat magnus princeps Presbiter Joes*." In his 1569 world map and his 1595 map of Africa, Mercator marked the empire of Prester John with an image of the sovereign seated on a throne, with a crown on his head and a scepter in his hand (Figure 3.4). As late as 1606, Ortelius's *Theatre of the Whole World*—the first full-size atlas published in England—devoted a folio spread to "The country of the ABYSSINES, or The Empire of PRESTER JOHN," which was

FIG. 3.3 This map of Africa is well known for the representation of the one-eyed Plinian monsters, known as Monoculi, who are depicted along the western central coast. As a "Nova Tabula," however, the map also includes symbols that denote kingdoms far to the south of those that had been known to classical authors. The castle that marks the royal seat of Prester John is one of these. Others include the crowns placed at "Melli" (or Mali), toward the Guinea coast, and at Melinde, to the west of the Horn of Africa.

Credit: "Africa XVIII nova tabula," in Sebastiani Munsteri, *Geographia universalis, vetus et nova, complectens Claudii Ptolemæi Alexandrini ennarrationis libros viii* (Basel, 1542; orig. pub. 1540), after fol. 46. G1005 1545*: Harvard Map Collection, Harvard University.

depicted as a region dotted with dozens of castles painted in red (Figure 3.5; also see Figure 3.6).

Even the midcentury descriptions of the world, which carried into English culture Plinian legends about the peoples of Africa, recorded as well the more recent opinion that Prester John reigned in the east. Prat, Waterman, Cuningham, Thevet, and Bateman thus all followed Pliny in the belief that much of Africa "lieth waste," as Waterman said, "voide of enhabitauntes, either to whote for menne to abide, or full of noisome and venomous vermine, and beastes," and that there were in all of Ethiopia no

FIG. 3.4 This is a detail from a map that appears in an edition of the Mercator-Hondius Atlas. The image of Prester John that appears at the center of this detail differs in one respect from those in most other editions of this atlas. In those works, the outline of the Abyssinian Emperor is not colored in, but rather is the same shade as the land under his dominion: white in black-and-white editions and green in color editions. In this map, the gown of Prester John is purple and his skin is brown. English reactions to the skin color of African peoples will be examined in depth in Chapter 5.

Credit: Detail from "Africa, Ex magna orbis terræ description Gerardi Mercatoris desumpta, Studio & industria G. M. Iunioris," in Gerardi Mercatoris, *L'Atlas de Gerard Mercator et d'Hondius: Atlas ou représentation du monde universel,* 2 vols. (Amsterdam, 1633), vol. 1: 62–63. MM 1.1633.2 pf*: Harvard Map Collection, Harvard University.

more than a small number of "dyvers peoples of sondry phisonomy and shape, monstrous and of hugly shewe." Even so, the opinion of Africa that was developed in the works of these authors was as complex as the one that had been present in the ancient world, and each author also described in detail the stories from Herodotus and Diodorus about the special attributes

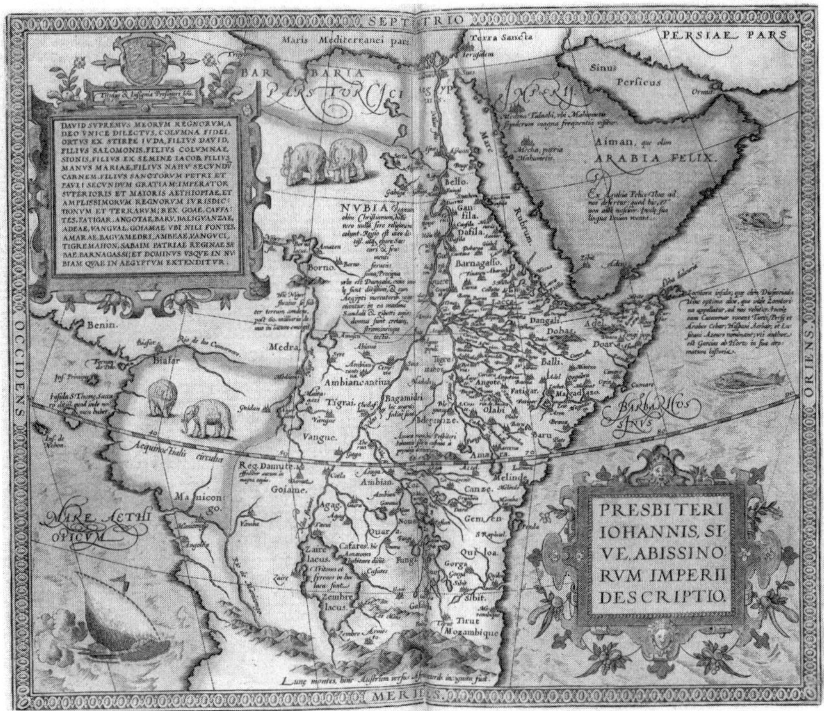

FIG. 3.5 This map contains a level of detail in the representation of eastern Africa that marks it as a distinct product of the second half of the sixteenth century. But it also retains certain features from earlier maps such as Münster's 1542 "Nova Tabula." The Mountains of the Moon remain the source of the Nile, and as in Münster's map, elephants are drawn over stretches of obscure terrain. The location for the empire of Prester John is another feature that Ortelius reproduced from the mapmakers of an earlier era.

Credit: "Presbiteri Johannis, Sive, Abissinorum Imperii Descriptio," in Abraham Ortelius, *The Theatre of the Whole World* (London, 1606), fol. 113. MO 1.1606 pf*: Harvard Map Collection, Harvard University.

of the eastern Ethiopians. These were said to have been "the fyrst of all men," according to Waterman, and they had devised "the first waie of worshippyng God." They had never been "under the bondage of any" and were "ever a free nacion." The people revered their king "as thoughe there ware in him a Godhead," and yet "for al that," Waterman marveled, the king was "governed by the lawe" and "bounde to all things after th'ordre of the contry."[23]

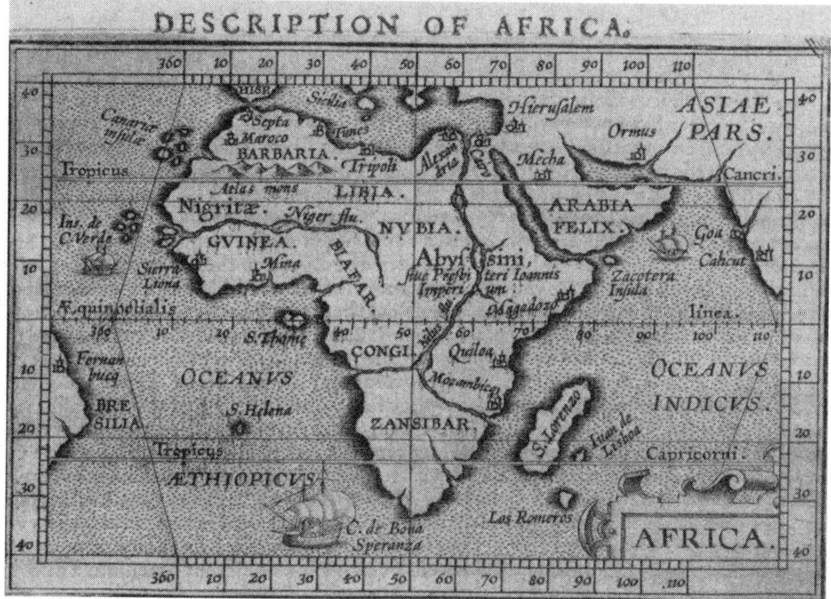

FIG. 3.6 Perhaps the most notable feature of this miniature map of Africa is one that befits an Ortelius production: the location of the immense "*Presbiteri Ioannis Imperium*" in the landlocked middle of the continent. Also notable in this map is the treatment of Africa's hydrographic system. The Nile River does not follow what was believed at this time to be its standard southern course into the Mountains of the Moon. By contrast, the Niger River does follow its standard early-modern course in an east-to-west direction through West Africa, from an obscure inland source to the western coast around Cape Verde.

Credit: "Africa," in Abraham Ortelius, *Abraham Ortelius His Epitome of the Theater of the Worlde* (London, 1603), A4. STC 18856: Houghton Library, Harvard University.

Waterman and his colleagues presented their accounts of the monstrous peoples of Africa as current information, but they spoke of these Ethiopians for the most part only as the original inhabitants of the region. "At this daye," Waterman said, the ancient capital at Meroë was under the control of a monarch named Prester John whose kingdom recalled the distinctive features of the wonderful civilization that it had succeeded. Its central institution was the church, and Prester John oversaw orders of priests, bishops, and archbishops as well as churches that were "much larger, much richer, and more gorgeous then ours." The political structure that Prester John oversaw was similarly elaborate. Under him, there were no fewer than sixty-two kings; in his court there were princes, dukes, and earls; and in each city in his realm there were judges who reported to governors who stood in for the king in local affairs. When Prester John went to war—as officials across Christendom had long hoped he would, against the Muslim states that seemed to surround the Holy Land—he led an army of one million men.[24]

In short, into the late sixteenth century, the English image of Africa was a study in contrast. As in classical Antiquity, English observers held that many African peoples were little advanced above the level of beasts in both physical features and cultural forms. Also as in Antiquity, however, the English believed that Africa was "in two parts parted," in the phrase of Homer, and that there was in the east a race of persons who could scarcely have been more different. Richard Eden had called the inhabitants of Africa "a people of beastly lyvynge, without a god, lawe, religion, or common welth." But Eden himself also said that, southward along the Nile from Meroë and still farther east toward the Red Sea, Africa held the dominion of "the greate and myghtye Emperour and Chrystian kynge Prester Iohan." What the people of beastly living lacked was what the empire of Prester John supplied: the possession of a god, law, religion, and commonwealth that "Chrystian kynge" captured in a phrase. The intricate systems of religion and politics that authors such as Eden described within the kingdom of Prester John served, in other words, as the mirror image of what such authors perceived to be the failure to live up to the most basic standards of human conduct across much of the rest of Africa.[25]

This double-sided aspect of the early English attitudes toward Africa has not been well understood. In the opinion of historians from Winthrop Jordan to Alden and Virginia Mason Vaughan, the English in the sixteenth century viewed the Africans as so "radically defective" and "uniquely deficient" in every measure of civility as to resemble beasts more than men—that is, as Eden's "people of beastly lyvynge," which was the phrase that these scholars took to have captured the common tenor of informed opinion. Not so much as the title of Prester John appeared in the accounts of these scholars, and neither did the tradition from Herodotus and Diodorus upon which the legend of Prester John had drawn. And in truth, we have established that in this period the English viewed Africa in more nuanced terms—with admiration as well as contempt, as home to both the lowest and the highest forms of human life.[26]

Around the turn of the seventeenth century, however, a dramatic shift took place in English perceptions of Africa. This was at root a shift not so much in what the English thought about Africa, although it was no doubt also that, as in how they came to think what they did: in other words, a shift in the sources rather than the content of their information.

The early English accounts were for the most part composed as commentaries upon classical texts, which themselves were often based upon conjecture. Even the more recent legend of Prester John had its origins in a letter from the twelfth century that seems to have been written in Europe and persisted over time as a trope that was used to describe a remote region in the African interior from which travelers' reports would not be readily accessible in England until the seventeenth century.[27]

To be sure, it took time for the old tropes to fade. The classical description of Africa that Richard Eden produced was reprinted in editions of the Hakluyt collection through 1600. In as late a production as *Othello,* Shakespeare had his titular African character dazzle Desdemona with tales of "the cannibals, that each other eat; / The Anthropophagi, and men whose heads / Do grow beneath their shoulders." Such phrases could well have been drawn from Eden, whose description of Africa had first been published almost half a century in the past. Moreover, as we will see, the accounts that introduced a new approach to the study of Africa around the turn of the century still repeated the convention that Prester John reigned over a powerful eastern empire about which there was only the most indirect information. But opinions such as these were now relics of an earlier era. Increasingly, English authors stated that their perceptions of Africa were informed by what recently had been seen there.[28]

The basis for the shift in English perceptions of Africa was, in other words, the rise of English contact with Africa in the second half of the sixteenth century. The accounts of Africa that appeared in the Hakluyt collection were not the work of classical scholars, aside from the brief interpolations of Eden. They were produced instead from the observations of seamen and merchants and reflected their particular concerns. At the height of the Second British Empire, in the Victorian period, the *Principal Navigations* was hailed as "the Prose Epic of the modern English nation." Nevertheless, the book was not an epic of discovery or conquest or even settlement, as the earlier epic narratives of the Iberian empires had been, but rather an epic that was concerned with commerce.[29]

Above all, the African materials that Hakluyt collected were narratives of navigation and trade. They covered the sea routes to the western coast, the currents near the shoreline, the terrain inland from the shore, the efforts of the English to form alliances with the French and the conflicts that so often marked relations with the Portuguese, the presents the native people sometimes demanded, their rituals of formal address, the commodities they favored and those they had to offer in return, the weights and measures they used, the struggles for power between members of the English crews, and the strong headwinds on the northward journeys home.

It was their mundane character that made the accounts in the Hakluyt collection so significant, for the image of Africa that was developed in these works little resembled the tales that ancient authors had told about the Torrid Zone. In the account of the first English voyage to the western coast, in 1553, the "smothering heate, with close and cloudie ayre," was said to have "rotted the coates off" the backs of the travelers. And yet as time went on, even as English travelers continued to fall sick and perish in Guinea, they attributed this to the water they consumed, the moisture of the air, and the sharp alterations in climate on the voyage from England rather than to the mythic scorching heat of the sun. The accounts of these travelers indicate, in fact, that Englishmen in Guinea did not much dwell upon what classical geographers would have led them to expect was the dominant fact of African life. Already in 1578, George Best was able to explain as much in an essay that he included in his *True Discourse* on the search for a Northwest Passage, which Hakluyt excerpted in the second edition of his collection. Best observed that "it may be gathered by experience of our Englishmen" in Guinea that the climate was far milder than "the old Philosophers" had imagined. For this reason, Best concluded with a Latin flourish, the "*Torrida Zona* may bee, and is inhabited."[30]

Moreover, the African inhabitants of the Torrid Zone were not the beastly peoples described in classical accounts. In a poem written in the style of an epic about the first of his two voyages to Guinea, in 1562, Robert Baker recalled that the ruler of a village on the coast had approached his crew "as naked as my naile." "By which I doe here gesse," Baker remarked, "That he from man and manlinesse / was void and clean astray." This poem was included in the first edition of the Hakluyt collection, but as with the Latin extract from Mandeville's fanciful *Travels,* it was left out of the much expanded second edition. In the more than two dozen accounts of travel to the western coast of Africa that Hakluyt printed in this text, the native people were said to cover at least their loins, and their participation in the commerce that was the focus of these narratives confirmed their human status. They were "a very warie people in their bargaining," as John Lok observed in 1554. At points on the Guinea coast, the people could be so "idle" as not to cultivate the land or so "wilde" that they did not know the proper customs of exchange. At other places, the people were seen to be "unreasonable" in their demands. That said, it was far more common for the Englishmen who went to Guinea over the course of this period to report that the people had acted "with confident love and good will towards us," in the assessment of one merchant who had been there in 1591. They had been "gentle and loving," as well as "courteous," and for the most part they had proven to be effective partners in trade.[31]

In addition to the men whom Lok had taken from Shamma to serve as interpreters, some local merchants in Guinea spoke French or Portuguese. When they lacked a common tongue, the English on occasion made an effort to learn Guinean languages. In the account of his first voyage, from 1555, William Towerson translated local phrases in lists that read as abstracts of early English activity in Guinea. "Bezow, bezow" was "their salutation," he said, and continued with the terms for "Hennes ynough," "Have you ynough," "Give me a knife," "Give me bread," "Hold your peace," "Ye lye," "Put foorth," and, with the routine interaction reflected in these phrases evidently at an end, "Rowe."[32]

What stood out from such accounts of African life, in context, was how ordinary it was. In 1599, the year in which the first two volumes of the second edition of the Hakluyt collection appeared, George Abbot and John Thorie published the first English descriptions of the world since the classical surveys of authors such as Waterman. "From beyond the hils *Atlas maior*" near the northern coast, Abbot declared, "unto the South of *Africa,* is nothing almost in antiquitie worthie the reading, and those things which are written for the most part are fables." The area was "in former times supposed by many not to bee much inhabited." But travelers from Portugal and, in recent times, from England had found that this was far from accurate. Thorie listed several of the unnamed creatures from Plinian texts—with no nose, no upper lip, or nose and mouth joined weirdly together—that were "thought by some men" to live in Africa. "But these," he concluded, "are but fained fables." With this conclusion, that classical authors had told little more than fables about the peoples of Africa, a new era in English perception had begun.[33]

Through the end of the seventeenth century, English descriptions of the world would continue to remark upon how inadequate classical accounts of Africa had been. The studies of the continent in such accounts as those of John Speed, Peter Heylyn, and Robert Morden all started from this criticism of their earliest predecessors. "What they knew not, and thought almost impossible to be known" about the continent, as Morden explained in 1680, "is now common: for the secrets of her deep and remotest shores, are now beaten up and tracted with continual Voyages." On the basis of such voyages, by 1652 Heylyn was able to conclude that classical observers "spoke upon conjecture, or more doubtful hear-say," when they said that "such strange people, as hardly did deserve to be counted men" were scattered across the barren lands that bordered the Torrid Zone.[34]

Scholars in recent years have often asserted that early English authors represented Africa as "a 'dark continent' whose clearest feature [was] its difference from England," as Emily Bartels has written in an essay on the Hakluyt collection. The term "dark continent" was an invention of the nineteenth century, however, and from the late sixteenth century, difference was not understood to be the clearest feature of Africa among the many English observers learned in classical texts. What struck them was rather that the people in Africa were less unusual than one had been led to expect. Travelers to the continent had found no "monstrous people" there, Speed observed in his 1627 world atlas: "They report not (upon their owne experience) of any other people then such as our selves are." The Africans had at last come to be seen as no more and no less than men.[35]

And as men do, the Africans came in many forms. In the decades that followed the second edition of the Hakluyt collection, the classical two-part scheme that had long set the structure for the English image of Africa almost entirely disappeared. What replaced it was not so much a new scheme of a similar kind as the view that no scheme could capture the range of African life.

The central document from this period was the next collection of travel narratives after that of Hakluyt: the *Pilgrimes* of Samuel Purchas, which came out in 1625. The aim of Purchas here was to some extent different from what Hakluyt had hoped to accomplish. Hakluyt's collection had arisen from his involvement in the project of westward expansion. He had worked to compile and publish as much as possible the record of English overseas enterprise. The full title thus described the contents of his work: this was a record of what had been *The Principal Navigations, Voyages, Traffiques and Discoveries of the English Nation.* In turn, Hakluyt hoped that in his efforts he would be able to establish that England had become a world power to compete with its Iberian rivals. In addition, of course, he wished to inspire the nation to ever more expansion abroad.

To be sure, Purchas was also involved in the colonial enterprise. He was a member of the Virginia company, and the discourse he composed in response to the massacre there in 1622 was the most learned and, indeed, the most important promotional tract from the Jacobean era. Purchas printed this discourse in his *Pilgrimes,* where almost two dozen narratives and other documents related to Virginia also appeared. Even so, the aim of Purchas in this work was far more expansive than that of Hakluyt. He had no less than "a World for the Subject" in his text, he said.

As it happened, in the period after the second edition of his own text had come out, Hakluyt's interests had expanded as well. He had overseen the translation of a number of important travel narratives that had come out in print in other languages, and in addition he had developed an enormous collection of oral accounts and manuscripts from English travelers abroad.

Sometime after Hakluyt's death, in 1616, Purchas came into the possession of the papers that Hakluyt had collected. In recognition of the debt he owed him, Purchas chose for his text the Latin title *Hakluytus Posthumus.* Here Purchas supplemented the materials that had come from his predecessor with new oral and manuscript accounts and narratives that had appeared in print in several languages. His book ran to four volumes. He intended for it to cover "the rarities and varieties of all." He meant for it to attest to the "remarkeable Varieties of Men and humane Affaires."[36]

Purchas approached Africa in this respect as a miniature of the world. The accounts that he printed covered the whole of the continent. As for many observers in the seventeenth century, it was for him a vast field for the remarkable varieties of men.

The attention to variety that defined the English image of Africa during this period was part and parcel of the spread of travelers' accounts from the continent around the turn of the century. It is true that, like their classical sources, earlier observers had assembled long lists of African peoples. As had Pliny, for example, Eden and Waterman appeared to revel in what Eden called the "marvelous and very strange" array that there was in Africa of Troglodytes, Blemmyi, and Atlantes as well as light-skinned (or albino) Leucæthiopes, "wylde and wanderynge" Getulians, and slender Ilophagi who leapt between trees, wrote Waterman, "like Cattes or Squirelles." Ptolemy had also named scores of African nations, and in editions of his *Geography,* cartographers of the sixteenth century such as Münster and Mercator included these in small-print inset captions and indexes that identified the Ptœmphanæ, Pesendaræ, Phorusij, Psilli, and dozens more. But insofar as anything about them was known in Europe, almost all of the peoples of Africa below the northern coast were connected by a common theme, for each diverged in some striking respect from what was understood to be normal for human beings. And to the extent that the eastern empire of Prester John, like the ancient civilization at Meroë, was regarded as a model of human perfection, the early English image of Africa was marked by a single stark contrast rather than genuine variety. It was "parted," as Homer had said of Ethiopia, not in many parts but "in two."[37]

During this early period, most English observers had taken Africa as a whole as the object of their interest. In their accounts, they had worked to incorporate all the peoples of the continent into one complex but coherent order. By contrast, the ambition of the travelers whose reports began to circulate in England around the turn of the seventeenth century was much more limited. They aimed only to relate their own experience, and since as a rule they were not explorers of the kind whose journeys into the interior would captivate the British public in the Victorian period, these authors confined themselves for the most part to the pockets of Africa that they had happened to see.

To begin, the African materials contained in the Hakluyt collection were limited in this sense: aside from the fabulous "brefe description of Africa" contributed by Eden, they covered no more than the thin stretch of land along the Guinea coast where the English had met the natives to trade. The same was the case for the *Report of the Kingdome of Congo,* which was translated in 1597 from an Italian text that gathered and supplemented the first-hand oral accounts of a Portuguese trader named Duarte Lopes who had spent five years in the region along and inland from the western central coast. In similar fashion, the passages that touched upon Africa in the *Voyages* of the Dutchman John Huighen van Linschoten, which was translated in 1598, were confined to the seaboard areas from Guinea to Congo to Mozambique, where the author had passed through on his way to the East Indies.[38]

The title of what would remain perhaps the most influential study of the continent through the end of the seventeenth century, *A Geographical Historie of Africa,* which was published in English in 1600, indicated a work that was comprehensive in scope. Its author was a former traveler and diplomat from Fez who had been presented to Pope Leo X as the prisoner of a Spanish pirate and baptized in 1520 under the name Joannes Leo.[39]

The account of Leo Africanus, as he came to be known across Europe in the period after his study appeared in the 1550 Ramusio collection of *Navigations and Voyages,* had already started to enter English culture in the second half of the sixteenth century. It was a fixture among the geographical books held in Tudor libraries, where, as the most prominent contemporary source on Africa, it sat uneasily beside the works of Pliny, Strabo, Ptolemy, and Waterman. It was also known to Eden and to Bateman, for even though neither author had much digested its findings, both included abstracts of Leo's work in separate sections from their own classical descriptions of Africa.[40]

Interestingly, the departure that Leo Africanus marked from the classical vision of Africa was best captured in the story that Shakespeare's Othello told to Desdemona about his early career. The cannibals and headless men whom Othello described could well have been drawn from the imagination of Richard Eden. But the character of Othello himself, as scholars of Shakespeare have shown, was modeled upon Leo—or at least upon the account of his life that John Pory, his English translator, added as a note to the reader in his edition of the *Geographical Historie*.

Both Leo and Othello were presented as learned travelers of noble birth. Both had converted from Muslim to Christian religion in Italy. Before their arrivals in Europe, both had had to contend with monstrous men, barren deserts, and what Othello called the "hills whose heads touch heaven" in Africa. Leo had survived "thousands of imminent dangers" in the course of his travels around the continent, according to Pory. He had often been "in hazard to have beene captived" by "prouling *Arabians,* and wilde Mores," even before he fell into the hands of pirates off the northern coast. Othello too was once "taken by the insolent foe, / And sold to slavery" before his eventual redemption. Famously foreign in their adopted European states, Othello and Leo were also seen to be out of place in their place of birth. Already, however, English perceptions of Africa had started to shift under their considerable influence.[41]

By the time the second edition of the *Principal Navigations* appeared, Hakluyt too had learned of Leo Africanus. He promised in an editor's note that Leo's "worthy worke" would be appended to his second volume. Hakluyt did not fulfill this promise. But he did oversee the translation of Leo's work that appeared the next year, and praised it as "the verie best" description of "the countries, peoples, and affaires of Africa" that "ever was written." Even so, the conception of the continent in the *Geographical Historie* was rather narrow, since Africa as Leo understood it was confined to the northwestern areas through which he had moved over the course of his peripatetic career. It extended no farther east than the Nile. In the south, according to Leo, Africa ended at the southern shore of the Niger River in the west and in the east at the lands of a people known as the Bugiha who lived on milk and camels' flesh 450 miles below the Mediterranean.[42]

Even within the borders he assigned to it, Leo almost never spoke in general of the peoples of Africa. He divided the continent into four regions—Barbaria, Numidia, Libya, and to the south of these "the land of Negros," which ran east and west along the Niger—and his broadest statements applied separately to the inhabitants of each region. In the first book of his account, for example, Leo reported that the people in Numidia lived longer than the Libyans and that the plague was common in Barbaria but unknown among the Negros. In a passage on the virtues and vices of the Africans, Leo continued in this vein: he reported that the Barbarians were studious and honest but proud and covetous; the Numidians were courteous and hospitable but base and servile; and while the Libyans appeared to be happy, they were brutish thieves. For their part, the Negros were loyal and convivial. Earlier in the first book, Leo had said that the Negros who lived in areas south of the Niger were rich and industrious. But he also remarked, in phrases that anticipated Richard Eden's distillation of ancient Mediterranean opinion, that they lived "a beastly kinde of life, being utterly destitute of the use of reason, of dexteritie of wit, and of all artes." In each of the subsequent books in his account, Leo considered one region or one area within one region. So distinct were they each from each other, he believed, that to compose a general account of Africa was to do no more than assemble a series of particular accounts of its parts.[43]

To be sure, this was also the method of Samuel Purchas, who came out in 1613 with the next English description of the world after that of George Abbot. Like Abbot, to whom he dedicated his work, Purchas had spent his career in the Church of England and confessed that he "never travelled 200. miles from *Thaxted* in *Essex,* where I was borne." Even so, in contrast to the crisp survey that Abbot had written, Purchas composed his *Pilgrimage* as a review of the reports from more than seven hundred travelers, whose works he sometimes copied to such an extent as to reproduce their own first-person pronouns and whose names he listed before the start of his book in what he called a "Catalogue of the Authors." Among these authors were several of the merchants whose narratives of travel to the Guinea coast had appeared in the Hakluyt collection as well as Lopes, van Linschoten, Leo, and several more of the travelers whose accounts Purchas would include as separate texts in his own 1625 collection, the *Pilgrimes.*[44]

Purchas started the two books of his *Pilgrimage* that were devoted to Africa with a short chapter in which he mainly reviewed the animals on the continent. He stated here in an aside that he would "neither beleeve, nor report" the tales of barely human "Monsters which *Pliny* and others tell." Beyond the statement that they were not monsters, however, Purchas followed Leo in that he gave almost no thought to what might have been supposed to be the common features of the peoples of Africa. As Leo had also done, he took care to avoid references to Africans as such, other than as the inhabitants of the former Roman province who were known by that name. The 133 pages of small-print text in which Purchas put forward his description of Africa were instead filled with a torrent of details drawn from a multitude of travel narratives about the myriad peoples who inhabited the various parts of the continent.[45]

Early in the first chapter on Africa in his *Pilgrimage,* Purchas had already started to divide the continent into parts. He took note of the four-part scheme that he had found in the work of Leo but observed that Leo had "thus excludeth Egypt" from Africa. To be sure, Leo himself had included in his study a final book on what he called "that most noble and famous province." Nevertheless, Purchas insisted that Leo had not covered the whole of the area that he considered to be Africa. On this point, Purchas followed John Pory. Even as he had brought the *Geographical Historie* into circulation in English, Pory had fixed upon its limited scope. He prefaced his edition with a "general description of all Africa" as well as a "particular description" of the areas that Leo "hath left undescribed." Here he introduced the stretch of the Guinea coast that fanned out to the south of the Land of Negros, the western central kingdoms of Congo and Angola, and the warring southern empires of Monomotapa and Mohenemugi. Purchas then took up Pory's task, as he set out to finish the description of Africa that Leo had begun. The first book on Africa in his *Pilgrimage* was an account of its five northern regions. In his second book, Purchas proposed that the area that remained be divided into two more parts, which in total would "make up seven parts of Africa."[46]

After the rejection of ancient fables about the Torrid Zone, this seven-part division of the continent would become the point of departure for English studies of Africa through the close of the seventeenth century. In the process, as with the tales of beastly peoples and semi-divine men, the basic coherence of the classical image was lost. Informed observers had come to believe that Africa was composed not of two parts but of many.[47]

Nowhere was the fragmentation of Africa during this period more clearly rendered than in cartography. In the context of the coherence their classical sources had ascribed to the peoples of Africa, and surely also as a result of how little of the continent ancient travelers had seen, such early cartographers as Münster and Mercator had not carefully mapped the borders between regions. Their editions of Ptolemy had split the extended area below the strip of land along the northern coast into only three parts, two of which were themselves parts of Ethiopia. The *Africa Tabula Nova* that appeared toward the end of Münster's 1540 *Geography* was even less complex. In this still largely classical representation, there were no borders between regions, and "AETHIOPIA," written in large print, stretched vaguely across the interior (see Figure 3.3).[48]

In the second half of the sixteenth century, the influence of classical sources slowly declined, as maps of Africa made on the basis of recent travelers' reports began to appear in Europe. Perhaps the first of these was the one printed in the 1554 second edition of the Ramusio collection. This map drew upon the work of Leo for the names that it assigned to the four northwestern regions of Africa, but it marked the rest of the continent as vaguely as had Münster or simply as Ethiopia. Toward the close of the century, the color editions of maps by Ortelius and Mercator became the first ones to separate the whole of Africa into regions: Ortelius counted nine, whereas Mercator had eleven. And in the first quarter of the seventeenth century, in the separately printed large-format works of the Dutchmen Blaeu and Hondius, cartographers started to attend to the division of Africa with a precision that far exceeded even that of authors such as Pory and Purchas in print.

In the 1617 map of Africa by Blaeu, and that of Hondius from 1623, the continent was split into more than two dozen regions, each one set off with borders that were drawn in green, yellow, orange, and purple. The works of Blaeu and Hondius became the models for the 1626 map of Africa that was

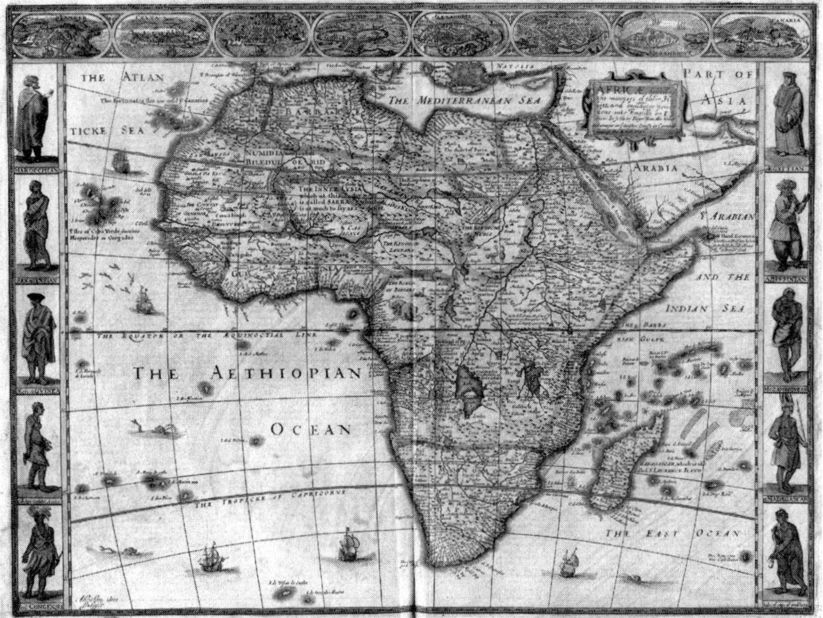

FIG. 3.7 The body of water in this map that borders the northwestern regions of Barbaria and Numidia appears under its common early-modern appellation: "THE ATLANTICKE SEA." However, a title that would soon vanish from European maps of Africa, "THE AETHIOPIAN OCEAN," is given for the body of water that stretches west from the western central coast. This title was common in early-modern maps. It refers to the region of southern Ethiopia, which was composed of the coastal areas that formed an upside-down arc around the former empire of Prester John.

Credit: "Africæ, described, the manners of their Habits, and buildinge," in John Speed, *A Prospect of the Most Famous Parts of the World* (London, 1662; orig. pub. 1627), between fols. 5 and 6. G1015.S64 1662: Reproduction courtesy of the Norman B. Leventhal Map & Education Center at the Boston Public Library.

printed in John Speed's *Prospect of the most Famous Parts of the World,* which was the first world atlas that was the work of an English author. The first edition of this work was done in black and white, and the regions were indicated only by name. But in 1662 the atlas was released in a color edition that reproduced almost exactly from its earlier models the patchwork of regions which each imagined Africa to be (Figure 3.7).[49]

In the same year that Speed's map of Africa appeared, a map of Africa that Hondius had made was inserted into the fourth and final edition of the

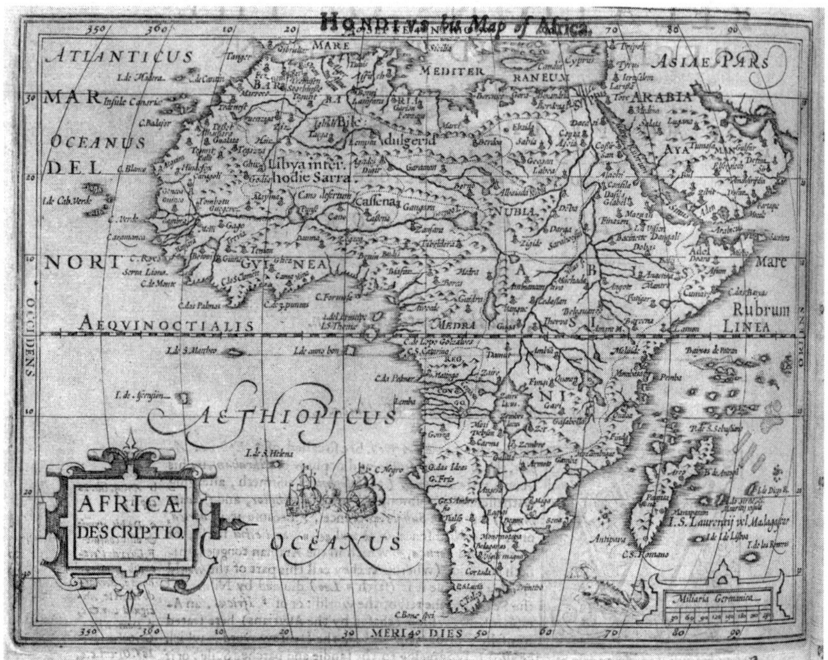

FIG. 3.8 Along with the works of Blaeu, the Hondius maps of Africa served as the models that Speed relied upon to produce his own image of the continent. The thin dotted lines that trace the borders between regions in this version of Hondius's Africa correspond to the thick and colorful borders that appear in the 1662 edition of the Speed atlas. In turn, the bodies of water to the west of the continent in this map appear under Latin titles similar to the English ones that Speed used.

Credit: "Hondius *his Map of* Africa," in Samuel Purchas, *Purchas His Pilgrimage,* 4th ed. (London, 1626), 620. STC 20508.5: Houghton Library, Harvard University.

Pilgrimage of Purchas (Figure 3.8). In this black-and-white representation, the regions were traced in thin lines that twisted and swirled across the continent. As did the mapmakers from the time, Purchas understood that to represent Africa was to arrange it into parts. And in the text of his *Pilgrimage,* after he had concluded his circuit of the five parts that Leo had covered, Purchas then set out to describe the two parts of Africa that it seemed to him Leo had left out.

Purchas began this section of his text in what might have seemed to his readers to be a familiar region: in northern Ethiopia, that is, within the empire of a "Christian Prince, called in Europe *Priest* or *Prester John*." For information about this region, Purchas turned to the first published report upon northern Ethiopia that was written by a European who had been there. This was the work of a Portuguese priest named Francisco Alvarez, who served as ambassador to the court of Prester John from 1520 to 1526. His account appeared next to that of Leo in the Ramusio collection, and this is where Hakluyt had come upon it, for he had commissioned from this edition an English translation, which Purchas then excerpted at length in his *Pilgrimes*.[50]

The official purpose of his voyage, Alvarez explained, was to assess how well the practices of the Ethiopians could be said to "agree with Christian Religion." However, his specific aim was to meet Prester John. After he had traveled through the various kingdoms of the empire for more than six months, when Alvarez was at last summoned to the capital, he was amazed. It was a moveable metropolis made up of "an infinite number of Pavilions and Tents," which housed more than forty thousand inhabitants. As he was led through the court, Alvarez took in the array of porters, guards, judges, nobles, governors, ambassadors, priests, and bishops as well as the kings, who paid tribute to the emperor in mules, horses, cotton, and gold. When he was admitted to the tent of the emperor, he was ushered into one crowded torchlit room and then another, and here at last was Prester John. "He seemeth to be young," Alvarez wrote, but "in his presence and pompe, he seemeth to be a great Lord, as in very deede he is."[51]

Toward the close of the sixteenth century, the new descriptions of Africa by Lopes and van Linschoten departed from their firsthand accounts of peoples on the western coast to expand upon Alvarez's assessment of Prester John in the east. He was the "greattest and richest Prince in all Africa," in the opinion of these authors, and both told of an annual feast in which officials assembled from around the empire to pay tribute, as a life-size gold-and-ruby model of the Virgin was paraded through crowds so dense that some spectators died of suffocation. In his description of the world, John Thorie reported that Prester John was even "accounted to be one of the cheefest Monarchs of our time." George Abbot noted that he was "reputed to be one of the greatest Emperours of the world." The reputation of Prester John had also reached the English Crown. In 1597, when Elizabeth sent one of her subjects on a diplomatic mission to meet him, she sent him with a letter addressed to "the most high and mightie Emperour of *Aethiopia.*" The Queen asked that as her representative traveled across "your highnesse dominions," he be maintained "under the safeguard and protection of your name."[52]

Already in the decades after Alvarez returned to Portugal, however, the news had started to circulate in Europe that some disaster had come upon the empire of Prester John. Alvarez himself was aware that the eastern border of the empire, along the Horn of Africa, was home to several Muslim kingdoms and that there was a general who made annual raids from here during Lent in order to take advantage of the fasting Ethiopians. Then around the middle of the century, Portuguese envoys reported that the ruler whom Alvarez had visited had perished in a civil war. His former lands were plunged so deep into chaos by Muslim incursions that a sailor known as Don John of Castro could lament, in a narrative that Purchas printed in his *Pilgrimes* just after the one from Alvarez, that he had witnessed "the ruine and losse of this Empire, in our unhappie days." Lopes and van Linschoten were dimly aware of such reports, and so was John Pory, but none of them appears to have had any source other than Alvarez upon which to draw for current information. Among English observers of Ethiopia, Purchas was the first to come to terms with "how that State decayed," in his phrase.[53]

Alvarez remained the author whom Purchas said he had "chiefly followed" in the long account of northern Ethiopia in his *Pilgrimage.* Like Alvarez, Purchas praised the manner in which the people there "copiously and eloquently interprete the Scripture" and found the two principal cities "populous and magnificent," with towers and temples "and the like tokens of Industrie, Antiquitie, and Maiestie." But Purchas also scolded Alvarez for applying what he concluded had begun as the title of a medieval monarch in Asia to a modern African ruler whose own people had never called him Prester John, "only *Acegue,* which signifieth Emperour, and Negus, that is, King." Moreover, to an extent that Alvarez had not done, Purchas focused upon the elements of culture that the peoples of Ethiopia did not possess: they did not have tablecloths, artillery, or wine, and although the land held rich deposits of silver and gold, "they have not Art to take it." Not even in their principal cities had they built walls to guard against Muslim attacks.

Purchas came to believe that Alvarez had seen the Ethiopian empire at its apex, in a period when its interlocked orders of politics and religion still recalled the classical legends of the civilization at Meroë and the medieval and Renaissance tales of the Christian kingdom of Prester John. In their place, Purchas was left to describe "the uncivill customes whereinto wild Maiestie and barbarous Greatnesse" had now "degenerated."[54]

A careful reader of Purchas here might well have been impressed at the drama that a single part of Africa could contain. When Alvarez had been there, northern Ethiopia was to a great extent a coherent region. Within the immense empire of Prester John, the people all spoke what Alvarez termed "the *Abissine* Tongue," and salt was the common currency. During this period, seventeen kingdoms paid tribute to the emperor—whose court, as Pory put it, was "alwaies flitting up and downe" the countryside, "sometimes to one place, and sometimes to another." Since then, the empire had fractured, and at present only four kings remained loyal to the successor to the monarch whom Alvarez had known. "All things are brought almost to nothing," Purchas wrote of the former empire in the third edition of his *Pilgrimage* in 1617, and as a result, northern Ethiopia had become not so much a coherent region as a scene of tumult, which extended from the coast along the Red Sea in the north to what were believed to be the deep inland sources of the Nile in the south.[55]

Far to the west, the Land of Negros was another part of Africa that was understood to be divided into parts. Leo Africanus had introduced into Western culture the claim that the peoples who lived on the Niger River were all the inhabitants of a single region. But in the section of his *Geographical Historie* in which Leo came to discuss this region in detail, he made clear that what the peoples here had in common was no more important than what drew them apart. Four different languages were spoken in the Land of Negros, and even as most of the Negros were Muslim, there were also Christians, as well as heathens of various kinds who worshipped fire or the sun or who seemed to have no religion at all.[56]

The section on the Land of Negros in his *Pilgrimage* came just before the account that Purchas gave of northern Ethiopia. But as the wild majesty and barbarous greatness of the empire of Prester John had degenerated into uncivil customs, as Purchas wrote, along the Niger the course of history had run in a different direction. When they first came into contact with Muslims from northern Africa, the peoples in the Land of Negros had "lived a brutish and savage life," Leo wrote, in terms that resembled his description of their vices in the present, "without any king, governour, common wealth, or knowledge of husbandrie." Since then, however, many of them had formed complex social orders on the basis of just these institutions. Now the Negros were subject to four main governors, and were sorted into no fewer than fifteen kingdoms. Only in the course of his tour through these kingdoms did Leo discuss the habits of the people in each one of them in depth—the crops they grew, the clothes they wore, the houses they built, and, in short, the kinds of lives they led.[57]

On the outskirts of kingdoms such as Gago and Gaoga, Leo explained, the peoples were shepherds and farmers who lived in "forlorne and base cottages" made of chalk and thatch that were gathered together into hamlets and villages. The inhabitants of Gago were "ignorant and rude," according to Leo; those of Gaoga were "rusticall and savage." In the mountains of Borno, where no proper names were used and wives and children were held in common, the people lived "after a brutish manner" that most closely recalled that of their earliest ancestors in the Land of Negros. In the capital cities of kingdoms such as Nubia, though, there were "exceeding rich and civill people" who were known to "excell all other Negros in witte, civilitie, and industry," as Leo said of the natives of Melli. The lands here yielded cotton, lemons, and rice, and merchants exchanged these and other goods such as ivory for horses, spices, and cloth from the other regions of Africa. In the old commercial hub at Tombuto (or Timbuktu) there was "great store of doctors, judges, priests, and other learned men." There was a temple here that Leo admired whose walls, like those of monasteries that Alvarez had seen chiseled into mountainsides in Ethiopia, were built with stone and lime.[58]

In the first book of his *Geographical Historie,* Leo had pioneered the division of Africa into regions. But even Leo was convinced that the real site of African life was not so much the region as the kingdom—that is, the bounded local communities that spread throughout the continent.[59]

English observers such as Pory and Purchas had learned from Leo to divide Africa into several principal parts, and they took from him as well this attention to the distinctive features of the many parts of which these parts were composed. Indeed, Pory and Purchas explained that there were at least five parts of the seventh and final region of Africa. Called in geographical terms "*Æthiopia Exterior,* or *Inferior,*" in contrast to "*Æthiopia Superior*" to the north, this was "that Southerly Tract of Africa," Purchas wrote, that ran along the coast in a long upside-down arc bordered to the inland side by the southern reaches of the former empire of Prester John. This final part of Africa started, in its northeastern corner, in the fertile Muslim lands of Aian; continued to the south along the Red Sea coast toward the wealthy corridor at Zanzibar, where ships from Portugal put in on the route to the East Indies; and extended down to the Cape of Good Hope, where the native people were rough and wild and referred to as Caphars, after the Arab term for "lawlesse people," according to Purchas. Northward from the Cape was the gold-rich mining empire of Monomotapa, whose conflicts with the empire of Mohenemugi were said to be "the most desperate and doubtfull battailes, that are performed in all those southern parts."[60]

Some of the parts of southern Ethiopia were further divided into parts. In Aian there were two kingdoms, Adel and Adea. Whereas the monarch of Adel was renowned for what Purchas said were the "Continuall warres" he made upon the Christian king of Ethiopia, the monarch of Adea paid tribute to that same king. Moreover, Purchas added, in Zanzibar there were the kingdoms of "Melinde, Mombaza, Quiloa, Mosambique, and others."[61]

However, nowhere was the division of Africa more intricately conceived than in the final part of its final region, the kingdom of Congo, which spread inland from the western coast and extended from the land of the Caphars in the south almost to the Bight of Biafra in the north. The most important source of information about Congo that was available in England through the first half of the seventeenth century was the *Report* upon the kingdom from Duarte Lopes, which Purchas published in excerpt in his *Pilgrimes* a little more than a quarter of a century after it had first come out in English. The structure of Congo was as complex as that of any region, and Lopes devoted much of his text to its reconstruction.[62]

To the south of Congo, Lopes began, there was Angola, whose ruler had long been subject to the king of Congo but had rebelled and now was "a great Prince, & a rich" and "an ally and not a vassal of the king." In the present,

Congo was made up of six provinces, and each one of these was under the control of its own lord. The province of Bamba, on the border with Angola, was the largest and most populous one, but in addition there were the provinces of Songo, Sundi, Pango, and Batta. The peoples of Batta in the east were "farre more rude and rusticall" than those in the rest of the kingdom. To the east of Batta, in the western reaches of the empire of Mohenemugi, were the areas patrolled by a fierce nomadic people known as the Gagas. Back in the center of the kingdom, the final province of Congo was Pemba. Here was the royal seat of San Salvatore, situated on a mountain built up with the houses of more than one hundred thousand inhabitants. The valleys below were planted with maize as well as palm trees that shaded the palaces of the nobles. Unlike the province to which it belonged, San Salvatore was under the direct rule of the king. And so by the count that Purchas kept, it was a seventh part of the sixth part of the seventh part of Africa.[63]

In short, the *Pilgrimage* of Purchas formed one long record of the fullness of Africa. The continent was twice as large as Europe, he observed, and although there were deserts such as the Sahara and mountains in Sierra Leone and above the Cape of Good Hope that were "beyond admiration for barrennesse," it was elsewhere "both fruitfull and populous." No doubt recent observers had marveled at how many people seemed to live within these fruitful areas. Their numbers at times seemed to be almost beyond measure. Pory had said that across the countryside in the empire of Prester John there were "verie manie villages, and infinite numbers of people." Moreover, Angola must have been "full of people beyond all credite," according to Lopes, for the ruler there could summon an army "to the number of a Million of soules." Some observers supposed that beyond the reach of their knowledge the peoples of Africa must extend without end into the interior. To the south of the Niger River, Leo explained, there were "infinite nations unknowen to us." Beside the lakes that spread around the empire of Mohenemugi, Purchas listed "other Kingdomes, of which we have little but the names to relate, Gorova, Colta, Anzuga, Moneulo, Baduis."[64]

Perhaps no remarks better demonstrate that the ancient image of Africa had by this time been turned on its head. Authors in the tradition of Pliny had assumed that the areas to which Leo and Purchas referred, because they were set within the Torrid Zone, were all but "voide of enhabitauntes," as William Waterman had written in 1555. Now, on the basis of little more direct information than Waterman had possessed, the best writers in Europe had started to imagine that the African interior was not void of inhabitants but full of them.

This principle of plenitude was applied as well in cartography from the period. The maps of Blaeu, Hondius, and Speed were marked with the borders between more than two dozen regions. These regions were covered over with the titles of kingdoms and empires and dotted with names and castles for what in total came to well over one hundred cities. The spaces in between were in many areas filled in with mountains, lakes, rivers, and deserts. The side edges on these maps were lined with figures of peoples from ten regions of the continent, from Morocco to Senegal to Guinea. The top edge on the map that Speed made was lined with models of eight cities from around the continent. The new midcentury productions from Robert Walton (Figure 3.9) and John Overton, whose renderings of Africa for the most part resembled the one from Speed, included models of cities on their bottom edges and also added the portraits of monarchs such as those of Congo and Abissina.[65]

The mapmakers from this period, as Purchas had done, sometimes placed peoples who existed only in rumor in areas that were not well known. They placed the Garamantes, whom Pliny had mentioned, in inner Libya, for example, and they noted that the Amazons were said to inhabit the lowlands between the two southern lakes in which the Nile River was believed to have its sources. In other obscure locations, these mapmakers drew animals. After Blaeu and Hondius, Speed had elephants, ostriches, lions, a monkey, a zebra, and a dragon in an arc that led from Biafra northeast into Nubia and west toward the Atlantic. Walton included fewer animals, but even his map was adorned with a lion, a horse, a camel, and an elephant. Later on, Jonathan Swift remarked acidly of practitioners in this tradition, "So Geographers in *Afric*-Maps / With Savage-Pictures fill their Gaps; / And o'er unhabitable Downs / Place Elephants for want of Towns." In a sense, of course, he was correct. However, what Swift appears not to have perceived was that the "Savage-Pictures" in "*Afric*-Maps" served as the details used to

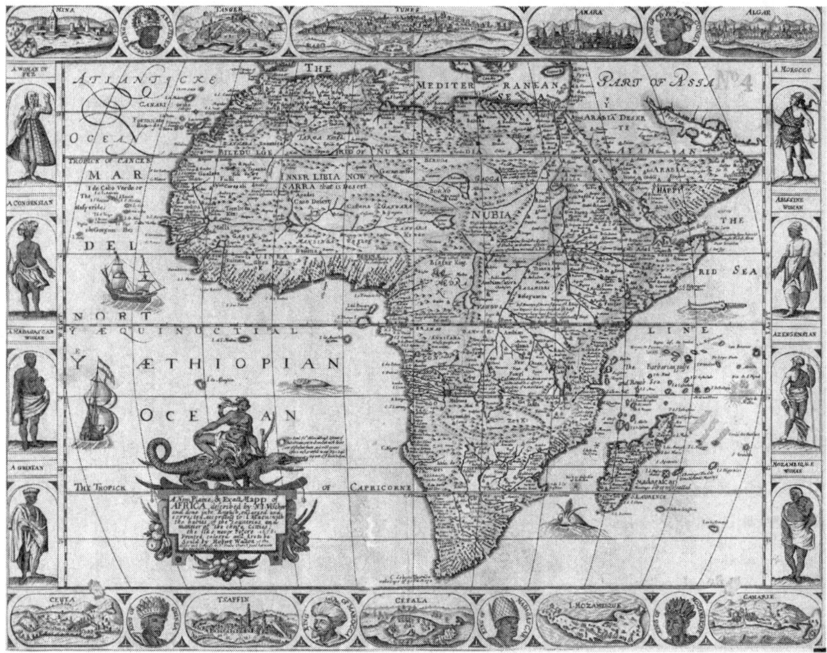

FIG. 3.9 This map for the most part resembles that of John Speed, but its more direct model was the work of the Dutch practitioner Pieter van den Keere. Van den Keere had drawn from the famous productions of Hondius and Blaeu, but he had added models of African cities on the bottom border of his maps and included the portraits of African rulers on both the top and bottom borders.

Credit: Robert Walton, "A New, Plaine, & Exact Mapp of Africa" (London, 1658). G8200. W37: Reproduction courtesy of the Norman B. Leventhal Map & Education Center at the Boston Public Library.

complete an image of the continent as a scene of abundance that would have been familiar to any reader of Purchas (see, for comparison, Figure 3.10).[66]

After he had finished the survey of Congo in his *Pilgrimage,* Purchas moved north into Loango, where Lopes had said the people were "altogether of the same nature, whereof the people of *Congo* are." Next Purchas touched upon the Anziques, whom he described as "the cruellest Canniballs, which the Sunne looketh on." Then, with his tour of Africa at an end, Purchas turned in two final chapters to the islands in the oceans that surrounded the continent. He reflected upon what had no doubt been a "long and tedious Journey over Land, where the steepe and Snowie Mountains, the myrie

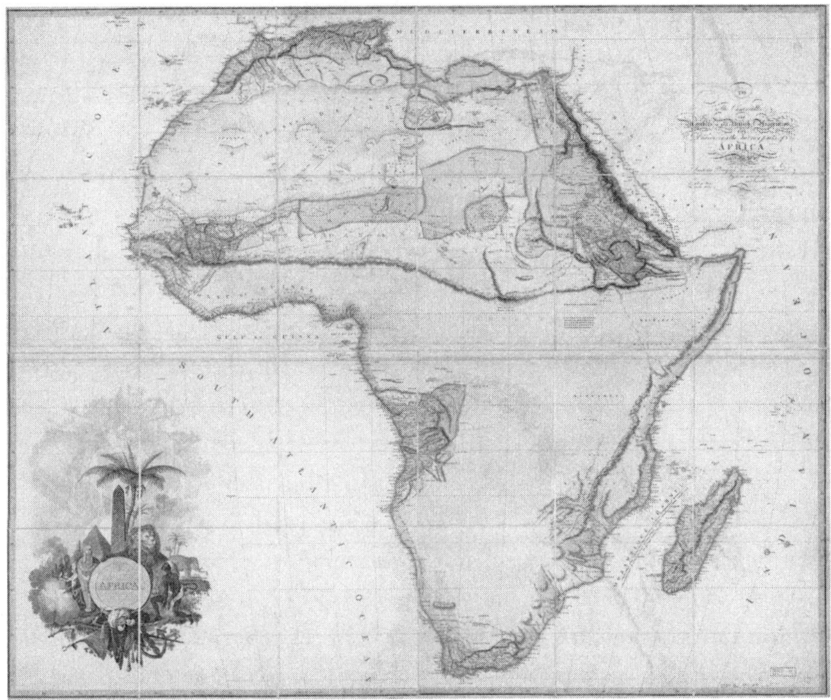

FIG. 3.10 The signature in the upper right-hand corner announces the dedication of this map to "the British Association for Discovering the Interior parts of Africa." Nevertheless, the most notable respect in which this map differs from the principal productions of the seventeenth century is the extent to which the interior of the continent is not filled in.

It was on the basis of maps such as this one that Joseph Conrad's Marlow, in the 1902 novel *Heart of Darkness,* learned as a child to consider the African interior "the biggest—the most blank, so to speak," of the "blank spaces on the earth." Early-modern observers of Africa had never said anything of the kind.

Credit: Aaron Arrowsmith, "Africa" (London, 1802). G8201.S2 1802.A7*: Harvard Map Collection, Harvard University.

and unwholesome Valleyes, the unpassable Wildernesses, swift Rivers, still Lakes, thicke Woods, and varietie of the Continent" had "thus long whiled us." As in the landscape, variety had been the rule in the peoples of Africa.[67]

The most elemental features of their lives attested to the variety of their experience. The materials from which they made their clothes and houses differed from place to place, as is evident in the figures on the edges of the maps from Speed and Walton. The languages they were known to use differed widely too. The Christians in northern Ethiopia spoke Abissin, while the Muslims who lived on the eastern coast had developed what one English traveler referred to as "a mish-mash of *Arabick* and *Portuguise.*" The peoples in Congo and Angola shared a common vocabulary but struggled to communicate because their accents differed, and neither could understand the Anzigues. In the Land of Negros, one could hear Sungai, Guber, and Borno, as well as what Leo said was the mixture spoken in Nubia of the "Chaldean, Arabian, & Egyptian toongs." The variety of the currencies in use across Africa resembled the variety of the languages. The shells of cowries were in use on the Niger and at points on the eastern Guinea coast, and the shells of a kind of snail called lumaches were traded in Congo. The currency in Angola was beads of glass, while in Mohenemugi it was red beads of clay. In Zanzibar, gold was more often accepted, as it was in northern Ethiopia, although salt was the more common form of money there.[68]

Confronted with this scene, European observers never attempted to fashion a single essential image from their impressions of the peoples of Africa. They rarely even paused to express surprise at how unlike one another the Africans seemed to be. Instead, authors such as Purchas focused their attention upon the events and customs particular to one nation—and then another and another. The Italian humanist Giovanni Botero was another author in this mold. In his *Relations, of the most Famous Kingdoms and Common-weales thorough the World,* which was first translated into English in 1601 and soon came out in five more expanded editions, Botero reproduced from Leo an account of several nations on the Niger River. He then announced that he would make no statements about the others. This was because "nothing can be spoken to, but their barrennesse and fertility, their poverty or riches, blessinges and curses, peculier more or less to every Nation." In turn, as Botero went on to describe the other nations of Africa, he made clear that the variety in the Land of Negros was also present across the continent.[69]

That said, now that they have been made so clear to us, we should observe that the varieties of African life were patterned after a single model, and in a word that model was Europe. Earlier authors such as Richard Eden had learned from classical texts to consider Africa in terms of the tenets of

European culture that it lacked. The institutions, customs, and beliefs that made Europe civil were on this account exactly the ones that, beyond the marvelous empire of Prester John, the peoples of Africa did not possess. So complete was their deficiency, in the opinion of such observers, that the Africans were often said to be not only different but almost inhuman. The consensus that had held this to be so had begun to unravel in England around the turn of the seventeenth century, when reports were received that travelers to the western coast had not found there "any other people then such as our selves are," in the phrase of John Speed. By the early decades of the seventeenth century, the negative formula that Eden had used had all but disappeared from informed discourse—or endured, as in Leo's account of the Land of Negros, only in reference to peoples in the distant past. Historians have long understood that early English and Iberian authors tended to describe the peoples of America in terms of analogies and resemblances to themselves. By the time Purchas wrote, a similar habit had developed among English observers of the peoples of Africa.[70]

This is not to assert that the English believed that African cultures resembled their own in a precise sense. The aspects of difference between them had always been apparent; in matters of religion in particular, the contrast between the Christians of Europe and the heathens and idolaters from Africa was said to be absolute and was believed by some to be irredeemable. What English observers perceived in Africa, though, was a part of the world that they thought they could comprehend, one that answered to the same categories and terms that they used to explain the structure of their own part of the world.

Almost none of the peoples of Africa spoke English, but they did have systems of communication that English travelers understood to be languages. They did not mint metal coins, but their measures of value were taken to be forms of money. In the initial period of European contact, they seemed hardly to know how to trade in commodities, but over time they learned. By 1623, the captain of a voyage up the Gambia River was able to report that the native people had been well prepared to take part in "the auncient and free Commerce, that uniteth nations." As the years passed, such commerce became more and more routine. The merchants who met on the western coast of Africa became more and more accustomed to one another. Often the merchants who arrived from Europe would remark upon the skill of their local counterparts. One commercial manual from 1638 explained that Europeans in West Africa should now expect to find local buyers for their wares who possessed "as good judgement in them as the sellers themselves."[71]

The points of resemblance that European observers were eager to establish between themselves and African peoples were most evident in what were taken to be their forms of social and political organization. The continent was divided into extended regions, which in turn held empires and nations. The borders between these were neatly drawn, such that "the difference between them," as Lopes observed with respect to Congo and Angola, was "as it commonly is between two nations that border one upon another, as for example between the *Portingalles* and the *Castilians.*" The nations of Africa were filled with villages and cities, and their rulers were monarchs and emperors.[72]

In this context, it is a telling fact that the account of Africa written on the Continent to which Pory and Purchas were most indebted was that of Giovanni Botero. As its title indicated, the premise of this account was that the kingdoms and commonwealths in Africa could be compared to those that there were to be found throughout the world. They could be incorporated into common conceptions of how people tended to live. They fit well within a pattern of human life that European authors supposed to be more or less universal.[73]

And in particular, there was one more feature of African life that such authors found familiar. Across the continent, there were peoples whom they had encountered or had read about who held and traded some persons as slaves.

As it happened, the classical descriptions of Africa produced in Europe around the middle of the sixteenth century had never mentioned slavery, either among what were said to be the beastly peoples in the western and southern areas of the continent or in the semi-divine culture that flourished in the east. In an observation borrowed from Diodorus, Waterman had noted that the civilization at Meroë had never been "under the bondage of any" and was "ever a free nacion." Into the seventeenth century, authors would continue to remark that certain African peoples led lives that were in some respect "brutish" or "beastly." The mountaineers around Borno, who neither used proper names nor lived within stable familial units, were included in this order, and so were the cannibalistic Gagas and Anzigues around Congo, the lawless Caphars at the Cape of Good Hope, and the herdsmen known as Fulbies, who ranged along the Gambia River and were so familiar with their cattle that they paid no mind to the flies that buzzed all around them. But for the most part these peoples were not known to hold or trade slaves.[74]

The slaves in Africa circulated almost entirely among the peoples who appeared to authors from Europe most complex, most civil, and most similar to themselves. Here such authors found it as easy to see that there were slaves as that there was currency, commerce, and government. They could even see that it was in the course of the routine operation of such institutions of civil life that some persons were made into slaves. Although scholars have argued that the cultural context for the English African slave trade was marked above all by the perception of difference and debasement, we have now started to establish that this was not the case. It is one of the terrible ironies in our collective past.

CHAPTER 4

The Sources of African Slavery

AROUND THE same time that English observers became aware that certain African peoples held slaves, they learned of certain peoples in America who did not. Michel de Montaigne had made one such people the subject of an essay, "Of Caniballes," which was published in English in the popular 1603 edition of John Florio. Montaigne reported here on a nation in Brazil whose culture was so simple that it could only be described in a list of what they did not have. They had "no kinde of traffike," he wrote, "no knowledge of Letters, no intelligence of numbers." There was among them neither riches nor poverty, "no name of magistrate, nor of politike superioritie," and in addition they had "no use of service." With this final item in his list, Montaigne meant that his subjects did not have servants under contract of the kind who tended his own estate in Bordeaux; after all, contracts were one more item he had said they did not possess. But he soon made clear that these people also did not possess slaves. The most important source of slaves in the early-modern Atlantic world was understood to be captives in war. What made this a nation of cannibals was that they ate their captives.[1]

One early reader of Montaigne was Shakespeare, who read the essay on cannibals in the Florio translation. In *The Tempest,* which was finished and first performed in 1611, Shakespeare has the counselor Gonzalo imagine himself as the ruler of a commonwealth on the island in the Mediterranean where he has been shipwrecked. Gonzalo explains that he would "(by contraries) / Execute all things." As in the Brazil of Montaigne, there would be upon his island no commerce, letters, magistrates, contracts, or "use of service," as well as labor, agriculture, "Mettall, Corne, or wine." Montaigne's report had become the model for Shakespeare's utopia. Both were communities defined by the absence of certain elements of European culture, ones framed, in the phrase of Gonzalo, "by contraries."[2]

In the decades after Shakespeare finished *The Tempest,* the themes in Montaigne's essay were taken up in the accounts of actual observers of the peoples of America. The most important one of these was the Dominican missionary Jean Baptiste Du Tertre, whose description of the Lesser Antilles came out in French in 1654. In his account of the native Caribs, Du Tertre recalled the negative method of Montaigne. The Caribs wore no clothes, he said, contracted no diseases, organized no police, acquired no luxury, and had had no education in the *sciences humaines.* They were "all equal," he continued, "without any sort of superiority or of servitude." They did hold slaves, but could not have had many of them, since Du Tertre reported that the Caribs ate the men they captured in war and enslaved only the women, whose children they also would consume.[3]

As well as a method of description, the accounts of Montaigne and Du Tertre shared a premise. Both authors believed that their subjects existed in the state of nature, the original condition of the species before humans had begun to alter and develop the bare aspect of Creation. The Brazilians of Montaigne and the Caribs of Du Tertre were not only without certain elements of culture but without human culture as such. What they had, Montaigne explained, was no more than "that which nature doth plainly imparte unto all creatures, even as she brings them into the world." They were "as nature made them," Du Tertre observed, "that is to say, in a great natural simplicity and *naïfveté.*" It was seen as a mark of their simplicity that neither one of these peoples had formed themselves into a stable hierarchical order and that, in this context, neither one held servants or what would have been any substantial number of slaves.[4]

In the eighteenth century, the richest and most complex description of the state of nature was the work of Jean-Jacques Rousseau. In his 1755 *Discourse on the Origin and the Foundations of Inequality Among Men,* he proposed that the original condition of the species was an earlier and even simpler one than previous authors had imagined. Humans in the state of nature, on his account, had no conception of morals and no use of language. They had developed no more than the most minimal attachments to one another. They had formed no families and instead tended to be "scattered in the Woods among the Animals," Rousseau said.

After a time these simple creatures had gathered together into families and then into little communities, and in certain remote areas these had survived down to the present day. Rousseau drew upon the work of Du Tertre when he observed that the Caribs were one such community. "Of all existing Peoples," he wrote, the Caribs had "so far deviated least from the state of Nature." Of course, elsewhere the species had continued to progress. Agriculture and metallurgy were invented, and systems of labor were established for the cultivation of the land. The institution of property followed, and soon states were founded as an attempt on the part of those who had them to secure their newfound possessions. In the process men were divided into rich and poor, ruler and ruled, and then at last into master and slave. This was "the last degree of inequality" and for this reason, as Rousseau insisted time and again, the relation characteristic of modern life.[5]

In short, for Rousseau, to develop an account of the manner in which humans came to be modern was to provide a description of the rise of slavery. And in his sense of slavery as a mark of the ambivalent progress of the species, Rousseau reflected upon a theme that also had been present in early-modern accounts of Africa.

Like the peoples whom Montaigne and Du Tertre described, the peoples of Africa who lived west and south of the empire of Prester John stood out from the earliest modern accounts for the deficiency of their forms of life. They were without the essential structure of law and commonwealth, according to the sixteenth-century editor Richard Eden, and had no "other knowleage of god," Eden remarked, "then by the lawe of nature." These peoples were not known to hold or trade persons as slaves, and in this respect too they resembled the American subjects of Montaigne and Du Tertre.[6]

In the first quarter of the seventeenth century, however, travelers' reports started to stream back into England that carried with them a new view of Africa. The peoples of the continent were not depicted in these works "by contraries," as was the method of Gonzalo. Rather, they were seen to have established forms of life that were varied and unusual but in essential respects civil by the standard of Europe. In these same works, English observers would first have learned that many of the peoples of Africa held slaves and were prepared to trade them for other commodities at points along the shore.

In Chapter 3, we traced the development of this new view of Africa, and now we will explain how slavery was understood to arise in African life. In the process we will expand upon the irony introduced at the end of that chapter: that slavery was said to have its sources in the attempts to maintain order in civil societies rather than in the absence of order in ones that were believed to be primitive.

❧

This irony was most vividly presented in the first half of the seventeenth century in the works authored and edited by Samuel Purchas. His survey of the peoples of the world, titled the *Pilgrimage* and published in four editions from 1613 to 1626, remained in this period the most detailed account of its kind. The other important English effort in the genre, the 1621 *Microcosmus* from Peter Heylyn, was considered even by the author to be an abstract of its sources, Purchas chief among them, as numerous unannotated marginal references made clear.[7]

The 1625 *Pilgrimes* of Purchas, his immense collection of travel narratives, was when published the largest work ever set for an English press. Its two books on Africa brought the studies of such authors as Leo Africanus and Duarte Lopes into much broader circulation and those of such authors as Francisco Alvarez and Don John of Castro, who had chronicled the decline of the Ethiopian empire, into English for the first time. In the quarter of a century after the *Pilgrimes* appeared, no significant new account of the areas south of the Senegal River would be published in England. As English ships began regularly to sail from Africa with persons held as slaves, the works of Purchas remained the best sources of information about the lives that would have led these persons to that point.

Of course, the works of Purchas included a torrent of information about almost every aspect of African life. They treated in careful detail such issues as the manner in which the people greeted visitors, the varieties of bread and wine they prepared, the animals they raised, the poisons they most feared, the vessels they built to navigate the rivers that cut across their lands, the festivals they held, and the lutes they fashioned from gourds that were strung with thin threads of wood, rushes, or hairs from the tail of an elephant. As did a number of his sources, Purchas took an intimate interest in the forms of African religion. Perhaps above all, however, the works that he authored and edited were concerned with the state—in other words, with the forms of government that had been established throughout the continent.

It was in the context of the state that Purchas and his contemporaries believed that slavery arose in African life. Even more than the old empire of Prester John or the kingdom of Congo, the region in which these authors had closely observed the structure of the state was the long Guinea littoral that stretched along the western coast from the Senegal River in the northwest to the Bight of Benin in the southeast. And so here is where we will begin our inquiry into what were understood to be the sources of African slavery.

From their earliest voyages to Guinea, around the middle of the sixteenth century, travelers from England had studied the forms of government there. They had learned that the men who controlled trade in many areas were called captains. These were rulers in the villages that were situated on the coast. They were also referred to as *alcaides,* which meant representatives, since their principal role was to represent the interests of a king who lived in a town farther inland. The English travelers whose accounts were printed in the Hakluyt collections most often worked with captains as well as with small independent merchants. It was because they had abducted the son of a captain at Shamma in 1554 that the company of John Lok had so offended the local people there. On occasion in this period, Englishmen were invited to come inland to meet with kings. In one such instance the merchant Edward Fenton had to decline the invitation and addressed a letter to a king named Fatima in which he expressed regret that he would be unable to visit "the Kinglike Place thowe mannageth." The merchants who did visit such places found that they were received into "a great houge haule longe and wyde" or into a walled settlement that could have been "as bigge in circuite as London."[8]

To initiate a trade in gold with kings deep in the interior was the ambition of Richard Jobson, whose 1623 book *The Golden Trade; or, A Discovery of the River Gambra* was a record of the attempt. As he rowed up the Gambra (or Gambia) River, which ran parallel to the Senegal and cut east across the continent, Jobson found little gold but did discover that there was one more level in the structure of local government than earlier English travelers in Guinea had understood. There were "petty Kings," he wrote, and then there were "great Kings." Leo Africanus had reported that most of the kings along the Niger, which was just to the north and east of the Gambia, had recently been brought under the rule of the king of Tombuto and made to pay him tribute. In a similar manner, according to Jobson, the several petty kings with whom he had traded were all under the rule of three great kings, who lived even farther inland and whom Jobson confessed he had never seen.[9]

An extract from the journal that Jobson kept during his voyage was published in the *Pilgrimes* of Purchas. But the most complete account of Guinea to appear in this collection had been translated from the work of the Dutchman Pieter de Marees. His *description and historicall declaration of the golden Kingdome of Guinea,* as Purchas titled the work, first came out in Amsterdam in 1602, and would continue to be an important source of English opinion well into the second half of the century.[10]

As had his English colleagues, de Marees noted that kings in towns in the interior commanded captains in villages along the shore. As would Jobson, he observed that there was a hierarchy even among kings. To a much greater extent than any English author from his era, though, de Marees, who had been there in the first period of intense Dutch interest in West Africa, was able to elaborate upon the entire structure of government that had been established in the great inland kingdoms of Guinea.

In the areas along the Gambia where Jobson had had occasion to trade, the office of the king was passed down in a line of descent from brother to brother and father to son. In contrast, in the parts of Guinea that were most familiar to de Marees, when one king died, "the common people" whom he had ruled would "choose another to governe them, and to possesse the Kingdome." The kingdom that this person possessed included a palace, which centered on a court that was protected by a company of armed guards. Even so, this king did not govern alone. He had the aid of a council of advisors and elders, and the most senior member of this council was a manager and treasurer, referred to as a *viador,* whose wealth looked to exceed that of the king. Below the council in status, there was a set of propertied gentlemen, whose houses were raised a couple of steps off the ground and had porches that were swept clean at the start of each day.[11]

In matters of justice, private disputes were heard before a judge, but when the issue at hand was a violation of the public law of the king, a more elaborate procedure was put in place. The king ordered an official known as the *catiff* to notify the common people of the town to gather in the marketplace. Here they met the gentlemen, the council, and the king. The accused person was held in the palace, where he was overseen by an executioner. From here, the accused was notified of the charges that had been made against him, and he was allowed to respond through the medium of the *catiff,* as the king and nobles sat in the marketplace and deliberated before the common people until the case was settled.[12]

We might pause for a moment to reflect upon this remarkable scene. In the telling of de Marees, a judicial procedure in a town set back from the coast of West Africa could best be described in terms derived from the courts of Europe. An entire political order had assembled here in a finely graded hierarchy that ran from common people to gentlemen to council to king. De Marees had given these titles in Dutch, and like the English translators of such foreign works as those of Leo and Lopes, the translator Purchas employed had rendered them in the lexicon of the English court, as though each one was at root a version of a form set in the nation of the observer.

The tendency of de Marees to describe Africa in terms derived from his own nation was present as well among early English travelers to Guinea. The rulers here were known to them as captains and kings, and these travelers noted, as would de Marees, that the local people themselves had begun to refer to their officials with titles they had learned from the Europeans with whom they had had the most regular contact. *Alcaide,* for example, the term used for the coastal representative of an inland king, was a Portuguese word that had become common among the local people; so was *viador,* as the treasurer of a kingdom was often called.[13]

The Englishmen who traveled to Guinea in the sixteenth century were on occasion surprised at how much what they found here seemed to resemble what they had left behind at home. The walled city into which one traveler was led thus appeared to him "as bigge in circuite as London." The canoes that John Hawkins found in use at Cape Verde looked so fast as that they could "make as much way, as a paire of oares in the Thames of London." According to one ship's master, the weather on the ocean near the Cape belied the legend of the Torrid Zone, for it was "as temperate as if we had beene in England."[14]

The merchant Jobson was struck in particular by how easily economic life along the Gambia could be brought within the bounds of the familiar. The local tradesmen were for the most part smiths, potters, and leather workers (or *sepateros* in Portuguese). The principal trader in the area urged Jobson to deal fairly with him, "because I am as you are," Jobson remembered the man had told him, "a Merchant, that goes from place to place." After their business was concluded, as Jobson went back down the river, he happened upon a gathering on the shore where the local people cooked and danced. "And amongst them likewise they had commerce, one thing for another," Jobson wrote, "so as it had a manner of resemblance to our fayres here in England."[15]

In the most thorough midcentury narrative of travel to the region, *A Relation of the Coasts of Africk Called Guinee,* which first appeared in an English edition in 1670, Nicolas Villault de Bellefond continued the search for points of resemblance well beyond the sphere of commerce. As had Jobson, Villault noted that the local people traded their best goods at markets "that resemble our Fairs." But he said as well that their huts were made "like our thatched houses in *Normandy,*" that some of their men had long beards "like the *Capuchins* with us," and that at sunset they would hold a dance that was "not much unlike one of our *Filoux* in *France.*" Even when he saw that their customs differed from what he understood to be his own, Villault made an effort to reconcile them. Although their clothes "be much different from ours," he once reflected, "yet they are as curious and as proud of them, as the best of us."[16]

Villault in essence reproduced the account of the political order in Guinea that had appeared in de Marees, whose work Villault seems to have known well. He described the captains who met his company to trade along the shore, the several kings whose authority extended into the interior, and the ruler upon whom these lesser authorities all depended, whose title was

Acanis le Grand and who in his opinion "may be called an Emperour." The account in Villault of the judicial process in Guinea was also similar to the one in de Marees. He said that "amongst these brutish, and barbarous Nations, Justice has its place." What de Marees had said about the criminal trials in Guinea was that even as the native people there were "wild, very useless and unmannered people in many things, herein they show a great piece of wisdom." Despite the deep resemblance that both authors perceived between themselves and the peoples of Guinea, de Marees in particular was appalled at certain aspects of their behavior. In trade with foreign merchants, according to de Marees, the native people stole, lied, and almost never kept their promises. The men took as many wives as they could, and both men and women were often unfaithful. They drank far too much palm wine. The scene of justice was never included in such assessments, however, and it was here that de Marees started to explain the role of slavery in African life.[17]

After all, slavery was present in almost every detail of this scene. The king who sat in judgment lived in a palace that was protected by a company of guards composed in part of slaves, and when he went abroad he was carried on the shoulders of slaves and trailed by other slaves who carried water, palm oil, and yams. The nobles who gathered around the king sat on stools supplied by slaves beneath shields that slaves held to protect them from the sun. In fact, these were nobles to the extent that they were able to own slaves, because this was the central privilege of nobility in Guinea, as ownership of land was the privilege of nobility in Europe. The official known as the *catiff,* who notified the common people of the trial and served as the medium between the nobles and king and the accused, was himself a slave.[18]

In another respect, too, slavery was present in this scene. In cases of murder, an offender could make an agreement with the king to "redeeme his life with money," as de Marees put it. If he was unable to do this, then he was put to death by the executioner, who would hang his severed head from a tree. On rare occasions, the killing of a person was met with a different punishment. When a dispute between nobles could not be resolved by a judge, the parties to the disagreement and their close friends and relatives would meet in a duel. In this case, if one man killed another, then he would be neither fined nor put to death but delivered as a slave to the widow of his victim. Slavery was also the punishment for several less serious offenses. If a merchant sold false gold to traders from Europe, then he was enslaved. Although de Marees had said that adulterers received a fine, Jobson and Villault later asserted that they were enslaved. Even petty criminals such as thieves could be enslaved if they were unable to pay the fine that a king demanded from them.[19]

Judicial enslavement—or slavery as punishment for crime—seemed to European observers to be most common in Guinea. But over the course of the seventeenth century, reports filtered back into England that claimed the practice was also in use across northern Ethiopia. There, it was said, a murderer was given to the nearest relation of his victim, who could "either kill him, or free him, or make him a Slave," in the phrase of Alvarez. In Guinea, slavery for crime was in each case said to be a permanent status: if he was unable to pay the fine that a king demanded from him, wrote de Marees, a thief "ever after, while he liveth, he must be a Slave." According to Villault, the same was the case for an adulterer, who would become a slave "without all hopes of redemption." Many slaves were kept in the possession of the nobles and kings in Guinea. But ownership of them could be transferred. All of the authors who noted that criminals in the region were enslaved were aware that on occasion they were sold to the Portuguese and eventually to the Dutch, French, and English merchants who arrived on the coast. These merchants would then take these persons across the Atlantic Ocean in order to sell them again in the New World. Once a slave was sold to merchants from Europe in order "to be sold into forreign Countries," Villault concluded, "he is never to appear in his own again."[20]

Observers from Europe thus understood judicial enslavement to be one source of African slavery, and believed that slavery of this kind inhered in the operations of at least some African states. Indeed, the central function of the states in Guinea in this period was seen to be the maintenance of order by means of a common judicial authority. The judicial procedure that authors such as de Marees described was attended by all of the members of a political community. In each case the settlement was reached by their rulers, who were nobles and kings in most inland towns and the captains who also served as judges in villages on the coast.[21]

In this period, there was also sometimes said to be one more kind of slavery that inhered in African states. Except in some rare cases, which will be treated later, slavery of this kind was not believed to be a source of persons who were traded across the Atlantic Ocean. Even so, in the course of an account of English perceptions of African slavery, it cannot be overlooked that the people in some places were said to be considered the slaves of their rulers.

To begin, in Guinea, observations of this kind had to do with the peculiar manner in which subjects seemed to address their rulers. From the first English voyage to the region, in 1553, travelers had remarked upon what Richard Eden called "the great reverence they gyve to their kynge." The nobles in his presence never looked him in the face, and as they left his court, they would not turn their backs but rather would "go creepynge backewarde with lyke reverence." For his part, Leo Africanus recalled that anyone who wished to have an audience with the king of Tombuto had to kneel to the ground and sprinkle dust over his head, which was a ritual that Richard Jobson also encountered in the petty kingdoms he visited along the Gambia River.

Some observers from Europe regarded such rituals with respect and even with envy. Eden lamented that if the English would treat with the same kind of reverence "owr saviour Chryst, we shuld remove from owr heads many plages." When Jobson first met with a king, he sat down and allowed dust to be scattered all around him and in his lap. However, it was also possible to see such gestures as the marks of a servile condition. According to one later Dutch merchant in Benin, the people there were "all Free-Men, notwithstanding which they are Treated as Slaves by their King."[22]

This had proven to be a remark most often made over the course of the seventeenth century about the people who lived under the Christian kings in northern Ethiopia, and here the situation was believed to be more serious. The common source of European opinion on this matter was Giovanni Botero's description of the kingdoms and commonwealths throughout the world, which first appeared in an English edition in 1601. As was the case for many English observers of Guinea, Botero's attention was drawn to the reverence accorded to the ruler whom Botero still knew as Prester John: at the mere mention of his name, Botero said, his subjects would "bow their bodies, and touch the earth with their hands." But Botero had also heard that the Ethiopian king exercised a measure of control over his subjects that no English observer had ever ascribed to any ruler on the western coast. He awarded noble status at his pleasure, and would rescind it for the smallest offense. Over time, through tributes and taxes and simple theft, he had impoverished the country to the point that his famous moveable court was the only town of any distinction that remained in the empire, as Muslim armies closed in from the east.[23]

Botero concluded from such reports that Prester John had treated the people under his control "more liker slaves then subiects." Well into the second half of the seventeenth century, English descriptions of the world would continue to draw from Botero for their accounts of northern Ethiopia. Even as English authors came to realize that the Christian rulers in the region had never used the title Prester John, such authors nevertheless repeated the refrain that the people of Ethiopia were treated "more like slaves then subjects," in the phrase of the cosmographer Peter Heylyn. As long as phrases of this kind continued to appear in English culture, however, they remained in the simile form. English authors were prepared to assert that the Ethiopian emperors treated their subjects like slaves, or more like slaves than subjects—but never that these people were in fact slaves. Prester John was said to hold slaves of his own, from whom his subjects were always distinguished: his subjects were not considered to be owned and could not be sold from person to person and place to place. At the least, no reports surfaced in this period to the effect that Prester John had sold his subjects as slaves beyond the borders of the realm.[24]

Botero's aim in his work had been to demonstrate the common causes of greatness (or as he put it in Italian, *grandezza*) in states. He believed that greatness was achieved and maintained by means of some complex combination of commerce and martial virtue, and he worked to explain the decline of the Christian empire in Ethiopia in these terms. He said that Prester John had sapped the wealth and degraded the spirit of his people to the point that they had been unable to defend themselves, as Botero was convinced free citizens were best able to do.[25]

Toward the end of the seventeenth century, Botero was succeeded as an authority on Ethiopia by the German linguist Job Ludolphus, whose *New*

History of Ethiopia appeared in English in 1682. Ludolphus too was concerned about the struggle of the Ethiopians against the "Barbarous *Idolaters*" that surrounded them. But unlike Botero, he saw the Ethiopians' submission to their ruler as an aid in their cause, since it seemed to him a measure of the "Concord and Unity" that prevailed within the realm. He advised that the private ownership of land be established on a much more stable basis, and promised that this would lead to the development of commerce and industry. Nevertheless, he concluded that the old refrain that the Ethiopians were treated like slaves reflected a simple confusion of terms. The Ethiopian language—for which Ludolphus also produced a Latin dictionary and grammar book—had a common word for *slave* and *servant:* the people had only ever been considered servants of the king.[26]

Even if slavery of this kind was understood to be no more than a figure of speech, it did share with judicial enslavement one important feature: both located the source of slavery within the context of a state—either in the procedure for the punishment of crime or in the particular relation between people and their ruler. As a matter of fact, until the seventeenth century, English observers had paid little attention to the relations between African states. The reception in the Renaissance of the classical litany of strange peoples who lived above the Torrid Zone had failed to inspire much reflection about how these peoples interacted with one another. The eastern empire of Prester John, according to Richard Eden, received tribute from dozens of kings, but it was bounded on the west by the Nile and to the north by a desert so immense that Eden referred to it as "the sea of sande." Even the travelers whose accounts were printed in the Hakluyt collections had tended to encounter each town one by one. Their method was to skirt the western coast about two leagues from the shore; for the most part, they would only send in a pinnace where they were waved in by people who seemed eager to trade or came across a river mouth in which they could gather fresh water before they would pull up anchor and move on across the coast.[27]

Indeed, only around the turn of the seventeenth century, in the accounts that were printed in the *Pilgrimes* of Purchas, did observers from England start to learn that Africa was a complex international system. And it was within this system that English observers found a second source of slavery. To be more exact, it was in the fissures within this system, in the conflicts between states, that the English perceived slavery to arise. Through the end of the seventeenth century, they were aware that most of the Africans who were sent across the Atlantic as slaves had started their journeys as captives taken in war.

The narratives that Hakluyt collected had presented Africa as essentially peaceful. The real discovery reflected in these reports, in comparison with the old legends that they aimed to discredit, was that the continent was the site of regular and profitable commerce. The most dramatic conflicts that appeared in these texts were those between the European powers that were in competition for the control of trade. Almost the only instance in which Hakluyt's travelers learned of violence between African states was when an *alcaide* on the coast at Cape Verde in 1591 told the merchants Richard Rainolds and Thomas Dassell that a truce had been declared in a "great warre" in order to accommodate their visit.[28]

The narratives that Purchas collected were altogether different in character. These works were preoccupied with war: as presented in them, Africa was violent almost as a matter of course. In Guinea, according to de Marees, the decision to make war was in the hands of the kings. Once a king had decided to make war, he would first call upon the soldiers who formed his personal guard. Then he would summon the armies of the captains who ruled in the towns under his command. On occasion there was a conflict so expansive that one king would enlist other kings to aid in his cause. Once their forces were assembled, they would meet in the court of the king who had sent for them. At this point, if the outcome of the conflict was seen to be in doubt, the combatants would "burne their owne Houses, and all their Townes," and take their wives and children with them into the field. In spite of this custom, the rulers in Guinea often took up arms in response to what seemed to be the most minor provocations, as well as in order to settle controversies about succession. "Warres," Purchas concluded, "are very rife among those Nations."[29]

If war was a common event among the nations of Guinea, across the two regions of Ethiopia it had become the essential condition. The accounts of northern Ethiopia that were published in the *Pilgrimes* were some of the first to report upon the decline of the empire of Prester John for an English public. These reports related how, in the time since Alvarez had returned to Portugal, the Muslim ruler of Adel had escalated his annual raids at Lent into a series of bloody campaigns that laid waste to several ancient kingdoms. At last in 1543, with the support of a company of Portuguese troops, Abissine forces beat back their enemies as far as the Red Sea coast. Already, however, from the desert territories in the southeastern Horn of Africa, a nomadic heathen tribe known as the Gallans had started to make inroads upon the weakened empire. Their advance had continued up to the time of the most recent reports that Ludolphus had received. He said that the Christians in northern Ethiopia were "always at war with these people."[30]

There were parts of southern Ethiopia as well where the wars seemed never to end. The powerful southeastern inland empires of Monomotapa and Mohenemugi were locked in what John Pory had called "continuall and bloudie warres" against each other. In addition to masses of their own troops, both sides were said to have enlisted fierce mercenaries on their behalf. The one had called upon the Amazons, who sheared off their left breast so as not to hinder their shot; the other had turned to the Gagas, who rased their cheeks and turned back their eyelids to terrible visual effect. When these forces met in battle, wrote Duarte Lopes, the Portuguese authority on Congo, their conflicts were "sometimes so blooddy, that it is hardely discerned who hath gotten the victorie."[31]

The wars in the riverine western central kingdom of Congo, Lopes believed, were more ordered affairs. As in Angola, which bordered on it to the south, the armies in Congo were divided into several regiments, each of which was under its own banner and captain. In the field, these forces were all under the command of a single general, who would direct them with signals from ivory fifes and iron triangles. To indicate that they had understood their directions, the captains and their deputies would then respond in kind, which produced what Lopes called "a warlicke and harmonious musicke." The southern province of Bamba was "the very keye, and the buckler and the sword," in defense of the kingdom from attacks from Angola. But in recent times, the most serious threat to Congo had come from the east. There, the lord of Batta had carried on "continuall warres" against the Gagas until, in 1568, the Gagas had invaded from Mohenemugi and chased the king of Congo onto the Island of Horses in the Zaire River. Only a long campaign with the aid of Portuguese harquebusiers had been able to restore him to the throne.[32]

Around the turn of the century, the area south of Angola into which the Gagas had now moved became the setting for perhaps the most remarkable English account of Africa from this period. "The strange adventures of Andrew Battell," as Purchas titled the text first printed in his *Pilgrimes,* was the narrative, Purchas said, of "my neere neighbour, dwelling at Leigh in Essex." Battell had sailed from England in 1589 on a privateer mission to Brazil, where he was captured by the Portuguese and sent as a prisoner to Angola. For a time, he was made to serve a colonial official as a trader on the coast, but after he attempted an escape, he was "banished for ever to the Warres" in which the Portuguese were engaged in the mountains around Angola. It was here that Battell met the Gagas and almost at once agreed to join them on a drive for plunder that led deep into the interior. Once Battell was captured by a hostile ruler and escaped to rejoin the Gagas. After a time, they allowed him to lead their soldiers into battle. "By this meanes," he recalled, "I have beene often carried away in their armes, and saved my life." Battell was with the Gagas for almost two years, but left them in hope of a return to England. At last, by around 1610, he was back in Essex and prepared to deliver an account of his adventures to a curious neighbor who himself had never traveled quite so far from home.[33]

In accounts of the battles of the Gagas, Battell fixed upon a regular point of interest among early observers of African wars. His attention was drawn to the precise scale of the conflicts he described. Heylyn noted that as late as 1559 the Abissine emperor could bring sixty thousand troops into the field and that his personal guard numbered twelve thousand horsemen. According to Pory, in Monomotapa the guard of the emperor was composed of four hundred mastiffs. Lopes reported that in Congo the lord of Batta led a force of seventy thousand men.[34]

When he had first come across them, Battell recalled, the Gagas only had five hundred men, but over time their camp swelled to sixteen thousand. When they arrived in a country they intended to conquer, they would build a round fort with twelve gates, one for each of their captains. Here they would rest for as long as two months until one night, under cover of darkness, their general would send out one thousand troops to imbosk themselves about a mile from the fort. In the morning he would present his army, as if to begin an assault, and when the enemy army marched out to meet it, "then the embosked men arise," Battell said, "so that very few escape." In this manner, when he was with them, the Gagas overran the kingdoms of Benguela, Calango, Shillambansa, and Casoch.[35]

The cruelty of the Gagas was renowned. In the invasion of Congo, Lopes recalled, they had "spared no mans life," and when they sacked Benguela, according to Battell, they had brought before their general the heads of more than one hundred lords of the kingdom. In the kingdoms they took, any people they did not kill they enslaved. Of these, they absorbed the young women into their camp as wives and made the young men fight in wars with collars around their necks as a mark of slavery until they brought the head of an enemy before their general, at which point they were freed and dignified as soldiers. These were the means by which the number of Gagas swelled while Battell was with them since, he noted, they buried their newborn children alive. The Gagas sold the rest of their slaves; in fact, in their first encounter, which took place when Battell was still attached to the Portuguese, the Gagas filled his ship with slaves over the course of seven days.[36]

In the first half of the seventeenth century, the Portuguese slave trade from western central Africa was well known across Europe. Lopes had noted that some of the natives of Congo who survived the invasion of the Gagas had been sold by merchants from the island of São Tomé to destinations as far off as Portugal. At Bamba, he continued, the Portuguese purchased five thousand persons on an annual basis and sent them "into divers parts of the worlde." And Purchas had heard that at the port town of Loando, in Angola, the Portuguese bought twenty-eight thousand slaves each year to send across the Atlantic to their colonial plantations in Brazil. It was a figure often repeated in English accounts in the decades that followed. These slaves had been "bought within the Land," according to Purchas, "and are captives taken in their warres."[37]

The captives taken in the wars in northern Ethiopia also were often enslaved. In the course of his "continuall war against the Abessine Christians," Botero reported, the king of Adel did "entreth their territories, burneth their villages, taketh prisoners." These prisoners then became the "innumerable slaves," in the phrase of Purchas, whom Muslims along the coast sent east across the Red Sea and into Arabia, Surat, Bengal, and Sumatra.[38]

The slaves in the kingdom of Borno, beyond the western border of Abissina in the Land of Negros, were sent north over the desert into Barbaria. Merchants would come down from there, according to Leo, and sell horses to the king. In exchange, when his army returned from conquests to the south, he would satisfy his creditors with prisoners at a rate of fifteen slaves for one horse. To the west along the Niger, the most powerful kingdom in the region was Tombuto. As did the monarch in Borno, the ruler here maintained a guard of three thousand horsemen. Soon after he came to power, he had conquered the kingdoms of Gualata, Agadez, Cano, Casena, and Guber. When he conquered Guber, Leo said, the "most part of the inhabitants were carried captive and kept for slaves." Since then, the army of the king had punished any ruler who refused to pay him tribute with attacks in which "so many as they take, they sell unto the merchants of Tombuto." The merchants of Tombuto had purchased so many persons in this manner that in the period when Leo visited the kingdom, he observed that the inhabitants kept "great store of men and women-slaves."[39]

Many of the persons enslaved in Guinea were kept there as well. De Marees even reported that, unlike in Angola or Congo, a merchant such as himself could "lade no ships full of Slaves" on the Gold Coast. The sources of slavery here resembled those that were in use in central Africa, as in addition to being a punishment for crime, slavery in Guinea was also known to begin in war. In war, de Marees explained, "whosoever is taken Prisoner they make him a slave all his life long." So close was the connection between war and slavery in Guinea that the people often used a Portuguese term, *morian,* to mean "Slave or Captive," according to de Marees, and the title of the enslaved official known as the *catiff* was taken from the French word *captif.*[40]

In short, across the states of Africa, slavery was understood to be a status attached to captives taken in war. In this sense, slavery had its origins in conflict. It arose from the attacks, battles, assaults, and raids that at times seemed to tear apart the continent in this period. However, in another sense, slavery was not a feature of conflict, because of course combatants only became captives once a war had reached its end. Seen differently, then, slavery arose not from war but rather from the delicate process by which states made peace.

Few observers understood the role of slavery in this process better than de Marees and Villault. They agreed that even though the rulers in Guinea would sometimes start wars in response to the most minor provocations, these conflicts were "not so cruell as they seeme," as de Marees said, because they "continueth not long." The conflicts in Guinea were "like a wisp of straw," according to Villault, "no sooner kindled, but extinguish'd." In combat, the people were as "Devils and not men." And yet as soon as one side accepted defeat, the victor would give quarter and "fall a taking of Prisoners." The parties to the conflict would hold a summit at which they would swear to do no harm in the future, and as security for this oath they would make an exchange of hostages, who were most often the sons of kings. Now at last commerce would resume. As Europeans in Guinea never failed to lament, commerce, including the commerce in slaves, could only take place in times of relative peace.[41]

Enslavement thus figured as an initial act in the attempt to establish peace between states. It set a limit to the violence of war. And the use of this limit would have been clear to observers of Africa in part because they had before them vivid evidence of the bloodshed that could result when the stronger party in a conflict had no interest in making slaves of its victims.

De Marees, for example, reported that in 1570 a company of Portuguese troops had been killed by the forces of a native kingdom near Mina in retaliation for an earlier attack; he had seen more than three hundred of their skulls, he said. Purchas too told of a massacre in Zanzibar in 1589 in which a people known as the Imbij, who came from around the Cape of Good Hope, had laid waste to Mombaza. Eighty thousand of them had marched on the kingdom, "destroying Townes, Cities, and Beasts, together with the Men" who happened to be in their path. Not content with "the destruction of all men," Purchas wrote, the ruler of the Imbij "shootes his arrows against the heavens."[42]

In their invasion of Congo, as we have seen, the Gagas had "spared no mans life." Nor did they relent once the king and his lords had retreated to the Island of Horses. Soon these men ran out of food. After "the most part of them dyed by famine," the rest sold themselves as slaves to the Portuguese merchants who sailed from São Tomé on ships stocked with provisions. Lopes explained that they had been "of necessitie constrayned" to do so. Slavery had been their only alternative to death.[43]

In truth it was a particular sort of death these persons feared, for the Gagas were known to eat their victims. Indeed, according to Battell, the Gagas were "the greatest Canibals and Man-eaters that be in the World." In the kingdoms they conquered, there were cattle in abundance, but they "fed chiefly upon mans flesh." Once, they held their camp for four months in an area they had overrun, "drinking, dancing, and banquetting with mans flesh." Even for someone who had seen as much as Battell, in the course of his travels across the Atlantic world, this was "an heavie spectacle to behold."[44]

The Imbij too were cannibals. At Mombaza, only a small number of the native people had escaped their "devouring mawes," Purchas wrote. They had buried the rest "in their bowels." Purchas also reported upon a people he called the Cumbæ, who were "devourers of mans flesh." Around 1550, the Cumbæ had invaded and plundered the lands of the native Capi in Sierra Leone. As it happened, the privateer and sea commander John Hawkins arrived in the area soon afterward, on his second voyage to the western coast of Africa to take slaves to sell in Spanish America. Hawkins and his men found the Cumbæ settled upon the land: the Capi were now their slaves. Elsewhere in Guinea, de Marees had heard that once prisoners in war were made slaves, "such as are slaine, their bodies are drest and eaten as good meate."[45]

Only in the parts of Guinea that de Marees knew best, however, was the distinction so well observed between prisoners in war, who were enslaved, and casualties in war, who were eaten. Among the other cannibals known to Purchas, prisoners were often eaten as well. The Gagas kept the young men and women whom they captured as slaves, but they would "kill and eat" their older captives, according to Battell. Lopes had explained that the reason their wars with the Amazons were so fierce was that the Amazons feared that if the Gagas took them captive, "they shall be devoured." In Sierra Leone, Purchas said, the Cumbæ held or sold "the meaner" rank of Capi as slaves but devoured all of the "chiefe men." Hawkins had said much the same. He had heard the Cumbæ would "keepe those that they take" in war as slaves only "untill such time as they want meate." For his part, on the road to Mombaza, the ruler of the Imbij "carried fire before him," according to Purchas, in order to announce his intention to "rost, and eate all such as he shall take." As on the Island of Horses in Congo, the native people at Mombaza who escaped from the Imbij sold themselves to Portuguese merchants on the coast. Pursued by enemies who would rather kill and eat them than enslave them, they made slaves of themselves.[46]

In cases such as these, slavery and cannibalism worked at cross purposes, since of course captives consumed were ones not enslaved. Indeed, a contrast began to take shape in the works of Purchas between peoples who enslaved their captives and those who ate them. Purchas had a theory that the Gagas, Cumbæ, and Imbij as well as the Gallans who lived in northern Ethiopia all descended from a common origin. They were nomads who traveled on remote inland corridors. When they came upon the settled kingdoms they intended to invade, they might have appeared to them more unusual than the Europeans who sailed in from the coasts. In war, they were almost perfectly cruel, which was the word Purchas and his colleagues most often used to describe their methods, and with few exceptions they were not known to hold slaves.[47]

For the most part, the slaves in Africa were held within the kingdoms that cannibals came to attack. From Guinea to Tombuto, Borno to Abissina, and Monomotapa to Congo, the wars of these states were limited to the extent that they tended to allow their captives to live, and then made use of them in order to strengthen their regimes. Slavery thus became a means to secure the political orders that conflicts could threaten. Some slaves were placed in the service of rulers as guards, administrators, or personal attendants; some were put to work as laborers for nobles or merchants; others were sold through markets over land and sea as a form of tribute or in return for commodities of various kinds.

In other words, slavery was the status attached to captives in states that in essence were civil, while—as Montaigne understood—cannibalism was often the response to captives among peoples who were not.

The "cruellest Canibals which the Sunne looketh on," according to Purchas, were the Anzigues, who lived up the Zaire River to the north and east of Congo. Lopes had said that they consumed not only the enemies they captured in war but also many of their slaves and even "their owne frendes and subiectes and kinsefolkes." They were a "savage and beastly people," he concluded, "saving onely in respect" that when the prices ran high in Congo they would travel down the river to sell their ivory, linens, and slaves. It was the one respect in which the Anzigues were not savage: on occasion they traded rather than ate their slaves.[48]

❧

Around the middle of the seventeenth century, as the regular English African slave trade began, authors in England were slow to register the event. Merchants from there had sent ships to Guinea to purchase slaves for Barbados as early as 1640. In the next two decades, around sixty thousand persons arrived in the English Caribbean colonies by such means. Even so, the most detailed description of the world from this period, Peter Heylyn's 1652 *Cosmographie,* was for the most part compiled from information in the much earlier works of Botero and Purchas. Like the authors of those works, Heylyn assumed that of the European powers that had established a presence in Africa only the Portuguese carried on a commerce in slaves. The same was the case in editions of the *Cosmographie* that came out in 1657 and in 1666. In that year, Robert Fage's compact *Cosmography* reported that even though ivory, ebony, sugar, ginger, and ostrich feathers were for sale around the continent, the one commodity that was known to interest the Englishmen in Africa was gold.[49]

Already by this time, however, the slave trade had started to become well known. In 1663, a charter issued to the African company had for the first time listed "negro slaves" in a list of the commodities to be purchased in Guinea. Although one description of the region printed in that year was titled *The Golden Coast,* its author was aware that the Englishmen who traveled there also sometimes traded for slaves. Over the course of the next quarter of a century, ships for the most part sponsored by the Company delivered almost two hundred thousand Africans into Barbados and Jamaica alone. By 1690, when one trader published a protest against the Company's monopoly over the expanding African trade, he started with an observation that would have surprised no well-informed English reader. The "Penury or Plenty" of their colonies in the Caribbean, the trader observed, "lies indispensably upon the Trade of *Negro* Servants from Africa."[50]

In the period that preceded this remark, the English had come to reflect upon their trade in slaves. The commerce that earlier they had condemned when practiced by Iberian powers was now one in which they participated and indeed upon which they relied. And in this context, the English sensed that they ought to produce some account of themselves in which their actions figured as legitimate.

And yet what most strikes the modern reader of this account is how little attention it seemed to English authors to require. Not so much as a pamphlet came out in this period that was devoted to a defense of the slave trade, and none was put out in order to condemn it. Even the several pamphlets that did appear toward the end of the seventeenth century in the controversy over the monopoly of the African company had to do with the organization of the slave trade rather than its moral character. Reflection upon this issue arose in phrases and passages in works that were more concerned with other matters: it had not cohered into a clear common opinion, much less into a debate. At this point it was instead made up of an interlocked set of imperfectly articulated assumptions. The central one of these was that to become a slave was a common fate in human affairs.[51]

The context in which the English had come to accept this assumption was not their experience of everyday life, because slavery in England had long since ended, but rather the reception of an ancient tradition of slavery that had best been preserved in the legal treatises of the Roman Empire. In what this book has described as the Roman tradition of slavery, all persons were considered to be free by nature, but as a result of accident or misfortune some persons could be made into slaves. These were most often captives in war and criminals, and they were placed into the hands of a master or of the state and could be bought and sold in the manner of other commodities.

Slavery had entered Roman law through the law of nations, which was understood to be composed of the customs that were common to all humankind. In the first half of the seventeenth century, as English observers came to believe that the peoples of Africa were more or less similar to those of Europe, they would have known that in at least one respect the more accurate model for Africa was the law of nations. Whereas the peoples of

Europe no longer took slaves, many of the peoples of Africa did so by the same means as the law of nations had allowed. It was in part for this reason that the English never registered even a hint of surprise when they learned of certain persons in Africa who had been reduced to a status that had no parallel in their own present social order.

Slavery in Africa was thus seen to arise from an image of the continent as a part of the world that was at once alien and familiar. As the works of Samuel Purchas had shown in the first half of the century, the structure of social and political life there may have been to some extent civil by the standard of Europe—even if it was this structure that produced a form of subjection that none of the nations of Europe now condoned.

The work that did the most to develop this image of the continent in the second half of the century was the grand volume *Africa* that John Ogilby published in 1670. Ogilby had had the work translated almost without alteration from the 1668 production of the Dutchman Olfert Dapper, who had compiled it from the best accounts published in Europe as well as Dutch and Portuguese reports that had circulated in manuscript. His section on Guinea, for example, was composed in this manner: it started with a survey of the inland kingdoms on the Niger River that was drawn from Leo, included passages on the Gold Coast that relied upon de Marees, and added to this original material on what Ogilby called "the great numbers of several Kingdoms" that spread west and east along the coast—from Kasangas and Guinala and Quoia around the mouth of the Gambia to Accra and Allada and Calabar toward the Bight of Benin. As Purchas had said was true across the continent, Ogilby said that some of the peoples in Guinea were nomads who had never established governments nor "ever scarce heard of any," while "the rest are all Monarchical, living under Laws, Order and Princes."[52]

Like Purchas, Ogilby held that the main source of slavery in Guinea was the wars in which the princes there were often engaged. The ruler of Guinala carried on "continual Wars" against the peoples of the Bissagos Archipelago, from whom, Ogilby said, he took "many Slaves." At Calabar, slaves arrived from the conflicts between eastern inland states in which, in a distinction that de Marees had also described, "they eat up whatever Enemies they kill, but their Prisoners they sell for Slaves." So common was the enslavement of such prisoners in Guinea that Ogilby took note when it did not take place. He remarked that the ruler of a people known as the Folgians, who lived under the monarch of Quoia, so feared the spirit of independence in an enemy whose forces he had subdued that he "resolved not to inflict any great Services upon them as Slaves, but live with them as Companions."[53]

Ogilby reported that often the prisoners who were enslaved in the wars in Guinea were sold on the coast to merchants from Europe and then carried to the West Indies: the ones at Guinala were purchased by the Portuguese, he said, and the ones at Calabar were acquired by the Dutch. Ogilby had also followed the progress of English commerce in the region, but he seems not to have known that his nation had entered the trade in slaves. By the time his work appeared, however, the news of this shift had filtered back into England. As it did, observers there took care to affirm that the persons whom their countrymen in West Africa carried to America had come to them by the same means as such persons had earlier come into the possession of their European rivals. "In *Guiny,*" explained Richard Blome, whose 1670 description of the world was an attempt to expand upon the famous atlas of the French cartographer Sanson, "there are several Petty *Kingdoms* who make *War* one against the other." "In which *Wars,* those they *kill,* they *eat;* those they *take,* they make *Slaves;* and such," Blome went on, as he blended novel English practices into what were now common European customs, "are those, that the *English, Dutch,* and other Nations buy of them."[54]

That the persons they bought in Guinea had been made slaves in war soon became a common refrain among the agents of the African company who had spent time there. In 1672 John Watts, the son of a surgeon from Kent who had been held hostage by the natives in Calabar for as long as four years, stated in a brief account of the region that "the Slaves they sell to the English are prisoners taken in war." On occasion, this had the effect that the traders in slaves would linger on the coast until they came upon a conflict on land that promised to deliver them their cargo. One such trader was Thomas Phillips, who captained a ship named the *Hannibal* that arrived near Sierra Leone in 1693. For six months, Phillips skirted east and traded for ivory and gold at English forts from Cape Coast to Cormantine until he reached the kingdom of Whidaw. The natives here were "constantly at wars" with their neighbors in Allada, in which "all the plunder is men and women to sell for slaves." Once Phillips had bought seven hundred of these men and women, the *Hannibal* sailed for Barbados.[55]

The extent to which the slave trade among the English depended upon the cycle of conflict in Guinea was apparent as well to foreign observers. Jean Barbot was a Huguenot merchant who had twice visited Guinea and, after the Edict of Nantes was revoked, fled to England, where he finished a manuscript on the region that was at least in part a record of his experience. Barbot recalled that during times of peace slaves were rare and their price was high; under such conditions, he said, the English slavers at Calabar would sometimes have to wait ten months in order to fill their vessels. In the aftermath of war, however, the pace of the slave trade so accelerated that on the Gold Coast in 1681 Barbot had seen three hundred prisoners delivered onto an English ship who had been captured in fighting in the interior earlier on that same day.[56]

Even if it seemed clear to Barbot as well as Ogilby that the main source of slavery in Guinea was war, European observers in this period became aware that some persons sold on the coast appeared to have been enslaved through other means—ones never considered to be legitimate in the long Roman tradition.

The thread that ran through accounts of slavery in the Roman tradition was the closeness between slavery and death. In the law of nations as this was set down in Roman legal texts, the term for slave, *servus,* was said to have derived from the term for preserve, *servare,* as slavery was a status reserved for persons who had been saved from death.

In the accounts of Africa written and edited by Purchas, slavery had been reserved for cases of this kind. Such were the cases in which prisoners in war were enslaved, since they might well have been killed in battle and then eaten by the cannibals who were so prominent in the image of the continent that Purchas had developed. For criminals, too, slavery figured as an alternative to death, since another punishment known to be in use for serious offenses was execution, and sometimes in West Africa persons accused of such offenses were made to undergo a trial by ordeal in which they drank a potion mixed with herbs or roots that often proved to be fatal. Even in the instances in the works of Purchas in which persons sold themselves—as, for example, on the Island of Horses in Congo or at Mombaza—this action was seen as the final recourse for those who otherwise would have been slaughtered.[57]

In their accounts of Guinea, Barbot and Villault had also reported that some of the slaves in the region had consented to their status; here again, both authors were careful to note that these persons had done so in order to preserve their lives. In addition to the prisoners of war and criminals who were enslaved, Villault explained, there were "such poor miserable Creatures" as had been unable "to maintain, or keep themselves alive." They had agreed to enter the service of a master in return for the goods and food they needed to survive, and in turn their children became "Slaves as well as the Parents." Barbot would add that in times of famine entire peoples could be driven to this fate, for he was on the coast in the spring of 1681 when in a fallow season thousands of the natives had "offered themselves for sale as slaves, in order to save their lives."[58]

This event made clear to Barbot "how all men have a natural love of life." Indeed, one more respect in which Africa figured as a model for the law of nations was that the choices of the people there confirmed its fundamental insight into the nature of slavery—that slavery had come to be accepted because there was no fate worse than death.

By the final third of the seventeenth century, however, reports had begun to spread that some of the persons whom Europeans purchased in Guinea had been sold into slavery when their lives had never been in peril. De Marees had known that parents could sell their children when they lacked "the means to bring them up or feed them." Blome agreed that parents could do so "when they are in need," but he also said that sometimes parents sold their children on occasions no more significant than "when they please them not." Watts heard that men could sell their wives and servants as well as their children if any of these persons argued with them more than once. And even though Ogilby had reported that the slaves sold at Calabar were prisoners in war, he also stated that the people who lived in the hills to the north of the kingdom were "so barbarously cruel, that the Parents sell their Children, the Husband his Wife, and one Brother and Sister the other" for no reason that he could discern.[59]

Among the kingdoms in Guinea, too, Ogilby found that slavery had grown into the structure of monarchical government. In the manner of certain earlier observers of Prester John, Ogilby believed that a number of the rulers in Guinea treated their subjects as though they were slaves. In Benin, he wrote, the king held "an unlimited Power, and so absolute a Soveraignty, that all his Subjects, how great soever, be no better than Slaves." For some of the rulers on the coast, the absolute power they held over their subjects had come to include the authority to sell them to European merchants. Thus the native people whom the Portuguese took from Kasangas, according to Ogilby, were "either purchas'd in War, or else under the pretext of some imperious and arbitrary Laws by the Kings and Great Men of the Countrey." In the inland kingdom of Gago, Blome reported, when men committed even a minor offense the king "sells their *Wives* and *Children* to strangers." Later on, at Whidaw, Phillips found in a similar vein that when the demand for slaves from foreign traders exceeded the supply of recent prisoners of war, the king sold hundreds of his wives to these traders in order "to compleat their number."[60]

Finally, even more unusual reports had surfaced to the effect that some persons whom the English had carried from the coast in Guinea had never been sold to them as slaves. It was a charge that recalled the abuses of the earliest English travelers to the region, from the crew of John Lok to the much larger companies of John Hawkins. When Watts asked the natives at Calabar in 1668 why they had taken him hostage when he had been there only to trade, they said that it was in response to the "unhandsome action" on the part of his countrymen "of carrying a Native away without their leave." By 1680, English commerce in Guinea had again been disrupted. According to the author of one pamphlet presented in defense of the African company, the cause was that separate traders had invited "some considerable Natives" to board their ship and "forthwith caryed them away, and sold them at the Plantations for Slaves." As had the natives at Calabar, the author condemned this as a "perfidious action." Through the end of the century, actions of this kind were met with swift reprisals. In 1698, when separate traders on the Gambia River seized sixteen local men to take to the Caribbean, the people surrounded the English fort at York Island and seized several Englishmen in response. Nevertheless, the word was now out in the open that some of the Englishmen in Guinea had broken all of the old customs and at least attempted to enslave anyone they could get their hands on.[61]

❧

Observers of Africa had, in short, come to realize that they could no longer smoothly assimilate the practice of slavery on the western coast to the ancient tradition from which it could have seemed to draw support. But the significance of this rupture was most apparent to authors who were concerned above all with America.

The first detailed account of slavery in the English American colonies was *A True & Exact History of the Island of Barbados,* which first appeared in 1657. The author of this account was a destitute businessman from London named Richard Ligon, who had worked as an overseer on sugar plantations toward the end of the previous decade. Already by this time, he estimated that the slaves on the island were "more then double the numbers of the Christians that are there." For the most part these persons arrived from areas on the western coast of Africa where "petty Kingdomes" sold to merchants from Europe "such as they take in Battle, whom they make slaves." Ligon observed that the enslaved Africans on Barbados marked the passage of time by the rotations of the moon. By this means they kept track of the time that had passed since important events in their lives. "So many Moons since one of these, and so many Moons since another," was what he imagined they told themselves. In this manner the Africans recorded the time that had passed since the birth of a child, or from the moment when they were forced to depart from their native land, or when they were "taken Prisoners" in war and enslaved "by some Prince or Potentate of their own Countrey."[62]

What Ligon had said about the sources of slavery in Africa soon became a common theme in English accounts of the Caribbean colonies. In 1672, Richard Blome published a survey of the English Caribbean that moved from Jamaica to Barbados to Saint Christopher to Bermuda. Blome predicted that Jamaica would soon become the "Richest *Plantation* that ever the English were, (or are like to be) Masters of," but for the moment Barbados was the nation's most important colonial possession in the region. The rich and fertile soil yielded cotton, ginger, indigo, and, most important, sugar on plantations stocked with slaves who came from Africa. It was "the custome in those parts," Blome explained, "for several petty *Kings* to go to Wars against one another; and the *Prisoners* that are taken of each side," he continued, as Blome more or less repeated what he had said about the customs of the slave trade on the western coast of Africa in the course of his 1670 description of the world, "they sell unto us, and other *European Nations* that come to *Traffique* with them."[63]

As Blome was well aware, the English merchants who sailed with slaves from the western coast of Africa now set course for Jamaica as well as Barbados. He noted in addition that the customs of slavery that had first been established on the one island were now also in place on the other. The first thorough report upon slavery as it had developed on Jamaica was the work of a former soldier from the Isle of Wight whose name was John Taylor. Taylor had served as a bookkeeper on sugar and indigo plantations in 1687. By this time, he estimated, there were as many enslaved as free persons on the island, and ever more of them arrived each day. What he said about the origins of the slaves on Jamaica was that most came from different parts of the western coast of Africa. There they were "under severall kings which have continuall warr at home one against another, and such prisoners which they take in the warrs they sell for slaves." These slaves were bought by "our English merchants, which sells them at Barbados and here."[64]

The simple statements that Taylor and Blome had at hand to describe the sources of African slavery recalled what Ligon had said about the matter, but neither covered all that Ligon had said. When he was on Barbados, Ligon had heard that there were routes into slavery in Africa other than the traditional one in which prisoners in war were made slaves. In some places on the western coast, kings would "sell their Subjects" on a whim; there were "some mean men," too, who would "sell their Servants, their Children, and sometimes their Wives."[65]

After he had called such men mean, however, Ligon did not pause in his account to reflect upon the moral character of their actions. Neither did he seem to pass judgment on the merchants who purchased the persons they sold. Among English authors, it was left to the nonconformist minister Richard Baxter to make the expansion of the sources of slavery in Africa into the basis for an attack upon English participation in the slave trade.

Baxter's *Christian Directory,* which came out in 1673, was presented as a detailed manual of practical advice for the application of the principles of religion. He allowed that there was a form of "slavery to which some men may be Lawfully put," and ran through a standard early-modern list of cases derived from Roman and Hebrew law. He noted that a man could be enslaved as a punishment for crime, if he was captured in war, or if poverty "do make a man consent to sell himself to a life of lesser misery, to escape a greater, or death it self." However, as Baxter turned his attention to the practice of slavery in the present, he said that he had been troubled to learn that some of the persons whom his countrymen considered to be their slaves had not been reduced to that condition in any one of the circumstances in which he understood this to be legitimate. In what could well have been a reference to the note that Watts had made about one such incident, Baxter asserted that "to go as Pirats and catch up poor *Negro's*" who had "never forfeited Life or Liberty" must be "one of the worst kinds of Thievery." Moreover, since it was a crime to enslave a person in this manner, Baxter reasoned that it was a crime to sell and buy them as a slave as well.[66]

Indeed, Baxter's central concern in this passage was not so much the sources of slavery in Guinea as the treatment of persons who were held as slaves in America. At this point in the *Directory,* he was concerned to define the duties of masters with respect to the persons who depended upon them: from wives to children to servants and at last to slaves. He maintained that even if the Negroes had lawfully been enslaved, they still were owed a measure of respect. Even "if their sins have enslaved them to you," Baxter observed, "yet Nature made them your equals." He worried that the "Masters in foraign Plantations who have *Negro's* and other Slaves" had instead started to "equal *Men* and *Beasts*" in the sense that both were purchased and used "meerly to the same end." As the planters came to treat both their animal and their human chattel as instruments for the production of profit, they defied the direction that they should have received from the principles of Christian religion: that their "chief end in buying and using slaves" should have been to treat them in such a manner as "to win them to Christ and save their souls."[67]

The conversion of persons who were enslaved in America was also the end pursued by the Anglican minister Morgan Godwyn, who referred to himself in the title of his 1680 polemic as *The Negro's & Indians Advocate, Suing for their Admission into the Church.* Like Baxter, Godwyn was concerned that "our Planters chief Deity" was none other than "*Profit,*" and "their God, INTEREST." In their determination to extract from their slaves as much labor as they could, the planters had refused to baptize and instruct them, and in so doing denied the "Right to *Religion*" that should have been guaranteed by the mere possession of a soul, "whether in a Bond, or *Freeman.*" Unlike Baxter, however, Godwyn had been to Barbados, where he served in the clergy for a decade, and he had seen that the abuses of the planters touched not only the souls but also the bodies of their slaves. Bare self-interest might have suggested a certain attention to the health of their laborers, so in this respect alone the planters had violated their most treasured principle. Godwyn wrote that what he witnessed on Barbados recalled what he had heard about the actions of the Spanish in the conquest of the Indies. The planters starved their slaves, kept them almost naked, and tortured them in their houses with special "*Engines,* and Devices to execute their *Cruelty.*"[68]

It was in the writings of the popular author of advice books Thomas Tryon that the cruelty of the planters moved toward the center of an attack upon the system of slavery in the Caribbean. Tryon had worked as a tradesman on Barbados for much of the 1660s, and in 1684 he put out a book of essays in which he offered *Friendly Advice to the Gentlemen-Planters of the East and West Indies.* After a treatise on the proper consumption of tropical fruits and herbs, he assumed the voice of a person who was enslaved in a treatise in which he put forward "The Negro's Complaint of their Hard Servitude, and the Cruelties Practiced upon them." "*Complaints* and *Lamentations,*" he observed, "are the natural Language of the *Miserable.*"[69]

According to Tryon, the cruelties practiced upon the persons enslaved on Barbados had started back on the routes over land to the port towns in Guinea, and had intensified on the ships that traversed the "Liquid Mountains" of the Middle Passage. In the New World, however, these cruelties had been perfected: it was a "*superlative Inhumanity*" that had met the Africans here. They might well have expected "another sort of Treatment," Tryon said, "from the Christians, who boast themselves the Sons and Favourites of the God of Love." Instead, they were worked past the point of exhaustion, whipped, burned, and raped. They could even be killed on a whim. Only in this final act did the planters in the Caribbean show some minimal form of consideration for the desires of their slaves—whose lives they had made into ones "far worse than Death."[70]

With this phrase the central argument of English authors against the system of slavery in the Caribbean had become clear. In the Roman tradition, slavery had seemed to represent a form of mercy in cases where death might well have been the crueler fate, and in reports from Africa, slavery was most often said to arise when the victors in battle were not so cruel as to kill and eat their victims. Toward the close of the seventeenth century, a rumor spread through the ports in Guinea where slaves were shipped to America that they were taken there not in order to work but rather to be fattened and then consumed. Already by this time, a number of English authors had come to believe that in a sense this rumor was correct. In the New World, the old balance had been upset. Here slavery was the essence of cruelty. To be condemned to this life was a fate worse than death.[71]

Nevertheless, there is perhaps no better measure of the continued influence of the Roman tradition of slavery than that even these authors did not reject it. Their arguments were directed toward abuses in the practice of slavery—in the sources of slavery, on the one hand, and in the treatment of slaves in America, on the other. None of them believed that slavery as such was illegitimate or looked forward to imagine a world without slaves.

In fact, even the more radical English critics had been quick to insist that reform in the practice of slavery would only tend to secure the institution. In 1671 the Quaker leader George Fox had sailed to Barbados in order to defend the members of his movement there who were held in suspicion due to a number of unusual customs, one of which was that they allowed their slaves to attend services with them. As Fox noted in a letter to the Governor and Assembly, this had given rise to "a most false Lye" that the Friends on the island had "*a Design to teach the Blacks to rebel.*" They had in mind nothing of the sort, he reported, and "the Lord knows it, who is the Searcher of all hearts." On the contrary, the prosperous Quaker planters assumed that instruction in Christ would inspire their human chattel to an ever more faithful and diligent performance of their duties. According to Fox, the love of the master would be repaid in kind by the love of the slave.[72]

Thomas Tryon also aimed to preserve the institution that he so severely condemned. The third and final essay in his book of *Friendly Advice* was presented as a dialogue between a master and his slave in America. At the end of the exchange, after he has again rehearsed the many "Cruelties and Oppressions" that he has suffered, the slave requests only that his master make several improvements to his conditions of labor. Once the master promises to do this, the slave announces that in return he will call upon all his fellows to be "obedient, humble, just and respective to all their Masters." "Good Night, my good dear Master!" the slave exclaims as the dialogue ends.[73]

Near the end of the seventeenth century, the work that most dramatically captured both the power and the limits of the English antislavery argument was Aphra Behn's prose narrative *Oroonoko,* which was printed in 1688. Although this work later gained fame as the first account of a slave revolt in modern literature, it is not, as readers from the eighteenth to the early twentieth century often said, an "emancipation novel."[74]

The book begins in the native country of its titular character, on the Gold Coast at Coramantien, where according to Behn the English find "the most advantageous Trading" for slaves. "For that Nation," she explains, "is very war-like and brave," and since they are "always in Hostility with one neighbouring Prince or other, they had the fortune to take a great many Captives; for all they took in Battel, were sold as Slaves." These slaves are sold by the general of the army, and Oroonoko has recently ascended to that rank. By the time an English merchant arrives on the coast, Behn is able to observe that this person is "very well known to *Oroonoko,* with whom he had traffick'd for Slaves."[75]

Already, though, the familiar routine of the slave trade at Coramantien has been disrupted. Oroonoko had in secret wed the daughter of the dead former general, a woman named Imoinda, who was soon summoned to join the harem of the king. Here she struggled to resist the king's advances, and once the king discovered that Oroonoko had sneaked into the royal palace to consummate his marriage, he ordered that both Imoinda and another woman who had come to her aid be "sold off, as Slaves, to another Country, either *Christian* or *Heathen;* 'twas no matter where."[76]

When the news of this event reached Oroonoko, he was back on the field of battle, and it is when he returns home that he meets the English merchant to sell the captives he has taken. He boards the merchant's ship in order to settle the terms of the sale, but then Oroonoko himself is seized and taken down to the hold. "Betray'd to Slavery" in an instant, he falls into despair. As the ship heads west from the shore, he laments he has been bound too tight to "quit himself of a Life that wou'd by no means endure Slavery."[77]

The ship next reaches land at the short-lived English sugar colony of Surinam, on the northern coast of South America. Oroonoko is purchased by a gentleman who comes to love him "as his dearest Brother." He is rarely made to work. When he learns that by chance Imoinda was sent to Surinam as well, the two lovers settle into a cottage and conceive a child. Still, Oroonoko finds that he cannot abide his condition and resolves to lead a revolt. He gathers together a number of enslaved men in order to exhort them to act. He reviews the tedium and drudgery of slavery, and then he comes to what seems to be the core of his case. "*And why,* said he," as Behn breaks into direct discourse,

> *Shou'd we be Slaves to an unknown People? Have they Vanquish'd us Nobly in Fight? Have they Won us in Honourable Battel? And are we, by the chance of War, become their Slaves? This wou'd not anger a Noble Heart, this wou'd not animate a Souldiers Soul; no, but we are Bought and Sold like Apes, or Monkeys, to be the Sport of Women, Fools and Cowards; and the Support of Rogues, Runagades, that have abandon'd their own Countries.*

"*Will you, I say,*" Oroonoko concludes, "*suffer the Lash from such Hands?*" His comrades respond, "with one accord, *No, no, no,*" and that night the revolt begins.[78]

For a call to arms, it is a careful address. Oroonoko does not dwell upon the cruelty of slavery. Nor does he complain that slaves have been denied access to the truths of Christian religion. He makes no mention of the manner in which Imoinda was sold off as a slave or he himself was betrayed to that condition. Over the course of his address, in fact, Oroonoko expresses no concern at all about the sources of slavery in Guinea—which must be due in part to the fact that, as he learned soon after his arrival in Surinam, he himself had enslaved most of the Africans there as captives in war. This is the route to slavery that Oroonoko accepts and almost even invites, as one that "wou'd not anger a Noble Heart." More so than any character we have encountered so far, he sees slavery as at root a matter of nobility or honor. It grates on him that the transatlantic trade has produced a situation in which to be a slave is the most acute form of dishonor. From this, he draws the conclusion that Tryon had pointed toward but never reached: in the New World, even if one "Dy'd in the attempt it wou'd be more brave" to take up arms in rebellion "than to live in perpetual Slavery."[79]

As it happens, Oroonoko does die in the attempt. It is not long before the militia of the colony tracks down the rebels under Oroonoko's command and offers that they will be pardoned if they surrender. Almost every one of them surrenders at once, and Oroonoko and Imoinda are taken prisoner. Once they realize that they cannot escape, Oroonoko kills his wife to save her from further enormities before at last he is tortured and then executed. Content to die rather than continue to live as a slave in Surinam, he smokes a pipe as he is hacked to pieces.

When his fellow rebels had abandoned him, Oroonoko said he was ashamed that he had attempted "to make those Free, who were by Nature *Slaves*." It was an offhand reference to the Aristotelian theory of slavery from a character who has been shaped much more by the legacy of Rome. Oroonoko "had heard of, and admir'd the *Romans*," according to Behn, even as a young man in Coramantien, and he is entertained in Surinam with stories of "the Lives of the Romans." The slave name that he receives here is Caesar.[80] In a sense, by the end of the narrative Oroonoko is out of time as well as out of place. The tradition of slavery in which he had participated has begun to break down, and he rebels against the one that has begun to replace it. He is the complex product of a transitional moment.

If Oroonoko was one complex character produced in English culture near the end of the seventeenth century, another was one who also took part in a rebellion against what he understood to be a form of slavery in 1688. This was the most important English author in the modern natural rights tradition: the political philosopher John Locke.

For it must be said that Locke was aware of the currents of thought and perception we have worked here to reconstruct. Locke was perhaps the greatest reader of books of geography and travel in his era, and at the time of his death, in 1704, his library held all but a few of the books on Africa that have so far been discussed. He owned the collections of Hakluyt and Purchas and the descriptions of the world from Abbot, Purchas, Heylyn, and Morden. He had the report upon Guinea from Villault, the Ethiopian history of Ludolphus, and the survey of the continent by Ogilby. He had the polemic on the conversion of slaves by Morgan Godwyn, whom he had taught at Oxford; and he owned a copy of *Oroonoko.*

For information about the English Caribbean colonies, Locke could have consulted his editions of the history of Barbados from Richard Ligon, and he could have read the massive 1671 survey of America that Ogilby had compiled. As it happened, Locke himself had been the principal author of the detailed section of this text that concerned the colony of Carolina. His own involvement here is, of course, well known. For a period of six years up to 1675, Locke served as Secretary to the Lords Proprietors of the colony. Founded in 1670 with settlers from Barbados, Carolina developed around the turn of the century into a slave society oriented around the cultivation of rice in the marshes on the coast.[81]

In this context it is curious that scholars have so often maintained that Locke could not have had the African slave trade in mind as he composed his own theory of slavery. In his *Two Treatises of Government,* which was printed in 1690, Locke presented a theory of the sources of slavery that was framed by close attention to the early-modern reception of Roman law. He said here that slavery should arise as a substitute for death for criminals and captives in war. And even though in the most important chapters about slavery in this work Locke made no mention of its practice in the present, there are subtle clues elsewhere that indicate he believed his theory could in essential respects describe the conduct of the English in the Atlantic world.[82]

The first one of these clues is to be found in the *Fundamental Constitutions* that Locke helped draft for Carolina in 1669 and then helped revise in 1682. The central article on slavery in the published version of this document granted to every freeman in the colonial settlement what it described as an "absolute power and authority over his negro slaves." In one of its earlier manuscript variations, this article had been even clearer in its intention to establish that a master would possess an "absolute arbitrary

Power over the Lives, Liberties and Persons of his Slaves." He could put them to death "for what cause soever he shall think fitt."[83]

This was no doubt an arresting provision, because the power of life and death that was granted to masters in Carolina was not allowed to the masters of slaves in any of the other English American colonies. From Barbados to Jamaica to Virginia, the slave codes of the seventeenth century made it a crime for any person willfully to kill a slave. That said, as we have seen, the most distinctive feature of Locke's theoretical account of slavery was that he insisted a slave was under the "absolute, arbitrary Power of another, to take away his Life, when he pleases." When Locke wrote this sentence in the *Second Treatise,* the sole contemporary source from which he could have drawn this vision of the awesome power that slavery involved was his own attempt to attach that same power to the masters of "negro slaves" across the ocean.[84]

The second clue that ties Locke closer to the practice of slavery in the present comes not from one of his own works but rather from a work of his associate James Tyrrell, whose *Patriarcha non Monarcha* came out in 1681. This book was so well known to Locke as to have given rise to a suspicion that Locke drafted one section of it. Tyrrell here put forward a natural rights theory that was fundamentally Lockean in character, and his account of the sources of slavery would have been familiar to Locke as well. Tyrrell held that what he called "the worst of Slaves" was the one taken as a captive in war. For his part, Locke had never considered whether a slave could flee from or resist a master, but Tyrrell insisted that a captive could do exactly this if not provided with the minimal "Comforts of Life. And if he cannot enjoy these," Tyrrell went on, "I believe there is no sober Planter in *Barbadoes* (who are most of them Assignees of Slaves taken in War) but will grant such a Slave may lawfully run away if he can."[85]

The content of this passage might not have been unusual, since in it Tyrrell aimed only to confirm what he believed to be the common opinion that a slave who was not well treated could run away from a master. Rather, it was his method that was worthy of note. In the course of a sentence, he had shifted from a consideration of ideas about slavery to the system in Barbados that seemed to be an instance of those ideas. In the course of a parenthetical aside, he had fit the transatlantic trade that made that system possible more or less into the consensus of his time about the lawful sources of slavery.

It was this consensus that Locke would accept and work to explain in the *Second Treatise.* And yet, as we have also seen, Locke rejected the broad provisions of the Roman tradition as he had found it. He argued that the lawful sources of slavery were far narrower than earlier authors had assumed: no person could consent to slavery, he said; none could be enslaved who had not taken part in an act of aggression that was unjust; and none could be enslaved other than the actual aggressors themselves. The children of slaves could not be made to inherit the condition of their parents, Locke continued, and he seems hardly to have imagined that slaves might be sold from one master to another.[86] This effort to limit the sources of slavery formed the basis for the revolutionary claims of the *Two Treatises* in the context of English politics. In turn, when laid aside the English African slave trade, the contrast was so great as to make Locke's theory the most complete indictment of that practice to appear in print in the seventeenth century.[87]

By the time the *Two Treatises* came out, as Locke would have known, the careful limits that he had placed upon the sources of slavery had all been set aside at one point or another in Guinea. Each one of the strictures set down by earlier theorists of natural rights had been discarded, and some persons had been made slaves by means that even the more permissive customs of the law of nations would not have authorized. It did still seem to be the case that most of the persons sold to English merchants had been enslaved in war or as a punishment for crime. But it had also become clear that the English never declined to purchase the slaves they were offered on legal or moral grounds. The example of Richard Jobson, who had rowed down the Gambia River in 1621, had long since been forgotten. We cannot help but ask, then, whether the ideas that were current in English culture about how slavery ought to arise shaped the actions of the English on the western coast of Africa at all or whether, from the middle of the seventeenth century, they went there prepared to buy all of the persons they could find.

As it happened, around the turn of the seventeenth century, a similar question had weighed upon the minds of some Portuguese observers of the actions of their countrymen on the western coast of Africa. By this time, authors from the Iberian nations had come to reflect more clearly upon their role in the development of slavery across the Atlantic world than would the English for quite some time. And since the manner in which the Portuguese most often acquired slaves in Africa resembled the practices that the English would put in place later in the century, their more sensitive authors can be seen to throw a certain light upon what were still more inchoate English beliefs.[88]

One such author was Baltasar Barreira, who arrived in Sierra Leone to serve in the small Jesuit mission there in 1605. The next year, in response to concerns that some of the persons whom Portuguese traders loaded onto their ships bound for America had been kidnapped into slavery, Barreira composed a report for his superiors in Rome. "What can in general be said about the blacks that are bought and sold in this part of Guinea," the report explained, "is that no examination into the legality of their captivity is made." The traders took "all of the blacks that are brought to them," and so accepted "their sale as sufficient proof of the legitimacy of their captive state." The traders never could have traced so many of the persons who were delivered to them on the shore back into the continent through old overland trade networks to the initial points at which they had been enslaved. In addition to the delays that such attempts would have caused, they would have been met with hostility from the native peoples, and one might never be able to discern who was telling the truth.[89]

"This is what can be said generally on the subject," Barreira wrote: the persons the Portuguese purchased in Guinea had been enslaved in circumstances that would have to remain "a matter of doubt." On the basis of the principle that "when in doubt, leave things as they are," Barreira concluded, "it seems that nothing should be changed." And of course little was changed in response to concerns of the kind that had prompted Barreira's report, either in the actions of the Portuguese in his time or among the English in the decades that followed. By inaction, they acted.

According to Barreira, there was one more point to be made on behalf of the traders in slaves. The source of their doubt was that "it cannot be denied," he observed, "that there exist in this Guinea reasons for genuine and legal captivity," such as war and crime. The Europeans there may not have been inclined to inquire too deeply into the past of each person who was sold to them as a slave. But they did seem to care that perhaps each one of them might legitimately have been reduced to that condition. To trade in slaves was not to be a criminal or a pirate. It was to work in conditions so uncertain that there was at least a chance that one's conscience could be clean. Here at last was the role for ideas in the origins of the African slave trade, for the English as for the Portuguese: to suggest that this event was possible from a moral point of view, that there were reasons to be offered in its defense, that the troubling questions about its conduct could be put off for a little while longer.

CHAPTER 5

The Causes of Complexion

ACCORDING TO a durable tradition of scholarship, the starkest contrast that the English drew between themselves and the peoples of Africa had to do with the color of their skin. From the early years of contact, the English may have known of Africans whom they understood to be more or less civil rather than savage and even Christian rather than heathen. But they had heard of almost no Africans who lived south of the Senegal River whose skin was not black rather than white.[1] The black color of the Africans, scholars have long maintained, arrested the attention of the English almost at once, and soon they had decided that it held deep meaning as a sign from God that here was an evil and inferior order of humankind. In turn, it was this perception of difference rooted in color that prepared the English to accept that the peoples of Africa were suited for a certain form of subjection to which no English person could be reduced. And after the end of slavery in America, this original and almost instinctual aversion of white for black remained, which was added proof for some scholars that it had been present from the start.

The present, however, can be an imperfect guide to the past, and this has proven to be the case in the study of skin color. As a matter of fact, much remains to be known about what the English thought about the blackness of African peoples in the period before 1700. The main historical accounts of racial attitudes have concentrated upon the eighteenth and nineteenth centuries, when the modern concept of race might be said to have emerged. To the extent that such works have touched upon earlier eras, they have often done so in order to find "the point of origin for traditions which are still with us," in the phrase of Winthrop Jordan, whose 1968 *White over Black: American Attitudes toward the Negro, 1550–1812,* helped to create the field named in its subtitle and to establish its central period of interest as in large part an examination of the revolutionary era and the early republic. Indeed, if we return to the earlier sources without a definite sense of what they must have said, in the light of later traditions or events, then we will find that what they did say was different from what we might have assumed.[2]

We will find, to begin, that the blackness of the Africans was not often seen to be an urgent concern. The observers of Africa whose accounts were current in early-modern England dwelled upon such natural features as the uneven shape of the coast, the cliffs that rose at points near the shore, the periodic inundations of the inland rivers, the richness of the soil, and the duration of the seasons. When such observers turned their attention toward the peoples of the continent, they tended to consider the manner in which the women gave birth, the reasons for which in many areas they circumcised their newborn male children, the fruits and vegetables they cultivated, the pipes they smoked, and the rituals they performed before they buried their dead. As we have seen, such observers were also interested in the forms of government that had been established among the peoples of Africa as well as their methods for the punishment of crime, conduct in war, and customs in the course of commerce.

Insofar as observers from this period were concerned with the bodies of the peoples of Africa, they studied the texture of their hair, how far they were able to see, the shape and size of their breasts and penises, how short or tall they were, and the diseases that tended to afflict them. The most sustained treatments of the Africans' skin color appeared in a pair of essays from around the middle of the seventeenth century. Elsewhere the topic was touched upon in items within lists, clauses within sentences, sentences within paragraphs, paragraphs within chapters, and chapters within immense and sprawling accounts. Here it appeared as one of many aspects of Africa that the English aimed to understand.

When English observers did remark upon the black skin of the Africans, they most often attempted to explain how it had come about. Some proposed that it was an effect of the heat of the sun over the Torrid Zone, and a small number asserted that it had its origins in an event described in the Bible that had come to be known as the Curse of Ham. But for the most part both of these ideas withered under examination. Over the course of the early-modern period, one more common opinion about black skin was that it was some kind of secret whose cause no person had been able to find out.

In general, a sense of indecision hovered over inquiries of this kind. By the end of the seventeenth century, English authors had long since come to a consensus that white was the natural or original color of humankind and that blackness was innate and permanent in African peoples. That said, the efforts of the English to account for these facts had led them to no clear conclusions about what they meant in social or political terms. English authors had not yet fastened upon skin color as the criterion for a hierarchical order of the types of humankind. That the color of a person might be presented as the reason for their status as a slave was still at this point far from certain.

In short, the argument of this chapter will be that in the period when slavery in the English Atlantic world began, we find in English culture not so much the development of the logic that would lead from blackness to slavery as an uncertain search after the causes of complexion.

So far it has been possible to describe the intellectual origins of American slavery almost without reference to skin color. Now we will see why that was so.

The English may not have been certain that they knew the cause of black skin, but they never doubted that the skin of the peoples whom they encountered along the western coast of Africa was black. It was not merely dark, they insisted, but black, and was indeed "very blacke," "exceedingly blacke," and "perfectly blacke." The Moors of northern Africa were dark, but these people were darker. From their earliest accounts, English authors repeated an old rumor that the Senegal River fixed the border between the tawny or brown Moors who lived to the north and the black Moors who lived to the south. The peoples who lived to the south of the Senegal River were thus sometimes referred to as "blacke Moores," "Blacke-Mores," and "Blackamores." Their skin was blacker than any the English had seen elsewhere. They were "the blackest nation of the world," in the phrase of one author.[3]

So unusual was the color of these peoples that in some cases an author needed only to name it in order to set them apart from the rest of humankind. In the 1623 account of his voyage up the Gambia River, Richard Jobson on occasion referred to the black skin of the men whom he met there. But several times he went so far as to say that they were "Black-men," "Blackmen," and "Blackes." These seem to have been the first uses in print English of Black as the word for a group of persons rather than the skin color of such persons—that is, as a proper noun rather than an adjective. In the final decades of the century, as English travelers abroad started to call themselves Whites—as opposed to Englishmen or Christians or persons who had white skin—so did a number of accounts appear in English that used the same word as Jobson had for the peoples of western Africa.[4]

From the sixteenth century, though, the more common term for these peoples had been Negros or Negroes. This was the plural form of the word in the Iberian languages for black, and English observers were aware that the skin of the Negroes was that same color. Nevertheless, it is a measure of the confusion of the era that English authors were unable to agree upon the origin of the term. Some held that the Negroes were so called because they lived in the basin of the Niger River, which had long appeared black to observers from the shore and whose name perhaps as a result was the Latin word for black. In fact, so similar did the word Niger seem to Negro that early English accounts at times used them in place of each other. The river thus became the "ryver Negro," and the peoples who lived along it were the "Nigers." Other authors maintained that the Negroes were named for the color of the soil in the region or the sediment that the river cast upon its shores. Still others said that they were named for the color of their skin. The compilers of the seventeenth century tended to list these as possible origins of the name without deciding between them.[5]

The learned English authors of the sixteenth century had also known the peoples of western Africa by one more name, and that was Ethiopians or Æthiopians. This name was derived from the works of the classical geographers, who had labeled as Ethiopia both the eastern area below Egypt and the vast western tract of land south of Libya. In the singular form, a person from this region was an Æthiope, which meant burnt-face in ancient Greek. Indeed, the geographers of Greece and Rome believed that the natives of

Ethiopia had been burned black by the sun. And in the Renaissance, when English authors started their own inquiries into the cause of black skin, this was the belief from which they began.[6]

In the ancient world, the classical belief about the cause of black skin had been set within a broad theory about the effect of the climate upon human life. This theory was first developed in the medical writings of Hippocrates, who proposed that the body be seen as a complex of inner elements or humors, which adjusted in response to external conditions. At the southern border of the habitable world, as Aristotle would explain in his *Problems,* the intense heat drew out the humors. As a result, the people here were cold and dry, and their skin was shaded only by the black bile or earthly humor that remained. This had left them with a number of virtues: classical observers from Aristotle to Strabo to Ptolemy remarked that the peoples of Ethiopia were subtle, sober, and wise. But they were also said to suffer from their climate, which made them feeble, jealous, and cruel. As the sun passed low over their part of the world, it wasted their fields and forced them to wander without end across the land in search of food and shelter. Over time, the Ethiopians had come to hate the sun. It was a common trope in classical accounts that the Ethiopians would curse the sun "when they behold it rising," as Strabo explained, "on the ground that it burns them and carries on war with them."[7]

The classical theory of the humors, and the image of the Ethiopians that it seemed to produce, were revived in the Renaissance by authors on the Continent. From around the middle of the sixteenth century, scholars from Bodin to Huarte to Charron elaborated upon the works of their predecessors in order to develop a more exact account of the character of each nation than any classical author had imagined. To be sure, these scholars still spoke in general about the traits that were to be expected from the people in the southern, middle, and northern parts of the world; but in addition they went on about the specific dispositions that would correspond to the climates in France, Spain, and England. As the inhabitants of a nation near the northern border of the habitable world, the English figured in this humoral discourse as the inverse of the Ethiopians: they were strong in body and courageous in spirit but dull in wit and, like the Ethiopians, altogether marginal in comparison to the peoples in more temperate areas. In part as a result of their position within it, the theory of the humors met an uncertain reception among the English. All of the recent works in which it had been developed were available in English or in Latin, but no English author appears to have used it as the basis for an account of the peoples of Ethiopia.[8]

What English authors in the sixteenth century did receive from humoral discourse was perhaps its most simple insight into the peoples of Ethiopia: that their skin was made black by the sun. In his 1559 *Cosmographical Glasse,* William Cuningham presented lessons in the form of a dialogue between student and teacher. "What will you coniecture," the teacher asks, "of those people that are blacke, face, body & all externe partes of them, doeth it not come of the heate of the Sonne?" "It muste nedes so be," the student responds, "& we call them Æthiopians." In similar fashion, the section on Ethiopia in the 1582 survey of the peoples of the world by Stephen Bateman started with a note that the region "hadde first that name of coulour of men. For the Sunne is nigh, and roasteth and toasteth them." In turn, Bateman continued, the color of the Ethiopians gave evidence of "the strength of the starre" overhead in their land.[9]

By the end of the century, as we have seen in Chapter 3, the classical image of Africa had for the most part come to seem out of date. English authors now rarely referred to the peoples of western Africa as Ethiopians. And yet at the same time, as it became more and more detached from its original context in the theory of the humors, the belief that the sun was the cause of black skin turned into a popular refrain in English works. The *Briefe Description of the Whole Worlde* that George Abbot published in 1599 was the first study of its kind openly to dismiss what it called the "fables" that ancient authors had told about the Torrid Zone. But even Abbot accepted that it was due to the heat that the peoples who lived there were "not only blackish like the Moores," he said, "but are exceedingly black." The category of the Moor was flexible during this period, for sometimes the black peoples of Africa were said to be Moors, and at other times the Moors themselves were said to be black. The poet John Davies was one author who considered them so: he observed in the same year that Abbot's study came out that it was the "Worlds *Sunne*" that "Makes the *More* blacke."[10]

Through the end of the seventeenth century, authors in England would continue to consider a popular one the opinion that the climate was the cause of black skin. As late as 1625, the geographer Nathanael Carpenter noted that in the region he called "the Land of *Blackmores,*" where the people were "all coleblacke," it was "the excesse of heat, which is taken to be the chiefe cause of this blackness." As it happened, Francis Bacon was another author who accepted this opinion. Toward the end of his life, as he also drew upon the civil law to press the case for war with Spain, the philosopher and former statesman composed a book that consisted of one thousand experiments and observations of the natural world, and one of these had to do with the cause of blackness. "The *Heat* of the *Sunne* maketh *Men Blacke,*" was what Bacon said. Nevertheless, he then added that the effect of this cause was not to draw the moisture from the body, as ancient authors had believed, but rather to draw it to the surface of the skin and hold it there. The color of the Negroes was thus more or less the inner color of the body made visible to the external world.[11]

In one form or another, then, the ancient opinion that the climate was the cause of black skin survived well into the seventeenth century. Even so, in this period no account of English travel to Africa accepted that this was the case. The one that came the closest was the 1555 report of Richard Eden upon the second English voyage to the western coast. To be sure, Eden did not make a direct attempt to account for the color of the people who lived there. He was even aware that though these people were "in oulde tyme cauled Ethiopes," they were now known as Negroes: this was the first use in print English of that term. But Eden drew upon his education in classical texts when he asserted that the people in this part of the world were "so scorched and vexed with the heate of the soonne, that in many places they curse it when it ryseth."[12]

As authors such as Eden were well aware, the classical effort to account for black skin was rooted in the belief that the heat of the sun rendered human life almost impossible in much of Africa. Several early English accounts reported in this vein that to the south of the northern coast the continent "must nedes be of heate almost importable" or was, in the phrase of Cuningham, for the most part "not inhabited" because of "th'extreme heat." Well into the second half of the sixteenth century, English authors could be found to repeat from their classical sources that this portion of Africa fell within the "*Torrida Zona*" or "burning zone" or "Torrid or burnt Zone."[13]

This was the image of Africa that the explorer George Best set out to correct. Best had sailed with Martin Frobisher on his voyages to the far northern mainland of America, and his 1578 *True Discourse* aimed at once to describe what had happened there and to encourage the expansion of English overseas enterprise. Into his description of Frobisher's search for a Northwest Passage, Best thus inserted an essay in which he hoped "to prove al partes of the world habitable" and in particular one part of the world that had been assumed not to be so.

In spite of what "the old Philosophers" had said, Best observed, Guinea and Benin had been discovered to be some of the "most frutefull and delectable" places in the world. Travelers from Portugal and France and in recent decades from England had settled down there to live, and had built castles and towns amid fields that abounded with grains, herbs, wood, and cattle. Since the air cooled off in the long nights near the Equator, the heat was not nearly so extreme as classical authors had supposed. In order to support this claim, Best turned to address what might have been interpreted as a stark piece of evidence of the heat in Africa—which was the "cole blacke" skin of the people who lived there. This must have come from some other source than the infamous "parching heate of the Sun."[14]

Although Best only aimed to prove that the African climate was far milder than "the old Philosophers" had supposed, his argument did not end at this point. Not only had classical observers mistaken the prospects for human life in the middle region of the earth: the entire attempt to ascribe black skin to heat had been an error. None of the geographers of Greece and Rome had imagined that a shift in climate would alter the color of a person. As in the Bible, they appear to have assumed both that a person could be black "because the Sunne hath looked upon" them and, at the same time, that for "the Ethiopian" to "change his skinne" was an appropriate expression for the impossible. But Best noticed the classical account required that color shift in response to climate in just this manner.[15]

As it happened, such a shift would soon be fashioned for the stage in Ben Jonson's *Masque of Blackness,* which was performed in 1605. In its first scene the masque presents the character of Niger, who represents the river in human form and appears in the "colour of an *Æthiope.*" Niger is surrounded by twelve of his daughters, who are the same color as their father, for the sun, Niger notes, has "shone / On their scorch'd cheeks." The daughters of Niger so dislike their complexion that each morning as the sun rises they have "charged his burning throne / With volleys of revilings." In the main action of the masque, Niger travels with his daughters to Britain, where they hope that the more temperate climate will turn their skin pale. They are pleased to hear that the sun here is one "Whose beams shine day, and night, and are of force / To blanch an Æthiope, and revive a *Cor's*" (or corpse). The promise that this wish will be fulfilled marks the end of the masque. By the time the action starts in its sequel, the 1608 *Masque of Beauty,* the daughters of Niger have been "washed white."[16]

Even the turn of phrase that Jonson used in *The Masque of Blackness* in order to describe this event, however, played upon its unlikelihood. To "blanch an Æthiope" was to work as much of a marvel as to "revive a *Cor's*." This phrase gestured as well toward the popular proverb on the early-modern English stage, which was present in several forms of shorthand, that "You labor in vain (to wash an Ethiop white)."[17] Some of the first persons from western Africa had arrived in England in 1554 aboard ships that were under the command of John Lok, and by the end of the century, the presence of such persons had come to be seen as more or less common. None of them seemed to have "blanched," in the usage of the *Masque of Blackness.* George Best himself reported that he had been surprised to come across the child of an African man who had been brought to England and a "faire Englishe woman" who was "as blacke as the Father was."[18]

In turn, Best continued, white skin had proven as impossible to change as skin that was black. He had heard that there were English mariners who, "though they be of valiant courage," had refused to travel to the Torrid Zone for fear that they would be "parched and broyled to death" or, even if they survived, that they would be "burned as black as a cole." As it happened, such a dramatic event set the context for the action in Jonson's *Masque of Blackness.* Here Niger recalls that his daughters had used to be "as fayre / As other Dames" in the time before the son of Apollo lost control of the chariot of the sun and "his heedless flames were hurled" down upon them. This was a myth that Jonson drew from Ovid. In the standard Elizabethan translation of Ovid's *Metamorphosis,* this was said to be the moment at which the Ethiopians, "(By reason that their bloud was drawne foorth to the outward part, / And there bescortched) did become ay after blacke and swart."[19]

In later decades, though, even as English travelers often remarked that the sun over Africa would tend to darken or tan the skin, they almost never said that it would blacken it. White skin would not turn black, just as black skin would not turn white.

Best believed that he knew why this was so—the causes of complexion cut deeper than the climate. The source of black skin among the peoples of Africa was to be found in "some naturall infection of the first inhabitants of that Countrey." In turn, the source of this "infection" was to be found in a story related in Genesis. During the Flood, the only men left alive were Noah and his sons Japhet, Sem, and Cham, who would possess the earth once the waters receded. Noah had ordered his sons to abstain from sex with their wives while aboard the Ark. But Cham disobeyed his father, in the hope that his child might be the first one born after the Flood and as a result inherit the earth for himself. For this "wicked and detestable fact," Best said, God had the wife of Cham bear a son, Chus, "who not only it selfe, but all his posteritie after him, should be so blacke and lothsome, that it might remaine a spectacle of disobedience to all the World." The black peoples of Africa were descended from Chus. The color of their skin marked the curse that God had placed upon their forefather.[20]

The story that Best told here was drawn from the historical 1561 *Cosmographicae* of the French scholar Guillaume Postel, but it differed in several respects from the one that appeared in the two most popular versions of Genesis in seventeenth-century England. In both the Geneva Bible and the King James Version, the offense of Ham, as the name was spelled in these works, was not the attempt to father a child aboard the Ark. It was rather that, once Noah planted a vineyard after the Flood and lay drunken in his tent, Ham "saw the nakednesse of his father, and told his two brethren without." Shem and Japhet walked backward into the tent and covered their father with a garment. When Noah awakened, he "knew what his yonger son had done unto him," and then he uttered a curse. Noah did not curse Cush, however, as Best said; he cursed another son of Ham whose name was Canaan. Most important, he did not curse him with blackness. "Cursed *bee*

Canaan," Noah said, "a servant of servants shall hee be unto his brethren." The marginal note for this line in the Geneva Bible added, "That is, a most vile slave." It was the first appearance of slavery in the sacred text.[21]

In short, Best introduced into English culture as a source of blackness a curse that in the Bible was a source of slavery. In recent decades, scholars have often seen this as a fateful event in the development of racial slavery. They have asserted that as the Atlantic slave trade began, the Curse was relied upon in order to tie blackness and slavery together. "The notion that Noah's curse justified enslaving black Africans," according to Robin Blackburn, "was probably more widely diffused in the sixteenth and seventeenth centuries than ever before." It was used during this time, as David Whitford has explained, "by a wide variety of authors seeking to exploit the text [of the Bible] as a support for the perpetual slavery of Africans." Such scholars have thus found in the early-modern era the origins of the antebellum American proslavery argument, in which the Curse had a central role as the biblical proof that slavery was the proper and specific fate of the black peoples of Africa.[22]

To be sure, at least one author in seventeenth-century England did use the Curse to this end. John Weemse was a learned Church of Scotland minister in Berwickshire whose 1626 *Portraiture of the Image of God in Man* explored the likeness between the Lord and the creature He had created who most resembled Him. Weemse insisted that before the Fall no man had endured "servile subjection." But he also knew that since then several kinds of men had been reduced to that status. Some were servants "*by nature,*" he explained, as were "the dull and blockish" who served men "of quicker wit." Others were "*servi belli*" who were captured in war, and still others were "servants *ex pacto*" who sold themselves. As Weemse ran through this familiar list of the Greek, Roman, and Hebrew sources of slavery, he made no mention of its practice in the present. He went on to note that slavery had first begun as a curse "upon a disobedient sonne *Cham.*" Only at this point did he find that he was able to assimilate the modern African slave trade to an ancient model. "Wee see to this day," he observed, "that the *Moores, Chams* posterity, are sold like slaves yet."[23]

Nevertheless, Weemse appears to have been the only author from this period to use the Curse in this manner in order to explain the African slave trade. The other author who came the closest was George Sandys, in an aside in his *Relation of a Journey* to the Middle East, which was published in 1615 and appeared in excerpt in the *Pilgrimes* of Purchas. In a caravan from Cairo to Jerusalem, Sandys recalled, he was approached by Muslim traders who "brought with them many *Negroes*" for sale. These the traders had bought from their parents in an area far up the Nile River where adults parted from their children with "little passion," Sandys explained, "regarding more the price then the condition of their slavery, who are descended of *Chus,* sonne of cursed *Cham,* as are all of that complexion." Sandys might well have seemed in this sentence to suggest that it was the particular disposition of the descendants of Chus to hold in little regard the freedom of their own children. And yet if this had been his aim, then his final phrase here would have been unusual.

Indeed, in what followed, Sandys made clear that he had referred to the Curse in an attempt to explain not so much the enslavement of certain Negroes as the complexion of all of them. This was not due to the heat of their climate. Nor did it owe to the black color of their sperm, as Herodotus had once proposed. Sandys dismissed as well the opinion of the Dutch traveler van Linschoten that the blackness of the peoples of Africa could be ascribed to the nature of the soil there. "For neither haply will other races in that soyl prove black," he remarked, "nor that race in other soils grow to better complexion." The blackness of the Africans came instead from "the curse of *Noe* upon *Cham* in the posterity of *Chus,*" Sandys concluded.[24]

This was in each respect the version of the Curse that Sandys would have found in the *True Discourse* of George Best. In the passages on Africa in that work, Best had never mentioned slavery. In turn, in English culture through the close of the seventeenth century, the Curse would be considered as a possible cause of the blackness of the Africans far more often than their status as enslaved.

Even so, during this time the Curse came to be understood by some authors as the reason for a number of other features of African life. As he reflected upon his journey along the Gambia River, the merchant Richard Jobson made no attempt to account for the color of the people whom he sometimes called Blacks. He had refused to buy or sell them as slaves. When he did posit that "these people originally sprung from the race of *Canaan,* the sonne of *Ham,* who discovered his father *Noahs* secrets, for which *Noah* awakeing cursed *Canaan,*" it was in the course of an effort to explain why their men were burdened with members of such size as made them unable to engage in intercourse with their wives when they were pregnant.[25]

In his 1625 treatise *Geography Delineated Forth,* Nathanael Carpenter drew upon the Curse in yet another context. Carpenter accepted what he observed to be the common opinion of the time: that the heat was the cause of black skin among the peoples of Africa. The idea that blackness had started "as a curse inflicted upon *Chams* posterity," he wrote, had "very little shew of probability." That said, as he considered the conditions of life near the Cape of Good Hope, where the land was barren and the people were brutish, Carpenter paused to speculate that this was a sign that the area bore "heavy as yet the curse of *Noah*" upon "the first father of that *African Nation.*" In a passage added to the second edition of his *Travels* to Africa and Asia, which was published in 1638, Thomas Herbert agreed that the Cape of Good Hope was "owned by an accursed Progeny of *Cham.*" The land there was fruitful, he maintained, but the people differed "in nothing from bruit beasts save forme." They were the lawless Caphars whom Purchas had earlier condemned. They had no religion and "no power or policie awing them."[26]

The line of thought that ran from Best to Herbert was thus a jagged one. Best had helped to make the Curse available to English authors as a possible cause of the black skin of the peoples of Africa. But in the early decades of the seventeenth century, the Curse was also available to observers of Africa as a cause of burdensome members, barren land, and an absence of religion and political order near the Cape of Good Hope.

Nor, of course, did the original biblical version of the Curse disappear from English culture in this period. One author who passed it on was a teacher named John Minsheu, who had produced what was the standard Spanish-English dictionary of the Elizabethan era. In 1617, he came out with an etymological dictionary in eleven languages that appeared under the title *The Guide into the Tongues.* Here he said that "Nief" derived from the French word *Naïf* and meant "a bond woman," for the reason that women were known for the most part to become bond by birth. Bondage had first begun, Minsheu then added, when Ham, "seeing the nakednesse of his *father Noe,* being *drunk* shewed it to his *brethren* in *derision*" and was "therefore punished in his sonne *Caanan*."[27]

Around this time it was common to believe that the Flood was the event in biblical time that could be seen to correspond to the transition from the law of nature to the law of nations, as these terms were defined in the Roman legal tradition. In his *Institutes of the Lawes of England*, which appeared in 1628, Edward Coke was careful to note that slavery marked a departure from the law of nature. He said that slavery had spread over time as the common status of captives in war, but then added that its ultimate origin was further in the past. After the Flood, Coke said, "bondage or servitude was first inflicted for dishonouring of parents" upon Ham, who was "punished in his sonne *Canaan*, with bondage."[28]

Of course, in early-modern English culture the fullest and most complex attempt to represent the events that were recorded in such minimal and obscure terms in Genesis was John Milton's poem *Paradise Lost*. Milton maintained that the original condition of Adam and Eve in the Garden of Eden must have been one of perfect freedom. This was in part the basis for his position, in the context of the English Civil War, that freedom was the natural status of humankind. God had given absolute dominion to humans over the animals, and in turn He was their absolute lord. "But Man over men," as Adam later realized, "He made not Lord." At the moment of the Creation, He had "human left from human free."

All the same, no English author from this period had as acute a sense as Milton of the consequences that had followed from the Fall. Toward the end of his poem, he had the Archangel Michael lead Adam to the top of a hill that looked out over the earth and relate to him what would be the future course of human events after he and Eve were exiled from Paradise. Soon subjection rather than freedom would become the rule. Rulers would seize unlimited power. Slavery would spread by means of conquest in war. Some nations would descend so far from virtue into vice as not to deserve to be free. In this regard, Michael told Adam, "Witness th' irreverent Son / Of him who built the Ark, / Who for the shame / Don to his Father, heard this heavie curse, / *Servant of Servants*, on his vitious Race."[29]

Milton did not mention Ham by name here and did not mention Canaan at all. No doubt the narrative context that he had developed was to a certain extent his own invention. The version of the "heavie curse" that he had Michael introduce, however, was none other than the one that Milton would have found in the text of the Bible.

For their part, after Coke and Minsheu had reproduced more or less this same version of the Curse, neither one went on to propose that the present inhabitants of Africa were descended from Canaan. In the seventeenth century, perhaps only Richard Jobson claimed that this was the case. Much less unusual was the opinion of John Weemse that the Africans, whom Weemse referred to as Moors, were descended from Ham. For example, John Pory, who translated the work of Leo Africanus, had said much the same. Before he started his description of the areas of the continent that Leo had not covered, Pory reported that "the greatest part" of the peoples of Africa were "thought to be descended from *Cham,* the cursed son of *Noah.*"[30]

Here Pory drew upon what was a popular opinion in English culture. Since at least the thirteenth century, scholars in Europe had aimed to establish that the three regions into which classical geographers had divided the world could be seen to correspond to the three sons of Noah whose progeny had filled the earth after the Flood. The peoples of Europe could be traced back to Japhet, those of Asia to Shem, and those of Africa to Ham. Around the turn of the seventeenth century, this scheme often appeared in works of biblical exegesis that were published in England. The *Devine Weekes* of Du Bartas, which was first translated into English in 1605, was one work of this kind. For Du Bartas, the placement of Ham in Africa had followed from his sin against his father. Whereas Japhet had been given "rich *Europe*" and Shem received "*Asia* rich in spice, / Pride of the World," Ham was sent to inhabit "poore *Affrica,*" which ran from "Sun-burnt *Guinne*" to "Hot *Concritan,* too-full of poysonie matter."[31]

That said, the three-part scheme upon which Du Bartas relied was not at all present in the text of the Old Testament. The dispersal of peoples that was described in Genesis did not fit within a strict division of the world into three parts. Each one of the sons of Noah had fathered sons who had then spread over more than one of the classical regions. For his part, Ham had fathered four sons, whose names were Cush, Phut, Mizraim, and Canaan. In the chapter in Genesis that over time had come to be known as the Table of Nations, Canaan was named as the forefather of the Canaanites, whose lands stretched southward from Sidon to Gaza, and among other peoples who were known to have lived in that area, the Philistines were said to have come from Mizraim.[32]

An attentive reader of the Old Testament could thus hardly maintain that all of the descendants of Ham had gone to live in Africa. The cartographer John Speed was one such reader. In 1611, Speed put out a brief volume of *Genealogies of Holy Scriptures.* In the first table in which he traced the lines of descent from Noah, he wrote Europe, Asia, and Africa under the lines that led, respectively, to Japhet, Shem, and Ham. That said, in the later tables in which he came to provide a more exact account of the descendants of Ham, Speed listed among them peoples such as the Caldeans and Hittites, in addition to the Philistines and Canaanites, who had never been believed to be Africans.[33]

According to Speed, among the sons of Ham, only Cush had been the source of the Ethiopians. Best and Sandys had also maintained that the black-skinned peoples of Africa descended not so much from Ham as from Cush (or Chus, as both authors spelled the name). Du Bartas, too, stated that the Hamitic line of descent that ran through Chus was "the *Æthiopian* strand." Nevertheless, again, the text of the Old Testament did not provide support for such claims. In the Table of Nations, Cush was said to have been the father of six sons. The most important one of these was Nimrod, who was the first ruler to appear in the Bible and the king of Babylon and conqueror of Assyria. In the most sophisticated work of biblical genealogy in this period, the 1614 *History of the World,* the former privateer and promoter of English overseas expansion Walter Raleigh went to pains to establish that "the seat of *Chush*" had been across the Red Sea "in *Arabia, not in Æthiopia.*" Raleigh proposed that to the west of Egypt, all of Africa had been peopled by Phut. Phut was the only son of Ham whose children were not mentioned in Genesis. Perhaps this was an appropriate point at which to arrive, since in truth there was not a single clear statement in the Old Testament about the origins of the peoples of Africa.[34]

According to Samuel Purchas, this fact should not have surprised any reader who understood the real purpose of that text. In the Table of Nations, as Purchas explained in the first book of his *Pilgrimage,* Moses had not intended to compose a "Geographicall Historie of all the Nations of the World." He had done no more than provide the names of "the first Fathers" who had peopled the areas near where Noah's Ark came to rest after the Flood. To determine even these was "a hard taske," Purchas observed. He said that the sons of Ham had dispersed into Africa and the southern part of Asia, but added that statements of this kind were "probable coniectures, not certaine proofes." What was much more important to Purchas was that, as hard as it would be to determine who had been the first father of each nation in the immediate aftermath of the Flood, it was "now after this confusion of Nations by wars, leagues, and otherwise, impossible" to state which nation in the present had come from whom. The increase in the number of people over time and the more or less continual movement of peoples from place to place had only multiplied the confusion.[35]

And so after a seven-page chapter on "the re-peopling of the world" after the Flood, Purchas moved on to the eighty-two chapters in which he described the peoples of Asia. In the thirty chapters of his *Pilgrimage* that he devoted to the peoples of Africa, Purchas came back just once—in a passage we will examine below—to the matter of their possible origins in a story related in Genesis. Similarly, John Pory had never returned, over the course of his survey of the peoples of Africa, to his early observation that these peoples were believed to be descended from Ham. None of the major travelers' reports from Africa that appeared in Purchas's *Pilgrimes* referred to a curse from the Bible in an effort to explain enslavement or black skin or indeed for any other reason.

By the middle of the seventeenth century, then, neither of the two most well-known opinions about the cause of black skin had come to be widely accepted. On the one hand, as skin color seemed not to change when white persons traveled south and black persons were made to come north, the ancient opinion that complexion was no more than a response of the body to the climate came to seem incredible. On the other hand, in a period when access to the text of the Bible expanded dramatically in England, any reader could see that the story of the curse in Genesis never mentioned blackness and might also have struggled to find among the figures named there anyone who could be believed to be the forefather of the black-skinned peoples of Africa.

To be sure, modern scholars have often asserted that the account that George Best developed "about the Africans' pigmentation was widely shared" in the early-modern era, in the phrase of Alden Vaughan. "In particular," as Peter Fryer has written, "that was how blacks were supposed to have come by their blackness." According to Mary Floyd-Wilson, once the climate had been dismissed as the reason for black skin, the narrative of a biblical curse "then emerges as an explanation of its origins and significance."[36]

Far more common in the seventeenth century, however, was the approach of the two most careful midcentury inquiries into the matter. The pair of essays on "*the Blacknesse of Negroes*" that were published by the scholar and physician Thomas Browne in 1646 and the natural philosopher and Christian theologian Robert Boyle in 1664 worked to discredit both well-known opinions about its cause as "Vulgar and Common *Errors,*" in the favored phrase of Browne. "How and when this tincture first began is yet a Riddle," Browne reflected, one that seemed as if it had "no lesse of darknesse in the cause, then blacknesse in the effect it selfe."[37]

Browne and Boyle were able to offer no more than the most tentative theories about the cause of black skin. Browne listed six of these theories, among them the "inward use of certaine waters," the "sootish and fuliginous matter proceeding from the sulphur of bodies torrified" in fire, and an obscure and ancient mutation in the species. Boyle proposed that persons had first come to be black as the result of "some Peculiar and Seminal Impression" of a black object upon the mind of a white woman who carried a fetus in her womb. And in the 1650 text *Anthropometamorphosis,* in the course of a treatment of the topic that for the most part followed that of Browne, the physician John Bulwer added that the first persons with black skin could have been Moors who became Negroes by painting their bodies black.[38]

Around the middle of the century, attempts to explain the origins of black skin thus started to proliferate. At the same time, a number of observers who doubted that they would be able to find its source focused instead upon an effort to determine the precise location of blackness in the body. Boyle had heard that "the Seat of that Colour" was in the thin outer layer of what he understood to be the two layers of the skin. In the decades that followed, several correspondents of the newly formed Royal Society aimed to establish that the seat of blackness was instead in a gelatinous third layer of the skin that was lodged between the other two. Others held that it was to be found in scales within the deepest layer of the skin. Still others claimed to have discovered, in the course of the dissection of black bodies, that the skin of the peoples of Africa received its color from their black blood.[39]

Claims of this kind—and the gruesome experiments from which they arose—had as their object not so much the cause of blackness as the point at which it was made manifest. Observers who were confident that they had found the one were still able to admit that they were uncertain about the other. This uncertainty was well captured in a passage from John Josselyn's 1674 narrative of a voyage to New England. In between observations about the diseases with which colonists in the area were afflicted and the plants that prospered there, Josselyn paused to consider "the blackness of the *Negroes.*" He reported that in the opinion of some authors, this had proceeded from "the curse upon *Cham*'s posterity," while in the opinion of others, it was "the property of the climate where they live." Josselyn only noted that once when he had had to remove an infection from the finger of "a *Barbarie-moor*" he noticed that it was the azure color of a deep third layer of skin, mixed with the tawny color of the outer two layers, which "makes them appear black. I do not peremptorily affirm this to be the cause," Josselyn hastened to add, "but submit to better judgment." As perhaps he was aware, no such better judgment was then available.[40]

We might pause here to record one thought that has no doubt already occurred to the reader. As authors such as Josselyn struggled to produce the cause of black skin, they seem hardly to have imagined that a reason for what they took to be their own white skin needed to be given. Each new inquiry into the matter tended to set black further apart from white, inasmuch as whiteness figured as a given fact and blackness as a departure that had to be explained.

In early-modern English culture, black skin was never considered to be so strange as to rank among the marvels that would often elicit the wonder of observers of the natural world.[41] It was not novel, because after all, classical geographers had been well aware of it among the Ethiopians. Nor was it so rare, since of course, as Thomas Browne observed, black was the color of "a mighty and considerable part of mankinde." That said, blackness had always been understood in England as the product of circumstances that were far from ordinary—either as the result of the extreme heat of the sun over the southernmost edge of the habitable world or as the mark of a divine malediction that was intended to serve as "a spectacle of disobedience to all the World," in the phrase of George Best.[42]

For authors around the middle of the seventeenth century who had rejected both of these accounts, black skin did not quite appear to be an effect whose cause would never be found. It looked to them less like a marvel than a riddle, which was the term that Browne chose. As they continued to offer insights into the sources and location of blackness, with all of the industry and optimism that suffused the practice of natural philosophy during this period, they only worried that their efforts would not be complete until submitted to better judgment, in the phrase of Josselyn. Even so, from the sixteenth century, another strain of authors had already started to doubt that such judgment would ever become available. To them, black skin looked less like a marvel and a riddle than a secret: a fact whose origins lay beyond the reach of human understanding.

The earliest English author to state the matter in these terms was Richard Eden, in his narrative of the second English voyage to Guinea. Toward the end of his account, Eden presented a list of several facts that the crew had observed there that they had been unable to explain. At night, the beams from the moon seemed to give off heat, and they claimed to have seen spouts of water the size of church pillars that fell from the air down into the sea. "This is also to be consydered as a secreate woorke of nature," Eden continued, that while the native peoples of the West Indies were olive in complexion, the people in Guinea were black. Earlier in his account, in the course of his brief classical description of Africa, Eden had written that the people who lived on the western coast were scorched by the heat of the sun over the Torrid Zone. But the theory of the humors upon which Eden drew here seemed to require that peoples whose lands stood in the same relation to the Equator be affected by the sun in a similar manner. The sun could not have made the Indians olive and the Africans black, he reasoned, and if the sun was not the source of black skin, then it would have to be considered one of the secrets of the natural world.[43]

Eden was not the only English author in this period for whom the complexion of the Indians posed a problem to the classical account of the color of the Africans. In the chapter on Ethiopia in his 1582 survey of the peoples of the world, Stephen Bateman had noted that the Ethiopians were black because they had been roasted and toasted by the sun. However, in a separate chapter on Africa that drew from modern sources, Bateman could not help but introduce the comparison to America. One had to "mervayle at this," he remarked, "that in all *America,* there are found no blacke men." If not the heat of the sun as it passed over the middle region of the Earth, what was "the efficient cause of this colour?" It would have to be "the drinesse of heaven, or of the earth, or perchaunce a certaine unknowen propertie of the soyle." Or else, Bateman concluded as he started to realize that perhaps his inquiry into the cause of black skin would not in the end produce an answer, it must have come from "a certayne reason hidden properlie in Nature unknowen unto man."[44]

Blackness "commeth of nature it selfe, who worketh it by some secreat reason," said Duarte Lopes, whose *Report of the Kingdome of Congo* was translated into English in 1597. Earlier in his narrative, Lopes had dismissed the opinion of classical authors that the climate was the cause of black skin, on the grounds that the children fathered by the Portuguese men who had settled in Congo seemed to be more or less white. At this point, he had accepted the view of Herodotus that blackness was passed on in "the nature of the seede" of African men. But now Lopes found himself stranded in the Spanish West Indies after his ship was blown off course on the route home to Lisbon. He was unsettled when he reflected that the brown- or tawny-skinned peoples on these islands lived in the same climate as the people whom he had encountered in Congo. In the manner of Eden and Bateman, he concluded from this fact that blackness must be some kind of secret, "which never yet to this day, eyther by auncient *Philosopher,* or new writer, hath beene fully set downe or understoode."[45]

According to the clergyman George Abbot, the cause of black skin was one of the only aspects of Africa that ancient philosophers had understood.

It was nothing more than an effect of the heat of the sun, he explained in his 1599 brief description of the world. In a passage added to the 1605 second edition of that text, however, Abbot revisited the issue. He noted that even though much of America fell within the Torrid Zone, the people there were all "of a reasonable faire complexion." If complexion was determined by what were known to be "the ordinarie rules of Nature," then this fact could not be accounted for. Abbot argued that skin color was not the work of nature, as earlier authors had assumed. It was instead determined by the author of nature—in other words, by God. The black skin of the peoples of Africa could only be ascribed to "Gods peculiar will" that made it so.[46]

In the decades that followed, what Abbot had said about the cause of black skin was repeated and refined in the works of Peter Heylyn. In his 1621 *Microcosmus,* which Heylyn referred to as his "little description of the great world," when he touched upon the color of the Africans he cited the classical myth from Ovid that they had been burned black by the sun, but he promised to deliver what he called its "true cause" when he came to the section of his book that was concerned with America. Here he started from what was now the familiar puzzle that even the peoples who lived at the same latitude as Ethiopia had been observed to be "little (if at all) inclining to blacknesse." This fact led him to reject the heat of the sun as the cause of black skin. Once he had also set aside the view that the complexion of the Africans reflected the color of their "generative seed," Heylyn decided that "wee must wholy ascribe it to Gods peculiar will and ordinance."[47]

Heylyn's *Microcosmus* would appear in eight editions through 1639, and when he enlarged upon it to produce his *Cosmographie* in 1652, his earlier position on the cause of the blackness of the Africans was more or less unchanged. He did add that "some will have this *Blackness* laid as a curse on *Cham,*" and went on to relate the version of this event that Best had told, but then said that this was "a fancie as ridiculous" as the view of Herodotus had been "false." "So that we must refer it wholly to Gods secret pleasure," Heylyn wrote. He then added, in a final clause, that "possibly enough the curse of God on *Cham*" had had what he termed "an influence" on the color of the Africans. Even so, according to Best, the story of the Curse laid out in detail the reason God had made the descendants of Ham black, and here Heylyn conceded, in a parenthetical aside, that God had done so "for some cause unknown to us." His pleasure or will was manifest in black skin—but one did not know what will this was.[48]

In short, authors from Eden to Heylyn saw in black skin a secret whose source was hidden within nature or God. In response to recent reports from the New World, they were led to reflect upon what they believed to be a certain unusual fact about the Old. They fastened upon the blackness of the Africans, which now no ancient account seemed able to explain. That said, during this time it was also possible to discern in the encounter with the light-skinned natives of America an occasion to reflect upon a secret broader in scope than black skin. For the most subtle authors of the era, the real secret was not blackness as such so much as the entire range of human colors.

The first author whose reflections upon this secret appeared in an English text was a Spanish historian named Francisco López de Gómara. In his 1555 *Decades of the Newe Worlde,* which was for the most part translated from Spanish and Italian accounts, Richard Eden published without attribution several excerpts from Gómara. One of these was a short chapter about "the colour of the Indians." Here Gómara observed that although in Africa the people were black to the south of what he referred to as "the burnt line," at an equal distance from the Equator in America, the people were almost the color of olives. From this, he drew the conclusion that the variety of complexions "proceadeth of man," in his phrase, "and not of the earth." What he meant was that certain colors inhered in certain peoples, and it could not be said that the total color scheme of mankind was an effect of the different climates in different parts of the world. It was the work of God alone. One could not know "the cause why god hath so ordeyned it," Gómara wrote,

> Otherwise then to consyder that his divine maiestie hath doonne this as infinite other to declare his omnipotencie and wisedome in such diversities of colours as appere not only in the nature of man, but the lyke also in beastes, byrdes, and floures, where dyvers and contrary colours are seene in one lyttle fether, or the leaves growynge owt of one lyttle stalke.

The colors of men resembled the colors that appeared in every kind of thing in the natural world. The most common of these, Gómara continued, were black, yellow, and white, but each of these came in an array of shades, since "men are whyte after dyvers sortes of whytenesse: yelowe after dyvers maners of yelowe; and blacke after dyvers sortes of blacknesse." Even these colors were only as points on a fully realized spectrum, for white graded into yellow through brown and red, and yellow turned to black through murrey and ash and the tawny complexion of the Indians. To many English observers, black skin stood out as a peculiar feature that at once demanded and often resisted explanation. By contrast, Gómara saw in blackness no more than one of the many colors of men. The sheer diversity was what drew his attention. He said that it was "to be marveyled at" and that it could not be considered "withowte great admiration" for the manifest and yet impenetrable wisdom of the divine.[49]

Among English authors, Purchas was the first to develop such reflections upon the secret source of skin color into a social vision for the peoples of the world. At the close of the chapter in his *Pilgrimage* about the Land of Negros, Purchas turned to discuss an issue that it seemed to him a reader would perhaps want him to address. "Now if any would looke that wee should here in our discourse of the Negro's assigne some cause of that their black colour: I answere, that I cannot well answere this question," Purchas said. The many causes that had been proposed all looked to be inadequate. He listed, and then dismissed, each of the reasons that he had found in the travel narratives in which he was so fully immersed: from the classical theory about the heat of the sun to the narrative of a biblical curse, from speculations on the particular character of the African soil to rumors about the black sperm of African men. Some authors would even "ascend above the Moone" in an effort to seek out the cause of blackness in some constellation of the stars. "And there I will leave them," Purchas wrote:

> Yea, I will send them further to him that has reserved many secrets of nature to himselfe, and hath willed us to content our selves with thinges reveiled. As for *secret thinges,* both in Heaven and Earth, *they belong to the Lord our God, whose holy name be blessed for ever,* for that he hath reveiled to us thinges most necessarie, both for body and soule, in the thinges of this life, and that which is to come. His incomprehensible *unitie,* which the Angells with covered faces in their *Holy, holy, holy* hymnes resound

and *Laude* in *Trinitie,* hath pleased in this varietie to diversifie his workes, all serving one humane nature, infinitely multiplyed in persons, exceedingly varied in accidents, that wee also might serve that *one-most God;* that the tawney Moore, black Negro, duskie Libyan, Ash-coloured Indian, olive-coloured American, should with the whiter Europæan become *one sheepe-fold,* under *one great shepheard,* till *this mortalitie being swallowed up of life,* wee may all *be one.*[50]

The essential fact of humankind was unity, not difference. Whereas Gómara had marveled at the common source of beasts, birds, and flowers of diverse colors, and Purchas focused his attention on the human, their purpose was the same. Both authors stressed what seemed to them as the limitless variety of life. According to Purchas, human nature was "infinitely multiplyed in persons, exceedingly varied in accidents," and the range of human colors ran from tawny to black to dusky to ash to olive to white (or at least "whiter"). It was none other than the extent of this variety that made clear the singularity of its source. Insofar as he felt that he was able to offer an opinion about the intention of the Creator, Gómara said that God had made men of different colors in order "to declare his omnipotencie." Purchas noted that "His incomprehensible *unitie*" was itself what "hath pleased in this varietie to diversifie his workes." For the variety of works that God gathered together into Himself in turn attested to His unity. The sweep of the sheep-fold offered evidence of the greatness of the shepherd. Only God could contain such plenitude.

❧

The black color of the people in the Land of Negros thus inspired Samuel Purchas to consider the unity of God's works. As he did so, he laid bare the fundamental theme in the early-modern search for the cause of black skin: the need to find a source for difference within the context of the single act of Creation revealed in Genesis.

To begin, the theory that the black-skinned peoples of Africa had been burned by the heat of the sun over the Torrid Zone, in spite of its origins in the works of the heathen geographers of classical Antiquity, fit well within the belief that all the peoples of the world were descended from

Adam and Eve. For this reason, even authors who had good cause to reject the classical account of black skin could also come to depend upon it. In the sections on America in his descriptions of the world, Heylyn asserted that blackness could only be ascribed to the will or pleasure of God. But in the historical introductions that appeared at the start of both works, he adopted a different position. Here he made cursory attempts to trace the first dispersal of the sons of Noah after the Flood, before he paused to marvel that the various peoples in the present had all descended from this common point of origin. "*O see how full of wonders strange is Nature,*" Heylyn remarked in verses he quoted from Du Bartas in his *Cosmographie,* that men so differed from one another "*not alone in stature, / Strength, colour, hair*" but "*in their humours, and their manners too. / The* Northern *man is fair,*" he went on, "*the* Southern *fowl; / That's white, this black.*" "The ground or reason of which difference," he explained, was none other than the effect over time of "the different tempers of those Countries" in which the progeny of Noah had gone to live.[51]

Nevertheless, Heylyn did admit that the variety of peoples was now so great as "that it might seem they had been made at first out of several Principles, and not all derived from one common Parent," as in the account in Scripture. The notion that not all the peoples of the world had come from a single original pair was in the early decades of the seventeenth century most often associated with such ancient pagan figures as Zoroaster and Julian the Apostate, who had proposed that the diversity of the world should be taken to indicate that it was the creation of more than one god. In the middle of the seventeenth century, though, the doctrine of plural origins received its most powerful early-modern statement from the French heretic Isaac La Peyrère. In *Men before Adam,* which was published in English in 1656, La Peyrère argued on the basis of detailed exegesis that the Old Testament had only told the story of the Jews. It had not described what must have been the separate origins of such ancient nations as the "*Caldeans, Egyptians, Scythians,* and *Chinensians,*" much less the far more obscure beginnings of the Mexicans in the New World.[52]

In the decades that followed the publication of *Men before Adam,* the doctrine that La Peyrère put forward received sympathetic attention from a small number of English authors. These authors approached the topic not in the course of the kind of scriptural criticism in which La Peyrère had been so adept, but rather in the context of natural philosophical inquiries into the physical composition and origin of the universe.

One such author was the linguist Francis Lodwick. In the 1670s, Lodwick produced several brief speculative accounts of the creation of the world. Here he elaborated upon the thesis of *Men before Adam* that the variety of peoples in the present was more or less preserved from the moment of the Creation. In this respect the present was the best evidence of the character of the distant past. Another author who endorsed the doctrine of plural origins was a scholar identified only as L.P., whose critical analysis of Genesis appeared in print in 1695. On the basis of an examination of "matter of Fact, as it stands in Nature," L.P. ridiculed the common claim that Genesis had described universal events. The sacred text could not explain the origins of the peoples of America, and L.P. added that the peoples of Africa must also have come from a separate source.[53]

In the second half of the seventeenth century, speculations of this kind were unorthodox and unusual. Lodwick never published his accounts, which remained in manuscript. L.P. chose to remain anonymous: his initials were in all likelihood a nod to the heretical Frenchman. Indeed, the challenge that La Peyrère had presented to the scriptural account of human origins was also met by dozens of works written in its defense. Among these were several histories of the world that were the most sophisticated English efforts in the genre since that of Walter Raleigh in 1614. The common aim of these books was to establish that the peoples of the world were all derived from the couple whom God had told in Genesis to be fruitful and multiply, and in the context of this attempt, authors found congenial the classical theory that the range of human colors had only to be attributed to the gradual effect of the climate in the various regions of the Earth. It was because he understood it from this point of view that the jurist Matthew Hale, in his 1677 *Primitive Origination of Mankind,* was not troubled by what he called the "strange variety" among humans in "Colour, Figure, Stature,

Complexion, Humor," as this all had arisen "from the difference of the Climate."[54]

To doubt that this was the case was to invite an unwelcome idea. Like La Peyrère, Lodwick and L.P. pointed to the New World as an exception to the standard account of human origins. But in a manner that the Frenchman had not, both English authors also fastened upon the Africans as people who must have been the product of a separate creation. The radical difference between the whiteness of the English and the blackness of the Africans was a central source of their concern. It was a concern that weighed upon the minds of even the most orthodox observers. "It may be urged, by way of Argument," warned the parson Thomas Robinson in his 1694 *Anatomy of the Earth,* "that if Blackness be natural to the *Æthiopian,* and Whiteness to the *European,* they do not derive their Original from one single Person." In an effort to confirm just such a claim, Lodwick and L.P. attacked the common accounts of the sources of blackness. They cast doubt upon the theories that aimed to derive blackness from seminal impression, the Curse of Ham, and the heat of the sun. In response, orthodox authors most often reverted to the position that the blackness of the Africans was simply a result of the climate in Africa. Upon reflection, Robinson believed it would be best to suppose that no color was natural to any people at all but rather that "the different Soyls, or various Modifications of Matter in several parts of the World, produced Men of different Colours and Complexions."[55]

To suppose that the climate had produced the men of different colors in the world was in some sense to accept that these colors had changed in the period since the Creation. Neither Hale nor Robinson made any clear statement to this effect. As we have seen, from the sixteenth century, the opinion that a change in climate might alter the color of a person had already come to seem incredible, and in the seventeenth century, no English observer made a serious effort to revive it. That said, in the second half of the seventeenth century, a small number of authors did take an interest in some version of this view. Near the end of his essay on the blackness of the Negroes, Robert Boyle recalled that he had been told the Negroes tended not to be black at birth. On the contrary, for several days their skin was "almost the like Reddish Colour with our *European* Children." For Boyle, this fact did not undermine the theory of seminal impression that he had advanced. Instead, it indicated that perhaps the impression of a black object upon the mind of a white mother could have mixed with the well-known darkening effect of the African sun to produce a person there as black as the persons who lived there in the present.[56]

In the decades after Boyle's essay appeared, members of the Royal Society that he had helped to found would on occasion compose lists of inquiries that they wished to have answered by travelers to Africa. The questions they posed reflected the range of interests among English observers of the continent since the early years of contact. These included requests for information about whether the rain there was very hot, what kinds of minerals were to be found in the ground, what kinds of sticks the people used to clean their teeth, and into how many months they divided the year. Travelers were asked to describe the weapons that the Africans carried into war and the stories they told about the creation of the world. Sometimes they were asked whether it was true that African children were born reddish, yellow, or even white—and then would turn black in a matter of days.[57]

Some English observers who were not convinced that a person could change color so dramatically over the course of an individual life nevertheless did accept that groups of persons had done just that over a longer period of time. In 1682, at a meeting of the Royal Society, its president Christopher Wren told his members "that Europeans, by continuing to inhabit in Africa, have been found to turn black, and that Blacks in England, after a few generations, become white." "We see the Blacks do not quit their complexion immediately by removing into another Climate," Thomas Burnet acknowledged in his 1684 *Theory of the Earth*, before he added that "their posterity changeth by little and little, and after some generations they become altogether like the people of the Country where they are."[58]

An interested reader of Burnet might well have wanted to ask whether this was the manner in which some humans had become white in the first place. In the seventeenth century, none of the English authors who maintained that the climate was the cause of black skin stated an opinion about what the original color of the human species had been. Many of them seemed to assume that it was white, and at the least not black, since their inquiries into the causes of complexion so often started in the course of attempts to explain the blackness of the Africans rather than their own whiteness. However, that the earliest humans had been white would have been a position difficult to reconcile with the version of scriptural history most common in early-modern English culture. The Garden of Eden was believed to have been in Asia, and so were the mountains of Ararat, where the Ark of Noah was said to have come to rest after the Flood. Perhaps for this reason, the authors who accepted that the climate had produced the variety of human colors in the present tended simply to state that this was the case and not to ask too eagerly after what the earliest one of these colors might have been.[59]

As a matter of fact, in the early-modern period, only those authors who dismissed the classical account of complexion articulated the position that the earliest humans must have been white. George Best was the first such author, for what made the curse of black skin such an arresting spectacle in his account was the fact of Noah's sons "all three being white, and their wives also." In the middle of the seventeenth century, even as Browne and Boyle dismissed the view that Best had advanced about the cause of black skin, their own remarks about the matter were informed by a similar opinion. Their several theories about the cause of blackness were so many efforts to "declare how and when the seede of Adam did first receave this tincture," according to Browne, and in the process to determine what Boyle said would have been the particular circumstances under which "a race of *Negroes* might be begun, though none of the Sons of *Adam* for many Precedent Generations were of that Complexion."[60]

Finally, the authors from this period who were not convinced by any of the reasons for blackness that had so far been advanced, and who concluded instead that it would have to be considered one of God's secret works, could have been taken to suggest that God had separately created the peoples of various colors in the world. In this context, none of these authors made at all clear how or when God had made these peoples—who were "all borne of Adam and Eve," as Gómara made certain to assure his reader, and in this sense were "all serving one humane nature," in the phrase of Purchas.[61]

This premise even framed the story of the Curse that Best had told. For Best, as well as for Sandys, the Curse fixed the origin of black skin within the context of the one family that had been left alive after the Flood. Ham's offense had been to disobey his father's order, in order that his son might rule over those of his brothers, and the curse that God placed upon Chus and all of his descendants was meant to warn children to obey their parents. Best's story of the Curse, in other words, drew at once upon a profound distinction between black and white persons and upon their closeness deep in the past—to the point of their common origin in an intimate struggle for power between father and son.

In short, in the early-modern period, English encounters with the peoples of Africa may at times have strained, but still had not started to cast serious doubt upon, the belief set down in Acts: that God "hath made of one blood all nations of men."[62]

This belief in the oneness of humankind could in some cases threaten to render the differences between persons almost trivial by comparison. In this vein, Purchas had called the shades of skin color no more than accidents on the surface of the essence of the human form. After all, it was form and not color that had figured as the central human feature for Richard Jobson when, in answer to an offer of slaves from a local merchant on the Gambia River, Jobson stated that "we were a people" who did not "buy or sell one another, or any that had our owne shapes." In moments such as these, we can discern in English culture a certain strain of indifference to color even among authors who did remark upon the black color of the Africans.

To be sure, as scholars of early-modern drama have established, the English tended to favor white over black as the standard for beauty. Ben Jonson had intended his *Masque of Blackness* and *Masque of Beauty* to complement each other as masque and anti-masque. In these works the desire of the daughters of Niger to be "blanched" by the sun over Britain reflected a familiar preference in English culture. This preference had figured as an aversion for Best, who described the fear among travelers to Africa that they would be burned black by the sun. Sandys reported "haply" that this would not happen, and by the same token he added that the black peoples of Africa would not "grow to better complexion" even if they moved elsewhere.

This assessment seemed correct to Purchas: in the chapter on the empire of Monomotapa in his *Pilgrimage,* he noted that it followed from the observation that the sun was not the source of blackness that Africans could not look to northward travel with "hope or hap of good colour." Black skin may have counted as one of the accidents of the human form, but Purchas still believed that it was an ugly and unfortunate one.[63]

In early-modern English culture, though, there were two ancient traditions that pointed toward an alternative evaluation of the appearance of the Africans. The first one of these was the classical tradition from Homer, Herodotus, and Diodorus in which the people of eastern Ethiopia were considered "the tallest and fairest and longest-lived of all men," as Herodotus had written. The second one could be traced back to the Old Testament, where in the Song of Songs the bride of Solomon had presented herself as "blacke, but comely." In the early-modern period, this was the tradition within which the beauty of African peoples was most often recorded. In the song that began the *Masque of Blackness,* the character of Niger was thus honored as the father of a "beautious race," even as his daughters are said to be "but blacke in face."[64]

In the second half of the seventeenth century, European travelers started to remark more often that the Africans were beautiful in spite of their complexion. According to such observers, the color of the Africans could be balanced against their open features, piercing white-and-brown eyes, and well-proportioned limbs. In England, the most famous example drawn from this tradition was Aphra Behn's Oroonoko. "Bating his colour," she said, "there cou'd be nothing in Nature more beautiful, agreeable and handsome" than he was. Browne and Boyle concluded from such remarks that blackness should not be seen as "inconsistent with Beauty, which even to our European Eyes," as Boyle explained, "consists not so much in Colour, as an Advantageous Stature, a Comely Symmetry of the parts of the Body, and Good Features in the face." These were qualities of shape, which Boyle believed the black peoples of Africa certainly could possess.[65]

Even if color was to be seen as one of the elements of beauty, the case against the Africans was far from certain. As Browne and Boyle both pointed out, the Africans tended to favor black over white as much as the English preferred white to black. "Navigators tell us of Black Nations,"

Boyle reported, that their own opinion of their color was so close to the opposite of the one that was current in the nations of Europe "that they paint the Devil White." In his classic treatment of Anglo-American attitudes, *White over Black,* Winthrop Jordan asserted that English observers perceived the peoples of Africa—in their supposed heathenism, barbarism, and blackness—as "little other than Devils incarnate." This was a phrase from the 1677 fourth edition of the *Travels* of Thomas Herbert, which described his voyages to Africa and Asia. The comparison appears to have been uncommon. In this period, many more observers of Africa reported that they had been struck to learn that the people there viewed white as the color most associated with evil.[66]

When travelers from Europe first arrived in towns on the Senegal River, Purchas wrote, the local people had huddled around them to study their skin. They rubbed it with spit to see whether its "whitenesse were naturall, or no," and when they discovered "it to bee no tincture, they were out of measure astonished" at what they had found. Their own sense of color was rather different. Over the course of the sixteenth century, as Europeans in Africa worked to establish regular contact with the peoples who lived along the western coast, they would on occasion note that their objects of worship were small black images. De Marees recalled that in Guinea, when he asked the people about their god, "they made answere, that hee is blacke like themselves." By the time he put out the 1617 third edition of his *Pilgrimage,* Purchas had learned that the Christians in northern Ethiopia held "their blacke colour in such estimation" that they would "paint CHRIST, the Angels, and Saints blacke." On the other hand, "the Divell, *Judas, Casphas, Pilate,* and wicked persons they paint white."[67]

Heylyn, too, reported in a poem that he printed in his descriptions of the world that in the Land of Negros the people "in their native beauty most delight, / And in contempt doe paint the Divell white." Heylyn was appalled: he said the Negros were "for the greater part Idolaters." Nevertheless, in the decades that followed, as more and more European observers learned that in Africa the devil was often painted white and the gods often depicted as black, Heylyn's harsh condemnation was almost never repeated. These observations were simply presented without further comment. For their part, Browne and Boyle took them to indicate that one reason blackness could not have come from an ancient curse was that it did not at all seem like a curse to the Africans.[68]

"Nor can I imagine," wrote the ship captain Thomas Phillips, in the journal of his 1694 voyage to Guinea, why the peoples there "should be despis'd for their colour." This was in May. In July the ship that Phillips captained, whose name was the *Hannibal,* would sail for Barbados with seven hundred enslaved persons. Three hundred and twenty of these persons would perish on the Middle Passage. Most of them died of dysentery, and some of smallpox, but a dozen of them leaped overboard and held themselves underwater until they drowned in the ocean. Phillips had been warned that a number of them might do this, "for 'tis their belief," he had heard, "that when they die they return home." He had been advised to cut off the arms or legs of "the most willful" members of his human cargo, because they also appeared to believe that in the event that they lost a limb, even their death would not bring their return. Phillips refused "to put in practice such barbarity and cruelty," however; and it was in order to account for this refusal that he turned for the first time in his account to discuss the cause of black skin.

Phillips said that the black skin of the peoples of Africa was caused by the climate there but that its ultimate source was God, since it was only the effect of "the climate it has pleas'd God to appoint them." He offered no reason why God might have appointed them such a climate, and seems to have believed that there might not have been one. Aside from their lack of Christian religion—which was "their misfortune more than fault," according to Phillips—the Africans were "as much the work of God's hands, and no doubt as dear to him as ourselves." Then, in a sentence that speaks at once to a broad cultural bias for white over black and the ease with which this bias could be set aside or even turned upside down in the early-modern period, Phillips went on to reflect, "I can't think there is any intrinsick value in one colour more than another, nor that white is better than black, only we think it so because we are so." No doubt the black people only did the same, who "in odium of the colour, say, the devil is white."[69]

For more than half a century, scholars have argued that when early English authors wrote about the peoples of Africa they in truth wrote only about themselves. According to Winthrop Jordan, the particular American fascination with the Africans developed out of "the need of transplanted Englishmen to know who it was they were." For "how it was with Negroes was how it was with themselves." This argument was the thread that bound up his narrative, Jordan explained, and it has as well bound his work to the more recent studies of a number of scholars, most of whom have been careful to record their debt to Jordan's classic text.[70]

In such studies, English observers seem to have seen the peoples of Africa not only as different from themselves but as different in an exact sense. They were their own perfect opposites. The Africans were savage rather than civil, heathen rather than Christian, and, as much as any people, beasts rather than men. Around the time when regular contact with the Guinea coast was established, Englishmen were troubled over what they took to be "the disintegration of social and moral controls at home," Jordan observed. They looked to Africa as a site upon which to project the disordered impulses and desires that they sensed within themselves. Their image of Africa thus came into focus over time as a sort of mirror into which the English reflected their own most shameful traits. If these could be found to be the characteristic traits of the people in some distant part of the world, then they safely could be believed not to be their own. *It is not we who are guilty,* Jordan imagined as the unwritten epigraph in English accounts of Africans, *but them.*[71]

In this charged context, a detail that might otherwise hardly have been noticed was seized upon to dramatic effect. The English were one of the fairest-skinned nations, whereas the peoples of Africa were some of the darkest in the world. It is a measure of the powerful impression that this fact had upon them that, almost from the first, the English stressed that the Africans were black, whereas they were white, "beinge coloures utterlye contrary," as Richard Eden remarked in 1555. In the decades that followed, Jordan asserted, the English fastened upon blackness as the visible emblem of the condition of the Africans as their own perverse negation. Jordan did discuss some of the inquiries from this period into the causes of complexion. In particular, he dwelled upon what he called "the extraordinary persistence" of the Curse of Ham, and said that this "was probably sustained by a feeling that blackness could scarcely be anything *but* a curse." At the same time, he held that the ultimate cause of the blackness that the English perceived upon the bodies of the Africans was the blackness that they had hidden within themselves. This was what Jordan meant when he said that "the Negro's color attained greatest significance not as a scientific problem but as a social fact." It was a fact that was all but created, loaded with meaning, and then turned to vicious effect in a context that was social above all else.[72]

I have a different sense of the sources that have been discussed in this chapter. To me, these sources do not seem to be responses to certain social pressures and do not seem so clearly to fulfill certain social needs. They do not seem to hold within them much of the inner lives of the persons who composed them. Nor do they seem to be attempts to explain and defend some particular treatment of the peoples of Africa, such as the enslavement of some of them. Rather, over the course of the period considered in this chapter, English efforts to discover the source of black skin seem above all to be attempts to solve what Jordan referred to as a scientific problem—but which might be described more broadly as an intellectual one.

During this period, inquiries into the causes of complexion were tied up with many of the issues that the English believed they had to understand in order to know their world. To ask whether the heat of the sun was the cause of blackness was also to ask what was the effect of the climate upon the human body, what was the climate like in the several regions of the world, and what kind of respect was owed to the works of the classical geographers. At a later date, to ask this same question would require one to ask, in addition, whether and at what rate the color of a person could change and whether the peoples of the world had all descended from the single act of Creation revealed in the Bible. On the other hand, to assert that the cause of blackness was to be found in a curse set down in the Old Testament was to make a statement about the proper interpretation of a brief but ominous passage in Genesis and about whether peoples in the present could be traced to persons named in the Table of Nations.

In turn, around the middle of the seventeenth century, those authors who proposed that blackness had come from the phenomenon known as seminal impression had to accept that the objects that mothers perceived could affect their children in the womb. Those who suggested that blackness had first been painted on the body drew upon novel theories about the effect of artifice upon human development. To focus instead upon the location of blackness was to seek to determine how many layers of skin there were and in what manner the color of the blood was communicated to the skin's surface. To reject all of these opinions was to put forward an alternative account of all or at least some of these issues. To conclude that blackness was a secret whose source was hidden within nature or God was to make some concession to the limits of human understanding.

We have seen throughout this book that English observers of Africa were not quite so concerned with the color of the peoples there as they would later become. Now we have also seen that when they did take an interest in blackness enough to inquire into its cause, their answers involved them in a larger and more diverse set of issues than has often been assumed. In his immense 1621 *Anatomy of Melancholy,* in the course of a digression about the effects of the air upon terrestrial affairs, Robert Burton gave some sense of this range when he asked, "Whence comes this variety of complections, colours, plants, birds, beasts, mettals, peculiar almost to every place?" Burton was struck by the variety of complexions and colors, which in the case of humans could be seen to include black, dun, and white. But this struck him in the same way as did the variety of plants, birds, beasts, and metals. It was one of many features of the world that a curious observer would want to explain. "Is it from the ayre," Burton wondered, "or from the soyle, or influence of starres, or some other secret cause?"[73]

Burton left these questions unanswered in his book—and this too was appropriate. Over the course of the early-modern period in English culture, discourse about the causes of complexion advanced rather little. The classical theory that blackness was produced by the heat of the sun was most often accepted until around the turn of the seventeenth century, then fell out of favor, and then came to the fore in a more modern form in the second half of the century. The view that blackness came from a biblical curse was introduced into English culture in a work that was first published in 1578, but was almost never endorsed in print, even if authors never ceased to discuss it as a possible but erroneous opinion. That the black sperm of African men could be the source of the black skin of African peoples was noted in a book translated into English in 1597, and that the particular features of the

African soil were the cause of blackness was proposed in a book that appeared in the next year; but neither one of these views ever received much support. Nor did the several proposals developed around the middle of the seventeenth century by Browne, Bulwer, and Boyle. In this period, perhaps the most revealing response to black skin was to admit that it must be some kind of secret, since so far each explanation that had been advanced for it had been flawed. No one theme emerged out of this thicket of positions. The search after the cause of black skin remained uncertain and incomplete. It was most properly framed, as Burton understood, in the form of a question.

What stands out to the modern reader is how little this state of affairs seems to have disturbed English observers of Africa in the early-modern period. They had tended to touch upon the causes of complexion in passing and then move on to other points of interest, as if no important affairs depended upon what they had written. As a matter of fact, not much did depend upon the digressions, asides, letters, verses, notes, and remarks that have appeared over the course of this chapter. The Atlantic commerce in enslaved persons from Africa, in particular, drew support from a different intellectual tradition. This was a period in English culture before blackness acquired its fatal association with slavery.

Epilogue

THIS BOOK has described the tradition of ideas from which slavery in the English Atlantic world first drew support. The roots of this tradition went deep in Western culture. Indeed, in early-modern England, its clearest and most powerful expression was understood to be the collection of texts known as the *Corpus Juris Civilis,* which had been produced for the governance of the Roman Empire. As has often been the case, however, the ideas in Roman law outlived the particular social order that these ideas were at first intended to describe. In early-modern England, Roman law was still seen to offer a current account of the standard structure of human affairs. As English authors worked to describe and explain the common customs of slavery, they often did so with reference to the Roman legal tradition.

The Roman tradition, as these authors understood it, defined slavery and freedom in simple terms. Freedom was the natural condition of humankind, but it was not necessarily a permanent one. Slavery had been introduced over time, as one of the institutions of modern life. Slavery arose when the natural freedom of all persons was taken from some persons as a result of accident and misfortune, most often for captives taken in war. It thus developed in the context of a world marked by radical reversals of fortune. At root it could be defined as the condition of persons who had been enslaved, and to speak about slavery was to refer back to an account of its sources.[1]

Early-modern English culture was saturated in accounts of the sources of slavery: the terrible and dramatic transformations of free persons into slaves. The drama of slavery on the Roman model was embedded in works of drama and literature, popular histories and studies of the common law, and philosophical reflections upon politics and detailed descriptions of the customs of the peoples of the world. To be sure, the prospect that free persons could be threatened with enslavement presented a special concern to

English authors at a time when it could have seemed the people of the nation had at last rid themselves of this ancient form of subjection.

There was one context in particular where English observers in this period received and focused their attention upon accounts of the sources of slavery. From around the turn of the seventeenth century, new descriptions of the peoples of Africa had started to circulate in English culture. As described in these reports, the customs of enslavement in Africa could be seen to fit more or less within the familiar Roman model. In the early decades of the English African slave trade, this simple observation was as much of a defense as English observers often bothered to provide. It was not America that mattered most in these efforts to defend the development of American slavery—it was Africa. Africa was the site of slavery that the Roman tradition was best prepared to explain.

In the Roman tradition, slavery was understood to arise from a stark and particular situation. Its most proximate condition was death, and enslavement was framed as the final alternative for persons who would otherwise have lost their lives. That said, what happened in the moment when free persons were enslaved could have permanent consequences. The authors of the *Corpus Juris* noted that to be enslaved was to become an article of property, which could be traded from person to person and place to place. They observed in addition that it was a tenet of the common law of all nations that slave status was passed down from mothers to their children. Slavery arose from a particular context but then entered others, as it produced property relations and became permanent and heritable over time.[2]

That the status of slaves was permanent and heritable was well known in the early-modern English Atlantic world. It was one of the principles of Roman law that was received and incorporated into the common law of England. From Bracton to Edward Coke, the most important authorities on the common law accepted that even if there were no more persons who were enslaved within the realm, the status of villeins bore some resemblance to that of slaves. Both ancient slavery and medieval villeinage had started in war, and both were permanent and heritable over time. If the common law departed from the civil law, it was on a more minor point about how to determine the status of children in cases in which one parent was free and the other was not. The common law held that in cases of this kind the status of children would follow that of their father. In contrast, the civil law held that the status of such children would follow that of their mother. It was a doctrine that had come to be referred to with the Latin phrase *partus sequitur ventrem*.[3]

From the start, almost all of the African persons in the English American colonies were considered to be slaves. Their status was for life, and it passed down to their children. This was a matter of common custom before it was ever set down in statute law. Indeed, the permanent and heritable character of slave status was the principal feature that marked it off from the status of English servants in the colonies. There was some dispute, in particular in the mainland American colonies, about how to determine the status of the children of mixed unions between enslaved and free persons. The colonial assembly in Virginia was the first to settle this dispute with the enactment of a statute. In 1662, the assembly codified what seems to have been the standard practice across English America. It declared that all children born in Virginia "shalbe bond or free only according to the condition of the mother."[4]

Indeed, in this period, America moved more and more toward the center of discourse on slavery in the English Atlantic world. The Atlantic slave trade fed the rapid development of colonial societies that were founded upon the forced labor of enslaved Africans. Here the sources of African slavery were far off in the distance. An entire creole generation of slaves were born who had never seen Africa. Toward the end of the seventeenth century, informed English observers across the Atlantic world started to come to terms with what their nation had done. Some sensed a certain pressure to defend the institution that they had established and were now so hard at work to expand. They turned their attention toward what American slavery was, and would become, as distinct from where it came from.

The importance of this shift cannot be overstated. In truth, it was the ultimate cause of all the shifts in discourse that now began to take place across the English Atlantic world. To describe the sources of African slavery was to explain how it happened that certain free persons had come to be enslaved. But this was less and less the central issue in the English American colonies, because here what was needed was the reason for which an entire order of persons who had been enslaved could never become free. The

Roman legal tradition was well prepared to explain the transformation of free persons into slaves. However, authors in the Roman tradition had always been much less focused upon the reasons for which slavery could be passed down and continue over time. Novel ideas and alternative traditions would need to be seized upon for this purpose. And English authors bent to the task—with all the perverse inventiveness that marked their nation's push into the Atlantic world.[5]

❧

Some authors never overcame the shock of this shift from the Old World to the New. From Morgan Godwyn to Thomas Tryon to Aphra Behn, a small number of English authors who had traveled across the ocean to the American slave colonies were all but overwhelmed at what they had seen. No ancient tradition of ideas had prepared them to encounter the vast and ordered cruelty of the plantation complex. These authors left more or less untouched the traditional Roman account of the sources of African slavery. They asserted that it was not an adequate defense to note that the persons held as slaves in the Caribbean had arrived there as slaves. No person deserved to be treated in this manner.

Some other observers of the Atlantic slave system in this period found that they were able to ease the pressure of this criticism. For if it was accepted that the masters of slaves in the Caribbean did have them in their lawful possession, then in truth no more than the most moderate reforms could be demanded. As the product of accident and misfortune in human affairs, slavery was never expected to be much more than barely preferable to death. It was perhaps for this reason that merchants and ship captains, such as Thomas Phillips and Jean Barbot, tended to respond with such cool unconcern to the mutinies and suicides to which their human cargo so often resorted on the Middle Passage. What was more, the traders in slaves could reassure themselves with the observation that the men and women who chose death over slavery in America had never made it as far as the sugar islands in order to form a more accurate opinion of the institution.[6]

As a matter of fact, some English authors had even started to entertain the idea that the slave colonies in the Caribbean could make some positive claim of their own. Remarks to this effect were little more than scattered traces of an incipient impulse. At this point, no one who understood the state of affairs on Barbados or Jamaica was much prepared to extol its social virtues. Even so, several observers who were aware of conditions in the Caribbean did propose that the slave system that had been established there offered a real benefit to the persons upon whose forced labor it depended. These authors moved to make a virtue out of what they understood to be a necessity.

One such author was none other than the ship captain Thomas Phillips. In the course of his passage across the Atlantic to deliver enslaved persons from Guinea to the Caribbean, several of these persons had starved themselves to death and a dozen had jumped overboard and drowned themselves in the ocean. Phillips had heard that this tended to happen. Sharks would follow slave ships across the Middle Passage and devour the persons who were left in their wake. Phillips noted that the Africans "had a more dreadful apprehension of *Barbadoes* than we can have of hell." But then he explained that this apprehension was unfounded. For "in reality," he wrote, "they live much better there than in their own country." Three weeks before his ship, the *Hannibal,* arrived in Barbados, the island was rocked by a hurricane. In the aftermath, plague had broken out. Phillips himself was seized with a case of vertigo that left him deaf. He maintained that the only reason the Africans did not realize that Barbados was much better for them than Guinea was that "home is home, &c." And with this piece of simple wisdom, he left the matter at that.[7]

Another English author from this period who was prepared to defend the slave system in the Caribbean was the eminent naturalist Hans Sloane. Sloane had served as a physician to the colonial governor of Jamaica for fifteen months from 1687 to 1689. In 1707, he published the first volume of his *Natural History of Jamaica.* His main aim in this work was to produce a complete description of the plants on the island, but he also included an introduction that in part described its human inhabitants—well over half of whom were enslaved Africans at the time when he was there.[8]

As Sloane started to explain how these Africans had come to the island of Jamaica, he reported upon the account of the slave trade that he had heard. He said that the adults on the western coast of Africa were "thought to be haters of their own Children, and therefore 'tis believed that they sell and dispose of them to Strangers for Money," who carried them as slaves to the Caribbean colonies. This was a rumor that had started to spread in English discourse in recent decades. As we have seen, Richard Ligon had heard it on Barbados and the geographer Richard Blome had included it in his description of Guinea. Even before the development of the English Atlantic slave trade, the idea had started to circulate that in some areas of Africa, parents did not hesitate to sell their children, "regarding more the price then the condition of their slavery." This was what some Muslim traders had told George Sandys near Cairo in 1611. It could have seemed to indicate that those who sold slaves approached their business with the same dispassionate attitude as those who purchased them.[9]

Nevertheless, for his part, Hans Sloane dismissed such reports out of hand. He had observed that the Africans on Jamaica were so attached to their children that masters dared not sell "one of their little ones, unless they care not whether their Parents hang themselves or no." What Sloane said about the slave trade to the Caribbean colonies was rather that the people on the western coast of Africa were "divided into several Captainships." When these went to war, "besides those slain in Battle many Prisoners are taken, who are sold for slaves and brought hither." This was the standard account at the time of the sources of African slavery, as even Ligon and Blome well understood. No doubt it carried the implication that precious few parents in Guinea had chosen to sell their children across the Atlantic Ocean. The Africans on Jamaica had arrived there due to accident and misfortune alone.[10]

That said, Sloane was not a man inclined to see either the human or the natural world as the product of accident. When his *Natural History of Jamaica* appeared in print, he was the secretary of the Royal Society. His deepest aim in this work was to recover and describe the order of the Creation within its evident and abundant variation. He concluded that observers were "ignorant in the History of Nature" who considered natural facts to be "the Productions of Chance." They were, rather, the products of divine intention. When he turned to the human facts he found on Jamaica, Sloane also hoped to find some providential pattern in place. He noted that the Africans who were enslaved on Jamaica had also been slaves back in Guinea. He was confident that they were "more easily treated by the *English* here, than by their own Country-People, wherefore they would not often willingly change Masters." An institution founded upon chance could thus be seen, from a different perspective, as one which could have been founded upon choice.[11]

After he had made this observation, Sloane moved to a topic whose connection to it he did not seem to perceive. He rehearsed with vivid precision the punishments that were inflicted upon the enslaved Africans on Jamaica. He said that slaves who committed minor offenses would have half of one foot chopped off with an axe. Slaves who refused to work were tied up and whipped with lance-wood switches and then salt and pepper were rubbed into their wounds. Slaves who attempted to escape from their masters had heavy iron rings fastened to their neck and ankles or a spur placed in their mouth. Those who rebelled were nailed to the ground, with each limb attached to a crooked stick, and then burned gradually from their hands and feet to their head. Sloane remarked that the victims of these measures endured them with "great Constancy." The Africans on Jamaica seemed almost to welcome death. They believed that when they died they returned home.[12]

The spectacular violence of the planters in the Caribbean no doubt could have been seen as one issue with the view that their slaves would willingly have accepted their status, even if in truth no such choice had ever been offered to them. But this was not even the most uncomfortable feature of the slave system in the English Caribbean for authors who worked to defend it. That was the fact that the planters had so far refused to allow the persons whom they owned and controlled to adopt the Christian faith that the planters at least claimed to profess. Even the Iberian nations were known to have held mass baptisms beside slave ships about to depart from the western coast of Africa. However cruel the Iberian Atlantic empires had been, it could not be denied that they had offered at least this measure of salvation to the persons whom they then tortured and worked to death. In their own most treasured Atlantic colonies, Englishmen had not even done this. They had no motive but their own interest to offer in defense of the slave system.

From the start of the Restoration, it had been the position of the English Crown that slaves in the American colonies should be instructed in the faith. Even before he issued the first charter to the royal African company that mentioned a commerce in slaves, Charles II had issued instructions to this effect. He demanded that learned and orthodox ministers be sent to the colonies to ensure that the persons who were sent there as slaves were "invited and made capable of baptism in the Christian faith." In the decades that followed, the officials who oversaw the colonies from London repeated such demands time and again to the colonial administrators and assemblies who worked to establish and maintain the slave system in America. The cause of conversion would soon receive a vital instrument with the foundation of the Society for the Propagation of the Gospel in Foreign Parts, which received its royal charter in 1701. Ministers were sent out across the English Atlantic world to preach the Gospel to those enslaved persons upon whose labor that world depended.[13]

To its metropolitan advocates, the cause of conversion in the colonies seemed as if it would advance the interests of the nation as well as the Kingdom of Christ. These men were convinced that slaves who received the Word would perform the duties of their office with all the meekness and forbearance that Christ had prescribed to the servants of masters. English visitors to the Caribbean, from Richard Ligon to the Quaker leader George Fox, tended to share this conviction. They started to envision a form of "Christian slavery," in the phrase of one scholar, that would contain the open resistance and rebellions that so often threatened the sugar islands in this period. Slave and master would be wrapped within reciprocal bonds of affection and obedience. As Christ had worked not for the destruction of the law but rather its fulfillment, so the Gospel would tend to secure the fragile social order at the lucrative outer rim of the English Atlantic empire.[14]

Through the end of the seventeenth century, calls for the baptism and conversion of slaves produced little action in the English Caribbean. As a rule, the planters opposed them. The most visceral and immediate concern the planters presented was that slaves who heard the Word would fail to understand the subtle promise of the Savior. The freedom that Christ held out was purely spiritual. Some slaves might wish to break their temporal bonds as well.

Concerns of this kind were especially acute on Barbados. As a matter of fact, it was in part in order to address such concerns that George Fox sailed there in 1671. He hoped to assure the planters that the Quakers who had started to invite slaves to attend their services had no intention to teach them to rebel. He received a skeptical audience. In 1675, another Friend named William Edmundson arrived on the island with plans to initiate the enslaved Africans into "the way of Life and Peace." Soon Edmundson was called before the colonial governor to answer an accusation from the planters that he had instead worked to make their slaves "Rebels, and rise and cut their Throats." This indeed seemed to have been their plan. In May 1675, a massive slave rebellion was discovered just before it was to have broken out. In the aftermath of this crisis, the colonial assembly passed an act to prevent "Quakers, from bringing Negroes to their Meetings." The planters on Barbados would well remember the lesson they drew from this episode. In 1680, when their representatives in London were presented with plans for the conversion of slaves, they responded that to pursue them would "endanger the island, inasmuch as converted negroes grow more perverse and intractable." This the planters were determined to prevent.[15]

However, the most common—and perhaps also the most resonant—concern that was presented in response to calls for the conversion of slaves in the English Atlantic world was one of a different kind. It had less to do with the effect of conversion upon the attitudes and actions of slaves and more with the effect upon the lawful duties of masters. In particular, it was the concern that masters who bestowed the blessed sacrament upon their slaves would then have to set them free.

This concern arose within a specific early-modern context of ideas. As we have seen, ideas about slavery in early-modern European culture were set within the broad reception of Roman law. In Roman law, slavery was understood to be a part of the law of nations, which was a collection of the customs common to all the nations of the world. But in early-modern Europe, it was well known that not all the nations of the world had continued to practice the old Roman customs of slavery. Over time, some important amendments and exceptions had been introduced. Perhaps the most important one of these was that at some point in the late medieval period, the nations that then understood themselves to compose a portion of the world known as Christendom had come to a consensus never to enslave each other. Outside the borders of Christendom, the law of nations would continue in full effect. Even within Christendom, Christian peoples would be allowed to hold people from outside the Christian sphere as slaves. But Christians would not do the same to one another.[16]

This exception to the law of nations was well known in early-modern culture, even as the nations that used to make up Christendom now understood themselves to make up a part of the world more often known as Europe. Perhaps the first modern author to describe and explain the consensus that Christian nations would not enslave their fellow Christians, even when taken captive in war, was the Spanish leader of the Second Scholastic, Francisco de Vitoria. His treatment of this issue was then repeated and elaborated upon in the work of the influential scholar of the civil law Alberico Gentili. From Bodin to Grotius, most of the principal early-modern interpreters of the Roman tradition commented with approval upon this modern departure from ancient custom. Soon learned studies of contemporary customs started to observe that the peoples of Europe had established an important exception to the common customs of enslavement.[17]

In the English Atlantic world, however, the prohibition upon enslavement between members of the Christian faith appeared to have an unintended consequence. If Christians could not enslave each other, then Christians could not hold one another as slaves. And yet this was exactly what would take place if the slaves of Christian masters were converted to the faith. The belief that conversion thus entailed emancipation was widespread across the English Atlantic world. It was cited in English court cases that affirmed the property status of enslaved Africans who had not been converted. On some rare occasions in the American colonies, enslaved Africans themselves pointed to their conversion in petitions for freedom. The planters too were well aware that Christian slaves would have to be freed. This was one of the main concerns the planters presented in response to calls for slave conversion.[18]

The proponents of slave conversion were assiduous in their efforts to respond to this concern. They assured the planters that the salvation of souls was their sole aim. They noted that the baptism of slaves had never seemed to undermine the development of slavery across the Iberian Atlantic world or indeed also in the French Atlantic empire. They admitted that perhaps some reforms would need to be introduced if the English colonial plantation was to become a site of salvation. The violence would need to be curtailed to some extent. Enslaved persons would need to be allowed to enter into Christian marriages. They would need to have some time off from work on Sundays to attend services. But almost never did the proponents of slave conversion indicate that the spiritual and temporal purposes of the plantation would conflict. Rather, what they said was that these purposes would work in tandem and reinforce each other.

The intentions and methods of the proponents of conversion were well captured in a brief conversation that took place on Barbados sometime late in the 1640s. In this period, Richard Ligon worked on a sugar plantation, where he became acquainted with an enslaved man he knew as Sambo. When Sambo expressed a desire to become a Christian, Ligon took the matter up with the master of the plantation. The planter opposed Sambo's conversion, he said, because "being once a Christian, he could no longer count him a Slave." Ligon replied that what he proposed was rather different: "I desired him to make a Slave a Christian." But the planter was steadfast in his opposition. He explained that the people on Barbados "were governed by the Lawes of *England*," and he noted that "by those Lawes, we could not make a Christian a Slave." To make a slave a Christian, in other words, was also to make him free. Were the planter to do this, he would open up a chain of unintended consequences that could threaten the entire plantation complex. He was sure that "all the Planters in the Iland would curse him" for what he had done.[19]

At the time, Ligon had no response to this concern. He could do no more than lament that in spite of his efforts "poor Sambo was kept out of the Church." However, in the decades that followed, the proponents of slave conversion across the English Atlantic world adopted an approach that Ligon had not anticipated. If the laws of England did seem to demand that conversion entailed emancipation, then the proponents of conversion would simply produce new laws.

The first unambiguous one of these laws was enacted in Virginia in 1667. The short preamble to the statute noted that some doubts had arisen as to whether slaves who received "the blessed sacrament of baptisme, should by vertue of their baptisme be made ffree." The answer the statute provided was that they should not. It declared that baptism "doth not alter the condition of the person as to his bondage or ffreedome." The *Fundamental Constitutions* that were drawn up as a plan of government for Carolina in 1669 made a similar declaration. The document allowed that slaves could become members of whatever church they pleased. But it said that no slave would on this basis be released from his master's dominion. Rather, he would remain "in the same state and condition as he was in before." As a matter of fact, it was in order to stress this point that the *Fundamental Constitutions* then included its most famous article, the one that defined the nature and extent of a master's dominion. It stated that a master in Carolina would have "absolute power and authority over his negro slaves," and then added the crucial provision that this would be the case for slaves "of what opinion or religion soever."[20]

The insight reflected in these documents was that in America an exception could be made to the common customs of Christendom—which were in themselves an exception to the common customs of the world. Soon this insight was reduced to a convenient shorthand and, in that form, started to circulate in statutes across the English Atlantic world. The first one of these statutes was the first comprehensive slave code for Jamaica, which was passed in 1684. This act removed all doubt about the consequences of conversion with one simple clause. It stated "that no Slave shall be free by becoming a *Christian*." The Jamaican slave code was then adopted with minor revisions as the first comprehensive code for Carolina in 1691. This act repeated the same clause. It stated "that no slave shall be free by becoming a christian."[21]

No such statement ever appeared in the comprehensive slave codes that were passed around this time on Barbados. But the proponents of conversion back in the metropole were hard at work to assure the planters that they posed no threat to their mode of production. A number of proposed statutes circulated in manuscript that aimed to make clear that the salvation of souls would not come at the cost of the plantation complex in the colonies. One of these documents, which appears to have been drafted in the first half of the 1680s, was titled "An Act on Barbados." This act noted that few of the enslaved Africans on the island would ever be converted if the planters continued to believe that "if they are soe converted they become free." What the act proposed instead was to establish that all enslaved Africans who "shall turne to the Christian faith" would be treated "as heretofore hath been used to be done as if they had never turned to the Christian faith." The conversion of slaves would result in "noe loss or Prejudice" to their masters.[22]

This document is held in manuscript in the papers of Robert Boyle. As we have seen, Boyle was a natural philosopher whose experiments and considerations from 1664 produced little more than tentative speculations about the cause of black skin. He denied that blackness could have come from either the heat of the sun or the Curse of Ham. He added that, no matter its cause, the blackness of the Africans could not be seen as a mark of inferior status. The preference for white over black in European culture mirrored, in Africa, the preference for black over white.

Boyle was also a Christian theologian, and in matters of faith he tended to speak and act with more conviction. Almost from the start of the Restoration, he had been a champion of the cause of conversion in the American colonies, where he focused his attention on the conversion of the native peoples of New England. Soon he turned to the "Laudable Design of Converting Infidels" in the Caribbean islands as well. Over time, he realized that in order to realize this aim he would need to act to remove "certain discouragements & Hinderances of the Conversion of the Infidels." He started to collect statutes that proposed to establish that the conversion of infidels in the colonies would not alter their civil status. One of these statutes was the "Act on Barbados."[23]

Another proposed statute from this period that Boyle collected and had transcribed was titled a plan "for the propagating of the Christian Religion and converting of Slaves" in the English colonies. This document declared that no slave, upon his profession of the faith, would be "freed of that service he oweth to his Master." Rather, he would remain "under the same Dominion to his Master as before." After this point, however, the document started to depart from the conventional script in proposals of this kind. It provided that each slave who embraced the Christian faith would be allowed to own property in some form and to provide evidence in court in some cases. The final provision in this document was perhaps the most unusual one. It said that in the small commercial outposts that the English maintained on the western coast of Africa, care should be taken to instruct the native people in the principles of Christian religion. Even the persons whom the English purchased there as slaves should hear the Word of God. Perhaps this would remove some of the dread the Africans were known to feel about their shipment to America. Perhaps the Africans could be persuaded that "by their slavery, their condition will be bettered by their access to knowledge Arts and Religion."[24]

This document seems to have been the work of a preacher and colonist from Scotland named William Dunlop, who would have written it in or around 1690, soon after his return to Britain from Carolina. In the course of his travels, Dunlop had come upon a novel idea in the discourse on slavery in the British Atlantic world. He had realized that the relation between slavery and Christian conversion could run deeper than most earlier authors had understood. It was not only the case that the continued enslavement of Africans in the colonies could be made compatible with their conversion to Christ. It was also that the prospect of conversion could be presented to the Africans in order to induce them to accept their enslavement in the first instance.

As novel as it was at the time, and as little precedent as there was for it in the customs of English merchants on the African coast, this idea drew upon a core conviction in early-modern English culture. The "Act on Barbados" had noted that for the pious Christian "the meanest soule" was endowed with "more real value than the whole world." There was no cause more important than the cause of conversion. And if this was the case, then it was difficult to accept that the spiritual salvation of the Africans would continue to depend upon the accidents of war and famine that worked to deliver some of them as slaves into the New World. All Africans should have access to such an inestimable benefit. The salvation of souls could thus come to seem as much more than the duty of Christian masters. It could become a rationale of its own for the slave trade.

One forum in which this rationale was put forward was a popular periodical named *The Athenian Mercury* that started its prolific print run in 1690. This was a weekly gazette whose editors called upon considerable wit and erudition to answer questions from readers on a broad span of topics. In 1691, the editors printed their first question on the topic of the African slave trade.[25]

A reader of the *Athenian Mercury* had written to ask whether it was "Lawful to Trade with Negroes, and to Buy 'em of one another?" The editors dispatched with the question in a brief response. It was "undoubtedly Lawful to Deal and Traffick with 'em," the editors wrote, "for how should we else convert 'em?" The commerce in persons rested upon the same stable basis. As for the Africans whom Englishmen purchased on the coast, "how hard soever they work afterwards, 'tis the greatest *Kindness* we can do 'em." Their shipment to the colonies as slaves would become the "means to *save* their *Souls*." The editors made a concession to the current state of affairs in the English Caribbean when they noted, in a final clause, that the salvation of the Africans would better be promoted were the kind of "care taken of 'em that ought to be."[26]

Were proper care taken of the Africans, then their enslavement would come to seem as the greatest kindness that Englishmen could perform on their behalf. Even the hard work that they were made to perform in America would be a useful form of discipline. Body and soul would both receive the appropriate instruction. After a time the Africans would ascend to Heaven on a path that Englishmen had laid out for them. This never would have happened if they had been allowed to remain in their native land. The editors of the *Athenian Mercury* had started to articulate an entire Atlantic vision. However, they had started from what was a simple and common premise—that the cause of conversion could be incorporated within the development of American slavery.

Still, the planters in the English Caribbean were unmoved. They continued to oppose the cause of slave conversion. Time and again the planters were assured that the conversion of slaves posed no threat to the extraction of their forced labor. Time and again the planters responded with steadfast opposition. Some observers of this conflict started to suspect that the planters must have some unstated reason for their position. The most sensitive of these observers was the Anglican minister Morgan Godwyn, who had worked for the conversion of slaves for a decade on Barbados.

In his 1680 polemic about the planters who had blocked his efforts, written when he was still on the island, Godwyn produced a vivid record of the mind of the planter class. His method was to describe and then dismantle each argument that had been presented to him to defend the exclusion of the slaves on Barbados from the Christian fold. These arguments all had a common form. They attested to the rapid development of a "strange and before unheard of conceit." Godwyn seems to have heard little of the familiar concerns from this period that slaves who received baptism and instruction in the faith would become intractable or would have to be freed. Rather, the planters on Barbados had told him that their slaves could never become the children of God.[27]

Godwyn reported that he had encountered two versions of this argument. On the one hand, the planters had told him that what prevented the conversion of the slaves on Barbados was the fact of their enslavement. To put on "the *Iron Chain* of Bondage" was to be deprived of all spiritual as well as temporal claims. The absolute power of a master extended over the soul as well as the body of a slave. Indeed, the domination of the one could be taken to entail the radical suppression and even denial of the other. Godwyn refused to accept what he took to be this novel opinion about the awesome power that slavery involved. He maintained that the fact of enslavement touched no more than the outward state of a person. No person could ever acquire control over the inward spirit of another. It was clear to Godwyn that this was the true Christian principle. The Christian God was no respecter of persons, and Christ had invited slaves and masters alike to dwell in the eternal mansion of the Lord.[28]

It was the second argument that Godwyn had heard on Barbados that most disturbed him. The planters had also told him that the reason the African persons held as slaves on the island could not be admitted to the Christian faith was that these were not persons at all. The planters had somehow come to believe, Godwyn reported, "that the *Negro's,* though in their Figure they carry some resemblances of Manhood, yet are indeed *no Men.*" They were treated as beasts of burden on Barbados by people who believed that this was what they were.[29]

Over the course of the early-modern period, English authors across the Atlantic world had often remarked that slaves were persons who had been reduced to the condition of beasts. They could be sold and purchased in the manner of horses and oxen. They could not acquire their own possessions, which was understood to be an entitlement of persons. Their owners used and abused them for their own ends. Like the lambs and calves of sheep and cattle, the children of slaves were born under the dominion of their masters. These were old themes in the discourse on slavery in the Roman tradition, and the learned Godwyn would not have been surprised to find them repeated on Barbados. What shocked him was that the planters there had started to maintain that the treatment of their slaves expressed some deep fact about them.

Godwyn upbraided the planters for their rush to embrace what he termed this "*horrid Principle.*" After his return to London, in 1680, he dedicated much of the rest of his life to an effort to make known what the planters had told him and to impress upon his audience in the metropole how far the planters across the Atlantic had moved from familiar tenets of English culture. As he was aware, none of the well-known descriptions of Africa from this period had made such a brazen attempt to "unman and unsoul" the peoples of the continent, in his phrase. The Europeans who had traveled there had for the most part sent back reports that stressed the resemblance between themselves and the peoples whom they encountered. It was not the supposed brutishness of the Africans that most struck them. It was their clear human status, which appeared to discredit classical fables about the Torrid Zone, and the civil institutions they had developed, which made possible the profitable commerce that was the central purpose of European involvement with Africa in this period.[30]

There was one more critical difference between European encounters with Africans in Africa and in the Atlantic slave colonies. Most of the Africans whom Europeans had met and read about in Africa had never been enslaved. Godwyn explained that on Barbados this was reversed. There the two terms, "*Negro* and *Slave,*" had over time become "Homogenous and Convertible." At the same time, the planters had worked to ensure that the terms "*Negro* and *Christian, Englishman* and *Heathen,*" were understood to be "*Opposites.*" Now the planters who had established this state of affairs had started to claim that it was no accident. It was not a result of chance or misfortune or brute force. It was an expression of the natural order.[31]

This was a new claim in the discourse on slavery in the English Atlantic world. But it was also an old claim. The planters with whom Godwyn had come into conflict were not known to be scholars of the most eminent philosopher of the ancient world. Their common discourse was derived from the Bible—even as Godwyn went to pains to demonstrate that the planters knew rather little of the Good Book. On point after point, they had twisted and distorted the Word to suit their own interest. On Barbados there had seemed to be "*no other* God *but* Money, *nor* Religion *but* Profit."[32]

All the same, when Godwyn heard the planters insist that the Africans were not men, his mind had not first turned to the possible biblical precedents for such an offensive notion. He was instead reminded of what the Spanish had said about the native peoples of America. In his opinion, the planters had advanced a "Conceit like unto which I have read, was some time since invented by the *Spaniards,* to justifie *their murthering the Americans.*" Godwyn was not aware that some Spanish authors had put forward an Aristotelian doctrine of natural slavery in order to defend their conquest of the Indies. What he had read was that the Spanish had denied the human status of their victims. It was this assertion that he connected to what he had heard on Barbados. He placed himself in the role of the famous Dominican friar Las Casas as the Apostle of the Africans. He condemned the actions of the English in America, which seemed to him at least as cruel as the actions of the Spanish had been.[33]

It so happened that, at the same time as Godwyn was at work on his polemic, another Englishman in the Caribbean published a short treatise that seemed to confirm what he said about the mind of the planter class. Thomas Trapham was a medical doctor who had studied at Oxford and departed for Jamaica around 1670. Since then he had lived and worked on the island, where he would become acquainted with Hans Sloane as well as the bookkeeper and memoirist John Taylor. His 1679 *Discourse of the State of Health in the Island of Jamaica* was the only book Trapham ever published. Here he described the air and water and terrain, the diet and habits of the people, and the diseases that tended to afflict them. When he came to the venereal diseases on Jamaica, he paused.

Trapham explained that in order to treat the venereal diseases on Jamaica, it would be useful to know where they had come from. He was certain that they had not come to the island from the English colonists who had made it their home. The first Europeans to suffer from them had been the Spanish, but the diseases had come from elsewhere, for the Spanish had first contracted them in the course of their conquest of the Indies. The most dreadful of the venereal diseases in circulation in the Caribbean had first appeared in the peoples whom the Spanish had conquered and enslaved in the establishment of their vast American empire. Trapham concluded with a flourish that the venereal diseases now found on Jamaica had first appeared in "the animal Indians, and the cursed posterity of the naked *Cham*."[34]

With this reference to the descendants of Ham, Trapham meant to refer to the native peoples of Africa. Godwyn had heard the planters on Barbados assert that the Africans who were enslaved on the island had descended from the same cursed son of Noah. This was one of the assertions that the planters had made in defense of their refusal to offer them baptism and instruction in the Christian faith. Godwyn drew upon the works of Thomas Browne and Robert Boyle to deliver the most detailed rebuke of this assertion in the seventeenth-century English Atlantic world. Godwyn denied that the Africans on Barbados were the descendants of Ham. He said it was impossible to determine which figure in Genesis the Africans had come from. He said no peoples in the present carried the burden of Noah's curse, which had applied only to Canaan and his immediate heirs. As Godwyn was aware, the association between a biblical imprecation and the present status of the Africans was much closer in the Caribbean than in the culture of the metropole. Trapham made reference to it as an accepted fact.[35]

According to Trapham, both the Africans and the native Americans had committed a sin so shameful that he was almost unable to describe it. What he said was that at some point in the past these peoples had seemed to "descend to an unsutable communication." They had entered a "too near alliance" and an "unhappy jumble of the rational with the brutal Nature." They had had sex with beasts. Yaws, the worst of the venereal diseases, had been one result. But Trapham explained that there was also another result of these "unheard of corruptions." God had made man the "Lord and Ruler" of the Creation. The man who so debased himself must relinquish his place in the natural order and submit to the rule of "whoso retains entire Humanity. Hence the Black may well become naturally Slaves," Trapham continued, "and the vast Territories of the Indians be easily invaded and kept in subjection." Spain had been the first of the European powers to act upon this principle. But the Spanish had soon entered into their own unsuitable communication with the peoples they had come to rule in the New World. Now the English had arrived to take over the same mission.[36]

Now, this was the distinctive idiom of Aristotle. The impression of Africa as a sliver of land on the northern border of the Torrid Zone, where animals mixed and bred to produce novel hybrid species, was the context for Aristotle's famous observation that, out of Africa, there was always something new. In turn, when Trapham declared that "the Black may well become naturally Slaves," he followed and filled in an Aristotelian doctrine. Aristotle never included the peoples of Africa, whom he would have known as the Ethiopians, in that order of persons whom nature marked out to be slaves. He believed the Ethiopians were weak but wise—and thus the perfect opposite of natural slaves. This was the distinctive idiom of the New World. Only in America could an Englishman in this era have drawn such a stark and absolute conclusion that the Africans were unfit for freedom. It was not an idea well suited to the discourse of Roman law, with its emphasis upon the natural freedom of all humankind and the sharp reversals of fortune back and forth between freedom and slavery. Trapham put the idea in terms derived from Aristotle.[37]

In the period that followed the publication of Trapham's *Discourse* on Jamaica, more and more information from the sugar islands filtered back into the metropolitan center of the English Atlantic world. Innovations in the Caribbean followed an extended circuit back east across the ocean. Ideas enlisted in support of the colonial slave systems started to transform the culture from which the colonists had first set out. This was the route of racial animus in the critical period for the development of American slavery.

Nevertheless, even at the end of the seventeenth century, ideas of the kind that had occurred to Thomas Trapham were still present at the margins of English culture. They had appeared in bits and pieces, in shards of assertions and tentative speculations. In this period, there was perhaps no better collection point for such ideas on the cusp of definite articulation than the *Athenian Mercury*, whose print run continued until 1697. As the title of the *Athenian Mercury* indicated, too, there was perhaps no place more appropriate for Aristotelian views to start to come into their own.

In 1694, three years after their first response to a question on the topic of the African slave trade, the editors of the *Mercury* printed a related question from a reader. The question was one that could well have occurred to a reader whose conscience had been pricked by an encounter with the works of Morgan Godwyn. The reader asked, "*Whether those Merchants and Planters in the* West Indies, *as well as all other parts of the World, that buy Negroes or other Heathen Servants or Slaves, are not indispensably bound to bring such Servants to be Baptised?*" The editors often answered several questions in the course of an issue, but they decided to respond to this one with an extended treatment. They focused on the case of the African persons held as slaves in the West Indian or Caribbean colonies.[38]

The editors were well aware that the merchants and planters had worked to prevent the baptism of the Africans held as slaves in the English Caribbean. They accepted as well what Godwyn had understood to be the deepest reason for the planters' actions. "Talk to a *Planter* of the *Soul* of a *Negro,*" the editors explained, "and he'll be apt to tell ye (or at least his actions speak it loudly) that the Body of one of 'em may be worth twenty Pounds, but the Souls of an hundred of 'em would not yield him one Farthing." The editors were decisive in their condemnation of the planters' contempt for the immortal souls of their human chattel. They concluded that of course the planters were bound to baptize the Africans they held as slaves. Christ was clear in his intention that "*all Nations of the Earth be blessed.*"

The editors had also heard about the common concern the planters had presented in their defense that the baptism of slaves would require their manumission. The editors made the common response that Scripture made no such requirement. Baptism and instruction in the Word would tend to teach slaves better to perform the duties of their office. After all, the lesson Christ had worked to impress upon His followers was that it was "their Duty, in whatever state they are call'd, therein to abide." Indeed, it was evident that some persons were called to serve. "Some Persons, nay, Nations seem to be born for Slaves," the editors observed:

> Particularly many of the *Barbarians in Africa,* who have been such almost from the beginning of the World, and who are in a much better condition

> of Life, when Slaves among us, then when at Liberty at Home, to cut Throats and Eat one another, especially when by the Slavery of their Bodies, they are brought to a capacity of *freeing* their Souls from a much more unsupportable Bondage.

It is important to appreciate how novel this claim would have been in early-modern English culture. In response to a question about the baptism of African persons enslaved in the Caribbean colonies, the editors of the *Mercury* had moved on to a discussion of slavery as such. They had maintained that it was the special allotment of some persons to serve, and they had observed that the peoples of Africa seemed to be some of such persons. As Aristotle had written, "From the hour of their birth, some are marked out for subjection." The condition of the Africans from time immemorial attested to the truth of this ancient principle. For them, baptism and instruction in the Word promised to provide useful lessons in how to fulfill their proper status in the natural order. According to the editors of the *Mercury,* this had to be seen as a powerful reason to advocate for the cause of conversion in the colonies.[39]

But the editors of the *Mercury* had not stopped at this point. They had also started to anticipate an even more complete kind of conversion. They had said that, once baptized, the Africans held as slaves in the Caribbean would not in truth be slaves, since their souls would be free. Back in their native land, the Africans had never been free in this sense. The nominal freedom that they experienced had been the most intolerable kind of spiritual bondage. They lived in a continual state of war. They cut each other's throats and ate each other. Any person would exchange that form of freedom for this form of subjection. For those who were known to be "fitter for *Slaves than Freedom,*" in the phrase of the editors, the two conditions were thus reversed. Freedom was enslavement, and the appropriate form of enslavement offered a truer form of freedom.

Perhaps it had always had to come to this. If some English observers of the Caribbean had started to maintain that the Africans there were destined to be slaves, then at some point attention would have to turn back to Africa. As it did, the detail and variety of early-modern descriptions of the continent would have to recede from view. The local situations in which persons there had been enslaved would have to become less important than these had been for earlier observers of the sources of the slave trade. The chance and misfortune that had delivered many thousands of Africans into the system of American slavery would come to seem as the instruments of an immense cosmic plan.

Soon the conceptual demands of American slavery would start to reverberate across the Atlantic. In order to defend it, English authors would have to make it consistent with a new view of Africa. In America or in Africa, it did not matter—the peoples of Africa could never be free. However debased their position in America, their lives in Africa would have to be said to be worse. Fables and rumors that had all but disappeared from current accounts of the continent would have to be revived. Some old conventions would have to be set aside, and some new ideas would have to be developed and pressed into service.

In the process, English discourse about Africa would become a silent reflection upon the conditions of oppression that Englishmen had imposed by force across the Atlantic. How it was with America was how it would have to become with Africa. Toward the close of the seventeenth century, the shift in ideas that would unfold in the context of such demands had started to take place. There were intimations of what was to come.

Notes

PROLOGUE

1. Morgan Godwyn, *The Negro's & Indians Advocate, Suing for Their Admission into the Church* (London, 1680), 39.

2. Joseph Conrad, "Heart of Darkness," in Joseph Conrad, *Youth: A Narrative and Two Other Stories* (London, 1902), 49–182, 108–109.

3. See, for example, Eric Eustace Williams, *Capitalism and Slavery* (Chapel Hill, NC, 1944); Wesley Frank Craven, *The Southern Colonies in the Seventeenth Century, 1608–1687* (Baton Rouge, LA, 1949); Oscar and Mary F. Handlin, "Origins of the Southern Labor System," *William and Mary Quarterly* 7, no. 2 (Apr. 1950): 199–222; Richard S. Dunn, *Sugar and Slaves: The Rise of the Planter Class in the English West Indies, 1624–1713* (Chapel Hill, NC, 1972); Carl and Roberta Bridenbaugh, *No Peace beyond the Line: The English in the Caribbean, 1624–1690* (New York, 1972); Richard B. Sheridan, *Sugar and Slavery: An Economic History of the British West Indies, 1623–1675* (Baltimore, 1974); Peter H. Wood, *Black Majority: Negroes in Colonial South Carolina from 1670 through the Stono Rebellion* (New York, 1974); David W. Galenson, *Traders, Planters, and Slaves: Market Behavior in Early English America* (New York, 1986); Nuala Zahedieh, "Trade, Plunder, and Economic Development in Early English Jamaica, 1655–89," *Economic History Review* 39, no. 2 (May 1986): 205–222; Hilary Beckles, *White Servitude and Black Slavery in Barbados, 1627–1715* (Knoxville, TN, 1989); Philip D. Curtin, *The Rise and Fall of the Plantation Complex: Essays in Atlantic History* (New York, 1990); Michael Craton, *Empire, Enslavement and Freedom in the Caribbean* (Kingston, Jamaica, 1997); Robin Blackburn, *The Making of New World Slavery: From the Baroque to the Modern, 1492–1800* (New York, 1997); B. W. Higman, "The Sugar Revolution," *Economic History Review* 53, no. 2 (May 2000): 213–236; Larry Gragg, *Englishmen Transplanted: The English Colonization of Barbados, 1627–1660* (New York, 2003); Max S. Edelson, *Plantation Enterprise in Colonial South Carolina* (Cambridge, MA, 2006); Russell R. Menard, *Sweet Negotiations: Sugar, Slavery, and Plantation Agriculture in Early Barbados* (Charlottesville, VA, 2006); Simon P. Newman, *A New World of Labor: The Development of Plantation Slavery in the British Atlantic* (Philadelphia, 2013); Trevor G. Burnard, *Planters, Merchants, and Slaves: Plantation Societies in British America, 1650–1820*

(Chicago, 2019); Christine Walker, *Jamaica Ladies: Female Slaveholders and the Creation of Britain's Atlantic Empire* (Chapel Hill, NC, 2020); Katherine Johnston, *The Nature of Slavery: Environment and Plantation Labor in the Anglo-American Atlantic World* (New York, 2022); and Nicholas Radburn, *Traders in Men: Merchants and the Transformation of the Transatlantic Slave Trade* (New Haven, CT, 2023).

4. At this point, two recent books deserve mention as exceptions that prove the rule stated in the text. See William A. Pettigrew, *Freedom's Debt: The Royal African Company and the Politics of the Atlantic Slave Trade, 1672–1752* (Chapel Hill, NC, 2013); and Abigail L. Swingen, *Competing Visions of Empire: Labor, Slavery, and the Origins of the British Atlantic Empire* (New Haven, CT, 2015). Both books work to show that political and ideological conflicts in Britain were an important context for the rise and development of the British Atlantic slave trade. The debates with which these books are concerned, however, as both authors are well aware, were debates about the proper organization and control of the slave trade rather than about the political or ideological issues that were at stake in the slave trade or the institution of slavery as such.

Finally, it should be mentioned that perhaps the most famous work in the field of American colonial history also had as its central concern the transition from servitude to slavery as the dominant form of labor. See Edmund S. Morgan, *American Slavery, American Freedom: The Ordeal of Colonial Virginia* (New York, 1974). Morgan noted that as the planters in Virginia started to purchase more and more enslaved Africans to cultivate their tobacco fields, there was "no conscious decision" for them to do so at the level of the colonial administration (292). The motive of the planters was simply that there was a higher return for investment in slaves. (His clearest statement to this effect was made here: Edmund S. Morgan, "Slavery and Freedom: The American Paradox," *Journal of American History* 59, no. 1 [Jun. 1972]: 5–29, 24–25.) But Morgan also noted—and this was the feature of his account that has attracted the most attention—that the transition from servitude to slavery allowed for a new kind of political rhetoric and political practice to emerge on the Chesapeake. "There may have been more than coincidence involved," he said, in what became the parallel establishment of republican freedom and equality for white Virginians and the imposition of ever stricter forms of oppression for Black Virginians (376).

Whatever the merits of this account as a description of events in colonial Virginia, it has to be said that the interdependence of freedom and slavery that so interested Morgan did not develop elsewhere in the slave societies of the seventeenth-century English Atlantic world. In this respect, as in others, Virginia may well have been distinctive. And regardless—as has been noted above and will be discussed in what follows in this book—the Caribbean colonies were the much more important context for the development of slavery in the English Atlantic world in this period.

The emergence and early development of slavery in Virginia has exercised a particular fascination over American historians and has received careful treatment in a number of important works. In addition to *American Slavery, American Freedom,* see, for example, Winthrop D. Jordan, *White over Black: American Attitudes toward the Negro, 1550–1812* (Chapel Hill, NC, 1968); T. H. Breen and Stephen Innes, *"Myne Owne Ground": Race and Freedom on Virginia's Eastern Shore, 1640–1676* (New York, 1980); Kathleen M. Brown, *Good Wives, Nasty Wenches, and Anxious Patriarchs: Gender, Race, and Power in Colonial Virginia* (Chapel Hill, NC, 1996); Ira Berlin, *Many Thousands Gone: The First Two Centuries of Slavery in North America* (Cambridge, MA, 1998); Anthony S. Parent, *Foul Means: The Formation of a Slave Society in Virginia, 1660–1740* (Chapel Hill, NC, 2003); Lorena S. Walsh, *Motives of Honor, Pleasure, and Profit: Plantation Management in the Colonial Chesapeake, 1607–1763* (Chapel Hill, NC, 2010); John C. Coombs, "The Phases of Conversion: A New Chronology for the Rise of Slavery in Early Virginia," *William and Mary Quarterly* 68, no. 3 (Jul. 2011): 332–360; and Rebecca Anne Goetz, *The Baptism of Early Virginia: How Christianity Created Race* (Baltimore, 2012).

5. See Williams, *Capitalism and Slavery.* For a nuanced and provocative reassessment of Williams's classic account, see H. Reuben Neptune, "Throwin' Scholarly Shade," *Journal of the Early Republic* 39, no. 2 (Summer 2019): 299–326.

6. David Brion Davis, *The Problem of Slavery in Western Culture* (Ithaca, NY, 1966), vii.

7. See David Brion Davis, *The Problem of Slavery in the Age of Revolution, 1770–1823* (Ithaca, NY, 1975); and David Brion Davis, *The Problem of Slavery in the Age of Emancipation* (New York, 2014).

8. Even if the thesis that Williams presented about the decline of the British slave system in the period of the antislavery movement has long since fallen from favor, it has provoked decades of learned commentaries and responses and still continues to be debated in the field. The controversy that has developed around *Capitalism and Slavery* has proven to be "perhaps one of the most complex in modern historical scholarship," in the view of one of its most prominent participants. Christopher Leslie Brown, *Moral Capital: Foundations of British Abolitionism* (Chapel Hill, NC, 2006), 15.

The historian who has done the most to challenge the so-called decline thesis most often associated with Williams—and to develop an account of the British antislavery movement that starts from the premise that the slave system in the Empire was viable, dynamic, and profitable up until the period of its demise—is Seymour Drescher. See, for example, Seymour Drescher, *Econocide: British Slavery in the Era of Abolition* (Pittsburgh, 1977); Seymour Drescher, *Capitalism and Antislavery: British Popular Mobilization in Comparative Perspective* (New York, 1987); and Seymour Drescher, *Abolition: A History of Slavery and Antislavery* (New York, 2009).

The most important one-volume account of the Anglo-American abolition movement is the recent work of Manisha Sinha. See Manisha Sinha, *The Slave's Cause: A History of Abolition* (New Haven, CT, 2016). Sinha presents an account of the abolition movement that is at odds with an interpretation of it as the instrument of powerful metropolitan interests. "Slave resistance," she writes, "not bourgeois liberalism, lay at the heart of the abolition movement" (1). Sinha aims to establish that over the entire course of its rise and development, abolitionism had a radical and interracial character.

9. See Christopher Leslie Brown, *Moral Capital: Foundations of British Abolitionism* (Chapel Hill, NC, 2006). The argument that Davis developed about the ideological function of the antislavery movement in the ascendant industrial capitalist order in Britain in *The Problem of Slavery in the Age of Revolution* was so subtle and provocative that it touched off an extended debate that was later presented in an edited volume: *The Antislavery Debate: Capitalism and Abolitionism as a Problem in Historical Interpretation,* ed. Thomas Bender, with essays by John Ashworth, David Brion Davis, and Thomas L. Haskell (Los Angeles, 1992).

10. See, for example, Orlando Patterson, *The Sociology of Slavery: An Analysis of the Origins, Development, and Structure of Negro Slave Society in Jamaica* (London, 1967); David Barry Gaspar, *Bondmen and Rebels: A Study of Master-Slave Relations in Antigua* (Baltimore, 1985); Hilary Beckles, *Natural Rebels: A Social History of Enslaved Black Women in Barbados* (New Brunswick, NJ, 1989); Paul Gilroy, *The Black Atlantic: Modernity and Double Consciousness* (Cambridge, MA, 1993); Jennifer L. Morgan, *Laboring Women: Reproduction and Gender in New World Slavery* (Philadelphia, 2004); Saidiya V. Hartman, *Lose Your Mother: A Journey along the Atlantic Slave Route* (New York, 2007); Stephanie E. Smallwood, *Saltwater Slavery: A Middle Passage from Africa to American Diaspora* (Cambridge, MA, 2007); Vincent Brown, *The Reaper's Garden: Death and Power in the World of Atlantic Slavery* (Cambridge, MA, 2008); Vincent Brown, *Tacky's Revolt: The Story of an Atlantic Slave War* (Cambridge, MA, 2020); and Jennifer L. Morgan, *Reckoning with Slavery: Gender, Kinship, and Capitalism in the Early Black Atlantic* (Durham, NC, 2021).

11. For seminal works in the field of African history that have aimed to position Africa and Africans in a complex and active role at the center of the history of the Atlantic slave trade—with particular attention to the precolonial period before 1700—see, for example, J. D. Fage, *A History of West Africa* (London, 1969); Walter Rodney, *A History of the Upper Guinea Coast, 1545–1800* (Oxford, 1970); Robin Law, *The Slave Coast of West Africa, 1550–1750* (Oxford, 1991); John K. Thornton, *Africa and Africans in the Making of the Atlantic World, 1400–1800* (Cambridge, UK, 1998); David Eltis, *The Rise of African Slavery in the Americas* (New York, 2000); G. Ugo Nwokeji, *The Slave Trade and Culture in the Bight of Biafra: An African Society in the Atlantic World* (Cambridge, UK, 2010); Roquinaldo Amaral Ferreira, *Cross-Cultural Exchange in the Atlantic World: Angola and Brazil during the Era of the Slave Trade* (Cambridge, UK, 2012); Mariana P. Candido, *An African Slaving Port and the Atlantic World: Benguela and Its Hinterland* (Cambridge, UK, 2013); Randy J. Sparks, *Where the Negroes Are Masters: An African Port in the Era of the Slave Trade* (Cambridge, MA, 2014); Linda M. Heywood, *Njinga of Angola: Africa's Warrior Queen* (Cambridge, MA, 2017); Michael A. Gomez, *African Dominion: A New History of Empire in Early and Medieval West Africa* (Princeton, NJ, 2018); and Toby Green, *A Fistful of Shells: West Africa from the Rise of the Slave Trade to the Age of Revolution* (Chicago, 2019).

12. For useful modern editions in which records of the royal companies that controlled English commerce with Africa in this period have been collected and published, see *Documents Illustrative of the History of the Slave Trade to America*, ed. Elizabeth Donnan, 4 vols. (Washington, DC, 1930–1935), vol. 1 (1440–1700); and in particular *The Local Correspondence of the Royal African Company of England, 1681–1699*, ed. Robin Law, 3 vols. (Oxford, 1997–2006).

1. FROM FREEDOM TO SLAVERY

1. The works of such scholars and historians will be cited throughout this book at length when appropriate. Here it will be most useful to mention a number of works that have developed a different understanding of the relation between race and slavery and have argued, to state a complex matter in simple terms, that racism was not a cause but almost entirely the result of slavery in America. See, for example, Eric Eustace Williams, *Capitalism and Slavery* (Chapel Hill, NC, 1944); Oscar and Mary F. Handlin, "Origins of the Southern Labor System," *William and Mary Quarterly* (hereafter *WMQ*) 7, no. 2 (Apr. 1950): 199–222; Edmund S. Morgan, *American Slavery, American Freedom: The Ordeal of Colonial Virginia* (New York, 1975); Peter Kolchin, *Unfree Labor: American Slavery and Russian Serfdom* (Cambridge, MA,

1987); Ira Berlin, *Many Thousands Gone: The First Two Centuries of Slavery in North America* (Cambridge, MA, 1998); and Karen E. Fields and Barbara J. Fields, *Racecraft: The Soul of Inequality in American Life* (New York, 2012). Each of these works has presented or at least started to outline its own account of the origins of American slavery. But none has drawn attention to the Roman tradition of ideas whose character and significance is examined in this book.

2. See, for example, W. W. Buckland, *The Roman Law of Slavery: The Condition of the Slave in Private Law from Augustus to Justinian* (Cambridge, UK, 1908); W. W. Buckland, *A Text-Book of Roman Law from Augustus to Justinian* (Cambridge, UK, 1921); Alan Watson, *Roman Slave Law* (Baltimore, 1987); and Barry Nicholas, *An Introduction to Roman Law,* rev. ed. (Oxford, 2008). On the development of Roman law, see also, for example, Aldo Schiavone, *The Invention of Law in the West,* trans. Jeremy Carden and Antony Shugaar (Cambridge, MA, 2012); and James Q. Whitman, *From Masters of Slaves to Lords of Lands: The Transformation of Ownership in the Western World* (Cambridge, UK, 2024).

3. For studies of the antebellum American proslavery argument, see William Sumner Jenkins, *Pro-Slavery Thought in the Old South* (Chapel Hill, NC, 1935); Clement Eaton, *Freedom of Thought in the Old South* (Durham, NC, 1940); Louis Hartz, *The Liberal Tradition in America: An Interpretation of American Political Thought since the Revolution* (New York, 1955), 145–200; Eugene D. Genovese, *The World the Slaveholders Made: Two Essays in Interpretation* (New York, 1969); George M. Fredrickson, *The Black Image in the White Mind: The Debate on Afro-American Character and Destiny* (New York, 1971); Drew Gilpin Faust, *A Sacred Circle: The Dilemma of the Intellectual in the Old South, 1840–1860* (Baltimore, 1977); *The Ideology of Slavery: Proslavery Thought in the Antebellum South, 1830–1860,* ed. Drew Gilpin Faust (Baton Rouge, LA, 1981); Larry E. Tise, *Proslavery: A History of the Defense of Slavery in America, 1701–1840* (Athens, GA, 1987); James Oakes, *Freedom and Slavery: An Interpretation of the Old South* (New York, 1990); Michael O'Brien, *Conjectures of Order: Intellectual Life and the American South, 1810–1860,* 2 vols. (Chapel Hill, NC, 2004); Eugene D. Genovese and Elizabeth Fox-Genovese, *The Mind of the Master Class: History and Faith in the Southern Slaveholders' Worldview* (New York, 2005); Lacy Ford, *Deliver Us from Evil: The Slavery Question in the Old South* (New York, 2009); and Walter Johnson, *River of Dark Dreams: Slavery and Empire in the Cotton Kingdom* (Cambridge, MA, 2013).

4. David Brion Davis, *The Problem of Slavery in Western Culture* (Ithaca, NY, 1966), 288, 62; and David Brion Davis, *The Problem of Slavery in the Age of Revolution, 1770–1823* (Ithaca, NY, 1975), 82. See also the final volume in what would become a three-

volume series about the antislavery movement in the Anglo-American Atlantic world: David Brion Davis, *The Problem of Slavery in the Age of Emancipation* (New York, 2014). For all their immense subtlety and erudition, the core of slavery, as Davis understood it, remained the same across these works. Davis only further developed the theme as, later in his career, he focused upon efforts to produce the "dehumanization" or "animalization" of the subject that had been "at the heart of slavery." See David Brion Davis, "At the Heart of Slavery," *New York Review of Books* 43, no. 16 (Oct. 17, 1996): 51–54.

In addition to that of Davis, the two most useful historical introductions to ideas of slavery remain Russell Parsons Jameson, *Montesquieu et l'esclavage: Étude sur les origines de l'opinion antiesclavagiste en France au XVIIIè siècle* (Paris, 1911); and Peter Garnsey, *Ideas of Slavery from Aristotle to Augustine* (Cambridge, UK, 1996).

5. Aristotle, *Politics,* in *The Complete Works of Aristotle: The Revised Oxford Translation,* ed. Jonathan Barnes, 2 vols. (Princeton, NJ, 2014), vol. 2, 1986–2129, 1990: 1254a30–31 and 1254a23–24.

6. Aristotle, *Politics,* in *Complete Works of Aristotle,* ed. Barnes, vol. 2, 1990: 1254b21; 2107: 1327b27; and 1987: 1252b5.

More likely than the opinion that Aristotle intended the discussion of slavery in his *Politics* as an attack upon the practice of slavery in the present is the view that in this work Aristotle adduced in support of his theory of natural slavery a belief popular in fifth-century Athens: that while Hellenes were destined to rule, barbarians were suited for slavery. For the origins and development of this belief, see, for example, Edith Hall, *Inventing the Barbarian: Greek Self-Definition through Tragedy* (New York, 1989); Paul Cartledge, *The Greeks: A Portrait of Self and Others* (New York, 1993); and Kostas Vlassopoulos, *Greeks and Barbarians* (Cambridge, UK, 2013).

7. Aristotle, *Politics,* in *Complete Works of Aristotle,* ed. Barnes, vol. 2, 1989: 1253b21; and *Justinian's Institutes,* trans. Peter Birks and Grant McLeod (Ithaca, NY, 1987), 37: I.2.2. In the passage cited above, the authors of the *Institutes* only reproduced the opinion of the jurists from whose commentaries the *Digest* had been composed. See, for example, the statement from Ulpian that "of course everyone would be born free by the natural law" and the one from Florentinus that slavery was "an institution of the *jus gentium,* whereby someone is against nature made subject to the ownership of another." *The Digest of Justinian,* trans. and ed. Alan Watson, 4 vols. (Philadelphia, PA, 1985), vol. 1: I.1.4 and I.5.4.

8. Aristotle, *Politics,* in *Complete Works of Aristotle,* ed. Barnes, vol. 2, 1991: 1255a2 (also 1990: 1254a18).

9. *Digest of Justinian,* trans. and ed. Watson, vol. 1: I.1.1 (on the law of nature, see also *Justinian's Institutes,* trans. Birks and McLeod, 37: I.2.1–2).

10. *Digest of Justinian,* trans. and ed. Watson, vol. 1: I.1.1; *The Institutes of Gaius,* trans. W. M. Gordon and O. F. Robinson (Ithaca, NY, 1988), vol. 1: I.1.1. For its part, the *Institutes* of Justinian referred both to the law of nature as "the law instilled by nature in all creatures," as had Ulpian, and to the law of nations as "the law which natural reason makes for all mankind," in terms that were borrowed from Gaius. *Justinian's Institutes,* trans. Birks and McLeod, 37: I.2.1.

11. *Digest of Justinian,* trans. and ed. Watson, vol. 1: I.1.4. For the two sources of slavery under the law of nations, see vol. 1: I.5.5.1. For the rules of enslavement under the civil law, as well as the relatively straightforward ones that were in place for enslavement under the law of nations, see Buckland, *Roman Law of Slavery,* 397–436; and Watson, *Roman Slave Law,* 7–22.

For several decades, historians have debated the relative importance of the different sources of the Roman slave supply. From this debate, it is evident both that capture in war and the natural reproduction of enslaved persons were the most important of these sources and that they were far from the only ones in practice in Rome. A number of routes into slavery that were still common in the period of Justinian, such as various forms of self-sale and the exposure of infant children, were not sanctioned and were rarely mentioned in the treatises of the *Corpus Juris.* See Keith Bradley, *Slavery and Society at Rome* (New York, 1994), 31–56; W. V. Harris, "Demography, Geography and the Sources of Roman Slaves," *Journal of Roman Studies* 89 (1999): 62–75; and Walter Scheidel, "The Roman Slave Supply," in *The Cambridge World History of Slavery, Volume 1: The Ancient Mediterranean World,* ed. Keith Bradley and Paul Cartledge (Cambridge, UK, 2011), 287–310.

12. For accounts of the development of the common law as an almost purely insular process, see, for example, Frederic William Maitland, *English Law and the Renaissance* (Cambridge, UK, 1901); J. G. A. Pocock, *The Ancient Constitution and the Feudal Law* (Cambridge, UK, 1957); Donald R. Kelley, "History, English Law, and the Renaissance," *Past and Present,* no. 65 (Nov. 1974): 24–51; and John H. Baker, *An Introduction to English Legal History,* 5th ed. (Oxford, 2019), 3–41. For subtler accounts of the relation between common and civil law, see Richard Helgerson, *Forms of Nationhood: The Elizabethan Writing of England* (Chicago, 1992), 63–104; Glenn Burgess, *The Politics of the Ancient Constitution: An Introduction to English Political Thought, 1603–1642* (University Park, PA, 1993); and Tamar Herzog, *A Short History of European Law: The Last Two and a Half Millennia* (Cambridge, MA, 2018), 73–151.

13. *Bracton on the Laws and Customs of England,* trans. Samuel E. Thorne, 4 vols. (Cambridge, MA, 1968–1977), vol. 2: 30. The remark that "liberty, which proceeds from the law of nature, cannot be taken away by the *jus gentium* but only obscured by it" is at vol. 2: 28.

14. Several of the older discussions of villeinage remain among the best: see, for example, Paul Vinogradoff, *Villainage in England: Essays in English Mediaeval History* (Oxford, 1892); Thomas Walker Page, *The End of Villainage in England* (New York, 1900); and R. H. Hilton, *The Decline of Serfdom in Medieval England* (London, 1969). As Bracton did not hesitate to point out, villeins were entitled to pursue an action against their lords in certain specified cases and could do so against third parties without special restriction. See, for example, *Bracton on the Laws and Customs of England,* trans. Thorpe, vol. 2: 34, 36–38, and 85–88.

15. *Britton,* trans. Francis Morgan Nichols, 2 vols. (Oxford, 1865), vol. 1: 194. In accord with the practical bent of his treatise, Britton wrote in French, which was then the vernacular language of the common law courts. His chapter on villeinage was thus titled "De nayfté," and here he moved smoothly between references to *vileyns* and *serfs,* both of whom were contrasted with *des fraunches gentz.* A similar account of the origin of villeinage can be found in a little-known treatise that also seems to have been written around the end of the thirteenth century under the influence of Bracton. The modern edition is Andrew Horne, *The Mirror of Justices,* trans. William Joseph Whittaker (London, 1895); see 76–77.

16. The additional causes of this impression among English authors in the late Tudor period will be examined in Chapter 2. Here it need only be observed that villeinage survived on a small scale through the close of the sixteenth century. See Diarmaid MacCulloch, "Bondmen under the Tudors," in *Law and Government under the Tudors,* ed. Claire Cross, David Loades, and J. J. Scarisbrick (Cambridge, UK, 1988), 91–110.

17. See Thomas Smith, *De republica Anglorum* (London, 1583), bk. 1, ch. 10: 10–12. After Aristotle's well-known remark that "the ox is the poor man's slave," Smith maintained that a slave was "but the instrument of his Lord" in the same manner as "the plow, the horse, the oxe or asse, be instruments of the husbandman." Smith, *De republica Anglorum,* bk. 1, ch. 10: 11.

18. See Smith, *De republica Anglorum,* bk. 3, ch. 8: 107–115.

19. On the movement for legal reform in England around the turn of the seventeenth century, see, for example, Brian P. Levack, *The Civil Lawyers in England, 1603–1641: A Political Study* (Oxford, 1973); as well as Helgerson, *Forms of Nationhood,*

63–104. The practical agreement between the common and the civil law was the consistent theme from, for example, William Fulbecke; see William Fulbecke, *A Parallele or Conference of the Civill Law, the Canon Law, and the Common Law of this Realme of England* (London, 1601).

20. John Cowell, *The Institutes of the Lawes of England,* trans. W.G. (London, 1651), 12. The original edition of the text appeared as John Cowell, *Institutiones juris anglicani* (Cambridge, UK, 1605). In this edition, Cowell used the term *servus,* or in the plural *servi,* to denote the persons who are referred to in this paragraph as "slaves" or as "enslaved." The English translation of Cowell's text referred to such persons as "servants," which was a common translation of the Latin term in the first half of the seventeenth century. Like *servi,* "servants" was often treated as a general class that included both free servants and unfree slaves. For Cowell, however, all servants were unfree, just as all *servi* had been slaves at Rome.

21. John Cowell, *The Interpreter: or Booke Containing the Signification of Words* (Cambridge, UK, 1607), unpaginated ("*Villein* [*villanus*]"). Curiously, then, in order to enlarge upon the status of villeins in England, Cowell turned not only to Bracton but also to Smith, and he never mentioned that Smith had held that there were no more villeins within the realm.

22. Edward Coke, *The First Part of the Institutes of the Lawes of England* (London, 1628), bk. 2, ch. 11, sect. 172: 116r–v.

23. The most sensitive treatment of Coke on the relation between common and civil law is Helgerson, *Forms of Nationhood,* 63–104. But see in addition J. G. A. Pocock, *The Ancient Constitution and the Feudal Law: A Reissue with a Retrospect* (New York, 1987; orig. pub. 1957), 30–69 and 255–305. Pocock maintained that Coke's mind "was as nearly insular as a human being's could be" (56). But even he was aware that this was more a matter of self-presentation than of ignorance. That Coke was more learned in the texts of the *Corpus Juris* than he often appeared is evident from the contents of his library: see *A Catalogue of the Library of Sir Edward Coke,* ed. W. O. Hassall (New Haven, CT, 1950), nos. 293–434 (English law) and 435–491 (civil law).

24. For the argument that Aristotle attributed to his opponents that slavery was founded upon the convention "by which whatever is taken in war is supposed to belong to the victors," see Aristotle, *Politics,* in *Complete Works of Aristotle,* ed. Barnes, vol. 2, 1991: 1255a6–7. For his part, Aristotle went so far as to maintain that war "against men who, though intended by nature to be governed, will not submit" was part of "the natural art of acquisition" and could even be considered a form of "hunting." Aristotle, *Politics,* in *Complete Works of Aristotle,* ed. Barnes, vol. 2, 1994: 1256b22-25.

25. For a remarkable collection of extracts, in which particular emphasis is placed upon Roman sources, see *Greek and Roman Slavery,* ed. Thomas Wiedemann (London, 1981).

26. For early-modern works that distilled the themes and lessons of classical works of history and literature, prominent among them being the association between war and slavery, see, for example, Clement Edmunds, *Observations upon the First Five Bookes of Cæsars Commentaries* (London, 1600), bk. 2, ch. 12: 98–102 and bk. 4, ch. 16: 155–157; and *The Treasurie of Auncient and Moderne Times* (London, 1613), 132–137.

27. For his role in the revival of the civil law in England, Gentili was praised, for example, by the legal scholar William Fulbecke as the author who "by his great industrie hath quickened the dead bodie of the Civil Law written by the auncient Civilians." William Fulbecke, *A Declaration or Preparative to the Study of the Lawe* (London, 1600), 26v. Fulbecke also produced what was in essence an abstract of Gentili's *Law of War* in the chapter on that topic in William Fulbecke, *The Pandectes of the Law of Nations* (London, 1602), 33v–52r.

28. Alberico Gentili, *De iure belli libri tres,* ed. James Brown Scott, trans. John C. Rolfe, 2 vols. (London, 1933), vol. 2, bk. 1, ch. 5: 29. Gentili's insistence that there was no conflict in the natural order led him to dismiss Aristotle's opinion that war could be waged in order to enslave enemies who were created by nature to be such; see vol. 2, bk. 1, ch. 12: 53–54. For the chapter in his work "Of Slaves," see vol. 2, bk. 3, ch. 9: 328–335.

29. Gentili, *De iure belli,* ed. Scott, trans. Rolfe, vol. 2, bk. 1, ch. 1: 8 (note that this phrase has been corrected from the Rolfe translation in order better to follow the Latin of Gentili, who said that the law of nations was that which "naturalis ratio inter omnes homines constituit" at Gentili, *De iure belli,* ed. Scott, vol. 1, bk. 1, ch. 1: 10). Gentili stated this principle of self-defense at Gentili, *De iure belli,* ed. Scott, trans. Rolfe, vol. 2, bk. 1, ch. 3: 18. It had appeared in the *Digest* under the law of nations, for example, at *Digest of Justinian,* trans. and ed. Watson, vol. 1: I.1.3 and IX.2.45.4.

30. For this reason, even though he clearly was incorrect in the assertion that Gentili's *Law of War* should be placed within the humanist tradition of ideas about war, Richard Tuck was right to draw attention to what he said was the "often extraordinarily brutal" character of that work. See Richard Tuck, *The Rights of War and Peace: Political Thought and the International Order from Grotius to Kant* (New York, 1999), 16. On the issues discussed in this section of the chapter, see the essays collected in *The Roman Foundations of the Law of Nations: Alberico Gentili and*

the Justice of Empire, ed. Benedict Kingsbury and Benjamin Straumann (New York, 2010).

31. So concerned was Grotius to establish the distinction between the law of nations and the law of nature in his masterpiece that it was later said that he had "at first design'd to have entitled it, *The Law of Nature and Nations.*" Jean Barbeyrac, "An Historical and Critical Account of the Science of Morality," in Samuel Pufendorf, *Of the Law of Nature and Nations,* trans. Basil Kennett, 4th ed. (London, 1729), 1–88, 79. The criticism of authors such as Gentili who had not made a clear distinction between these two sources of law was a consistent theme in "The Preliminary Discourse" and in particular in Hugo Grotius, *The Rights of War and Peace,* trans. John Morrice (London, 1738), xiii–xxxvi, xxvii–xxviii.

32. The original manner in which Grotius thus placed rights at the foundation of his theory of natural law has led a number of English translators of his text to render its title as *The Rights of War and Peace,* as the Latin term that Grotius used to mean both law and right, *ius,* has no similarly ambivalent English equivalent. This was of course how the title of the work appeared in the 1738 edition that was cited in the previous note, which remains the best English translation of the complete text. The ambivalence of the original Latin was reflected as well in the titles of the two seventeenth-century translations: see *The Illustrious Hugo Grotius of the Law of Warre and Peace,* trans. Clement Barksdale (London, 1654); and *The Most Excellent Hugo Grotius His Three Books Treating of the Rights of War & Peace,* trans. William Evats (London, 1682).

33. Grotius, *Rights of War and Peace,* trans. Morrice, bk. I, ch. III, pt. VII.1: 65 and II.V.XXXII: 213.

34. Grotius, *Rights of War and Peace,* trans. Morrice, II.V.XXIX.2: 211. For the limits that Grotius placed upon slavery in order to ensure, in his phrase, that the practice would be "confined within the Bounds of Nature," see Grotius, *Rights of War and Peace,* trans. Morrice, II.V.XXVII–XXXII: 209–214.

35. Grotius, *Rights of War and Peace,* trans. Morrice, III.VII.I.2: 602; III.VII.II: 603; and III.VII.III.1: 603.

36. Grotius, *Rights of War and Peace,* trans. Morrice, III.XII.VIII.1: 657 and III.X.I.1: 626.

For scholars in recent decades who have maintained that Grotius himself endorsed the doctrine of the law of nations with regard to slavery, see, for example, Tuck, *Rights of War and Peace,* 171; James Farr, "Locke, Natural Law, and New World Slavery," *Political Theory* 36, no. 4 (Aug. 2008): 495–522, 502; and Mary Nyquist, *Arbitrary Rule: Slavery, Tyranny, and the Power of Life and Death* (Chicago, 2013), 226.

37. Grotius, *Rights of War and Peace,* trans. Morrice, xxviii and III.VII.I.1: 602. The most detailed accounts of Grotius's gradual rejection of the Aristotelian culture in which he had been educated are in Richard Tuck, *Natural Rights Theories: Their Origin and Development* (Cambridge, UK, 1979), 58–81; and Richard Tuck, *Philosophy and Government, 1572–1651* (Cambridge, UK, 1993), 154–201.

In support of his assertion that "Slavery is against Nature," Grotius turned to the Roman jurists he referred to as "the Lawyers" and cited the passage in which this phrase appeared in the *Digest.* See Grotius, *Rights of War and Peace,* trans. Morrice, III.VII.I.1: 602. As a matter of fact, in spite of the departure that his system marked from their own conception of it, Grotius was eager to acknowledge his debt to the authors of Roman law, as well as to the many more recent scholars who had contributed to the development of the civil law tradition. See, for example, Grotius, *Rights of War and Peace,* trans. Morrice, xxxiv–xxxv.

Grotius's immersion in such sources is now well understood, and has been examined in important recent studies such as Benjamin Straumann, *Roman Law in the State of Nature: The Classical Foundations of Hugo Grotius' Natural Law,* trans. Belinda Cooper (Cambridge, UK, 2015); Daniel Lee, *Popular Sovereignty in Early Modern Constitutional Thought* (Oxford, 2016), 255–272; and Francesca Iurlaro, *The Invention of Custom: Natural Law and the Law of Nations, ca. 1550–1750* (New York, 2021), 105–123.

38. Barbeyrac, "Historical and Critical Account of the Science of Morality," in Pufendorf, *Law of Nature and Nations,* trans. Kennett, 4th ed. (1729), 79. The scholar who has done the most to trace this Grotian tradition is Richard Tuck, in the works cited above and also in Richard Tuck, *The Sleeping Sovereign: The Invention of Modern Democracy* (Cambridge, UK, 2015).

39. Thomas Hobbes, *De Corpore Politico. Or The Elements of Law* (London, 1650), 31.

40. Thomas Hobbes, *Leviathan, or, The Matter, Forme, and Power of a Common-wealth Ecclesiasticall and Civil* (London, 1651), 76. The most subtle interpretation of his account of equality and its full contemporary context is Kinch Hoekstra, "Hobbesian Equality," in *Hobbes Today: Insights for the 21st Century,* ed. S. A. Lloyd (Cambridge, UK, 2013), 76–112.

41. John Milton, *The Tenure of Kings and Magistrates,* 2nd ed. (London, 1650), 8 and 11. To be sure, he drew his doctrine of the natural freedom of all mankind from his impression of the condition of the species before the Fall in Genesis: this was what he referred to as the "Mosaical" source for his account (8). That said, Milton also found support for his doctrine in the *Institutes* of Justinian, as is clear, for example, from "Commonplace Book," in *The Complete Prose Works of John Milton,* gen.

ed. Don M. Wolfe, 8 vols. (New Haven, CT, 1953–1982), vol. 1: 344–513, 410 and 470.

42. Sir Robert Filmer, *Patriarcha. The Naturall Power of Kinges Defended against the Unnatural Liberty of the People,* in Sir Robert Filmer, *Patriarcha and Other Writings,* ed. Johann P. Sommerville (Cambridge, UK, 1991), 1–68, 3. Filmer said he had been disappointed to find this same "conceit of original freedom" not only in the writings of defenders of the royalist cause but also in those of "the authors of the principles of the civil law, and Grotius, Selden, Hobbes, Ascham and others." Sir Robert Filmer, *Observations upon Aristotles Politiques,* in Filmer, *Patriarcha and Other Writings,* ed. Sommerville, 235–286, 237.

For a rich and learned treatment of the development of natural freedom as a premise in seventeenth-century English political discourse and of the variety of positions that this premise could be seen to support, see Michael P. Zuckert, *Natural Rights and the New Republicanism* (Princeton, NJ, 1994).

43. *Aristotles Politiques, or Discourses of Government,* ed. Louis Le Roy, trans. I.D. (London, 1598), 32 and 33. The accounts of his library that Hobbes composed are described and in part reproduced in James Jay Hamilton, "Hobbes's Study and the Hardwick Library," *Journal of the History of Philosophy* 16, no. 4 (Oct. 1978): 445–453.

44. Hobbes, *De Corpore Politico. Or The Elements of Law,* 92, 111, and 93. The most detailed description of the dramatic change in the meanings that he attached to slavery and freedom over the course of his career is in Quentin Skinner, *Hobbes and Republican Liberty* (Cambridge, UK, 2008).

It should be noted that, even as the main thrust of Hobbes's argument in *The Elements of Law* was to hold that the natural right had to be surrendered without reserve in the formation of a civil society, he did also include in this work several statements to the opposite effect, which in turn prefigured the position that he would take up and defend in his later works: that the natural right of each person to defend their own life could never be entirely surrendered. See, for example, Hobbes, *De Corpore Politico. Or The Elements of Law,* 69.

45. Thomas Hobbes, *On the Citizen,* trans. and ed. Michael Silverthorne and Richard Tuck (Cambridge, UK, 1997), 111 and 103. This edition has the best English translation from the original Latin text that Hobbes started to circulate in 1642 and had printed in a revised second edition in 1647 as Thomas Hobbes, *Elementa philosophica de cive* (Amsterdam, 1647). This was first translated into English in an imperfect and unauthorized edition as Thomas Hobbes, *Philosophicall Rudiments Concerning Government and Civil Society* (London, 1651). For the distinction between

ergastuli and *servi,* see Hobbes, *On the Citizen,* trans. and ed. Silverthorne and Tuck, 103.

46. Hobbes, *Leviathan, or, The Matter, Forme, and Power of a Common-wealth Ecclesiasticall and Civil,* 109 and 107.

47. Hobbes, *Leviathan, or, The Matter, Forme, and Power of a Common-wealth Ecclesiasticall and Civil,* 104. The critical passage in *On the Citizen* in which Hobbes marked the distinction between two kinds of *servus* is on Hobbes, *On the Citizen,* trans. and ed. Silverthorne and Tuck, 103–104. Nevertheless, as noted above, Hobbes observed that the unfree class of *servi* were also referred to with "the particular appellation of *workhouse slaves* [*ergastuli*]." Hobbes, *On the Citizen,* trans. and ed. Silverthorne and Tuck, 103.

48. It should be noted that what is described above as Hobbes's classical treatment of slavery was perhaps drawn as much from Greek sources as from Roman ones. His first printed book had been a translation of Thucydides, and in the final decade of his life, Hobbes produced a translation of the two works of Homer. See *Eight Bookes of the Peloponnesian War Written by Thucydides,* trans. Thomas Hobbes (London, 1629); and *The Iliads and Odyssey of Homer,* trans. Thomas Hobbes, 2nd ed. (London, 1677). Hobbes did also observe, in a later passage in *Leviathan,* that there was a parallel in Greek for the distinction that he drew between the status of servants and that of slaves. "Slaves taken in war, and their Issue" had been called "Δουλοι, that is properly, Slaves, and their Service, Δουλεια," in contrast to the labor under contract of those persons who were called "Θητεξ; that is, Domestique Servants." Hobbes, *Leviathan,* 358.

49. Hobbes, *Leviathan,* 104.

50. For the role of consent in the context of slavery as punishment, see the discussion that appears in the long chapter on punishment in Grotius, *Rights of War and Peace,* trans. Morrice, II.XX.I.3: 403.

51. Samuel Pufendorf, *Of the Law of Nature and Nations,* trans. Basil Kennett (Oxford, 1703), III.II.VIII: 180; and Barbeyrac, "Historical and Critical Account of the Science of Morality," in Pufendorf, *Law of Nature and Nations,* trans. Kennett, 4th ed. (1729), 81.

Tuck has argued that the theory of natural rights that Pufendorf developed marked a "repudiation of Grotius" in the sense that it "laid stress on the fact that general agreements for social utility confer rights" rather than persons "having rights or property *in themselves,* outside the network of social obligations." See Tuck, *Natural Rights Theories,* 156–173, 157 and 161. That said, Pufendorf only ever put forward the claim that property rights in objects were conferred in this manner: see, for example, Pufendorf, *Law of Nature and Nations,* trans. Kennett, IV.IV: 318–333. With respect to the rights that persons had in themselves, he made the same claim as had Grotius, that is, that persons could be said to have such rights "outside the network of social obligations," in the phrase of Tuck. See, for example, Pufendorf, *Law of Nature and Nations,* trans. Kennett, II.II.III: 82–84. This claim was also clearly stated in the abridgement of his major work that was printed in 1673 and soon appeared in an English edition; see Samuel Pufendorf, *The Whole Duty of Man According to the Law of Nature,* trans. Andrew Tooke (London, 1691), II.I: 207–219.

52. Pufendorf, *Law of Nature and Nations,* trans. Kennett, VI.III.VI: 123 and 124.

53. Filmer was a keen reader of Aristotle. See, for example, Filmer, *Observations upon Aristotles Politiques,* in Filmer, *Patriarcha and Other Writings,* ed. Sommerville, 235–286. His principal concern here was to deny Aristotle's premise that the family and the state were under two different kinds of rule. But he was also clear in his rejection of Aristotle's doctrine of natural slavery: see, for example, Filmer, *Patriarcha,* in Filmer, *Patriarcha and Other Writings,* ed. Sommerville, 15. In the course of an aside on the civil law in this same work, Filmer explained his own position that "no man is born a servant, or subject to the power of a master by the law of nature, yet every man is born subject to the power of a father." Filmer, *Patriarcha,* in Filmer, *Patriarcha and Other Writings,* ed. Sommerville, 65.

54. For the recommendation that Locke made of *The Law of War and Peace* and *Law of Nature and Nations,* of which he said the latter "perhaps is the better of the two," see John Locke, *Some Thoughts Concerning Education,* ed. John W. Yolton and Jean S. Yolton (Oxford, 1989), 239. See also "Mr Locke's Extemporè Advice &c.," in Locke, *Thoughts Concerning Education,* ed. Yolton and Yolton, 319–327, 321–322.

55. John Locke, *Two Treatises of Government* (London, 1713), Preface (unpaginated). The edition from 1713 was the definitive edition of the work and incorporated the many alterations to the text that Locke had made in the period since its original publication.

56. Locke, *Two Treatises of Government,* 2T §6: 183; and Anonymous [James Tyrrell], *Patriarcha non Monarcha. The Patriarch Unmonarch'd* (London, 1681), 105. For scholars who have treated Locke's doctrine of natural law as the basis for his conclusion that a person could not consent to be enslaved, see, for example, Ruth W. Grant, *John Locke's Liberalism* (Chicago, 1987), 68–71; and Jeremy Waldron, *God, Locke, and Equality: Christian Foundations of John Locke's Political Thought* (Cambridge, UK, 2002), 141–142 and 198–199.

57. Locke, *Two Treatises of Government,* 2T §24: 198. For references in the works of Grotius and Pufendorf to self-enslavement under Hebrew law, see Grotius, *Rights of War and Peace,* trans. Morrice, I.III.VIII.1: 64; and Pufendorf, *Law of Nature and Nations,* trans. Kennett, VI.III.IV: 124.

58. Locke, *Two Treatises of Government,* 2T §6: 183 and 2T §23: 197.

59. Locke, *Two Treatises of Government,* 2T §172: 320 (see Hobbes, *Leviathan,* 103); 2T §16: 191; and 2T §24: 197.

60. Locke, *Two Treatises of Government,* 2T §179: 326.

61. *Digest of Justinian,* trans. and ed. Watson, vol. 1: I.6.1.1 (this phrase appeared in a passage that was drawn from Gaius; see *Institutes of Gaius,* trans. Gordon and Robinson, 1: I.52); and *Digest of Justinian,* trans. and ed. Watson, vol. 4: L.17.209. For the derivation of the term *servus,* see *Digest of Justinian,* trans. and ed. Watson, vol. 1: I.5.4.2.

This derivation of the term *servus* was well known to early-modern authors. It had been disputed in the humanist tradition, for example by the French jurist Jacques Cujas, who asserted that *servus* more likely would have come from the term for serve, *servire.* For reference, see Daniel Lee, *The Right of Sovereignty: Jean Bodin on the Sovereign State and the Law of Nations* (Oxford, 2021), 126. But that *servus* came from *servare* was affirmed, for example, in Gentili, *De iure belli,* trans. Rolfe, vol. 2, bk. 2, ch. 16: 215; Jean Bodin, *The Six Bookes of a Commonweale,* trans. Richard Knolles (London, 1606), bk. 1, ch. 5: 34; and Grotius, *Rights of War and Peace,* trans. Morrice, III.IV.X.1: 565. Neither Hobbes nor Pufendorf was much interested in this dispute, but Hobbes did mention it; see Hobbes, *Leviathan,* 104.

The classic treatment of the paired themes of slavery and death is Orlando Patterson, *Slavery and Social Death: A Comparative Study* (Cambridge, MA, 1982). Patterson's principal aim in this work was to develop a definition of slavery, which he did by means of what has become the famous metaphor of social death. Slavery, according to Patterson, was best understood as a condition of social death—that is, a relation of domination marked by a maximum of alienation and dishonor. That said, as he considered the processes in which persons were reduced to this condition, Patterson was well aware that slavery also had to be seen in close relation to physical death. Slavery "always originated (or was conceived of as having originated) as a substitute for death, usually violent death," he observed (5; see also 105–147). The relation between slavery and physical death—which was so prominent in descriptions of the sources of slavery, in particular—is my own focus in this book.

62. Gentili, *De iure belli,* trans. Rolfe, vol. 2, bk. 3, ch. 9: 328.

63. Pufendorf, *Law of Nature and Nations,* trans. Kennett, VI.III.VI: 125; and Pufendorf, *Whole Duty of Man According to the Law of Nature,* trans. Tooke (London, 1691), II.IV: 240.

64. The term that Locke used to describe this form of authority was of course "despotical power," which arose, he explained, when one person "puts himself into the state of War with another. For having quitted Reason, which God hath given to be the Rule betwixt Man and Man, and the common bond whereby human kind is united into one Fellowship and Society," Locke continued, the aggressor in such an instance, "so revolting from his own Kind to that of Beasts, by making Force, which is theirs, to be his Rule of Right, he renders himself liable to be destroyed by the injur'd Person, and the rest of Mankind, that will join with him in the execution of Justice, as any other wild Beast, or noxious Brute with whom Mankind can have neither Society nor Security." Locke, *Two Treatises of Government,* 2T §172: 320–321. Slavery was the condition in which what Locke called here "the execution of Justice" was delayed and the person who had transgressed against the natural law was put into the service of the person against whom this person had transgressed. For other passages in which Locke spoke in a similar manner of despotical power as a form of authority proper to wild beasts, see, for example, Locke, *Two Treatises of Government,* 2T §16: 191–192; and 2T §181: 327–328.

65. For scholars who have asserted that the account of slavery that Locke developed in his principal political works was composed with the contemporary practice of slavery in the English Atlantic world in mind, even if of course these scholars have held a wide variety of views about what Locke intended to be the effects of his account, see, for example, John Locke, *Two Treatises of Government,* ed. Peter Laslett (Cambridge, UK, 1960), 2T §24: 284–285 (editorial note); Davis, *Problem of Slavery in Western Culture,* 118–121; Martin Seliger, *The Liberal Politics of John Locke* (London, 1968), 116; Jennifer Welchman, "Locke on Slavery and Inalienable Rights," *Canadian Journal of Philosophy* 25, no. 1 (Mar. 1995): 67–81; Charles W. Mills, *The Racial Contract* (Ithaca, NY, 1997), 62–89; Brad Hinshelwood, "The Carolinian Context of John Locke's Theory of Slavery," *Political Theory* 41, no. 4 (Aug. 2013): 562–590; Nyquist, *Arbitrary Rule,* 326–361; Holly Brewer, "Slavery, Sovereignty, and 'Inheritable Blood': Reconsidering John Locke and the Origins of American Slavery," *American Historical Review* 122, no. 4 (Oct. 2017): 1038–1078; and Chris Taylor, "Divine Servitude against the Work of Man: Dispossessive Subjects and Exoduses to and from Property," *Religion* 50, no. 2 (2020): 215–236.

66. Davis, *Problem of Slavery in Western Culture,* 108.

2. ENGLISH FREEDOM IN A WORLD OF SLAVES

1. There are several recent accounts that have worked to provide an account of English thoughts and actions with respect to African peoples in the Atlantic world and, in so doing, to examine the period that is covered in this chapter in closer detail than had so far been the case. This chapter is indebted to these accounts and has relied upon their research and insight even as it has worked to build upon them. See Miranda Kaufmann, "Africans in Britain: 1500–1640" (D.Phil. thesis, University of Oxford, 2012); Michael Guasco, *Slaves and Englishmen: Human Bondage in the Early Modern Atlantic World* (Philadelphia, 2014); Cassander Smith, *Black Africans in the British Imagination: English Narratives of the Early Atlantic World* (Baton Rouge, LA, 2016); Miranda Kaufmann, *Black Tudors: The Untold Story* (London, 2017); Philip D. Morgan, "Virginia Slavery in Atlantic Context, 1550 to 1650," in *Virginia 1619: Slavery and Freedom in the Making of English America,* ed. Paul Musselwhite, Peter C. Mancall, and James Horn (Williamsburg, VA, 2019), 85–107; and Onyeka Nubia, *England's Other Countrymen: Black Tudor Society* (London, 2019).

2. One additional, although less important, element of the context for the conviction on the part of English authors in the second half of the sixteenth century that theirs was a nation dedicated to freedom was the repeal, in 1549, of a statute that had imposed enslavement to a master for two years as a punishment for able-bodied persons who were deemed to be vagrants for their refusal to labor. Notable as this act certainly was, it had been passed just two years prior and had never been enforced. See C. S. L. Davies, "Slavery and Protector Somerset; the Vagrancy Act of 1547," *Economic History Review* 19, no. 3 (1966): 533–549. The statute is 1 Edw. VI. c. 3 in *The Statutes of the Realm* (Burlington, CA, 2007), vol. 4, pt. 1: 5–8.

3. See Raphael Holinshed, *The First and Second Volumes of Chronicles* (London, 1587), a revised and expanded version of the 1577 original edition. See William Camden, *Britain, or a Chorographicall Description of the most flourishing Kingdomes, England, Scotland, and Ireland,* trans. Philemon Holland (London, 1610); this was the first English edition of the work, which had been printed in six Latin editions from 1586 to 1607.

4. Thomas Smith, *De republica Anglorum* (London, 1583), bk. 2, ch. 24: 86. Smith had perhaps come to this account of the nature of the nation in the course of reflection upon the failure and repeal of the 1547 statute on vagrancy, since Davies has had good reason to speculate that Smith, who was clerk of the Privy Council at the time, may himself have been the author of that statute. See Davies, "Slavery and Protector Somerset," 543–545.

5. For the best recent accounts of Bodin's original doctrine of sovereignty, see Richard Tuck, *The Sleeping Sovereign: The Invention of Modern Democracy* (Cambridge, UK, 2015), 1–62; and Daniel Lee, *The Right of Sovereignty: Jean Bodin on the Sovereign State and the Law of Nations* (Oxford, 2021). Due to the particular context in which he came to consider the matter of slavery, to represent Bodin as an "abolitionist," in the term that has been used by one recent scholar, is to see his position as more absolute than in fact it was. See Mary Nyquist, *Arbitrary Rule: Slavery, Tyranny, and the Power of Life and Death* (Chicago, 2013), 168.

6. Jean Bodin, *The Six Bookes of a Commonweale,* trans. Richard Knolles (London, 1606), bk. 1, ch. 5: 33.

7. Bodin, *Six Bookes of a Commonweale,* trans. Knolles, bk. 1, ch. 5: 34 (and, for his extended criticism of the two positions on slavery that were derived from Aristotle on the one hand and from Roman jurists on the other hand, see 34–38).

8. Bodin, *Six Bookes of a Commonweale,* trans. Knolles, bk. 1, ch. 5: 44 and 45.

9. Bodin, *Six Bookes of a Commonweale,* trans. Knolles, bk. 1, ch. 5: 42; John Rushworth, *Historical Collections of Private Passages of State, Weighty Matters in Law, Remarkable Proceedings in Five Parliaments,* 6 vols. (London, 1680–1701), vol. 2: 468; and William Harrison, "An Historicall Description of the Iland of Britaine," in Holinshed, *First and Second Volumes of Chronicles,* 1–250, bk. 2, ch. 5: 1.

10. Melchor de Santa Cruz de Dueñas, *Floresta española,* ed. María Pilar Cuartero and Maxime Chevalier (Barcelona, 1997), 197 (cited in translation from Kaufmann, *Black Tudors,* 13); and Bodin, *Six Bookes of a Commonweale,* trans. Knolles, bk. 1, ch. 5: 32 and 40. The line cited above did not appear in the English edition of *Floresta española* that was printed in 1595, though readers would have found in this text several references to Africans held as slaves in Spain; see, for example, *Wits Fittes and Fancies,* trans. Anthonie Copley (London, 1595), 23, 84, and 111. See also, for example, William D. Phillips Jr., *Slavery in Medieval and Early Modern Iberia* (Philadelphia, 2014).

11. On these issues, see, for example, Anthony Pagden, *Lords of All the World: Ideologies of Empire in Spain, Britain, and France c. 1500–1800* (New Haven, CT, 1995), 11–62; J. H. Elliott, *Empires of the Atlantic World: Britain and Spain in America, 1492–1830* (New Haven, CT, 2006); Geoffrey Parker, *Imprudent King: A New Biography of Philip II* (New Haven, CT, 2014); and Geoffrey Parker, *Emperor: A New Life of Charles V* (New Haven, CT, 2019).

12. Walter Bigges, *A Summarie and True Discourse of Sir Frances Drakes West Indian Voyage* (London, 1589), 27. This episode appeared in the version of this account

printed as Thomas Cates, "A summarie and true discourse of sir Frances Drakes West Indian voyage," in Richard Hakluyt, *The Principal Navigations, Voyages, Traffiques and Discoveries of the English Nation,* 3 vols. (London, 1599–1600), vol. 3: 534–548, 541. In addition, this episode also appeared in Samuel Purchas, "Virginias Verger," in Samuel Purchas, *Hakluytus Posthumus or Purchas His Pilgrimes,* 4 vols. (London, 1625), bk. 9, ch. 20, 4: 1809–1826, 1817. Hereafter these collections will be cited as Hakluyt, *Principal Navigations* (1599); and Purchas, *Hakluytus Posthumus or Purchas His Pilgrimes.*

13. Thomas Hobbes, *The Life of Mr. Thomas Hobbes of Malmesbury* (London, 1680), A2v; and "Ordering Martial Law against Possessors of Papal Bulls, Books, Pamphlets [Greenwich, 1 July 1588, 30 Elizabeth I]," in *Tudor Royal Proclamations,* ed. Paul L. Hughes and James F. Larkin, 3 vols. (New Haven, CT, 1964–1969), vol. 3 (*The Later Tudors*): 13–17, 14 and 15. See also Colin Martin and Geoffrey Parker, *Armada: The Spanish Enterprise and England's Deliverance in 1588* (New Haven, CT, 2023).

14. Rycharde Eden, "Rycharde Eden to the Reader," in Peter Martyr, *The Decades of the Newe Worlde or West India,* trans. Rycharde Eden (London, 1555), A1r–D3v, A2v. The other book on America that Eden printed was a translation from parts of Sebastian Münster's colossal description of the world; see *A treatyse of the newe India,* trans. Rycharde Eden (London, 1553).

15. Eden, "Rycharde Eden to the Reader," in Martyr, *Decades of the Newe Worlde,* trans. Eden, B1v. Perhaps one measure of this shift in English attitudes toward Spain is that when *The Decades of the Newe Worlde* was brought out in a revised edition in 1577, the former Preface by Eden had been excised from the text and replaced with an Epistle and Preface by the new editor, Richard Willes, who was much more neutral with respect to the depiction of Spanish actions and at least to some extent critical of the work of his predecessor. See Peter Martyr, *The History of Travayle in the West and East Indies,* trans. Richarde Eden and ed. Richarde Willes (London, 1577).

16. Bartholomew de las Casas, *The Spanish Colonie, or Briefe Chronicle of the Acts and gestes of the Spaniardes in the West Indies,* trans. M.M.S. (London, 1583), R2r–v.

17. Several of the classic accounts of this debate remain some of the best. See, for example, Lewis Hanke, *The Spanish Struggle for Justice in the Conquest of America* (Philadelphia, 1949); Lewis Hanke, *Aristotle and the American Indians: A Study in Race Prejudice in the Modern World* (Chicago, 1959); José A. Fernández-Santamaria, "Juan Ginés de Sepúlveda on the Nature of the American Indians," *The Americas* 31, no. 4 (Apr. 1975): 434–451; and Anthony Pagden, *The Fall of Natural Man: The American Indian and the Origins of Comparative Ethnology* (Cambridge, UK, 1982).

18. It should be noted that Aristotle himself had not devoted much attention to the methods by which natural slaves might be compelled to submit to their natural masters. He was far more concerned with the particular character of the relation that would develop between them. All the same, and as Sepúlveda hastened to point out, Aristotle did express approval for war that was waged for this purpose. He once referred in the *Politics* to "the art of acquiring slaves, I mean of justly acquiring them," as "a species of hunting or war." Aristotle, *Politics,* in *The Complete Works of Aristotle: The Revised Oxford Translation,* ed. Jonathan Barnes, 2 vols. (Princeton, NJ, 2014), vol. 2, 1986–2129, 1992: 1255b37–39.

19. Las Casas, *Spanish Colonie,* trans. M.M.S., Q3r and R1r. For "The summe of the disputation between Fryer Bartlemewe de las Casas or Causas, and Doctor Sepulveda," see Las Casas, *Spanish Colonie,* trans. M.M.S., Q3r–R2v. One central theme in the Valladolid debate that did not appear in this short report was the extreme care that Las Casas had taken there to demonstrate that the Indians were not natural slaves. Over the course of his career, he had accumulated a tremendous amount of empirical evidence in an effort to make plain what he took to be the fullness and rational character of Indian culture. Both major works in which Las Casas expanded upon this theme, his *History of the Indies* and his *Apologetic History of the Indies,* were begun long before he drew upon their findings in the confrontation with Sepúlveda, but neither one of these works came out in print before the nineteenth century, and neither one was at all well known in early-modern England. Moreover, little trace of this deep interest in Indian culture would have been evident from what Las Casas said about the Indians in the *Brevísima Relación.* Here they figured for the most part as the innocent victims of a massacre. Las Casas did at points mention the large and thriving nations to which the Spanish had laid waste, but more often in this work he compared the Indians to mere lambs, whom the Spanish had set upon like ravenous wolves. See, for example, Las Casas, *Spanish Colonie,* trans. M.M.S., A1r–A3r.

20. Francisco de Vitoria, "On the American Indians (*De Indis*)," in Francisco de Vitoria, *Political Writings,* trans. and ed. Anthony Pagden and Jeremy Lawrence (Cambridge, UK, 2010; orig. pub. 1991), 231–292, 239 and 250. For his reaction to the reports about the conquest of Peru, see Francisco de Vitoria, "Letter to Miguel de Arcos, OP, Salamanca, 8 November [1534]," in Vitoria, *Political Writings,* 331–333.

21. For the full text, in English as well as in Latin, of these Bulls of Donation, see *European Treaties Bearing on the History of the United States and Its Dependencies to 1648,* ed. Frances Gardiner Davenport, 4 vols. (Washington, DC, 1917–1937), vol. 1: 56–83. For early versions printed in England, in English as well as in Latin, see, for example, Martyr, *Decades of the Newe Worlde,* trans. Eden, 167r–173r; and Purchas,

Hakluytus Posthumus or Purchas His Pilgrimes, bk. 2, ch. 1, 1: 13–18. Finally, for his assessment, see Vitoria, "On the American Indians," in Vitoria, *Political Writings,* 258–264.

22. Vitoria, "On the American Indians," in Vitoria, *Political Writings,* 291.

23. Gentili thus held that "the law which is written in those books of Justinian is not merely that of the state, but also that of the nations and of nature." Alberico Gentili, *De iure belli libri tres,* ed. James Brown Scott, trans. John C. Rolfe, 2 vols. (London, 1933), vol. 2, bk. 1, ch. 3: 17. The lectures that Vitoria composed on the law of war were delivered soon after his lectures on the affairs of the Indies and were indeed presented as an effort to expand upon certain themes that he had introduced there. See Vitoria, "On the Law of War," in Vitoria, *Political Writings,* 293–327.

24. For his dismissal of the argument that the Spanish war upon the Indians was authorized by their natural slavery, see Gentili, *De iure belli,* trans. Rolfe, vol. 2, bk. 1, ch. 12: 53–57 (and in particular 55); for his rejection of the claim that the absence of Christian religion among the Indians could be considered as a reason to make war in order to convert them, see vol. 2, bk. 1, ch. 10: 38–41 (in particular 39) and ch. 25: 123. On this point, see Vitoria, "On the American Indians," in Vitoria, *Political Writings,* 243–246 and 265–272.

25. Gentili, *De iure belli,* trans. Rolfe, vol. 2, bk. 1, ch. 25: 122 (also 124). See Vitoria, "On the American Indians," in Vitoria, *Political Writings,* 272–275. On the bestiality and cannibalism of the Indians, see, for example, *A treatyse of the newe India,* trans. Eden, G6r–H2v; and Eden, "Rycharde Eden to the Reader," in Martyr, *Decades of the Newe Worlde,* trans. Eden, A2v–A3r; as well as Vitoria, "On the American Indians," in Vitoria, *Political Writings,* 273. Vitoria was the only source that Gentili cited on this point.

26. See, for example, Gentili, *De iure belli,* trans. Rolfe, vol. 2, bk. 1, ch. 14: 64–65, and ch. 16: 78.

27. Richarde Hackluyt, *A particular discourse concerninge the greate necessitie and manifolde commodyties that are like to growe to this Realme of Englande by the westerne discoveries lately attempted . . . Known as Discourse of Western Planting,* ed. David B. Quinn and Alison M. Quinn (London, 1993). This volume includes a facsimile version of the text, which was not printed at the time and seems to have been unknown until the nineteenth century outside of the small circle in which it was originally circulated. The title the work received in the period after it was rediscovered—that is, *Discourse of Western Planting*—to some extent mistook the character of Hakluyt's interest in America, which, as will be noted below, had more

to do with maritime commercial enterprise than with the effort to settle and maintain "plantations." On Hakluyt, see Peter C. Mancall, *Hakluyt's Promise: An Elizabethan's Obsession for an English America* (New Haven, CT, 2007).

28. In the chapter in which he put forward his own "aunswer to the Bull of the donacion of all the west Indies graunted to the kinges of Spain," Hakluyt did follow Vitoria in his assertion that this was not valid because the Pope had not had the authority to grant it. He also held, as had Vitoria, that the limited power of the Pope in temporal affairs was the main reason he could not have given dominion over the Indians to the Castilian Crown. That said, it will be no surprise that the Protestant Hakluyt did not come to this point from a reading of Aquinas, as had Vitoria, and based it instead upon the observation that, even if the Pope was admitted to be the Vicar of Christ, Christ had said that "his kingdomme was not of this worlde." "Why then doth the Pope that would be Christes servaunte," Hakluyt inquired, "take upon him the devision of so many kingdommes of the worlde?" Hackluyt, *Discourse of Western Planting,* ed. Quinn and Quinn, 96.

29. For a study of Raleigh's career, see Alan Gallay, *Walter Raleigh: Architect of Empire* (New York, 2019).

30. Hackluyt, *Discourse of Western Planting,* ed. Quinn and Quinn, 11 and 43. For the chapter in which he described and reflected upon "the incredible and more then barbarous and savage endeles cruelties" that the Spanish had inflicted upon the native peoples of America, which in turn would cause these people to "ioyne with us or any other moste willinglye to shake of their moste intolerable yoke," see 52–63. In the course of this chapter, Hakluyt quoted at length from the 1583 English edition of the *Brevísima Relación,* though he is also likely to have read the original Spanish version of the text.

31. "1607. 'A Justification for Planting in Virginia,'" in *New American World: A Documentary History of North America to 1612,* ed. David B. Quinn, 5 vols. (New York, 1979), vol. 3: 417–418.

On the early English efforts to establish the justice of their American enterprise, on the one hand, against the Spanish claim to complete dominion and, on the other hand, against the claims of the Indians, see, for example, Robert A. Williams Jr., *The American Indian in Western Legal Thought: The Discourses of Conquest* (New York, 1990), 121–225; Pagden, *Lords of All the World,* 63–102; Patricia Seed, *Ceremonies of Possession in Europe's Conquest of the New World, 1492–1640* (New York, 1995), 16–40; Richard Tuck, *The Rights of War and Peace: Political Thought and the International Order from Grotius to Kant* (New York, 1999), 109–139; David Armitage, *The Ideological Origins of the British Empire* (New York, 2000); Andrew Fitzmaurice,

Humanism and America: An Intellectual History of English Colonisation, 1500–1625 (Cambridge, UK, 2003); Ken MacMillan, *Sovereignty and Possession in the English New World: The Legal Foundations of Empire, 1576–1640* (Cambridge, UK, 2006); Christopher Tomlins, *Freedom Bound: Law, Labor, and Civic Identity in Colonizing English America, 1580–1865* (New York, 2010), 1–190; Andrew Fitzmaurice, *Sovereignty, Property and Empire, 1500–2000* (Cambridge, UK, 2014), 59–84; and Michael Guasco, *Slaves and Englishmen: Human Bondage in the Early Modern Atlantic World* (Philadelphia, 2014), 155–194.

32. Hackluyt, *Discourse of Western Planting,* ed. Quinn and Quinn, 8; and "April 10, 1606. The Charter That Created the Virginia Companies," in *New American World,* ed. Quinn, vol. 5: 191–197, 192.

33. See *The Digest of Justinian,* trans. and ed. Alan Watson, 4 vols. (Philadelphia, 1985), vol. 1: I.1.3–5.

34. See Vitoria, "On the American Indians," in Vitoria, *Political Writings,* 278–284; and Gentili, *De iure belli,* trans. Rolfe, vol. 2, bk. 1, ch. 19: 89–90. As Gentili thus observed, even though "commerce is in accordance with the law of nations," the Spanish in the Indies "were aiming there, not at commerce, but dominion." For his part, Vitoria had treated this matter with extreme caution. He held that the Spanish would have had a just cause for war if the Indians had prevented the Spanish from carrying on trade with them, but he also never indicated that he believed that this had happened and, moreover, never made an effort to defend what of course he knew was the complex colonial enterprise of the Spanish in the Indies in such terms.

See George Peckham, *A True Reporte, of the late discoveries, and possession, taken in the right of the Crowne of Englande, of the New-found Landes* (London, 1583); George Pecham, "A true Report of the late discoveries," in Richard Hakluyt, *The Principall Navigations, Voiages and Discoveries of the English Nation* (London, 1589), 701–718; and George Peckham, "A true Report of the late discoveries," in Hakluyt, *Principal Navigations* (1599), vol. 3: 165–181. Hereafter the former collection will be cited as Hakluyt, *Principall Navigations* (1589).

Of course, it was Hakluyt who had thus reprinted the work of Peckham. Later on in this chapter, we will introduce Hakluyt as an editor in addition to an author. As an author, the clearest statement that he made in defense of the English enterprise in America, after the 1584 report that he submitted to the Queen, was the "Notes Ascribed to Richard Hakluyt, 1598," in *The Original Writings and Correspondence of the Two Richard Hakluyts,* 2 vols., ed. E. G. R. Taylor (London, 1935), vol. 2: 420–425.

35. See *Digest of Justinian,* trans. and ed. Watson, vol. 4: XXXXI.1.1–7; *Justinian's Institutes,* trans. Peter Birks and Grant McLeod (Ithaca, NY, 1987), 55–57: II.1.1–24; and *The Institutes of Gaius,* trans. W. M. Gordon and O. F. Robinson (Ithaca, NY, 1988), 153–155: II.65–68.

36. See John Donne, *A Sermon upon the VIII. Verse of the I. Chapter of the Acts of the Apostles* (London, 1622), in particular 25–27. See also *The Holy Bible, Conteyning the Old Testament, and the New* (London, 1611), Genesis, ch. 1, ver. 28, and Genesis, ch. 9, ver. 1. It should be noted that, for Donne, the acquisition of land that was considered to be unused and thus unowned was an act that he understood to be legitimate under "a *Power* rooted in *Nature,* and a *Power* rooted in Grace," but was in addition authorized by what he said was "a power yssuing from the Law of *Nations.*" What Donne meant here was that, with respect to the acquisition of unowned land, a principle that at first inhered in the law of nature had then been enacted so widely in the legal codes of particular states that it had entered the law of nations, which was a collection of the customs all nations had in common. Donne, *Sermon upon the VIII. Verse of the I. Chapter of the Acts of the Apostles,* 25–26.

Both Vitoria and Gentili did mention this Roman principle of natural law, and did also accept in general terms that it was valid. But it is a measure of how little this principle was used in connection with the Spanish conquest of the Indies that neither author believed that it could have been at all useful in this context. Gentili, for example, maintained that it would be a mistake to focus upon unoccupied land in the Indies because there was unoccupied land in all parts of the world, including in Spain. See Vitoria, "On the American Indians," in Vitoria, *Political Writings,* 280–281; and Gentili, *De iure belli,* trans. Rolfe, vol. 2, bk. 1, ch. 17: 80–81.

37. Robert Johnson, *Nova Britannia: Offering Most Excellent fruites by Planting in Virginia* (London, 1609), B4v. This was a common comparison; see also, for example, William Symonds, *Virginia* (London, 1609), 15. The point made in this paragraph is well put in Fitzmaurice, *Humanism and America,* 164–166.

38. "1607. 'A Justification for Planting in Virginia,'" in *New American World,* ed. Quinn, vol. 3: 418. For an important account of Virginia that also treated the three arguments that have been described here as ones that could be seen to complement one another in a defense of the colonial enterprise, see William Strachey, *The Historie of Travell into Virginia Britania (1612),* eds. Louis B. Wright and Virginia Freund (London, 1953), in particular 7–29 ("A Praemonition to the Reader"). Even though this work circulated in manuscript in London from 1611, it did not come out in print until the nineteenth century. A separate shorter work from Strachey, which described the shipwreck of his fleet on the sea route to Virginia in 1609,

was composed in 1610; it became a source for Shakespeare in *The Tempest* and later appeared in print as William Strachey, "*A true reportory of the wracke, and redemption of Sir Thomas Gates Knight; upon, and from the Ilands of the Bermudas,*" in Purchas, *Hakluytus Posthumus or Purchas His Pilgrimes,* bk. 9, ch. 6, 4: 1734–1758.

39. Strachey, *Historie of Travell into Virginia Britania,* 26. For this principle, described as one that came in under the law of nations, see *Digest of Justinian,* trans. and ed. Watson, vol. 1: I.1.3 and IX.2.45.4.

40. Peckham, *True Reporte,* Ciir.

41. [Edward Waterhouse], *A Declaration of the State of the Colony and Affairs in Virginia* (London, 1622), 22. See also, for example, Christopher Brooke (with introduction by Robert C. Johnson), "A Poem on the Late Massacre in Virginia," *Virginia Magazine of History and Biography* 72, no. 3 (Jul. 1964): 259–292; John Frederick Fausz, "The Powhatan Uprising of 1622: A Historical Study of Ethnocentrism and Cultural Conflict" (Ph.D. diss., College of William and Mary in Virginia, 1977); and Alden T. Vaughan, "'Expulsion of the Salvages': English Policy and the Virginia Massacre of 1622," *WMQ* 35, no. 1 (Jan. 1978): 57–84; as well as James Horn, *A Brave and Cunning Prince: The Great Chief Opechancanough and the War for America* (New York, 2021).

42. Donne, *Sermon upon the VIII. Verse of the I. Chapter of the Acts of the Apostles,* 19; and [Waterhouse], *Declaration of the State of the Colony and Affairs in Virginia,* 22.

43. [Waterhouse], *Declaration of the State of the Colony and Affairs in Virginia,* 23; and "Virginia Company. A Letter to the Governor and the Council in Virginia. October 7, 1622," in *The Records of the Virginia Company of London,* ed. Susan M. Kingsbury, 4 vols. (Washington, DC, 1906–1935), vol. 3: 683–690, 683.

44. See Samuel Purchas, "Virginias Verger: Or a Discourse shewing the benefits which may grow to this Kingdome from American English Plantations," in Purchas, *Hakluytus Posthumus or Purchas His Pilgrimes,* bk. 9, ch. 20, 4: 1809–1826. On Purchas, see, for example, *The Purchas Handbook: Studies of the Life, Times and Writings of Samuel Purchas, 1577–1626,* ed. L. E. Pennington, 2 vols. (London, 1997).

45. See "A briefe Narration of the destruction of the Indies by the Spaniards: written by a Frier Bart. de las Casas a Spaniard," in Purchas, *Hakluytus Posthumus or Purchas His Pilgrimes,* bk. 8, ch. 4, 4: 1569–1603 (for the short report on the Valladolid debate, which like the rest of this text was drawn from the 1583 English edition, see 1601–1603); "Of the Popes Bull made to Castile, touching the New World," in Purchas, *Hakluytus Posthumus or Purchas His Pilgrimes,* bk. 2, ch. 1, 1: 13–18; and "Animadversions on the Said Bull of Pope Alexander," in Purchas, *Hakluytus*

Posthumus or Purchas His Pilgrimes, bk. 2, ch. 1, 1: 18–25. On these issues, see Armitage, *Ideological Origins of the British Empire,* 61–99.

46. Purchas, "Virginias Verger," in Purchas, *Hakluytus Posthumus or Purchas His Pilgrimes,* bk. 9, ch. 20, 4: 1816, 1811, and 1813.

47. Purchas, "Virginias Verger," in Purchas, *Hakluytus Posthumus or Purchas His Pilgrimes,* bk. 9, ch. 20, 4: 1819. Purchas also looked forward to consider what he said would be the "Iust advantage" the colonists would derive from the native people, insofar as the colonists would "make use of their labours" at Purchas, "Virginias Verger," in Purchas, *Hakluytus Posthumus or Purchas His Pilgrimes,* bk. 9, ch. 20, 4: 1811 and 1826. A similar plan had been proposed in the account of events in 1622 that the Virginia company had put out. According to this document, one of the benefits that would come from the massacre was that now the Indians could "justly be compelled to servitude and drudgery, and supply the roome of men that labour." [Waterhouse], *Declaration of the State of the Colony and Affairs in Virginia,* 24–25. A similar proposal was put before the company: "John Martin. 'The Manner Howe to Bringe the Indians into Subiection.' December 15, 1622," in *Records of the Virginia Company of London,* ed. Kingsbury, vol. 3: 704–707.

48. Las Casas, *Spanish Colonie,* trans. M.M.S., A2v.

49. Aristotle, *Politics,* in *Complete Works of Aristotle,* ed. Barnes, vol. 2, 1990: 1254a23; and 2029: 1278b36–37.

50. Hackluyt, *Discourse of Western Planting,* ed. Quinn and Quinn, 119.

Even the English observers of America from this period who were most well versed in the works of Aristotle never made an attempt to connect his doctrine of natural slavery to what would be the relations between the English settlers and the Indians. Hakluyt himself presented to the Queen a Latin abstract of the *Politics* in the same interview in which he also submitted to Her Majesty his report on westward expansion. Nevertheless, neither one of these works so much as entertained what was known to have been the common Spanish claim that the Indians were slaves as a matter of nature. Hakluyt appears to have accepted that as a matter of nature the Indians were free and that their relations with the Spanish fell under another type of rule that Aristotle had defined. It was a tyrannical regime that the Spanish had established over the Indians, according to Hakluyt. In this respect Hakluyt followed what had also been the opinion of Las Casas. For the abstract, see Richard Hakluyt, "Analysis, seu resolution perpetua in octo libris Politicorum Aristotelis," British Library MS Royal 12, G. XIII.

51. John Bonoeil, *His Maiesties Gracious Letter to the Earle of South-Hampton* (London, 1622), 85–86.

52. On the political situation in this period, see Thomas Cogswell, *The Blessed Revolution: English Politics and the Coming of War, 1621–1624* (Cambridge, UK, 1989), esp. 265–307; as well as Jason Eliot Eldred, "Imperial Spain in the English Imagination, 1563–1662" (Ph.D. diss., University of Virginia, 2010), 283–365.

53. Francis Bacon, *Considerations Touching a Warre with Spaine,* in *Certaine Miscellany Works of the Right Honourable Francis Lo. Verulam, Viscount S. Alban,* ed. William Rawley (London, 1629), 1–76, 12.

54. For his statement of the doctrine of *justus metus* and its application to the case for war with Spain, see Bacon, *Considerations Touching a Warre with Spaine,* in *Certaine Miscellany Works,* ed. Rawley, 12–23. For this doctrine in Gentili, see Gentili, *De iure belli,* trans. Rolfe, vol. 2, bk. 1, ch. 14: 61–66; and for its appearance in Roman law, see, for example, *Digest of Justinian,* trans. and ed. Watson, vol. 1: IV.2.5–6 and vol. 3: XXXIX.2.27. Bacon had pursued his aim for legal reform since the sixteenth century, and his most detailed proposal in this regard was first printed after his death in the same volume that also included his case for war with Spain: see Francis Bacon, *An Offer to our Late Soveraigne King James, of a Digest to be Made of the Lawes of England,* in *Certaine Miscellany Works,* ed. Rawley, 135–159.

55. For Bacon in the 1609 charter, see "May 23, 1609. The Second Virginia Charter, the First to the London Company Alone," in *New American World,* ed. Quinn, vol. 5: 205–212, 207. For Hobbes's admission, see "At a Virginia Court Held the 19th of June 1622," in *Records of the Virginia Company of London,* ed. Kingsbury, vol. 2: 39–56, 40.

56. Francis Bacon, "Of Plantations," in *The Essayes or Counsels, Civill and Morall, of Francis Lo. Verulam, Viscount St. Alban* (London, 1625), 198–204, 198.

57. The complex textual history of this account is as follows. It first appeared in print as "The seconde vyage to Guinea," in Peter Martyr, *The Decades of the Newe Worlde or West India,* trans. Rycharde Eden (London, 1555), 349v–360r. Then it was printed as "The second viage to Guinea," in Peter Martyr, *The History of Travayle in the West and East Indies,* trans. Richarde Eden and ed. Richarde Willes (London, 1577), 342v–353r. Hakluyt relied upon this edition for the account that he printed as "The second voyage to Guinea," in Hakluyt, *Principall Navigations* (1589), 89–98; and then as "The second voyage to Guinea," in Hakluyt, *Principal Navigations* (1599), vol. 2, pt. 2: 14–23. In the first two editions listed here, no member of the crew was identified by name as the source of Eden's information. Hakluyt was the first to identify Lok as Eden's source, which Hakluyt first did in the 1599 second edition of his collection.

58. "The seconde vyage to Guinea," in Martyr, *Decades of the Newe Worlde,* trans. Eden, 359v. See "The first voyage made by M. William Towrson Marchant of London, to the coast of Guinea," in Hakluyt, *Principall Navigations* (1589), 98–112, 107 and 109. For a useful survey of European enterprise in this period, see John W. Blake, *West Africa: Quest for God and Gold, 1454–1578* (London, 1977).

59. "The first voyage made by M. William Towrson Marchant of London," in Hakluyt, *Principall Navigations* (1589), 110 and 107.

60. "The first voyage made by M. William Towrson Marchant of London," in Hakluyt, *Principall Navigations* (1589), 108; and "The second voyage made by M. William Towrson to the coast of Guinea," in Hakluyt, *Principall Navigations* (1589), 112–120, 115. The man named Anthony does not appear in English sources after this point, but the return of Binny is mentioned in the narrative of the next Towerson voyage; see "The third and last voyage of Maister William Towrson, to the coast of Guinie," in Hakluyt, *Principall Navigations* (1589), 120–130, 126. One of the other men whom Lok had taken was said to be on an English ship at Mina in the narrative of the second Towerson voyage; see "The second voyage made by M. William Towrson," in Hakluyt, *Principall Navigations* (1589), 115.

The practice of early English merchants in Guinea of bringing local men home with them in order to prepare them to facilitate trade back in Guinea is discussed, for example, in Kaufmann, *Black Tudors,* 169–195. The practice received the support of officials in London; see "The Instructions," in *The Troublesome Voyage of Captain Edward Fenton, 1582–1583,* ed. E. G. R. Taylor (Cambridge, UK, 1959), 50–59, 56.

61. Walter Wren, "The voyage of M. George Fenner to Guinie," in Hakluyt, *Principall Navigations* (1589), 142–150, 144.

62. "The first voyage made by M. William Towrson Marchant of London," in Hakluyt, *Principall Navigations* (1589), 107.

63. For the full text of the 1455 Bull *Romanus Pontifex,* in English as well as in Latin, see *European Treaties Bearing on the History of the United States and Its Dependencies to 1648,* ed. Davenport, vol. 1: 9–26; for the Treaty of Tordesillas, see vol. 1: 84–100.

64. See Wren, "The voyage of M. George Fenner to Guinie," in Hakluyt, *Principall Navigations* (1589), 144–146 and 150. On occasion in this period, Englishmen in Guinea insinuated themselves into the Iberian trade in African persons as buyers rather than sellers of slaves. In 1582, a crew under the command of Edward Fenton stopped in Sierra Leone toward the start of an ill-fated voyage intended for China. The crew had been much depleted by disease. Before their departure from the coast, Fenton purchased four Africans from local Portuguese merchants in

order to replenish his ranks. See Luke Ward, "The voyage intended towards China, wherein M. Edward Fenton was appointed Generall," in Hakluyt, *Principall Navigations* (1589), 647–672, 655; and for clarification, see "Private Diary of John Walker," in *Troublesome Voyage of Captain Edward Fenton, 1582–1583,* ed. Taylor, 198–218, 209.

65. "The first voyage of the right worshipfull and valiant knight, sir John Hawkins . . . made to the West Indies 1562," in Hakluyt, *Principall Navigations* (1589), 521–522, 521–522.

66. See John Sparke, "The voyage made by the worshipful M. John Hawkins . . . to the coast of Guinea, and the Indies of Nova Spania . . . begunne in An. Dom. 1564," in Hakluyt, *Principall Navigations* (1589), 523–543; and John Hawkins, "The 3. Unfortunate voyage . . . to the partes of Guinea, and the West Indias, in the yeeres 1567. and 1568," in Hakluyt, *Principall Navigations* (1589), 553–557. This description of Hawkins's third voyage had previously appeared as John Hawkins, *A true declaration of the troublesome voyadge of M. John Hawkins to the parties of Guynea and the west Indies* (London, 1569).

67. "The first voyage of the right worshipfull and valiant knight, sir John Hawkins . . . made to the West Indies 1562," in Hakluyt, *Principall Navigations* (1589), 522. For a fuller discussion of Hawkins's methods in Guinea, see P. E. H. Hair, "Protestants as Pirates, Slavers, and Proto-Missionaries: Sierra Leone 1568 and 1582," in *Journal of Ecclesiastical History* 21, no. 3 (Jul. 1970): 203–224.

68. In 1607, on the route to India, William Finch and his crew stopped at Sierra Leone. They met a local ruler who seemed to possess the "power to sell his people for slaves." Finch noted that this ruler "proferred unto us" some of these persons. It is perhaps an indication of the lack of English interest in the slave trade in this period that Finch did not record his response. "Observations of William Finch, Merchant, taken out of his large Journall," in Purchas, *Hakluytus Posthumus or Purchas His Pilgrimes,* bk. 4, ch. 4, 1: 414–440, 414.

69. Richard Jobson, *The Golden Trade: or, A Discovery of the River Gambra, and the Golden Trade of the Aethiopians* (London, 1623), 89. For a useful modern edition, see *The Discovery of the River Gambra, 1623, by Richard Jobson,* ed. David P. Gamble and P. E. H. Hair (London, 1999). For the most detailed treatment of English trade with Guinea in this period, see J. W. Blake, "The Farm of the Guinea Trade," in *Essays in British and Irish History,* ed. H. A. Crone, T. W. Moody, and D. B. Quinn (London, 1949), 86–106. For the charter issued to the African company in 1618, see "African Company. (Patent Rolls, 16 Jac I. pt. vi.)," in *Select Charters of Trading Companies, A.D. 1530–1707,* ed. Cecil T. Carr (London, 1913), 99–106.

70. "The voyage of Richard Rainolds and Thomas Dassel to the rivers of Senega and Gambra adjoyning upon Guinea, 1591," in Hakluyt, *Principal Navigations* (1599), vol. 2, pt. 2: 188–192, 192; and Samuel Purchas, *Purchas His Pilgrimage. Or Relations of the World and the Religions Observed in All Ages and Places Discovered, from the Creation unto this Present* (London, 1613), 581. Of course, Jobson was well aware of the Iberian transatlantic slave trade from Guinea; see, for example, Jobson, *Golden Trade,* 29.

71. Robin Blackburn, *The Making of New World Slavery: From the Baroque to the Modern, 1492–1800* (London, 1997), 220; and Morgan, "Virginia Slavery in Atlantic Context, 1550 to 1650," in *Virginia 1619: Slavery and Freedom in the Making of English America,* ed. Musselwhite, Mancall, and Horn, 95. For examples of a similar approach to the relationship between Iberian and English practices in the early-modern Atlantic world, see James H. Sweet, "Spanish and Portuguese Influences on Racial Slavery in British North America, 1492–1619," in "Collective Degradation: Slavery and the Construction of Race," Proceedings of the Fifth Annual Gilder Lehrman Center International Conference at Yale University (Nov. 7–8, 2003), 1–33; and April Lee Hatfield, "A 'Very Wary People in Their Bargaining' or 'Very Good Marchandise': English Traders' Views of Free and Enslaved Africans, 1550–1650," in *Slavery and Abolition* 25, no. 3 (Dec. 2004): 1–17.

The most detailed and flexible work in the field is Michael Guasco, *Slaves and Englishmen: Human Bondage in the Early Modern Atlantic World* (Philadelphia, 2014), in particular 41–120. This chapter is much indebted to the work of Guasco, even if my own points of emphasis sometimes differ from his.

72. See "A discourse written by one Miles Phillips Englishman, one of the company put a shore in the West Indies by M. John Hawkins in the yeere 1568," in Hakluyt, *Principall Navigations* (1589), 562–580, 572.

One more source of particular insight into English perceptions of Spanish America, including into the institution of African slavery in the Spanish West Indies, is the richly illustrated unpublished document from the 1580s that has come to be known as the Drake Manuscript; see *Histoire Naturelle des Indes: The Drake Manuscript in the Pierpont Morgan Library* (New York, 1996).

For essential discussions of English actions at the margins of Spain's American empire in this period, see Kenneth R. Andrews, *The Spanish Caribbean: Trade and Plunder 1530–1630* (New Haven, CT, 1978); and Kenneth R. Andrews, *Trade, Plunder and Settlement: Maritime Enterprise and the Genesis of the British Empire 1480–1630* (Cambridge, UK, 1984).

73. The most judicious assessment of what Drake could have done with the Africans he took with him from Santo Domingo and Cartagena, as well as of the various

interpretations in the scholarship on this episode, is Guasco, *Slaves and Englishmen,* 109–120.

74. On Bermuda, whose Black population grew to around one hundred between 1616 and 1619, see Michael J. Jarvis, *Isle of Devils, Isle of Saints: An Atlantic History of Bermuda, 1609–1684* (Baltimore, 2022). On the broad Atlantic context for the arrival of the first Africans in Virginia, see April Lee Hatfield, *Atlantic Virginia: Intercolonial Relations in the Seventeenth Century* (Philadelphia, 2004); Peter C. Mancall, ed., *The Atlantic World and Virginia, 1550–1624* (Williamsburg, VA, 2007); and Paul Musselwhite, Peter C. Mancall, and James Horn, eds., *Virginia 1619: Slavery and Freedom in the Making of English America* (Williamsburg, VA, 2019).

75. Guasco, *Slaves and Englishmen,* 89. Guasco has provided the most complete account of the alliance that formed between Englishmen and *cimarrones* in this period; see 80–120.

For the standard accounts of Drake's exploits with the *cimarrones* in 1572, see "The first voyage, attempted and set foorth by the expert, and valiant Captaine M. Francis Drake himself . . . about the yeere 1572," in Hakluyt, *Principall Navigations* (1589), 594–595; "The first voyage attempted and set foorth by the expert and valiant captaine M. Francis Drake himself . . . about the yeere 1572," in Hakluyt, *Principal Navigations* (1599), vol. 3: 525–526; and Philip Nichols, *Sir Francis Drake Revived* (London, 1626).

For the encouragement from English colonial promoters to enlist the *cimarrones* in a challenge to the Spanish American empire, see, for example, William Alexander Stirling, *An Encouragement to Colonies* (London, 1625), 7; and Thomas Gage, *The English-American his Travail by Sea and Land: or, A New Survey of the West-India's* (London, 1648), 130.

76. Hackluyt, *Discourse of Western Planting,* ed. Quinn and Quinn, 43 and 60. Hakluyt no doubt had much of his information about the *cimarrones* from Drake himself, whom he said was "already in credite with the Symerons" and would be able to lead them in a combined attack upon the Spanish Empire in which English, Indian, and African forces could "bringe great thinges to passe, and that with greate ease" (119).

77. "The Discourse and Description of the voyage of Sir Frawncis Drake & Master Frobisher," in *Sir Francis Drake's West Indian Voyage, 1585–86,* ed. Mary Frear Keeler (London, 1981), 179–210, 189.

78. "A large Relation of the Port Ricco voiage, written as is reported, by that learned man and reverend Divine Doctor Layfield," in Purchas, *Hakluytus Posthumus or*

Purchas His Pilgrimes, bk. 6, ch. 3, 4: 1155–1176, 1166; and John King, *Lectures upon Jonas* (Oxford, 1597), 179. See also *An Elizabethan in 1582: The Diary of Richard Madox, Fellow of All Souls,* ed. and trans. Elizabeth Story Donno (London, 1976), 191–192; and "The admirable adventures and strange fortunes of Master Antonie Knivet," in Purchas, *Hakluytus Posthumus or Purchas His Pilgrimes,* bk. 6, ch. 7, 4: 1201–1242, 1233.

79. Stirling, *Encouragement to Colonies,* 7.

80. William Camden, *Annales: The True and Royall History of the famous Empresse Elizabeth Queene of England France and Ireland &c.,* trans. Abraham Darcie (London, 1625; orig. pub. 1615), bk. 1: 173.

Another author from this period who condemned Hawkins for his participation in the African slave trade was Samuel Purchas. In the course of a short report upon English travel to America, Purchas said that when the final Hawkins crew was attacked and all but demolished by the Spanish near Vera Cruz, Hawkins's "iniustice to Savages was chastised by uniustice of Christians." Samuel Purchas, "The first Voyages made to divers parts of America by Englishmen," in Purchas, *Hakluytus Posthumus or Purchas His Pilgrimes,* bk. 6, ch. 4, 4: 1177–1187, 1179.

81. Jobson, *Golden Trade,* 89; and "Observations collected out of the Iournall of Sir Thomas Roe, Knight, Lord Embassadour from His Maiestie of Great Britaine, to the Great Mogol," in Purchas, *Hakluytus Posthumus or Purchas His Pilgrimes,* bk. 4, ch. 16, 1: 535–591, 575.

82. John Wheeler, *A Treatise of Commerce, Wherein Are Shewed the Commodies Arising by a Wel Ordered and Ruled Trade* (Middelburg, 1601), 3. Wheeler was at this time the secretary of the Company of Merchant Adventurers, which controlled the cloth trade between England and the Continent.

In turn, with respect to the status of the slave in the Roman legal tradition as a person who could be owned, recall the influential statement from Florentinus in the *Digest* that slavery was "an institution of the *jus gentium,* whereby someone is against nature made subject to the ownership of another." *The Digest of Justinian,* trans. and ed. Alan Watson, 4 vols. (Philadelphia, 1985), vol. 1: I.5.4.

83. On the momentous transition to sugar cultivation and enslaved African labor on Barbados, see the suite of historical accounts cited in the notes in the Prologue. Perhaps the most exact chronological account of this transition is one not listed there: John J. McCusker and Russell R. Menard, "The Sugar Industry in the Seventeenth Century: A New Perspective on the Barbadian 'Sugar Revolution,'" in *Tropical Babylons: Sugar and the Making of the Atlantic World, 1450–1680,* ed. Stuart B. Schwartz (Chapel Hill, NC, 2004), 289–330.

84. "George Downing to John Winthrop, Jr.," in *Documents Illustrative of the History of the Slave Trade to America,* ed. Elizabeth Donnan, 4 vols. (Washington, DC, 1930–1935), vol. 1 (1440–1700): 125–126. One enslaved African on Barbados from this period was reported to have expressed doubt as to whether the Lord had blessed the sugar revolution on the island. "The Devel was in the English-man," this person was said to have observed, and explained that "he makes every thing work; he makes the Negro work, the Horse work, the Ass work, the Wood work, the Water work, and the Winde work." [Anonymous], *Great Newes from the Barbadoes* (London, 1676), 6.

85. For the charter issued to the new Royal African Company in 1660, see "African Company. (Patent Rolls, 12 Car. II, pt. xxi.)," in *Select Charters of Trading Companies, A.D. 1530–1707,* ed. Cecil T. Carr (London, 1913), 172–177, 174. For the 1663 charter, see "African Company. (Patent Rolls, 14 Car. II., pt. xxvii.)," in *Select Charters of Trading Companies,* ed. Carr, 177–181, 181.

86. "The Company of Royal Adventurers to Francis Lord Willoughby," in *Documents Illustrative of the History of the Slave Trade to America,* ed. Donnan, vol. 1 (1440–1700): 156–157, 156. For a discussion of the activities of the African company formed in 1630, see George Frederick Zook, *The Company of Royal Adventurers Trading into Africa* (Lancaster, PA, 1919).

87. For the 1672 charter, see "African Company. (Patent Rolls, 24 Car. II, pt. iii.)," in *Select Charters of Trading Companies,* ed. Carr, 186–192.

88. John Cary, *An Essay on the State of England, in Relation to Its Trade* (Bristol, 1695), 47 and 75 (and for Cary's advice on the organization of the slave trade, see 65–86); and Dalby Thomas, *An Historical Account of the Rise and Growth of the West-India Collonies* (London, 1690), 28 and 30 (and for Thomas's awareness that almost all of the labor in the West Indian sugar colonies was done by enslaved Africans, see 13–29).

3. THE ENGLISH IMAGE OF AFRICA

1. The region of the continent that has come to be known as sub-Saharan was in the period considered here marked not by reference to a desert but rather by reference to a river—the Senegal—which was said to set the border between the "tawny" or "brown" peoples to the north of it and the black-skinned peoples who lived to the south. The original source in this respect was the fifteenth-century account of the Venetian trader Alvise Cadamosto. See *The Voyages of Cadamosto and Other Documents on Western Africa in the Second Half of the Fifteenth Century,* trans. and ed. G. R. Crone (London, 1937), 27–28. What Cadamosto said on this

point was then later repeated by Richard Eden. See "The seconde vyage to Guinea," in Peter Martyr, *The Decades of the Newe Worlde or West India,* trans. Rycharde Eden (London, 1555), 349v–360r, 355v. In turn, what both Cadamosto and Eden said was more or less in accord with an opinion expressed in the most influential account of northwestern Africa in the early-modern period: that the northernmost black-skinned peoples lived along the Niger River, which was believed to feed into both the Senegal River and the Gambia River at some undetermined point near the western coast. See John Leo, *A Geographical Historie of Africa,* trans. John Pory (London, 1600), 2–5.

2. In early-modern England, the most influential account of this kind was that of Acosta, which first came out in English as Joseph Acosta, *The Naturall and Morall Historie of the East and West Indies,* trans. Edward Grimeston (London, 1604). It appeared in several excerpts in the Purchas collection—for example, as "Civill Customes and Arts of the Indians taken out of Acosta's 6. Booke," in Purchas, *Hakluytus Posthumus or Purchas His Pilgrimes,* bk. 5, ch. 6, 3: 1050–1065.

The method of cultural classification that was developed in such accounts has best been described in the works of Anthony Pagden: see, for example, Anthony Pagden, *The Fall of Natural Man: The American Indian and the Origins of Comparative Anthropology* (Cambridge, UK, 1982); as well as Anthony Pagden, *European Encounters with the New World: From Renaissance to Romanticism* (New Haven, CT, 1993).

3. For the charters issued to the African companies in 1660 and 1672, respectively, see "African Company. (Patent Rolls, 12 Car. II, pt. xxi.)," in *Select Charters of Trading Companies, A.D. 1530–1707,* ed. Cecil T. Carr (London, 1913), 172–177; and "African Company. (Patent Rolls, 24 Car. II, pt. iii.)" in *Select Charters of Trading Companies,* ed. Carr, 186–192.

For detailed discussions of these themes, see K. G. Davies, *The Royal African Company* (London, 1957), 213–290; P. E. H. Hair and Robin Law, "The English in Western Africa to 1700," in *The Origins of Empire: British Overseas Enterprise to the Close of the Seventeenth Century,* ed. Nicholas Canny (Oxford, 1998), 241–263; David Eltis, *The Rise of African Slavery in the Americas* (New York, 2000), 137–163; and Simon P. Newman, *A New World of Labor: The Development of Plantation Slavery in the British Atlantic* (Philadelphia, 2013).

4. Winthrop Donaldson Jordan, "White over Black: The Attitudes of the American Colonists toward the Negro, to 1784" (Ph.D. diss., Brown University, 1960), 19. As Christopher Brown has noted, the dissertation from which Jordan developed *White over Black* contained "in its essentials" the first half of the book. This was the case for the famous first chapter of the book, except for several incautious but revealing

statements such as the one quoted above. See Christopher Leslie Brown, "Foreword," Winthrop D. Jordan, *White over Black: American Attitudes toward the Negro, 1550–1812,* 2nd ed. (Chapel Hill, NC, 2012; orig. pub. 1968), vii–xvi, xii. "What enabled Europeans to buy Negroes as slaves," Jordan maintained here, "was the blackness and barbarism which placed the Africans beyond the pale of civilization."

For more recent statements of some version of this essential position, see Dorothy Hammond and Alta Jablow, *The Myth of Africa* (New York, 1977); Anthony J. Barker, *The African Link: British Attitudes to the Negro in the Era of the Atlantic Slave Trade, 1550–1807* (Totowa, NJ, 1978); Alden T. Vaughan, "The Origins Debate: Slavery and Racism in Seventeenth-Century Virginia," in Alden T. Vaughan, *Roots of American Racism: Essays on the Colonial Experience* (New York, 1995), 136–174; Betty Wood, *The Origins of American Slavery: Freedom and Bondage in the English Colonies* (New York, 1997); David Eltis, *The Rise of African Slavery in the Americas* (New York, 2000); Mary Nyquist, *Arbitrary Rule: Slavery, Tyranny, and the Power of Life and Death* (Chicago, 2013); Keith Thomas, *In Pursuit of Civility: Manners and Civilization in Early Modern England* (Waltham, MA, 2017); and Jennifer Morgan, *Reckoning with Slavery: Gender, Kinship, and Capitalism in the Early Black Atlantic* (Durham, NC, 2021).

5. *The excellent and pleasant worke of Julius Solinus Polyhistor,* trans. Arthur Golding (London, 1587), Qiiiv; *Julius Solinus Polyhistor,* trans. Golding, Siv; and Aristotle, *Generation of Animals,* trans. A. L. Peck, 2 vols. (Cambridge, MA, 1943), vol. 2, ch. 7: 245 (see also Aristotle, *History of Animals,* trans. D. M. Balme, 3 vols. [Cambridge, MA, 1991], vol. 3, ch. 7: 203).

Please note that the standard modern English translations are used for quotations from classical texts for which there were no well-known early-modern vernacular print editions.

6. *The Rare and Singuler Worke of* Pomponius Mela, trans. Arthur Golding (London, 1590), 8.

The most important editions of Pliny that were current in early-modern England were *A Summarie of the Antiquities, and wonders of the worlde, abstracted out of the sixtene first bookes of the excellente Historiographer Plinie,* trans. I.A. (London, 1566); and above all *The Historie of the World. Commonly called, The Naturall Historie of C. Plinius Secundus,* trans. Philemon Holland (London, 1601).

For the deviant human forms that there were to be found in Ethiopia, see *A Summarie of the Antiquities, and wonders of the worlde,* trans. I.A., Biiiv–Biiiiv; and *Historie of the Worlde,* trans. Holland, bk. 5, chs. 1–8: 90–96 and bk. 6, ch. 30: 146–148. See also *Rare and Singuler Worke of Pomponius Mela,* trans. Golding, 8 and 14–15; and *Julius Solinus Polyhistor,* trans. Golding, Tr–Uiir; as well as Herodotus, *The Persian*

Wars, trans. A. D. Godley, 4 vols. (Cambridge, MA, 1920–1925), vol. 2, bk. 4: 351–364.

7. *Diodorus of Sicily,* Library of History, trans. C. H. Oldfather, 12 vols. (Cambridge, MA, 1933–1967), vol. 2, bk. 3: 105 (for the broader discussion of these peoples, see vol. 2, bk. 3: 85–133); and *Julius Solinus Polyhistor,* trans. Golding, Uiv. See also *The Geography of Strabo,* trans. Horace Leonard Jones, 8 vols. (New York, 1917–1933), vol. 8, bk. 17.

On the Atlantes, see, for example, Herodotus, *Persian Wars,* trans. Godley, vol. 2, bk. 4: 357; *Rare and Singuler Worke of Pomponius Mela,* trans. Golding, 15; *Geography of Strabo,* trans. Jones, vol. 8, bk. 17: 147; and *Historie of the Worlde,* trans. Holland, bk. 5, ch. 8: 96.

The work of Diodorus had been rendered into English in the late fifteenth century by the poet John Skelton, but this edition did not appear in print until the twentieth century; see *The Bibliotheca Historica of Diodorus Siculus,* trans. John Skelton, ed. F. M. Salter and H. L. R. Edwards (London, 1956–1957).

8. For a useful edition, see J. Lennart Berggren and Alexander Jones, *Ptolemy's* Geography*: An Annotated Translation of the Theoretical Chapters* (Princeton, NJ, 2000).

9. See *Ptolemy's Cosmographia: A Facsimile of the First Atlas: Bologna, 1477* (Greenwich, CT, 2007), fols. 12–15.

10. The best references are Oscar I. Norwich, *Norwich's Maps of Africa: An Illustrated and Annotated Carto-Bibliography,* rev. and ed. Jeffrey C. Stone (Norwich, VT, 1997); Rodney W. Shirley, *The Mapping of the World: Early Printed World Maps, 1472–1700* (Riverside, CT, 2001); and Richard L. Betz, *The Mapping of Africa: A Cartobibliography of Printed Maps of the African Continent to 1700* (Utrecht, 2007). See also Henry N. Stevens, *Ptolemy's* Geography*: A Brief Account of All the Printed Editions down to 1730* (London, 1908). Mercator's Ptolemaic map of Africa is not listed in these works but was printed as "Africae Tabula IIII" in Gerardum Mercatorem, *Tabulae Geographicae Cl: Ptolemei admentem autoris restitutæ & emendate* (1578), unpaginated (after fol. O).

11. See, in order, *The Discription of the Contrey of Aphrique,* trans. Wyllyam Prat (London, 1554); *The Fardle of Facions,* trans. William Watreman (London, 1555); William Cuningham, *The Cosmographical Glasse* (London, 1559); Andrewe Thevet, *The New Found Worlde,* trans. Anonymous (London, 1568); and Bartholomaeus Anglicus, *Batman uppon Bartholome, His Booke De Proprietatibus Rerum,* trans. John Trevisa and rev. and supp. Stephen Batman (London, 1582). The works of Prat and Waterman were made from the French edition of Johann Boemus, *Omnium gentium mores, leges et ritus* (1520). An English edition was later made from this impor-

tant work: Ioannes Boemus, *The Manners, Lawes, and Customes of All Nations,* trans. Edward Aston (London, 1611).

12. "The seconde vyage to Guinea," in Martyr, *The Decades of the Newe Worlde,* trans. Eden, 355v.

13. "The seconde vyage to Guinea," in Martyr, *Decades of the Newe Worlde,* trans. Eden, 349v.

Eden's use of classical sources to describe parts of Africa where European travelers had just started to explore can be seen to resemble the reliance of Spanish authors upon the works of classical authorities in the course of their own efforts to describe America in the early period of Spanish overseas exploration. This theme has received careful treatment in, for example, J. H. Elliott, *The Old World and the New, 1492–1650* (Cambridge, UK, 1970); Anthony Pagden, *The Fall of Natural Man: The American Indian and the Origins of Comparative Anthropology* (Cambridge, UK, 1982); Anthony Grafton (with April Shelford and Nancy Siraisi), *New Worlds, Ancient Texts: The Power of Tradition and the Shock of Discovery* (Cambridge, MA, 1992); David A. Lupher, *Romans in a New World: Classical Models in Sixteenth-Century Spanish America* (Ann Arbor, MI, 2003); and Sabine MacCormack, *On the Wings of Time: Rome, the Incas, Spain, and Peru* (Princeton, NJ, 2007).

14. *Homers Odysses,* in *The Whole Works of Homer: Prince of Poetts in His Iliads and Odysses,* trans. George Chapman (London, 1616), 1–376, 2.

15. This point has been best developed in the works of Malvern van Wyk Smith, who has observed that from classical Greece to imperial Rome, perceptions of Africa were "dialectically established, negotiated and interrogated along lines suggested by the trope of 'two Ethiopias': 'worthy' and 'noble' or 'other' and 'savage,' with many surprises in between." Malvern van Wyk Smith, *The First Ethiopians: The Image of Africa and Africans in the Early Mediterranean World* (Johannesburg, 2009), 62 (see esp. 281–378).

16. Herodotus, *Persian Wars,* trans. Godley, vol. 2, bk. 4: 395 (for the complete description, see vol. 2, bk. 4: 347–395); and Herodotus, *Persian Wars,* trans. Godley, vol. 2, bk. 3: 141 (and also vol. 2, bk. 3: 25–35).

17. *Geography of Strabo,* trans. Jones, vol. 8, bk. 17: 141; and *Diodorus of Sicily,* trans. Oldfather, vol. 2, bk. 3: 91. For his complete description of the eastern Ethiopians, see *Diodorus of Sicily,* trans. Oldfather, vol. 2, bk. 3: 89–113. For accounts of Ethiopian burial rituals, see *Geography of Strabo,* trans. Jones, vol. 8, bk. 17: 147; and *Diodorus of Sicily,* trans. Oldfather, vol. 1, bk. 2: 399 and vol. 2, bk. 3: 95 and 109.

18. *Diodorus of Sicily,* trans. Oldfather, vol. 2, bk. 3: 93 (see Herodotus, *Persian Wars,* trans. Godley, vol. 2, bk. 3: 35); and *Historie of the Worlde,* trans. Holland, bk. 6, ch. 29: 145.

19. *The Famous and Memorable Workes of Josephus,* trans. Thomas Lodge (London, 1602), bk. 8, ch. 2: 202 (see *The Holy Bible, Conteyning the Old Testament, and the New* [London, 1611], 1 Kings, ch. 10, ver. 1–13); and *Holy Bible,* Psalm 68, ver. 31. For Phillip, see *Holy Bible,* Acts, ch. 8, ver. 27–39. For Matthew, see *The Auncient Ecclesiastical Histories of the First Six Hundred Yeares after Christ,* trans. Meredith Hanmer (London, 1607; orig. pub. 1584), 534.

20. *The Voyages and Travailes of Sir John Maundevile Knight* (London, 1582), Riiir (see in general chs. 86–99: Riiir–Tiir).

21. For the chapters on Prester John in the extract from the work of Mandeville that appeared in the first edition of the Hakluyt collection, see "The Voyages and Discoveries of S. J. Mandevil," in Hakluyt, *Principall Navigations* (1589), 24–77, 65–72. It is a reflection of the shift in location of Prester John from Asia to Africa that had taken place in the period between Mandeville and Hakluyt that, in the index to the Hakluyt collection, the Asian ruler described in the Mandeville extract was identified as "Presbiter John Emperor in Affrike."

For a valuable discussion of this period, see Matteo Salvadore, *The African Prester John and the Birth of Ethiopian-European Relations, 1402–1555* (New York, 2016).

22. See, for example, Michael E. Brooks, "Prester John: A Reexamination and Compendium of the Mythical Figure Who Helped Spark European Expansion" (Ph.D. Diss., University of Toledo, 2009), esp. 51–173. Even one of the most careful scholars in the field has said that "the gradual demise of the Prester John legend in inner Africa" was "a dominant trend from the early sixteenth century." Francesc Relaño, *The Shaping of Africa: Cosmographic Discourse and Cartographic Science in Late Medieval and Early Modern Europe* (Burlington, VT, 2001), 66 (for the full discussion, see 51–74).

23. *Fardle of Facions,* trans. Watreman, Bviiir, Ciir, Ciir, Ciir, Ciir, and Ciiv. For the description of eastern Ethiopia most similar to that of Waterman, see the one that appeared in the other work that was done in this period from the survey of Boemus, which was *Discription of the Contrey of Aphrique,* trans. Prat, Dvv–Eiiv.

At this point it must be noted that although both Waterman and Prat repeated the classical opinion that the Ethiopians had been generated by the earth as the first men, both authors also were well aware of the radical departure that what they referred to as this "false opinion" marked from "the true opinion of the devine, concerning the beginnyng of man." *Fardle of Facions,* trans. Watreman, Bivv and Biir (and see also *Discription of the Contrey of Aphrique,* trans. Prat, Ciiir–Diiiv). Indeed, the Christian account of the origin of humankind, and the place of the peoples of Africa within this account, will be touched upon in Chapter 5.

24. *Fardle of Facions,* trans. Watreman, Civv, Cvr, Cvr, and Cvir. For accounts of the empire of Prester John, see *Fardle of Facions,* trans. Watreman, Civv–Cviir; and *Discription of the Contrey of Aphrique,* trans. Prat, Eiir–Evr. For briefer acknowledgments that eastern Ethiopia was now under the dominion of Prester John, see Cuningham, *Cosmographical Glasse,* 187; Thevet, *New Found Worlde,* trans. Anon., 24r; and Bartholomaeus, *Batman uppon Bartholome,* trans. Trevisa and rev. and supp. Batman, 251r.

25. Rycharde Eden, "A breefe description of Affrike," in Martyr, *Decades of the Newe Worlde,* trans. Eden, 344r–345r, 344v. For references to "the dominion of the greate Emperoure of Ethiope cauled Prester John" and "the sayde Christian Emperoure Prester John," see the description of Africa from Eden that appeared in "The seconde vyage to Guinea," in Martyr, *Decades of the Newe Worlde,* trans. Eden, 356r.

26. Jordan, *White over Black,* 20; and Alden T. Vaughan and Virginia Mason Vaughan, "Before Othello: Elizabethan Representations of Sub-Saharan Africans," *WMQ* 54, no. 1 (Jan. 1997): 19–44, 42. For their uses of Eden's phrase, see Jordan, *White over Black,* 24 and 28; and Vaughan and Vaughan, "Before Othello," *WMQ*, 25.

27. The most learned inquiries into what nevertheless remains the indeterminate authorship of this twelfth-century letter are Karl F. Helleiner, "Prester John's Letter: A Mediaeval Utopia," *Phoenix* 13, no. 2 (Summer 1959): 47–57; and Vsevolod Slessarev, *Prester John; The Letter and the Legend* (Minneapolis, MN, 1959).

28. William Shakespeare, *The First Quarto of* Othello, ed. Scott McMillin (Cambridge, UK, 2001), act 1, scene 3: 67.

29. J. A. Froude, *Short Studies in Great Subjects,* 4 vols. (London, 1891), vol. 1: 446. On the fundamentally commercial concerns of the Hakluyt collection, which is perceptively considered in this context as "an epic of commerce," see Richard Helgerson, *Forms of Nationhood: The Elizabethan Writing of England* (Chicago, 1992), 149–191, 190.

30. "A voyage made out of England into Guinea in Affricke . . . in the yeere of our Lorde. 1553," in Hakluyt, *Principall Navigations* (1589), 83–87, 86; and George Best, "A true Discourse of the three Voyages of discoverie, for the finding of a passage to Cathaya, by the Northwest," in Hakluyt, *Principal Navigations* (1599),

vol. 3: 47–96, 48, 49, and 48. See also George Best, *A True Discourse of the Late Voyages of Discoverie . . . under the conduct of Martin Frobisher Generall* (London, 1578), 19, 22, and 19–20.

31. William Garrard, "The first voyage of Robert Baker to Guinie, with the Minion, and Primrose, set out in October, 1562," in Hakluyt, *Principall Navigations* (1589), 130–135, 132; "The second voyage to Guinea," in Hakluyt, *Principall Navigations* (1589), 89–98; "The first voyage made by M. William Towrson Marchant of London, to the coast of Guinea," in Hakluyt, *Principall Navigations* (1589), 98–112, 102; "The second voyage made by M. William Towrson to the coast of Guinea," in Hakluyt, *Principall Navigations* (1589), 112–120, 114; "The voyage of Richard Rainolds and Thomas Dassel," in Hakluyt, *Principal Navigations* (1599), vol. 2, pt. 2: 191; Anthony Ingram, "The voiage set forth by M. John Newton, and M. John Bird marchants of London to the kingdome and Citie of Benin in Africa," in Hakluyt, *Principal Navigations* (1599), vol. 2, pt. 2: 129; and James Welsh, "A voyage to Benin beyond the Countrey of Guinea," in Hakluyt, *Principal Navigations* (1599), vol. 2, pt. 2: 129.

For studies of English perceptions of the native people in Guinea in this period, see, for example, Emily C. Bartels, "Othello and Africa: Postcolonialism Reconsidered," *WMQ* 54, no. 1 (Jan. 1997): 45–64; P. E. H. Hair, "Attitudes to Africans in English Primary Sources on Guinea up to 1650," *History in Africa,* vol. 26 (1999): 43–64; and Jennifer L. Morgan, *Laboring Women: Reproduction and Gender in New World Slavery* (Philadelphia, 2004), 12–68.

32. "The first voyage made by M. William Towrson Marchant of London, to the coast of Guinea," in Hakluyt, *Principall Navigations* (1589), 102 (also 108). Also see the Guinean vocabulary translated into Latin in the diary of a chaplain aboard the Fenton voyage that was first printed as *An Elizabethan in 1582: The Diary of Richard Madox, Fellow of All Souls,* trans. and ed. Elizabeth Story Donno (London, 1976), 177.

33. George Abbot, *A Briefe Description of the Whole Worlde* (London, 1599), Cviir and Ciiiv; and John Thorie, *The Theatre of the Earth* (London, 1599), Bivv. In this transitional period in English attitudes, even Abbot could repeat as current information legends from the classical authors whom he otherwise dismissed. "According to the Proverbe, *Africa semper aliquid apportat novi,*" Abbot wrote, in a version of the Latin phrase that Pliny had adapted from Aristotle, "new and strange shapes of beastes are brought forth there . . . where oftentimes contrarie kinds have conjunction the one with the other." Abbot, *Briefe Description of the Whole Worlde,* Civv.

34. Robert Morden, *Geography Rectified: Or, A Description of the World* (London, 1680), 318 (reprinted in Robert Morden, *Geography Rectified: Or, A Description of the World,* 2nd ed. [London, 1700], 462); and Peter Heylyn, *Cosmographie in Four Bookes* (London, 1652), bk. 4, pt. 1: 2 (and reprinted in Peter Heylyn, *Cosmographie in Four Books,* 5th ed. [London, 1677], bk. 4, pt. 1: 2).

35. Emily C. Bartels, "Imperialist Beginnings: Richard Hakluyt and the Construction of Africa," *Criticism* 34, no. 4 (Fall 1992): 517–538, 525; and John Speed, *A Prospect of the Most Famous Parts of the World* (London, 1627), 5.

The seventeenth-century critique of ancient opinion about Africa was perhaps best expressed in a passage in a book that was for the most part a translation from the atlas of the famous French cartographer Sanson. "But it is time to finish *Affrica,*" as the author wrote toward the end of his account, "and to say that if we would have believed certain *Authors* among the *Antients,* this *Affrica* had been represented to us with unsupportable *heates,* unsufferable *drought,* fierce and cruel *beasts,* perfidious *Men,* horrible and affrightful *Monsters,* whereas time, which daily discovers things unknown to the *antients,* hath made us see that the greatest *heates* of *Affrica* have some *refreshments;* that the dryest *sands* have some *wells,* some *waters;* that the vastest *solitudes* have some *green fields,* some *fruits;* that the *beasts* are not so dangerous, but that *Men* may defend themselves from their fury; nor the *Men* so *faithless,* but that they have *Commerce* and *Society* among themselves, as also with *Strangers.*" Richard Blome, *A Geographical Description of the Four Parts of the World* (London, 1670), pt. 2: 82.

36. Purchas, "The Epistle Dedicatorie," in Purchas, *Hakluytus Posthumus or Purchas His Pilgrimes,* vol. 1: unpaginated (after title page); and Purchas, "To the Reader," in Purchas, *Hakluytus Posthumus or Purchas His Pilgrimes,* vol. 1: unpaginated (after title page). Hereafter this collection will be cited in an even more abbreviated form as Purchas, *Pilgrimes.* For reference, see C. R. Steele, "From Hakluyt to Purchas," in *The Hakluyt Handbook,* ed. David B. Quinn, 2 vols. (London, 1974), vol. 1: 74–96; and *The Purchas Handbook: Studies of the Life, Times and Writings of Samuel Purchas, 1577–1626,* ed. L. E. Pennington, 2 vols. (London, 1997).

37. Eden, "The seconde vyage to Guinea," in Martyr, *Decades of the Newe Worlde,* trans. Eden, 356r and 355v; and *Fardle of Facions,* trans. Watreman, Fvir. See "Aphricæ Tablua IIII," in Munsteri, *Geographia universalis* (1542), fol. 16 (figure 4); and "Africae Index," in Gerardum Mercatorem, *Tabulae Geographicae Cl: Ptolemei admentem autoris restitutæ & emendate* (1578).

38. See "Drawen out of the writings and discourses of Odoardo Lopes, a Portingall, by Philippo Pigafetta," *A Report of the Kingdome of Congo, a Region of Africa,*

trans. Abraham Hartwell (London, 1597); and John Huighen van Linschoten, *Discours of Voyages into ye Easte and West Indies,* trans. W.P. (London, 1598), bk. 1, chs. 3–4: 5–11; and bk. 2: 198–216.

39. For an excellent contextual biography, see Natalie Zemon Davis, *Trickster Travels: A Sixteenth-Century Muslim Between Worlds* (New York, 2006). Still in 1704, in an informed assessment of the field, Leo was judged to have "given the best light into [*Africk*] of any Writer." "The Catalogue and Character of most Books of Travels," in *A Collection of Voyages and Travels,* 4 vols. (London, 1704), vol. 1: lxxvi–c, lxxvi.

40. For geography books held in Tudor libraries, see E. G. R. Taylor, *Tudor Geography, 1485–1583* (London, 1930), 193–243 (appendix II). See Eden, "A breefe description of Affrike," in Martyr, *Decades of the Newe Worlde,* trans. Eden, 344r–345r; as well as Bartholomaeus, *Batman uppon Bartholome,* trans. Trevisa and rev. and supp. Batman, 250r–251r.

41. Shakespeare, *First Quarto of* Othello, ed. McMillin, act 1, scene 3: 66; and John Pory, "To the Reader," in John Leo, *A Geographical Historie of Africa,* trans. John Pory (London, 1600), unpaginated.

On the parallels between Othello and Leo Africanus, see Lois Whitney, "Did Shakespeare Know Leo Africanus?" *PMLA* 37, no. 3 (Sept. 1922): 470–483; and Emily C. Bartels, *Speaking of the Moor: From Alcazar to Othello* (Philadelphia, 2008), 138–190.

42. Hakluyt, "[editor's note]," in Hakluyt, *Principal Navigations* (1599), vol. 2, pt. 2: 193; and Hakluyt, "An approbation of the historie ensuing," in Leo, *Geographical Historie of Africa,* trans. Pory, 57.

Pory attested in this edition of the work of Leo that Hakluyt had been "the onely man that moved me to translate it." Pory, "To the Right Honorable sir Robert Cecil Knight," in Leo, *Geographical Historie of Africa,* trans. Pory, unpaginated. In this period, Hakluyt had also overseen the English translations of the works of Lopes and van Linschoten that were mentioned above—as well as that of the work of Alvarez, which will be mentioned later in this chapter, and the description of the Guinea coast by Pieter de Marees that will appear in Chapter 4. See D. B. Quinn, C. E. Armstrong, and R. A. Skelton, "The Primary Hakluyt Bibliography," in *The Hakluyt Handbook,* ed. David B. Quinn, 2 vols. (London, 1974), vol. 2: 461–575, 528–569 ("Works in which Hakluyt's influence is known or acknowledged").

43. Leo, *Geographical Historie of Africa,* trans. Pory, 2 (for example) and 42.

44. Purchas, "[editor's note]," in Purchas, *Pilgrimes,* bk. 1, ch. 6, 1: 74.

See "To the Most Reverend Father in God, George, By the Divine Providence, Lord Archbishop of Canterburie," in Samuel Purchas, *Purchas His Pilgrimage. Or Relations of the World and the Religions Observed in All Ages and Places Discovered, from the Creation unto this Present* (London, 1613), unpaginated (after title page). As is indicated here, Abbot was at this time the Archbishop of Canterbury: he was appointed to the position in 1611 and would serve in it until his death in 1633. At some point between the publication of the first and the second edition of his *Pilgrimage,* Purchas was appointed to serve Abbot as his chaplain. It was a role in which he would remain until his death in 1626. In this year he published the fourth and final edition of his text, which also was dedicated to Abbot. See "To the Most Reverend Father in God, George, by the Divine Providence, Lord Archbishop of Canterburie," in Samuel Purchas, *Purchas His Pilgrimage. Or Relations of the World and the Religions Observed in all Ages and Places Discovered, from the Creation unto this Present* (London, 1626), unpaginated (after title page).

Hereafter these works will be cited in abbreviated form as Purchas, *Pilgrimage* (date); unless otherwise indicated, all citations will be from the 1613 first edition.

45. Purchas, *Pilgrimage,* 468. On the ancient Africans, see Purchas, *Pilgrimage,* 527–533. For the pages that Purchas devoted to Africa, see Purchas, *Pilgrimage,* 463–599; and in turn the section on Africa had already swelled to 160 pages in the second edition of the work: see Samuel Purchas, *Purchas His Pilgrimage. Or Relations of the World and the Religions Observed in All Ages and Places Discovered, from the Creation unto this Present,* 2nd ed. (London, 1614), 555–715.

46. Purchas, *Pilgrimage,* 464; Leo, *Geographical Historie of Africa,* trans. Pory, 296 (and on Egypt, see Leo, *Geographical Historie of Africa,* trans. Pory, 296–328); Pory, "A generall description of all Africa," in Leo, *Geographical Historie of Africa,* trans. Pory, 1–8, 1; Pory, "A particular description of all the knowne borders, coastes and inlands of Africa, which John Leo hath left undescribed," in Leo, *Geographical Historie of Africa,* trans. Pory, 8–60; and Purchas, *Pilgrimage,* 464.

47. See—though each author would add that the islands that surrounded the continent amounted to an eighth and final part of Africa—Speed, *Most Famous Parts of the World,* 5; Heylyn, *Cosmographie,* bk. 4, pt. 1: 3; and Morden, *Geography Rectified,* 318–319; as well as, for example, Peter Heylyn, *Microcosmus, or A Little Description of the Great World* (London, 1621), 370; Lewes Roberts, *The Merchants Mappe of Commerce* (London, 1638), 67; and John Ogilby, *Africa: Being an Accurate Description of the Regions of Ægypt, Barbary, Lybia, and Billedulgerid* . . . (London, 1670), 8–9.

48. See "Africae Tabula IIII" in Gerardum Mercatorem, *Tabulae Geographicae Cl: Ptolemei admentem autoris restitutæ & emendate* (1578), unpaginated (after fol. O).

49. The maps mentioned above appear in order in Betz's carto-bibliography, *Mapping of Africa,* as "1554 Giovanni Battista Ramusio—Giacomo Gastaldi: Prima Tavola," 95–97; "1570 Abraham Ortelius: Africæ Tabula Nova (Fifth State 1595)," 120–121; "1595 Gerard Mercator II: Africa," 162–165; "1617 Willem Janszoon (Blaeu): Africæ nova descriptio," 225–228; "1623 Jodocus Hondius Jr.: Africæ nova Tabula (Second State 1623)," 236; and "1626 John Speed: Africæ, described, the manners of their Habits, and buildinge," 241–243. (To be clear, Speed's map of Africa was finished and dated in the year before his 1627 world atlas was published.)

50. Purchas, *Purchas His Pilgrimage,* 548. See Purchas, "[marginal note]," in "The Voyage of Sir Francis Alvarez, a Portugall Priest, made unto the Court of Prete Ianni, the Great Christian Emperour of Ethiopia," in Purchas, *Pilgrimes,* bk. 7, ch. 5, 2: 1026–1121, 1026–1027. See, in addition, C. F. Beckingham, "North and North-East Africa and the Near and Middle East," in *Purchas Handbook,* ed. Pennington, vol. 1: 219–240, 223.

As has been indicated above, Leo included almost no material about Ethiopia in his text. Of course, he was well aware that the northeastern region, "called by the Latines *Aethiopia,*" was inhabited by Christians who were under the rule of "an Emperour, which they call *Prete Gianni.*" Nevertheless, he said that his four-part scheme of Africa was drawn from the works of African cosmographers and that these authors maintained that while the southern border of Africa was the Niger River, its eastern border was the Nile—such that the position of Egypt within Africa was ambiguous and Ethiopia was "not to be called any member or portion of Africa." Leo, *Geographical Historie of Africa,* trans. Pory, 3 (on the Nile, see 1).

51. "Voyage of Sir Francis Alvarez, a Portugall Priest, made unto the Court of Prete Ianni," in Purchas, *Pilgrimes,* bk. 7, ch. 5, 2: 1027, 1079, and 1079.

52. Lopes, *Reporte of the Kingdome of Congo,* trans. Hartwell, 209 (see also van Linschoten, *Voyages into the Easte and West Indies,* trans. W.P., 214); Thorie, *Theatre of the Earth,* B1r; Abbot, *Briefe Description of the Whole Worlde,* Cviiir; and "The letters of the Queenes most excellent Maiestie sent by one Laurence Aldersey unto the Emperour of Aethiopia, 1597," in Hakluyt, *Principal Navigations* (1599), vol. 2, pt. 2: 203–204, 204.

53. "A Rutter of Don John of Castro, of the Voyage which the Portugals made from India to Zoez," in Purchas, *Pilgrimes,* bk. 7, ch. 6, 2: 1122–1148, 1128; and Purchas, "[marginal note]," in "A Rutter of Don John of Castro," in Purchas, *Pilgrimes,* bk. 7, ch. 6, 2: 1122.

See Lopes, *Report of the Kingdome of Congo,* trans. Hartwell, 209–210; van Linschoten, *Voyages into the Easte and West Indies,* trans. W.P., 214; and Pory, "Particular description," in Leo, *Geographical Historie of Africa,* trans. Pory, 16. For example, Pory often cited Alvarez in his description of "*Abassia, or the empire of* Prete Ianni," in Pory, "Particular description," in Leo, *Geographical Historie of Africa,* trans. Pory, 12–19; and here he included a summary of the work of Alvarez from the Ramusio collection, under the title of "Certaine answeres of Don Francisco Alvarez . . . in the countrey of Prete Ianni," in Pory, "Particular description," in Leo, *Geographical Historie of Africa,* trans. Pory, 20–25.

54. Purchas, *Pilgrimage,* 565, 571, 571, 571, 562, and 564; and Purchas, "[marginal note]," in "The Voyage of Sir Francis Alvarez," in Purchas, *Pilgrimes,* bk. 7, ch. 5, 2: 1027.

After this point, the ruler of Ethiopia would never again widely be known to English observers as Prester John, and the title had all but disappeared by the time of the maps from Blaeu, Hondius, and Speed, each of whom simply referred to the region by what had become its far more common title, Abissina. For a fuller treatment of this period, see John Samuel Harpham, "The Late Career of Prester John" (research note in progress).

55. "The Voyage of Sir Francis Alvarez," in Purchas, *Pilgrimes,* bk. 7, ch. 5, 2: 1050; Pory, "Certaine answeres of Don Francisco Alvarez," in Pory, "Particular description," in Leo, *Geographical Historie of Africa,* trans. Pory, 20; and Samuel Purchas, *Purchas His Pilgrimage, or Relations of the World and the Religions Observed in All Ages and Places Discovered, from the Creation unto this Present,* 3rd ed. (London, 1617), 854.

56. Leo's work appeared in the Purchas collection in an abbreviated form as "Observations of Africa, taken out of John Leo his nine Bookes, translated by Master Pory," in Purchas, *Pilgrimes,* bk. 6, ch. 1, 2: 749–851.

57. Leo, *Geographical Historie of Africa,* trans. Pory, 284. On the four main governors in the Land of Negros, see Leo, *Geographical Historie of Africa,* trans. Pory, 5.

58. Leo, *Geographical Historie of Africa,* trans. Pory, 291, 289, 294, 293, 295, 287, and 288.

59. On the view of Africa that was presented in this text, see, for example, Davis, *Trickster Travels,* 125–152. For reflection upon "what is crucial to this text and its early modern ethnogeographic vision," which is understood to be "its insistence on the primacy and contingency of Africa's discrete communities," see Bartels, *Speaking of the Moor,* 138–154 (quoted phrase appears on 150).

60. Purchas, *Pilgrimage,* 572 and 578; and Pory, "Particular description," in Leo, *Geographical Historie of Africa,* trans. Pory, 32. Among sources available in English, this seventh region of Africa received the most detailed descriptions in Lopes,

Report of the Kingdome of Congo, trans. Hartwell, 186–217; van Linschoten, *Voyages into the Easte and West Indies,* trans. W. P., 7–11 and 210–214; Pory, "Particular description," in Leo, *Geographical Historie of Africa,* trans. Pory, 25–36; and Purchas, *Pilgrimage* (1626), 754–764; as well as in an account not mentioned so far: "Collections out of the Voyage and Historie of Friar Ioaõ dos Sanctos his Æthiopia Orientalis, & Varia Historia," in Purchas, *Pilgrimes,* bk. 9, ch. 12, 2: 1535–1567, 1535–1558.

61. Purchas, *Purchas His Pilgrimage,* 572 and 572.

62. For the excerpt in the *Pilgrimes,* see "A Report of the Kingdome of Congo, a Region of Affrica: Gathered by Philippo Pigafetta, out of the Discourses of Master Edward Lopes a Portugall, translated out of Italian into English, by Master Abraham Hartwell, and here abbreviated," in Purchas, *Pilgrimes,* bk. 7, ch. 4, 2: 986–1026.

For the debt that they expressed to the work of Lopes in their own accounts of the region, see van Linschoten, *Voyages into the Easte and West Indies,* trans. W.P., 205; Pory, "Particular description," in Leo, *Geographical Historie of Africa,* trans. Pory, 41; and Purchas, *Purchas His Pilgrimage,* 580. Moreover, for accounts of Congo that were drawn from that of Purchas, see Heylyn, *Microcosmus* (1621), 386–387; and John Smith, *The True Travels, Adventures, and Observations of Captaine John Smith* (London, 1630), 37–39.

63. Lopes, *Report of the Kingdome of Congo,* trans. Hartwell, 44, 21, and 103. For the discussion of "the confines of the kingdome of *Congo* towards the South," in which Angola in particular was treated, see Lopes, *Report of the Kingdome of Congo,* trans. Hartwell, 43–58. For the survey of "the sixe Provinces of the kingdome of *Congo,*" see Lopes, *Report of the Kingdome of Congo,* trans. Hartwell, 60–106. And on the "Royall Cittie of the Kingdome of Congo," see Lopes, *Report of the Kingdome of Congo,* trans. Hartwell, 107–117.

64. Purchas, *Pilgrimage* (1617), 704; Purchas, *Pilgrimage* (1613), 464 (see also Purchas, *Pilgrimage* [1617], 704); Pory, "Particular description," in Leo, *Geographical Historie of Africa,* trans. Pory, 20; Lopes, *Report of the Kingdome of Congo,* trans. Hartwell, 54; Leo, *Geographical Historie of Africa,* trans. Pory, 285; and Purchas, *Pilgrimage* (1613), 574.

65. For the maps of Walton and Overton, see "1658 Robert Walton: A New, Plaine, & Exact Mapp of Africa," in Betz, *Mapping of Africa,* 302–303; and "1668 John Overton: A New and most Exact map of AFRICA," in Betz, *Mapping of Africa,* 350–351. Both of these maps were modeled upon one made by Pieter van den Keere, which was in turn copied from a Hondius map similar to the one that would become

the model for Speed: see "1614 Pieter van den Keere, Amsterdam: AFRICAE NOVA DESCR.," in Betz, *Mapping of Africa,* 54–56; and "1606 Jodocus Hondius, Amsterdam: NOVA AFRICÆ TABULA," in Betz, *Mapping of Africa,* 51–53.

66. Jonathan Swift, *On Poetry: A Rapsody* (London, 1733), 12.

67. Lopes, *Report of the Kingdome of Congo,* trans. Hartwell, 31; and Purchas, *Pilgrimage,* 588 and 592.

68. Thomas Herbert, *Some Yeares Travels into Divers Parts of Asia and Afrique* (London, 1638), 27; and Leo, *Geographical Historie of Africa,* trans. Pory, 9. For the other references, see, in order, "The Voyage of Sir Francis Alvarez," in Purchas, *Pilgrimes,* bk. 7, ch. 5, 2: 1050; Lopes, *Report of the Kingdome of Congo,* trans. Hartwell, 57 and 37; Lopes, *Report of the Kingdome of Congo,* trans. Hartwell, 24 (copied in Roberts, *Merchants Mappe of Commerce,* 85–86) and 56; Purchas, *Pilgrimage,* 574; and "The Voyage of Sir Francis Alvarez," in Purchas, *Pilgrimes,* bk. 7, ch. 5, 2: 1043 and 1055. On the use of cowrie shells, see Jan Hogendorn and Marion Johnson, *The Shell Money of the Slave Trade* (Cambridge, UK, 1986).

69. Giovanni Botero, *Relations, of the most Famous Kingdoms and Common-weales thorough the World,* trans. Robert Johnson, 2nd ed. (London, 1608; orig. pub. 1601), 174. The passage on the Land of Negros in which the quoted sentence appeared was not present in the much shorter first English edition of the work. Heylyn repeated this sentence without attribution in Heylyn, *Cosmographie,* 4.2: 57.

70. For sophisticated treatments of this theme in European descriptions of the native peoples of America, see—in addition to the works of Anthony Pagden cited earlier in this chapter—Margaret T. Hodgen, *Early Anthropology in the Sixteenth and Seventeenth Centuries* (Philadelphia, 1964); J. H. Elliott, *The Old World and the New, 1492–1650* (Cambridge, UK, 1970); Karen Ordahl Kupperman, *Settling with the Indians: The Meeting of English and Indian Cultures in America, 1580–1640* (Totowa, NJ, 1975); Karen Ordahl Kupperman, *Indians and English: Facing off in Early America* (Ithaca, NY, 2000); and Joyce E. Chaplin, *Subject Matter: Technology, the Body, and Science on the Anglo-American Frontier, 1500–1676* (Cambridge, MA, 2001), 7–198.

71. Richard Jobson, *The Golden Trade: or, A Discovery of the River Gambra, and the Golden Trade of the Aethiopians* (London, 1623), 86; and Roberts, *Merchants Mappe of Commerce,* 86.

For later remarks in a similar vein, about the skill of the local merchants in West Africa, see, for example, "Wilhelm Johann Müller's Description of the Fetu Country, 1662–1669," trans. Adam Jones, in *German Sources for West African History, 1599–1669,* ed. Adam Jones (Wiesbaden, Germany, 1983), 134–259, 247–253;

Nicolas Villault de Bellefond, *A Relation of the Coasts of Africk Called Guinee,* trans. Anonymous (London, 1670), 135; *Barbot on Guinea: The Writings of Jean Barbot on West Africa, 1678–1712,* ed. P. E. H. Hair, Adam Jones, and Robin Law, 2 vols. (London, 1992), vol. 2: 334; Charles Davenant, *Reflections upon the Constitution and Management of the Trade to Africa* (London, 1709), 10; and John Atkins, *A Voyage to Guinea, Brazil, and the West-Indies* (London, 1735), 105.

72. Lopes, *Report of the Kingdome of Congo,* trans. Hartwell, 57.

73. The work on the Continent whose African materials most closely followed Botero in this period was Pierre D'Avity, *The Estates, Empires, & Principallities of the World,* trans. Edward Grimeston (London, 1615), 1077–1107.

74. The mountaineers around Borno as well as the Gagas, Anzigues, and Caphars are mentioned above. For a rare account of "the poore *Fulbies* life, whereunto he is so enured, that in a manner he is become bestiall," see Jobson, *Golden Trade,* 35.

4. THE SOURCES OF AFRICAN SLAVERY

1. Michaell de Montaigne, "Of Caniballes," in Michaell de Montaigne, *The Essayes or Morall, Politike and Millitarie Discourses,* trans. John Florio (London, 1603), 100–107, 102. Montaigne did claim that he had learned all that he related about the supposed cannibals of Brazil from a servant of his who had lived there: see Montaigne, *Essayes,* trans. Florio, 100–101. Even so, the negative formula that he relied upon in the course of this account drew upon what was already an old method in European travel narratives and descriptions of the peoples of the world: see Margaret T. Hodgen, "Montaigne and Shakespeare Again," *Huntington Library Quarterly* 16, no. 1 (Nov. 1952): 23–42; Bernard Weinberg, "Montaigne's Readings for *Des Cannibales,*" in *Renaissance and Other Studies in Honor of William Leon Wiley,* ed. George Bernard Daniel Jr. (Chapel Hill, NC, 1968), 261–279; and Kenji Go, "Montaigne's 'Cannibals' and 'The Tempest' Revisited," *Studies in Philology* 109, no. 4 (Summer 2012): 455–473.

2. William Shakespeare, *The Tempest,* in *Mr. William Shakespeares Comedies, Histories, & Tragedies* (London, 1623), 1–19, 7.

3. Jean Baptiste Du Tertre, *Histoire Generale, des isles de S. Christophe, de la Guadeloupe, de la Martinique, et autres dans l'Amerique* (Paris, 1654), 397 (trans. my own). For a general description of the Caribs, see Du Tertre, *Histoire Generale,* 396–400; and for an account of their treatment of captives, see Du Tertre, *Histoire Generale,* 449–453. Du Tertre was an important source of information for the author César de Rochefort, whose *Histoire Naturelle & Morale des Iles Antilles de l'Amerique* (1658)

soon appeared in an English edition as *The History of the Caribby-Islands,* trans. John Davies (London, 1666).

4. Montaigne, "Of Caniballes," in Montaigne, *Essayes,* trans. Florio, 104; and Du Tertre, *Histoire Generale,* 397 (trans. my own).

5. Jean Jacques Rousseau, "Discourse on the Origin and the Foundations of Inequality Among Men," in *Rousseau: The* Discourses *and Other Early Political Writings,* trans. and ed. Victor Gourevitch (Cambridge, UK, 1997), 111–222, 144, 156 (see also 196), and 182 (see also for example 173 and 185).

6. Rycharde Eden, "A breefe description of Affrike," in Peter Martyr, *The Decades of the Newe Worlde or West India,* trans. Rycharde Eden (London, 1555), 344r–345r, 344v.

7. Heylyn did note in defense of his book that, although "the matter I derive from others, the wordes for the most part are mine owne." Peter Heylyn, *Microcosmus, or A Little Description of the Great World* (Oxford, 1621), Preface. The marginal references in the section of the book about Africa were for the most part to the descriptions of the world from Botero and Abbot as well as that of Purchas. On the early development of the field, see, for example, E. G. R. Taylor, *Late Tudor and Early Stuart Geography, 1583–1650* (London, 1934); John Parker, *Books to Build an Empire: A Bibliographical History of English Overseas Interests to 1620* (Amsterdam, 1965); and Lesley B. Cormack, *Charting an Empire: Geography at the English Universities, 1580–1620* (Chicago, 1997).

8. "Sea Journal of Edward Fenton in the Galleon Leicester," in *The Troublesome Voyage of Captain Edward Fenton, 1582–1583,* ed. E. G. R. Taylor (Cambridge, UK, 1959), 83–149, 108; "The fyrst vyage to Guinea," in Martyr, *Decades of the Newe Worlde,* trans. Eden, 346v; and "The second voyage made by M. William Towrson to the coast of Guinea," in Hakluyt, *Principall Navigations* (1589), 112–120, 118. For other instances in which English merchants from this period visited kings in inland towns, see Anthony Ingram "The voiage set forth by M. John Newton, and M. John Bird marchants of London to the kindome and Citie of Benin in Africa," in Hakluyt, *Principal Navigations* (1599), vol. 2, pt. 2: 129–130; and "The voyage of Richard Rainolds and Thomas Dassel to the rivers of Senega and Gambra adjoyning upon Guinea, 1591," in Hakluyt, *Principal Navigations* (1599), vol. 2, pt. 2: 188–192.

9. Richard Jobson, *The Golden Trade: or, A Discovery of the River Gambra, and the Golden Trade of the Aethiopians* (London, 1623), 47. Jobson also often made reference to the hierarchy of kings in the extract from his voyage journal that Purchas later printed: Richard Jobson, "A True Relation of Master Richard Jobsons Voyage," in

Purchas, *Pilgrimes,* bk. 7, ch. 1, 2: 921–927. See John Leo, *A Geographical Historie of Africa,* trans. John Pory (London, 1600), 5 and 287–288.

10. For the account of de Marees in the Purchas collection (which was an excerpt significantly reduced from the original), see [Pieter de Marees], "A description and historicall declaration of the golden Kingdome of Guinea," trans. G. Artus Dantise, in Purchas, *Pilgrimes,* bk. 7, ch. 2, 2: 926–970. For a modern edition made from this original text, see Pieter de Marees, *Description and Historical Account of the Gold Kingdom of Guinea (1602),* trans. Albert van Dantzig and Adam Jones (Oxford, 1987).

11. [de Marees], "Golden Kingdome of Guinea," trans. Dantise, in Purchas, *Pilgrimes,* bk. 7, ch. 2, 2: 948–949. For hereditary succession in Jobson, see Jobson, *Golden Trade,* 58–59.

12. For the procedure described in this paragraph, see [de Marees], "golden Kingdome of Guinea," trans. Dantise, in Purchas, *Pilgrimes,* bk. 7, ch. 2, 2: 950–951; and de Marees, *Gold Kingdom of Guinea,* trans. van Dantzig and Jones, 98–104.

13. For a reference to an *alcaide,* see "The voyage of Richard Rainolds and Thomas Dassel," in Hakluyt, *Principal Navigations* (1599), vol. 2, pt. 2: 189. The title was also rendered, for example, as *almade, Alcade,* and *Algaier:* in order, see Towerson, "The second voyage made by M. William Towrson to the coast of Guinea," in Hakluyt, *Principall Navigations* (1589), 119; Jobson, "A True Relation of Master Richard Jobsons Voyage," in Purchas, *Pilgrimes,* bk. 7, ch. 1, 2: 922; and [de Marees], "golden Kingdome of Guinea," trans. Dantise, in Purchas, *Pilgrimes,* bk. 7, ch. 2, 2: 927.

14. Towerson, "The second voyage made by M. William Towrson to the coast of Guinea," in Hakluyt, *Principall Navigations* (1589), 118; John Sparke, "The voyage made by the worshipful M. John Hawkins . . . to the coast of Guinea, and the Indies of Nova Spania . . . begunne in An. Dom. 1564," in Hakluyt, *Principall Navigations* (1589), 523–543, 526; and James Welsh, "A voyage to Benin beyond the Countrey of Guinea, set foorth by Master Bird and Master Newton Marchants of London," in Hakluyt, *Principal Navigations* (1599), vol. 2, pt. 2: 126–129, 128.

15. Jobson, *Golden Trade,* 142 and 111. On the local tradesmen, see Jobson, *Golden Trade,* 119–122.

16. Nicolas Villault de Bellefond, *A Relation of the Coasts of Africk Called Guinee,* trans. Anonymous (London, 1670), 173, 25, 140, 218, and 144.

17. Villault, *Relation of the Coasts of Africk Called Guinee,* trans. Anon., 139 and 261; and de Marees, *Gold Kingdom of Guinea,* trans. van Dantzig and Jones, 99. For de Marees as a source for Villault, who would have read the earlier account in its 1605 French edition, see Adam Jones, "Semper Aliquid Veteris: Printed Sources for the History of the Ivory and Gold Coasts, 1500–1750," *Journal of African History* 27, no. 2

(1986): 215–235, 216. For discussions of the political order in Guinea, see Villault, *Relation of the Coasts of Africk Called Guinee,* trans. Anon., 20, 225, and 139. For the aspects of Guinean behavior that appalled de Marees, which are treated in passages only parts of which were printed in the abridged version in Purchas, see de Marees, *Gold Kingdom of Guinea,* trans. van Dantzig and Jones, 105–109, 37–38, and 32.

18. On the slaves of the king, see [de Marees], "golden Kingdome of Guinea," trans. Dantise, in Purchas, *Pilgrimes,* bk. 7, ch. 2, 2: 949 and 966. On slaves of the nobles, see de Marees, *Gold Kingdom of Guinea,* trans. van Dantzig and Jones, 34 and 229. On eligibility to own and trade slaves as the privilege of nobility in Guinea, see [de Marees], "golden Kingdome of Guinea," trans. Dantise, in Purchas, *Pilgrimes,* bk. 7, ch. 2, 2: 958–960.

19. [de Marees], "golden Kingdome of Guinea," trans. Dantise, in Purchas, *Pilgrimes,* bk. 7, ch. 2, 2: 951. Punishments for crime are noted at [de Marees], "golden Kingdome of Guinea," trans. Dantise, in Purchas, *Pilgrimes,* bk. 7, ch. 2, 2: 950–951. On slavery as punishment for adultery, see Jobson, *Golden Trade,* 53; and Villault, *Relation of the Coasts of Africk Called Guinee,* trans. Anon., 264. On slavery as punishment for petty criminals who could not pay their fines, see (as well as de Marees) Villault, *Relation of the Coasts of Africk Called Guinee,* trans. Anon., 207; and *The Golden Coast, Or A Description of Guinney* (London, 1665), 73. In addition, the narrative of the second Guinea voyage of John Hawkins noted that a person could be enslaved for theft; see Sparke, "The voyage made by the worshipful M. John Hawkins . . . to the coast of Guinea," in Hakluyt, *Principall Navigations* (1589), 527.

20. "The Voyage of Sir Francis Alvarez, Portugall Priest, made unto the Court of Prete Ianni, the Great Christian Emperour of Ethiopia," in Purchas, *Pilgrimes,* bk. 7, ch. 5, 2: 1094; [de Marees], "golden Kingdome of Guinea," trans. Dantise, in Purchas, *Pilgrimes,* bk. 7, ch. 2, 2: 950; Villault, *Relation of the Coasts of Africk Called Guinee,* trans. Anon., 264 (see also Jobson, *Golden Trade,* 53); and Villault, *Relation of the Coasts of Africk Called Guinee,* trans. Anon., 266.

For reports about the use of judicial enslavement in northern Ethiopia, see also, for example, John Ogilby, *Africa: Being an Accurate Description of the Regions of Ægypt, Barbary, Lybia, and Billedulgerid . . .* (London, 1670), 648; Job Ludolphus, *A New History of Ethiopia. Being A Full and Accurate Description of The Kingdom of Abessinia, Vulgarly, though Erroneously called the Empire of Prester John,* trans. J. P. Gent (London, 1682), 237; and Robert Morden, *Geography Rectified: Or, A Description of the World,* 2nd ed. (London, 1688; orig. pub. 1680), 489.

21. The importance of judicial authority to the states in Guinea was indicated by a passage in his *Pilgrimage* in which Purchas described the ritual in which a ruler would ascend to the throne in one inland kingdom. He would receive "a Hatchet

into his hand which they use in Executions, and after this all acknowledge subjection," was what Purchas said. Purchas, *Pilgrimage* (1626), 712.

22. "The fyrst vyage to Guinea," in Martyr, *Decades of the Newe Worlde,* trans. Eden, 347r; and William Bosman, *A New and Accurate Description of the Coast of Guinea,* trans. Anonymous (London, 1705), 430. The original Dutch edition of this latter work was published in 1704. For the report from Leo on the king of Tombuto, see Leo, *Geographical Historie of Africa,* trans. Pory, 288; and for a similar ritual, see Jobson, *Golden Trade,* 48–49.

23. Giovanni Botero, *The Travellers Breviat, or An historicall description of the most famous kingdomes in the World,* trans. Robert Johnson (London, 1601), 171 (on Prester John, see 169–177). Johnson put out five more expanded editions through 1616 that generally used the title that first appeared in the 1608 second edition: *Relations, of the most Famous Kingdoms and Common-weales thorough the World.* That said, the sections on Ethiopia in these editions remained more or less unchanged from the original 1601 edition.

24. Botero, *Travellers Breviat,* trans. Johnson, 171; and Peter Heylyn, *Cosmographie in Four Bookes* (London, 1652), bk. 4, pt. 1: 71. The phrase quoted here still appeared in the final edition of Heylyn's text; see Peter Heylyn, *Cosmographie in Four Books,* fifth ed. (London, 1677), bk. 4, pt. 1: 59.

For similar remarks about the treatment of the people of Ethiopia, see, for example, John Pory, "A particular description of all the knowne borders, coastes and inlands of Africa, which John Leo hath left undescribed," in Leo, *Geographical Historie of Africa,* trans. Pory, 8–60, 16; and Richard Blome, *A Geographical Description of the Four Parts of the World* (London, 1670), pt. 2, 58.

25. For the English translation of Botero's well-known separate text on the causes of greatness in states, see Giovanni Botero, *A Treatise, Concerning the causes of the Magnificencie and greatnes of Cities,* trans. Robert Peterson (London, 1606). This text was far more limited than Botero's survey of the kingdoms of the world in its argument that commerce and industry, rather than virtue, were the true causes of greatness. On the reception of this argument, see Andrew Fitzmaurice, "The Commercial Ideology of Colonization in Jacobean England: Robert Johnson, Giovanni Botero, and the Pursuit of Greatness," *WMQ* 64, no. 4 (Oct. 2007): 791–820.

26. Ludolphus, *New History of Ethiopia,* trans. Gent, "To the Courteous Reader" (unpaginated) and 203. For his advice on the private ownership of land, see in particular Ludolphus, *New History of Ethiopia,* trans. Gent, 200 and 202–206. For his observation that "*Gabre,* or *Servant,* has a more diffusive signification among Them

than among Us. For it extends not to real Slaves alone, but their Subjects and Domesticks," see Ludolphus, *New History of Ethiopia,* trans. Gent, 235.

27. Eden, "Breefe description of Affrike," in Martyr, *The Decades of the Newe Worlde,* trans. Eden, 344v.

28. "The voyage of Richard Rainolds and Thomas Dassel," in Hakluyt, *Principal Navigations* (1599), vol. 2, pt. 2: 189.

Even if the English travelers whose accounts appeared in the Hakluyt collections were not much aware of wars between African states, Hakluyt himself did include in the second edition of his text several short indirect reports upon conflicts that will be mentioned in what follows in this chapter: see, for example, "An Advertisement sent to Philip the second king of Spaine from Angola by one Baltazar Almeida de Sousa, touching the state of the foresayd countrey, written the 21 of May, 1589," in Hakluyt, *Principal Navigations* (1599), vol. 2, pt. 2: 133; and Laurence Madoc, "Another briefe relation concerning the late conquest and the exceeding great riches of the cities and provinces of Tombuto and Gago, written from Marocco the 30 August 1594," in Hakluyt, *Principal Navigations* (1599), vol. 2, pt. 2: 192–193.

29. [de Marees], "Golden Kingdome of Guinea," trans. Dantise, in Purchas, *Pilgrimes,* bk. 7, ch. 2, 2: 947; and Purchas, *Pilgrimage* (1626), 717.

30. Ludolphus, *New History of Ethiopia,* trans. Gent, 86 (and on the Gallans, see 81–87). The best report from the Adelian wars of the sixteenth century was printed in the Purchas collection just after those of Alvarez and Don John of Castro that were discussed in Chapter 3; see "A briefe Relation of the Embassage which the Patriarch Don John Bermudez brought from the Emperour of Ethiopia . . . to the . . . King of Portugall," in Purchas, *Pilgrimes,* bk. 7, ch. 7, 2: 1149–1174. The works on these events that Purchas published were in turn digested in a series of accounts that closely resembled one another: Botero, *Travellers Breviat,* trans. Johnson, 169–177; Pierre D'Avity, *The Estates, Empires, & Principallities of the World,* trans. Edward Grimeston (London, 1615), 1077–1091; and Heylyn, *Cosmographie,* bk. 4, pt. 1: 59–72.

31. Pory, "Particular description," in Leo, *Geographical Historie of Africa,* trans. Pory, 31; and "Drawen out of the writings and discourses of Odoardo Lopes, a Portingall, by Philippo Pigafetta," *A Report of the Kingdome of Congo, a Region of Africa,* trans. Abraham Hartwell (London, 1597), 204. On the wars between these two empires, see also Lopes, *Report of the Kingdome of Congo,* trans. Hartwell, 192–206; van Linschoten, *Voyages into the Easte and West Indies,* trans. W.P., 212–213; Pory, "Particular description," in Leo, *Geographical Historie of Africa,* trans. Pory,

30–34; Purchas, *Pilgrimage* (1626), 757–761; and Heylyn, *Cosmographie,* bk. 4, pt. 1: 75–77.

32. Lopes, *Report of the Kingdome of Congo,* trans. Hartwell, 49, 61, and 102. On the military order in Congo and Angola, see Lopes, *Report of the Kingdome of Congo,* trans. Hartwell, 47–54. On the Gagas' invasion and on the campaign that expelled them from Congo, see Lopes, *Report of the Kingdome of Congo,* trans. Hartwell, 159–164. Lopes remained the sole printed source on this event. As on many aspects of Congo, he was relied upon by sources in English: see, for example, D'Avity, *Estates, Empires, & Principallities of the World,* trans. Grimeston, 1095–1107; and Heylyn, *Cosmographie,* bk. 4, pt. 1: 78–82.

33. Purchas, *Pilgrimage* (1626), 765; and "The strange adventures of Andrew Battell of Leigh in Essex," in Purchas, *Pilgrimes,* bk. 7, ch. 3, 2: 970–985, 973 and 976. The text printed in the *Pilgrimes* seems to have been recorded and edited by Purchas as well as by an anonymous transcriber in a process that is not well understood. As early as the first edition of his *Pilgrimage,* in 1613, Purchas had obtained information from conversations with Battell and referred to it in his discussions of western central Africa; see Purchas, *Pilgrimage,* 580–592. The modern edition of the text is *The Strange Adventures of Andrew Battell of Leigh, in Angola and the Adjoining Regions,* ed. E. G. Ravenstein (London, 2010; orig. pub. 1901).

34. Heylyn, *Cosmographie,* bk. 4, pt. 1: 68; Pory, "Particular description," in Leo, *Geographical Historie of Africa,* trans. Pory, 32; and Lopes, *Report of the Kingdome of Congo,* trans. Hartwell, 103.

35. "The strange adventures of Andrew Battell," in Purchas, *Pilgrimes,* bk. 7, ch. 3, 2: 476.

36. Lopes, *Report of the Kingdome of Congo,* trans. Hartwell, 160. The sack of Benguela is on "The strange adventures of Andrew Battell," in Purchas, *Pilgrimes,* bk. 7, ch. 3, 2: 974; for the uses to which the Gagas put their slaves, see 977.

37. Lopes, *Report of the Kingdome of Congo,* trans. Hartwell, 62; and Purchas, *Pilgrimage* (1626), 765. On the natives of Congo who were sold as far as Portugal after the invasion of the Gagas, see Lopes, *Report of the Kingdome of Congo,* trans. Hartwell, 161.

The source for the figure that Purchas reported was "Relations of Master Thomas Turner who lived the best part of two yeeres in Brasill," in Purchas, *Pilgrimes,* bk. 6, ch. 8, 4: 1243. This figure was then repeated in Lewes Roberts, *The Merchants Mappe of Commerce* (London, 1638), 89; Heylyn, *Cosmographie,* bk. 4, pt. 1: 78–79; and Blome, *Geographical Description of the Four Parts of the World,* pt. 2, 62.

38. Botero, *Travellers Breviat,* trans. Johnson, 175–176; and Purchas, *Pilgrimage* (1626), 754. On the origin and destinations of the Abessine slaves traded by Muslims on the coast, see, for example, in addition to the passages from Botero and Purchas, Pory, "Particular description," in Leo, *Geographical Historie of Africa,* trans. Pory, 26–27; D'Avity, *Estates, Empires, & Principallities of the World,* trans. Grimeston, 1085; Heylyn, *Cosmographie,* bk. 4, pt. 1: 68; and Ludolphus, *New History of Ethiopia,* trans. Gent, 70.

39. Leo, *Geographical Historie of Africa,* trans. Pory, 290, 288, and 288. On Borno, see Leo, *Geographical Historie of Africa,* trans. Pory, 293–294 (also Botero, *Travellers Breviat,* trans. Johnson, 171). On the conquests of Tombuto, see Leo, *Geographical Historie of Africa,* 284–296.

As reported in a dispatch included in the second edition of the Hakluyt collection, the Moroccan army conquered Tombuto in 1589: see Madoc, "Another briefe relation," in Hakluyt, *Principal Navigations* (1599), vol. 2, pt. 2: 192–193. However, even John Pory, Leo's English translator, seems not to have known about this event. Purchas only mentioned it in passing (see Purchas, *Pilgrimage* [1626], 722), and Heylyn was under the impression that after a short time the ruler of Tombuto had been restored to the throne and was now "in as eminent power, as ever in any times before." Heylyn, *Cosmographie,* bk. 4, pt. 1: 58.

40. [de Marees], "Golden Kingdome of Guinea," trans. Dantise, in Purchas, *Pilgrimes,* bk. 7, ch. 2, 2: 960, 948, and 960. De Marees did note that to the east of the Gold Coast, on the Allada River, the Portuguese bought a "great number of slaves . . . to carry to other places, as to Saint *Thomas,* and to *Brasilia*" (965). For the origin of *catiff,* see de Marees, *Gold Kingdom of Guinea,* trans. van Dantzig and Jones, 101n2.

41. [de Marees], "Golden Kingdome of Guinea," trans. Dantise, in Purchas, *Pilgrimes,* bk. 7, ch. 2, 2: 948; and Villault, *Relation of the Coasts of Africk Called Guinee,* trans. Anon., 256 and 255.

For laments from European merchants that war in Guinea had disrupted commerce, see, for example, "Samuel Brun's Voyages of 1611–20," in *German Sources for West African History, 1599–1669,* ed. Adam Jones (Wiesbaden, Germany, 1983), 44–96, 67–68; Villault, *Relation of the Coasts of Africk Called Guinee,* trans. Anon., 136 and 259; Thomas Phillips, "A Journal of a Voyage Made in the Hannibal of London, Ann. 1693, 1694," in *A Collection of Voyages and Travels,* 6 vols. (London, 1732), vol. 6: 171–239, 199 and 201; and James Barbot, "An Abstract of a Voyage to New Calabar River, or Rio Real, in the year 1699," in *A Collection of Voyages and Travels* (1732), vol. 5: 455–466, 455.

42. Purchas, *Pilgrimage* (1626), 755. For the event that de Marees described, which did not appear in the abridgement in the *Pilgrimes,* see de Marees, *Gold Kingdom of Guinea,* trans. van Dantzig and Jones, 91.

43. Lopes, *Report of the Kingdome of Congo,* trans. Hartwell, 160 and 161.

44. "The strange adventures of Andrew Battell," in Purchas, *Pilgrimes,* bk. 7, ch. 3, 2: 974 and 975. What Battell said about the cannibalism of the Gagas was repeated in Purchas, *Pilgrimage* (1626), 772–773; and Heylyn, *Cosmographie,* bk. 4, pt. 1: 80.

45. Purchas, *Pilgrimage* (1626), 755 (see also Heylyn, *Cosmographie,* bk. 4, pt. 1: 78); Purchas, *Pilgrimage* (1626), 712; and [de Marees], "Golden Kingdome of Guinea," trans. Dantise, in Purchas, *Pilgrimes,* bk. 7, ch. 2, 2: 948. This remark from de Marees was repeated in *The Golden Coast, Or A Description of Guinney,* 82; Ogilby, *Africa,* 482; and Blome, *Geographical Description of the Four Parts of the World,* pt. 2, 50. For what Hawkins said about the Cumbæ and the Capi, whom he knew as the Samboses and the Sapies, see Sparke, "The voyage made by the worshipful M. John Hawkins . . . to the coast of Guinea," in Hakluyt, *Principall Navigations* (1589), 526–527.

46. "The strange adventures of Andrew Battell," in Purchas, *Pilgrimes,* bk. 7, ch. 3, 2: 977; Lopes, *Report of the Kingdome of Congo,* trans. Hartwell, 205; Purchas, *Pilgrimage* (1626), 712; Sparke, "The voyage made by the worshipful M. John Hawkins . . . to the coast of Guinea," in Hakluyt, *Principall Navigations* (1589), 526; and Purchas, *Pilgrimage* (1626), 755.

47. For Purchas's theory about the common origin of the peoples listed here, a theory that was no doubt indebted to the accounts of earlier Portuguese travelers in Guinea, see Purchas, *Pilgrimage* (1626), 722 and 755. For the characterization of such peoples as "cruel," see "A briefe Relation of the Embassage which the Patriarch Don John Bermudez brought from the Emperour of Ethiopia . . . to the . . . King of Portugall," in Purchas, *Pilgrimes,* bk. 7, ch. 7, 2: 1167; Purchas, *Pilgrimage* (1626), 773; Heylyn, *Cosmographie,* bk. 4, pt. 1: 76; and Ludolphus, *New History of Ethiopia,* trans. Gent, 81.

48. Purchas, *Pilgrimage* (1626), 772; Lopes, *Report on the Kingdome of Congo,* trans. Hartwell, 36, 35, and 35. On the Anzigues, see also Purchas, *Pilgrimage* (1626), 772; Thomas Herbert, *Some Yeares Travels into Divers Parts of Asia and Afrique* (London, 1638), 10–11; and Heylyn, *Cosmographie,* bk. 4, pt. 1: 76.

49. The materials on Africa are in Heylyn, *Cosmographie in Four Bookes* (1652), bk. 4, pt. 1: 1–90; Peter Heylyn, *Cosmographie in Four Books,* 2nd ed. (London, 1657),

bk. 4, pt. 1: 917–1007; and Peter Heylyn, *Cosmographie in foure Bookes,* 3rd ed. (London, 1666), bk. 4, pt. 1: 931–1007. The materials on Africa are in Robert Fage, *Cosmography* (London, 1666), 96–111; on gold, see Fage, *Cosmography,* 106.

50. For the charter issued to the royal African company in 1663, see "African Company. (Patent Rolls, 14 Car. II., pt. xxvii.)," in *Select Charters of Trading Companies, A.D. 1530–1707,* ed. Cecil T. Carr (London, 1913), 177–181: the phrase "negro slaves" is from 181. For the trader's protest against the monopoly of the African company, see William Wilkinson, *Systema Africanum: or a Treatise, Discovering the Intrigues and Arbitrary Proceedings of the Guiney Company* (London, 1690): the phrase quoted above appears on 7. See also *The Golden Coast, Or A Description of Guinney,* 62 and 68.

For additional works that were presented in the context of debate about the monopoly of the African company, and in turn registered the recent expansion in the slave trade and its importance to the Caribbean colonies, see *Certain Considerations Relating to the Royal African Company of England* (London, 1680), 5; R.B. [Nathaniel Crouch], *A View of the English Acquisitions in Guinea* (London, 1686), 11; Edward Littleton, *The Groans of the Plantations* (London, 1689), 7; and Dalby Thomas, *An Historical Account of the Rise and Growth of the West-India Colonies* (London, 1690), 30–53.

51. For studies of this controversy, see K. G. Davies, *The Royal African Company* (London, 1957), 97–152; William A. Pettigrew, *Freedom's Debt: The Royal African Company and the Politics of the Atlantic Slave Trade, 1672–1752* (Williamsburg, VA, 2013); and Abigail Leslie Swingen, *Competing Visions of Empire: Labor, Slavery, and the Origins of the British Atlantic Empire* (New Haven, CT, 2015).

52. John Ogilby, *Africa: Being an Accurate Description of the Regions of Ægypt, Barbary, Lybia, and Billedulgerid . . .* (London, 1670), 377 and 318. Dapper is not mentioned on the title page of this text, which has led some scholars to refer to it as "Ogilby's Africa." However, there is no doubt that Ogilby understated the extent of his reliance upon the Dutchman when he remarked in his Preface that he had already started to research and write when he came across Dapper, "whose large Addition, added to my own Endeavors, hath much Accelerated the *Work.*"

On Dapper, see, for example, G. Thilmans, "Le Sénegal dans l'oeuvre d'Olfried Dapper," *Bulletin de l'Institut Fondamental d'Afrique Noire* 33, no. 3 (Jul. 1971): 508–563; P. E. H. Hair, "Barbot, Dapper, Davity: A Critique of Sources on Sierra Leone and Cape Mount," *History in Africa,* vol. 1 (1974): 25–54; and Jones, "Semper Aliquid Veteris."

53. Ogilby, *Africa,* 364, 482 (for this distinction, see also 483 and 462), and 407–408.

54. Richard Blome, *A Geographical Description of the Four Parts of the World* (London, 1670), pt. 2, 50. The subtitle explained that the work was "Taken from the Notes & Workes of the Famous Monsieur Sanson, Geographer to the French King, and other Eminent Travellers and Authors." On the prisoners at Guinala who were purchased by the Portuguese, see Ogilby, *Africa,* 364; and on those at Calabar who were acquired by the Dutch, see Ogilby, *Africa,* 483 (marginal note). For further reports that the Portuguese bought prisoners to transport to the West Indies, see Ogilby, *Africa,* 363 and 469. Ogilby wrote of the progress of English commerce in Guinea (and of the conflicts in which their attempts to establish settlements there had involved them with the agents of the Dutch in recent decades) in particular in the section of his work that concerned the Gold Coast: see Ogilby, *Africa,* 419–433.

55. [Anonymous], *A True Relation of the Inhumane and Unparallel'd Actions, and Barbarous Murders of Negroes or Moors: Committed on Three English-men in Old Calabar in Guinny* (London, 1672), 16; and Thomas Phillips, "A Journal of a Voyage Made in the Hannibal of London, Ann. 1693, 1694," in *A Collection of Voyages and Travels,* 6 vols. (London, 1732), vol. 6: 171–239, 220. The author of the former work said that it was composed "verbatim" from the oral account of John Watts (3).

Like Phillips, the principal Dutch official in Guinea in this period had been frustrated to find that at points on the coast, "It sometimes happens that when the In-land Countries are at Peace, here are no slaves to be got." Bosman, *New and Accurate Description of the Coast of Guinea,* trans. Anon., 327.

56. The manuscript described here was composed in French and finished in 1688 but never published. Barbot would never again visit Guinea but did translate his work into English and vastly expanded it upon the basis of recent travel books until the time of his death in 1712. This version of the text became well known when it was printed as John Barbot, "A Description of the Coasts of North and South-Guinea," in *A Collection of Voyages and Travels,* 6 vols. (London, 1732), vol. 5: 1–420. The version of the text used here is of course the 1688 manuscript, which is available in an excellent English edition as *Barbot on Guinea: The Writings of Jean Barbot on West Africa, 1678–1712,* ed. P. E. H. Hair, Adam Jones, and Robin Law, 2 vols. (London, 1992). On the scarcity of slaves in peacetime, see *Barbot on Guinea,* vol. 2: 440, 518, and 550; on English slavers at Calabar, see vol. 2: 672; on the acceleration of the slave trade in the aftermath of war, see vol. 2: 439 and 518; and on the 1681 episode, see vol. 2: 550 (as well as, for the version Barbot gave in the 1732 edition, 350).

57. For the use of trial by ordeal in West Africa, see, for example, de Marees, *Gold Kingdom of Guinea,* trans. van Dantzig and Jones, 102–103; Purchas, *Pilgrimage*

(1626), 720; Villault, *Relation of the Coasts of Africk Called Guinee,* trans. Anon., 263–264; Ogilby, *Africa,* 405–406 (at Quoia) and 497–499 (at Loango); and *Barbot on Guinea,* ed. Hair, Jones, and Law, vol. 2: 503 and 640.

58. Villault, *Relation of the Coasts of Africk Called Guinee,* trans. Anon., 206 and 207; and *Barbot on Guinea,* ed. Hair, Jones, and Law, vol. 1: 76 (also 107 and, in vol. 2, 549).

59. De Marees, *Gold Kingdom of Guinea,* trans. van Dantzig and Jones, 176; Blome, *Geographical Description of the Four Parts of the World,* pt. 2, 46; [Anonymous], *True Relation of the Inhumane and Unparallel'd Actions, and Barbarous Murders of Negroes or Moors: Committed on Three English-men in Old Calabar in Guinny,* 18; and Ogilby, *Africa,* 483. For a similar report, see the 1665 survey of Guinea in which it was stated without explanation that there were "Slaves and Children, which the Parents will trappan to the Sea side, and sell away for a Crown." [Anon.], *Golden Coast, Or A Description of Guinney,* 62.

60. Ogilby, *Africa,* 474 and 363; Blome, *Geographical Description of the Four Parts of the World,* pt. 2, 46; and Phillips, "Journal of a Voyage Made in the Hannibal of London," in *A Collection of Voyages and Travels* (1732), vol. 6: 219. For other kingdoms in Guinea where the monarch was said to hold absolute power over his subjects, see Quoia, Accra, and Allada at Ogilby, *Africa,* 399, 434, and 468. Barbot had also heard that the kings in Guinea "can enslave their subjects," but he maintained that "they never carry out this extreme measure unless there is some dire need domestically or unless the particular subjects have committed some great misdeed." *Barbot on Guinea,* ed. Hair, Jones, and Law, vol. 1: 107.

61. [Anon.], *True Relation of the Inhumane and Unparallel'd Actions, and Barbarous Murders of Negroes or Moors: Committed on Three English-men in Old Calabar in Guinny,* 6; and *Certain Considerations Relating to the Royal African Company of England,* 8. For testimony about the events on the Gambia River in 1698, see Charles Davenant, "Reflections upon the Constitution and Management of the Trade to Africa, Part II," in *The Political and Commercial Works of that Celebrated Writer Charles Davenant, LL.D.,* 5 vols. (London, 1771), vol. 5: 167–246, 170–171.

62. Richard Ligon, *A True & Exact History of the Island of Barbados* (London, 1657), 46 and 52. Ligon's account came out in a widely circulated second edition: the passages cited above were reproduced in Richard Ligon, *A True & Exact History of the Island of Barbadoes* (London, 1673), 46 and 52.

63. Richard Blome, *A Description of the Island of Jamaica; With the other Isles and Territories in America to which the English are Related* (London, 1672), 15 and 91. Blome's description of Barbados was indebted to that of Ligon, which he acknowledged on

Blome, *Description of the Island of Jamaica,* 96. Moreover, he noted that what he said about slavery in his description of Barbados could also be applied to the institution as it had more recently been established on Jamaica: see Blome, *Description of the Island of Jamaica,* 93.

64. *Jamaica in 1687: The Taylor Manuscript at the National Library of Jamaica,* ed. David Buisseret (Kingston, Jamaica, 2008), 273. Taylor's three-volume account, which included records of his own life and travels as well as a comprehensive description of Jamaica, seems to have been prepared for publication but did not appear in print until the useful modern edition cited here. For Taylor's estimation that there were as many enslaved as free persons on Jamaica when he was there, see *Jamaica in 1687: The Taylor Manuscript at the National Library of Jamaica,* ed. Buisseret, 236. As a matter of fact, Taylor was mistaken on this point: there were as many enslaved Africans as free persons on Jamaica at least from 1673, and by 1690, the ratio of enslaved to free persons was about three to one. In his own earlier assessment of the ratio of enslaved to free persons on Barbados, Ligon was also mistaken—although his mistake was to overstate rather than to understate the ratio. Not until around 1660 were there more slaves than colonists on Barbados.

65. Ligon, *A True & Exact History of the Island of Barbados,* 46.

66. Richard Baxter, *A Christian Directory: Or, A Summ of Practical Theologie, and Cases of Conscience* (London, 1673), 558, 558, and 559.

67. Baxter, *Christian Directory,* 557, 557, 558, and 560. For the chapter on "The Duties of Masters towards their Servants," see Baxter, *Christian Directory,* 556–560.

68. Morgan Godwyn, *The Negro's & Indians Advocate, Suing for their Admission into the Church* (London, 1680), 13, 83, 80, and 81. For the comparison between the cruelty of the planters on Barbados and that of the Spanish in the Indies, see Godwyn, *The Negro's & Indians Advocate,* 12 and 82. Despite the title he chose for his polemic, Godwyn did not mention the conversion of Indians, and even though Godwyn served in the clergy in Virginia before he moved to Barbados, in 1670, he only discussed slavery on the Caribbean island. He would return to the same themes in Morgan Godwyn, *A Supplement to the Negro's & Indians Advocate* (London, 1681). On Godwyn, see Alden T. Vaughan, "Slaveholders' 'Hellish Principles': A Seventeenth-Century Critique," in Alden T. Vaughan, *Roots of American Racism: Essays on the Colonial Experience* (New York, 1995), 55–81.

69. Philotheos Physiologus [Thomas Tryon], *Friendly Advice to the Gentlemen-Planters of the East and West Indies* (London, 1684), 75. For "The Negro's Complaint of their Hard Servitude," see Physiologus [Tryon], *Friendly Advice to the Gentlemen-Planters of the East and West Indies,* 75–145.

70. Physiologus [Tryon], *Friendly Advice to the Gentlemen-Planters of the East and West Indies,* 80, 77, 85–86, and 81. See also Philippe Rosenberg, "Thomas Tryon and the Seventeenth-Century Dimensions of Antislavery," *WMQ* 61, no. 4 (Oct. 2004): 609–642. On Baxter and Godwyn as well as Tryon, see David Brion Davis, *The Problem of Slavery in Western Culture* (Ithaca, NY, 1966).

71. For word of this rumor, see, for example, *Barbot on Guinea,* ed. Hair, Jones, and Law, vol. 2: 639 and 774–775; and Bosman, *New and Accurate Description of the Coast of Guinea,* trans. Anon., 365.

72. [George Fox], "For the Governour, and His Council & Assembly," in George Fox, *To the Ministers, Teachers, and Priests, (So called, and so Stileing your Selves) in Barbadoes* (London, 1672), 65–79 (79 is labeled 69), 77 and 69. On the ambivalence of the early Quakers, see Davis, *Problem of Slavery in Western Culture,* 291–332; and in particular Katharine Gerbner, *Christian Slavery: Conversion and Race in the Protestant Atlantic World* (Philadelphia, 2018).

73. Physiologus [Tryon], "A Discourse in way of Dialogue, Between an Ethiopian or Negro-Slave and a Christian, that was his Master in America," in Physiologus [Tryon], *Friendly Advice to the Gentlemen-Planters of the East and West Indies,* 146–222, 212 and 222.

74. Ernest A. Baker, *The Novels of Mrs Aphra Behn* (London, 1905), xxiii. Readers of *Oroonoko* have come to be far more careful in recent decades; for informed contextual treatments, see Katharine M. Rogers, "Fact and Fiction in Aphra Behn's *Oroonoko,*" *Studies in the Novel,* vol. 20 (1988): 1–15; Joanna Lipking, "'Others', Slaves, and Colonists in *Oroonoko,*" in *The Cambridge Companion to Aphra Behn,* ed. Derek Hughes and Janet Todd (Cambridge, UK, 2004), 166–187; and in particular Rebekah Mitsein, *African Impressions: How African Worldviews Shaped the British Geographical Imagination across the Early Enlightenment* (Charlottesville, VA, 2022), 77–97.

One issue that is addressed in studies such as the ones listed above is whether *Oroonoko* is a work of history or of fiction. The work seems to have elements of both genres, which in the seventeenth century were not often rigorously distinguished. What is clear is that Behn intended for the book to be read as a record of real events: she had in all likelihood lived in Surinam in the 1660s, which serves as the setting for the second half of the book, whose subtitle was of course *A True History.* It also seems clear that *Oroonoko* was frequently read as truthful by its early readers. One such reader was the very author who first adapted it for the stage: see Thomas Southerne, *Oroonoko: A Tragedy* (London, 1696), "The Epistle Dedicatory."

75. Mrs. A. [Aphra] Behn, *Oroonoko: or, the Royal Slave* (London, 1688), 14 and 86.

76. Behn, *Oroonoko,* 69.

77. Behn, *Oroonoko,* 90 and 91.

78. Behn, *Oroonoko,* 187–188 and 189.

79. Behn, *Oroonoko,* 193. Oroonoko learns from the African slaves in Surinam that "he was that Prince who had, at several times, sold most of 'em to these Parts" (Behn, *Oroonoko,* 110), and he remarks, after he has finished his address quoted above, "*That Honour was the First Principle in Nature, that was to be Obey'd*" (Behn, *Oroonoko,* 190).

80. Behn, *Oroonoko,* 203, 19, and 141.

81. For the full catalogue of Locke's final library, see John Harrison and Peter Laslett, eds., *The Library of John Locke* (Oxford, 1971; orig. pub. 1965). The books of geography and travel contained herein are treated in detail in John Samuel Harpham, "Locke and the Churchill Catalogue Revisited," *Locke Studies,* vol. 17 (2018): 233–241. The argument of this article is that Locke was intimately involved in the production of the 1704 *Collection of Voyages and Travels,* published by Awnsham and John Churchill, whose expanded 1732 edition first printed the accounts of Thomas Phillips and Jean Barbot cited above.

The literature on the involvement of Locke with the Carolina colony is immense, but much of the evidence has been collected in several informative articles; see David Armitage, "John Locke, Carolina, and the 'Two Treatises of Government,'" *Political Theory* 32, no. 5 (Oct. 2004): 602–627; James Farr, "Locke, 'Some Americans,' and the Discourse on 'Carolina,'" *Locke Studies,* vol. 9 (2009): 19–94; Brad Hinshelwood, "The Carolinian Context of John Locke's Theory of Slavery," *Political Theory* 41, no. 4 (Aug. 2013): 562–590; and James Farr, "'Absolute Power and Authority': John Locke and the Revisions of the *Fundamental Constitutions of Carolina,*" *Locke Studies,* vol. 20 (2020): 1–49. The attribution to Locke of the discourse on Carolina in the Ogilby collection is made on the basis of rather sound evidence in Farr "Locke, 'Some Americans,' and the Discourse on 'Carolina.'" It should also be noted that Locke owned stock in the Royal African Company from 1672 to 1675, when the Company's investment in the transatlantic slave trade was well known.

82. For the most sophisticated attempts to detach Locke's theory of slavery from the contemporary practice of the African slave trade, see James Farr, "'So Vile and Miserable an Estate': The Problem of Slavery in Locke's Political Thought," *Political Theory* 14, no. 2 (May 1986): 263–289; and James Farr, "Locke, Natural Law, and New World Slavery," *Political Theory* 36, no. 4 (Aug. 2008): 495–522.

83. "The Fundamental Constitutions of Carolina," in *The Statutes at Large of South Carolina,* ed. Thomas Cooper (Columbia, SC, 1836), vol. 1: 43–56, 55; and "Coppy

of the Modell of Government Prepared for the Province of Carolina &c," Ford Collection, New York Public Library (unfoliated), art. 73.

84. John Locke, *Two Treatises of Government* (London, 1713; orig. pub. 1690), 2T §23. Armitage has even suggested that Locke wrote the chapter that contains this passage in the same period in 1682 when he also helped to revise the *Fundamental Constitutions:* Armitage, "John Locke, Carolina, and the 'Two Treatises of Government,'" 610–619.

For a contextual account of the slave codes in the early English Caribbean colonies, see Edward B. Rugemer, *Slave Law and the Politics of Resistance in the Early Atlantic World* (Cambridge, MA, 2018).

85. James Tyrrell, *Patriarcha non Monarcha* (London, 1681), 105. On whether Locke drafted a section of Tyrrell's *Patriarcha,* see, for example, Richard Tuck, *The Rights of War and Peace: Political Thought and the International Order from Grotius to Kant* (Oxford, 1999), 169–170 (fn. 8).

For a similar conviction—that the slaves on Barbados who attempted to escape from their masters were "therein justified by the Law of Nature"—see Physiologus [Tryon], *Friendly Advice to the Gentlemen-Planters of the East and West Indies,* 111.

86. In the *Second Treatise,* Locke wrote about slavery as the intimate relation between the aggressor in an unjust war and that person's intended victim, who acquired absolute and arbitrary power over the individual who had wrongly attempted to acquire that same power over them. Only in an aside in the *First Treatise* on the nature of monarchical authority did Locke acknowledge, without reflection, that "A Planter in the *West Indies*" might have within his household "Sons of his own, Friends, or Companions, Soldiers under Pay, or Slaves bought with Money." Locke, *Two Treatises of Government,* 1T §130 and 131.

87. For the argument that Locke had a deep animosity to slavery, which does touch upon his views in the *Two Treatises* but centers on his efforts to curtail the use of African slaves in Virginia in the period when he was a member of the Board of Trade from 1696 to 1700, see Holly Brewer, "Slavery, Sovereignty, and 'Inheritable Blood': Reconsidering John Locke and the Origins of American Slavery," *American Historical Review* 122, no. 4 (Oct. 2017): 1038–1078.

88. See, for example, "Brother Luis Brandaon to Father Sandoval," in *Documents Illustrative of the History of the Slave Trade to America,* ed. Elizabeth Donnan, 4 vols. (Washington, DC, 1930–1935), vol. 1 (1440–1700): 123–124; André Alvares d'Almada, *Brief Treatise on the Rivers of Guinea,* trans. and ed. P. E. H. Hair, 2 vols. (Liverpool, 1984); and the reports collected in *Jesuit Documents on the Guinea of Cape*

Verde and the Cape Verde Islands, 1585–1617, trans. and ed. P. E. H. Hair (Liverpool, 1989).

For scholarship in this field, see in particular Davis, *Problem of Slavery in Western Culture,* 165–196; Herman L. Bennett, *African Kings and Black Slaves: Sovereignty and Dispossession in the Early Modern Atlantic* (Philadelphia, 2018); Anna More, "Necroeconomics, Originary Accumulation, and Racial Capitalism in the Early Iberian Slave Trade," *Journal for Early Modern Cultural Studies* 19, no. 2 (Spring 2019): 75–100; and Daniel Nemser, "Possessive Individualism and the Spirit of Capitalism in the Iberian Slave Trade," *Journal for Early Modern Cultural Studies* 19, no. 2 (Spring 2019): 101–129.

89. Baltasar Barreira, "Concerning the slaves that come from the parts of Guinea which are called Cape Verde," in *Jesuit Documents on the Guinea of Cape Verde and the Cape Verde Islands,* trans. and ed. Hair, doc. 16.

5. THE CAUSES OF COMPLEXION

Note: The title of this chapter has been taken from that of ch.1, pt. 2, in Winthrop D. Jordan, *White over Black: American Attitudes toward the Negro, 1550–1812* (Chapel Hill, NC, 1968), 11–20.

1. From at least the time of Pliny, who reported upon the light-skinned Leucæthiopes, foreign observers had been dimly aware of albinism among the peoples of Africa. They never doubted, however, that it marked a strange departure from the norm, and in the seventeenth century, English observers learned that it was seen as such by the peoples in many areas of the continent. Andrew Battell had found that to the north of Congo, in Loango, there were sometimes born "white children, which is very rare among them, for their Parents are *Negroes.*" These persons were referred to as *Dondos,* and they were placed in the service of the king. "If they goe to the Market," Battell continued, "they may take what they list, for all men stand in awe of them." "The strange adventures of Andrew Battell," in Purchas, *Pilgrimes,* bk. 7, ch. 3, 2: 980. Similar reports later came to the attention of the compiler John Ogilby. When he noted that the Portuguese referred to the "white *Moors*" in Loango as *Albinoes,* this was in all likelihood the first use of the term in a book printed in English. See John Ogilby, *Africa: Being an Accurate Description of the Regions of Ægypt, Barbary, Lybia, and Billedulgerid*... (London, 1670), 509.

It should also be noted that the skin color of the Ethiopian ruler known as Prester John was a matter of some dispute in early-modern Europe, in particular in the sixteenth century. On the one hand, a number of observers reported that the people in Ethiopia were brown or black, and they seem to have assumed that their ruler was the same. On the other hand, some authors observed that the Ethiopian monarchs themselves traced their line of descent back to a union between King Solomon and the Ethiopian Queen of Sheba, whose visit to Jerusalem was mentioned in the Bible. Since Solomon was assumed to be white, these authors maintained that Prester John must be the same. Not mentioned in this dispute was the famous report of the Portuguese ambassador Francisco Alvarez, who in the 1520s had visited the Christian emperor he knew as Prester John and found him "not very blacke, but of the colour of a Chest-nut, or of ruddy Apples, which are not very Tawny." "The Voyage of Sir Francis Alvarez, a Portugall Priest, made unto the Court of Prete Ianni, the Great Christian Emperour of Ethiopia," in Purchas, *Pilgrimes,* bk. 7, ch. 5, 2: 1026–1121, 1079.

2. Winthrop Donaldson Jordan, "White over Black: The Attitudes of the American Colonists toward the Negro, to 1784" (Ph.D. diss., Brown University, 1960), 34. For studies of British racial attitudes that focus in similar fashion upon the eighteenth and nineteenth centuries, see Wylie Sypher, *Guinea's Captive Kings: British Anti-Slavery Literature of the XVIIIth Century* (Chapel Hill, NC, 1942); Philip D. Curtin, *The Image of Africa: British Ideas and Action, 1780–1850* (Madison, WI, 1964); Dorothy Hammond and Alta Jablow, *The Myth of Africa* (New York, 1977); Anthony J. Barker, *The African Link: British Attitudes to the Negro in the Era of the Atlantic Slave Trade, 1550–1807* (Totowa, NJ, 1978); P. J. Marshall and Glyndwr Williams, *The Great Map of Mankind: British Perceptions of the World in the Age of Enlightenment* (London, 1982), 227–257; Ivan Hannaford, *Race: The History of an Idea in the West* (Baltimore, 1996); Roxann Wheeler, *The Complexion of Race: Categories of Difference in Eighteenth-Century British Culture* (Philadelphia, 2000); David Bindman, *Ape to Apollo: Aesthetics and the Idea of Race in the 18th Century* (London, 2002); George Boulukos, *The Grateful Slave: The Emergence of Race in Eighteenth-Century British and American Culture* (New York, 2008); Andrew S. Curran, *The Anatomy of Blackness: Science and Slavery in an Age of Enlightenment* (Baltimore, 2011); Simon Gikandi, *Slavery and the Culture of Taste* (Princeton, NJ, 2011); Catherine Molineux, *Faces of Perfect Ebony: Encountering Atlantic Slavery in Imperial Britain* (Cambridge, MA, 2012); Suman Seth, *Difference and Disease: Medicine, Race, and the Eighteenth-Century British Empire* (New York, 2018); and Devin Vartija, *The Color of Equality: Race and Common Humanity in Enlightenment Thought* (Philadelphia, 2021).

Finally, for broad and well-informed accounts that have drawn attention to the development of racial attitudes over time and to their differences from place to place, see George M. Fredrickson, *Racism: A Short History* (Princeton, NJ, 2002); Colin Kidd, *The Forging of Races: Race and Scripture in the Protestant Atlantic World,*

1600–2000 (Cambridge, UK, 2006); Francisco Bethencourt, *Racisms: From the Crusades to the Twentieth Century* (Princeton, NJ, 2013); and Jean-Frédéric Schaub and Silvia Sebastiani, *Race et histoire dans les sociétés occidentales (XVe–XVIIIe siècle)* (Paris, 2021).

3. The phrases that are quoted in this paragraph appear, in order, in Rycharde Eden, "A breefe description of Affrike," in Peter Martyr, *The Decades of the Newe Worlde or West India,* trans. Rycharde Eden (London, 1555), 344r–345r, 344r; George Abbot, *A Briefe Description of the Whole Worlde* (London, 1599), Cviir; Richard Jobson, *The Golden Trade: or, A Discovery of the River Gambra, and the Golden Trade of the Aethiopians* (London, 1623), 37; Thomas Blundeville, *M. Blundevile His Exercises* (London, 1594), 262v; "Drawen out of the writings and discourses of Odoardo Lopes, a Portingall, by Philippo Pigafetta," *A Report of the Kingdome of Congo, a Region of Africa,* trans. Abraham Hartwell (London, 1597), 10; Lewes Roberts, *The Merchants Mappe of Commerce* (London, 1638), 81; and Benjamin Jonson, *The Queenes Masques. The first, of blacknesse,* in *The Workes of Benjamin Jonson* (London, 1616), 893–901, 893.

4. Jobson, *Golden Trade,* 83, 9, and 36.

5. For references to the "ryver Negro," see, for example, Eden, "Breefe description of Affrike," in Martyr, *Decades of the Newe Worlde,* trans. Eden, 344r; and *Abraham Ortelius His Epitome of the Theater of the Worlde* (London, 1603), 107v. This same river is called the "Blacke River" in as late a map as the "New and accurate Mappe of the World" in Roberts, *Merchants Mappe of Commerce,* unpaginated (before 1). In turn, for references to the people who lived near the Niger River as "Nigers," or in the singular form as a "Niger," see, for example, Reginald Scot, *The Discoverie of Witchcraft* (London, 1584), 153; and Robert Stafforde, *A Geographicall and Anthological Description of all the Empires and Kingdomes, both of Continent and Islands in this terrestriall Globe* (London, 1607), 40.

Leo Africanus introduced the name of the Niger into early-modern European culture when he said "the lande of Negros hath a mightie river, which taking his name of the region, is called Niger." But he had not made clear the reason why this region was called by its name. John Leo, *A Geographical Historie of Africa,* trans. John Pory (London, 1600), 2.

For speculations about the origin of the term "Negro," see, for example, Purchas, *Pilgrimage,* 537; Peter Heylyn, *Microcosmus, or A Little Description of the Great World* (London, 1621), 379; Roberts, *Merchants Mappe of Commerce,* 81; Robert Morden, *Geography Rectified: Or, A Description of the World* (London, 1680), 337; and in particular Ogilby, *Africa,* 315.

6. A number of the classically informed midcentury English surveys of the peoples of Africa, which were introduced in Chapter 3, drew attention to the etymology of "Æthiope." They tied the word more directly to the heat of the sun in Ethiopia than the skin color of the Ethiopians, although, as we have already begun to see, the one was often taken to be an effect of the other in the classical discourse that these works in large part followed. For example, William Prat noted that the name for the peoples of Ethiopia was formed from the Greek "*Atho* whiche signifieth burne, and *Oph* which signifieth take hede & that because of the approchyng & nyghe to the soone" in that part of the world. *The Discription of the Contrey of Aphrique,* trans. Wyllyam Prat (London, 1554), Cvir. See also *The Fardle of Facions,* trans. William Watreman (London, 1555), Ciir.

7. *The Geography of Strabo,* trans. Horace Leonard Jones, 8 vols. (New York, 1917–1933), vol. 8, bk. 17, ch. 2, sect. 3: 147. See Hippocrates, "Airs, Waters, Places," in *Hippocratic Writings,* ed. G. E. R. Lloyd and trans. J. Chadwick and W. N. Mann (London, 1983), 148–169; Aristotle, *Problems,* trans. Robert Mayhew, 2 vols. (Cambridge, MA, 2011), vol. 1, bk. 14: 439–449; and Ptolemy, *Tetrabiblos,* trans. F. E. Robbins (Cambridge, MA, 1940), bk. 2, ch. 2: 121–127; as well as Pliny, *Natural History,* trans. H. Rackham, 10 vols. (Cambridge, MA, 1942), vol. 1, bk. 2, sect. 130: 321–323 and vol. 2, bk. 5, sect. 8: 249–253.

8. For attempts on the part of Continental authors in the Renaissance to elaborate upon the classical theory of the humors, see, for example, John Bodin, *Method for the Easy Comprehension of History,* trans. Beatrice Reynolds (New York, 1945), 85–152; Juan Huarte, *The Examination of Mens Wits,* trans. R.C. [Richard Carew] (London, 1594); and Pierre Charron, *Of Wisdome,* trans. Samson Lennard (London, 1608), 163–168. On the theory of the humors, which is referred to with the artful term "geohumoralism," and its complex reception in England, see Mary Floyd-Wilson, *English Ethnicity and Race in Early Modern Drama* (New York, 2003).

9. William Cuningham, *The Cosmographical Glasse* (London, 1559), 66–67; and Bartholomaeus Anglicus, *Batman uppon Bartholome, His Booke De Proprietatibus Rerum,* trans. John Trevisa and rev. and supp. Stephen Batman (London, 1582), 223v–224r.

10. George Abbot, *A Briefe Description of the Whole Worlde* (London, 1599), Cviir; and John Davies, *Nosce Teipsum* (London, 1599), 40. On the flexible category of the Moor, see Emily C. Bartels, *Speaking of the Moor from Alcazar to Othello* (Philadelphia, PA, 2008). For a survey of references to the view that the sun was the cause of black skin in verse from this period, see Kim F. Hall, *Things of Darkness: Economies of Race and Gender in Early Modern England* (Ithaca, NY, 1995), 92–107.

11. Nathanael Carpenter, *Geography Delineated Forth in Two Bookes* (Oxford, 1625), bk. 2: 48; and Francis Bacon, *Sylva Sylvarum: or A Naturall Historie* (London, 1626), 105.

12. "The seconde vyage to Guinea," in Peter Martyr, *The Decades of the Newe Worlde or West India,* trans. Rycharde Eden (London, 1555), 349v–360r, 355v.

13. *Fardle of Facions,* trans. Watreman, Ciir; Cuningham, *Cosmographical Glasse,* 185 (a similar opinion can even be found in the work of an author who was as oriented toward the modern view of Africa as John Pory; see John Pory, "A generall description of all Africa," in Leo, *Geographical Historie of Africa,* trans. Pory, 1–8, 2); and George Best, *A True Discourse of the Late Voyages of Discoverie . . . under the conduct of Martin Frobisher Generall* (London, 1578), 19, 19, and 20.

14. Best, *True Discourse of the Late Voyages of Discoverie,* 19, 22, 20, 28, and 28.

15. *The Holy Bible, Conteyning the Old Testament, and the New* (London, 1611), The Song of Solomon, ch. 1, ver. 6; and Jeremiah, ch. 13, ver. 23.

16. Benjamin Jonson, *The Queenes Masques. The first, of blacknesse,* in *Workes of Benjamin Jonson,* 894, 897, 897, 897, 898; and Benjamin Jonson, *The Second Masque. Which was of beautie,* in *Workes of Benjamin Jonson,* 901–910, 903.

17. For the use of this proverb, see, for example, Morris Palmer Tilley, *A Dictionary of Proverbs in England in the Sixteenth and Seventeenth Centuries* (Ann Arbor, MI, 1950), E186: 190; as well as Hall, *Things of Darkness,* 107–116.

18. Best, *True Discourse of the Late Voyages of Discoverie,* 29. For studies of persons from western Africa who were present in England around the turn of the century, see, for example, Imtiaz H. Habib, *Black Lives in the English Archives, 1500–1677: Imprints of the Invisible* (Burlington, VT, 2008); Miranda Kaufmann, *Black Tudors: The Untold Story* (London, 2017); and Onyeka Nubia, *England's Other Countrymen: Black Tudor Society* (London, 2019).

19. Best, *True Discourse of the Late Voyages of Discoverie,* 18; Jonson, *The Queenes Masques. The first, of blacknesse,* in *Workes of Benjamin Jonson,* 896; and *The xv. Bookes of P. Ovidius Naso, Entitled, Metamorphosis,* trans. Arthur Golding (London, 1587; orig. pub. 1567), 20v.

20. Best, *True Discourse of the Late Voyages of Discoverie,* 30 and 31.

21. *The Holy Bible,* Genesis, ch. 9, ver. 22, 24, and 25; and *The Bible: that is, The Holy Scriptures conteined in the Old and New Testament* (London, 1601; orig. pub. 1560), Genesis, ch. 9, ver. 25 (note f). The parts of the work upon which Best would have drawn are Guliemo Postel, *Cosmographicæ Disciplinæ Compendium* (Basil, 1561), 17–19

and 37–46. Postel had associated the descendants of Cham with both slavery and black skin, whereas Best only associated the Curse with blackness. Postel is given as the source for the version of this story that Best told in David Whitford, *The Curse of Ham in the Early Modern Era: The Bible and the Justifications for Slavery* (Burlington, VT, 2009), 118–120.

22. Robin Blackburn, "The Old World Background to European Colonial Slavery," *WMQ* 54, no. 1 (Jan. 1997): 65–102, 95; and David Whitford, "A Calvinist Heritage to the 'Curse of Ham': Assessing the Accuracy of a Claim about Racial Subordination," *Church History and Religious Culture* 90, no. 1 (2010): 25–45, 27. For efforts by these same scholars to expand upon these assertions, see Robin Blackburn, *The Making of New World Slavery: From the Baroque to the Modern, 1492–1800* (New York, 1997), 64–76; and Whitford, *Curse of Ham in the Early Modern Era,* 105–176. For similar assertions, see, for example, Christopher Hill, *The English Bible and the Seventeenth-Century Revolution* (New York, 1993), 29; David M. Goldenberg, *The Curse of Ham: Race and Slavery in Early Judaism, Christianity, and Islam* (Princeton, NJ, 2003), 3; Floyd-Wilson, *English Ethnicity and Race in Early Modern Drama,* 10; Susan Dwyer Amussen, *Caribbean Exchanges: Slavery and the Transformation of English Society, 1640–1700* (Chapel Hill, NC, 2007), 22; and Naomi Tadmor, *The Social Universe of the English Bible: Scripture, Society, and Culture in Early Modern England* (Cambridge, UK, 2010), 113–115.

23. John Weemse, *The Portraiture of the Image of God in Man* (London, 1633; orig. pub. 1626), 236–237.

24. George Sandys, *A Relation of a Journey begun An. Dom. 1610* (London, 1637; orig. pub. 1615), 136.

The excerpt that appeared in the Purchas collection was "Relations of Africa, taken out of Master George Sandys his larger discourse observed in his Journey, begun Ann. 1610," in Purchas, *Pilgrimes,* bk. 6, ch. 8, 2: 896–920. The relevant passage was on 912–913. The text at this point was slightly altered from Sandys's original edition to make even clearer that he understood the Curse as a cause of blackness rather than slavery. After the remark that the parents of the "*Negros*" who had sold their children paid more regard to "the price then condition of their slavery," the sentence ended. The next sentence then continued, "These are descended of *Chus,* the Sonne of cursed *Cham,* as are all of that complexion. Not so by reason of their Seed, nor heat of the Climate: Nor of the Soyle . . . but rather from the Curse of *Noe* upon *Cham* in the Posteritie of *Chus.*" Purchas included a marginal note: "Black colour whence." For the passage in which van Linschoten wrote, about the color of the peoples on the western coast of Africa, that "it is not the heat of the Sunne, but the nature of the Countrey that maketh them blacke," see John Huighen van Linschoten, *Discours of Voyages into ye Easte and West Indies,* trans. W.P. (London, 1598), bk. 2: 211.

25. Jobson, *Golden Trade,* 52.

26. Carpenter, *Geography Delineated Forth,* bk. 2: 48 and 41; and Thomas Herbert, *Some Yeares Travels into Africa & Asia the Great,* second ed. (London, 1638), 16. The first edition of this work had appeared in 1634, and Herbert would continue to revise it through the appearance of a fourth edition in 1677. Earlier in the 1638 edition, as he considered the peoples along the western coast of Africa, Herbert had remarked that "the raging Sunne has scorcht their bodies" but had not also made clear that he believed this was the cause of their black skin. Herbert, *Some Yeares Travels into Africa & Asia the Great,* 8.

27. John Minsheu, *The Guide into the Tongues* (London, 1617), 327: no. 8606. See also John Minsheu, *A Dictionarie in Spanish and English, first published into the English tongue by Ric. Percivale Gent.* (London, 1599).

28. Coke, *The First Part of the Institutes of the Lawes of England* (London, 1628), bk. 2, capt. 11, sect. 172.

29. John Milton, *Paradise Lost. A Poem Written in Ten Books* (London, 1667), bk. 10: lns. 960–962 and 992–995.

In recent decades, it has become common to assert that in the lines quoted above from *Paradise Lost,* Milton intended to endorse or at least accepted without criticism the enslavement of African peoples in the contemporary English Atlantic world. This claim has been put forward in, for example, Steven Jablonski, "Ham's Vicious Race: Slavery and John Milton," *Studies in English Literature, 1500–1900* 37, no. 1 (Winter 1997): 173–190; Mary Nyquist, *Arbitrary Rule: Slavery, Tyranny, and the Power of Life and Death* (Chicago, 2013), 146–147; Daniel Shore, "Was Milton White?," *Milton Studies* 62, no. 2 (2020): 252–265, 254–259; and Feisal G. Mohamed, "On Race and Historicism: A Polemic in Three Turns," *ELH* 89, no. 2 (Summer 2022): 377–405, 394.

The claim put forward in such accounts depends upon a connection between the "vitious Race" of Ham and the peoples of Africa in the present. Milton never mentioned such a connection. What is more, for reasons that will be discussed in what follows in this chapter, it is not clear that Milton would have believed that the peoples of Africa were descended from Ham or were at least the only descendants of Ham that there were in the present. There is one final point to be made here. In *Paradise Lost,* Milton never mentioned the contemporary enslavement of Africans. To what extent Milton was aware of the practice of African slavery in the Atlantic world is a question that requires more research. When the blind poet at last came out with his epic rendition of events described in Genesis, in 1667, news of the establishment of slave systems in the English Atlantic world had only started to reach the best-informed observers back in the metropole.

30. John Pory, "A generall description of all Africa," in Leo, *Geographical Historie of Africa,* trans. Pory, 1–8, 6.

31. [Guillaume de Salluste, Sieur du Bartas], *Bartas: His Devine Weekes and Workes,* trans. Joshua Sylvester (London, 1605), 440. Perhaps the earliest significant attempt to establish the scheme noted above was recorded in the so-called T-O maps that were included in the *Etymologiae,* by Isidore of Seville, from the thirteenth century; see *Mappemondes, A.D. 1200–1500,* ed. Marcel Destombes (Amsterdam, 1964), 29–34. Among early seventeenth-century works of biblical exegesis in which this scheme also appeared, see, for example, Thomas Cooper, *The Blessing of Japheth* (London, 1615), 3.

32. For the Table of Nations, in both the Geneva Bible and the King James Version, see *The Holy Scriptures conteined in the Old and New Testament,* Genesis, ch. 10; and *The Holy Bible,* Genesis, ch. 10. In turn, for an important discussion of these issues, see Benjamin Braude, "The Sons of Noah and the Construction of Ethnic and Geographic Identities in the Medieval and Early Modern Periods," *WMQ* 54, no. 1 (Jan. 1997): 103–142. On the original context for what the author terms the "Hamitic myth" and its development up to the fifteenth century in Christian and Muslim sources, see William McKee Evans, "From the Land of Canaan to the Land of Guinea: The Strange Odyssey of the 'Sons of Ham,'" *American Historical Review* 85, no. 1 (Feb. 1980): 15–43.

33. See John Speed, *The Genealogies of Holy Scriptures* (London, 1611). The tables referred to here are on 2 and 4–5.

34. [du Bartas], *Bartas: His Devine Weekes and Workes,* trans. Sylvester, 440; and Walter Ralegh, *The History of the World* (London, 1614), bk. 2, ch. 8, sect. 10: 126. On Phut and the peopling of Africa, see Ralegh, *History of the World,* bk. 2, ch. 8, sect. 11: 131–132. Raleigh's judgment about the location of "the seat of *Chush,*" as he spelled the name, was affirmed in, for example, Peter Heylyn, *Cosmographie in Four Bookes* (London, 1652), 13–14.

35. Purchas, *Pilgrimage,* 39 and 38. The method that Purchas used here in order to determine which of the descendants of Noah had first peopled which areas of the earth was to compare the names assigned to each person in the Table of Nations to those that had been used for certain nations in ancient languages. By this method—which, of course, Purchas wanted to emphasize could provide no more

than conjectures—he was able to posit that, of the sons of Ham, Canaan had gone to Canaan, Mizraim to Egypt, Cush to Ethiopia and Arabia, and Phut to Libya.

36. Alden T. Vaughan, "The Origins Debate: Slavery and Racism in Seventeenth-Century Virginia," in Alden T. Vaughan, *Roots of American Racism: Essays on the Colonial Experience* (New York, 1995), 136–174, 164; Peter Fryer, *Staying Power: The History of Black People in Britain* (London, 1984), 142; and Floyd-Wilson, *English Ethnicity and Race in Early Modern Drama,* 5.

37. Thomas Browne, *Pseudodoxia Epidemica: or, Enquiries into very many received tenents, and commonly presumed truths* (London, 1646), bk. 6., ch. 10: 322; bk. 6, ch. 10: 322–323; bk. 6, ch. 10: 327; and bk. 6, ch. 10: 323. Browne devoted three interconnected essays to this topic; see Browne, *Pseudodoxia Epidemica,* bk. 6, chs. 10–12: 322–338. For Boyle's essay on the "the Cause of the Blackness of those many Nations, which by one common Name we are wont to call *Negroes,*" see Robert Boyle, *Experiments and Considerations Touching Colours* (London, 1664), 151–167 ("Experiment XI"), 151.

38. Browne, *Pseudodoxia Epidemica,* bk. 6, ch. 10: 327; Browne, *Pseudodoxia Epidemica,* bk. 6, ch. 12: 334; and Boyle, *Experiments and Considerations Touching Colours,* 161. For his discussion of the cause of black skin, see J.B. [John Bulwer], *Anthropometamorphosis: Man Transform'd; or, the Artificial Changeling* (London, 1650), 253–255.

The proposal that Robert Boyle put forward here was not uncommon in classical sources that were well known to early-modern English authors; see, for example, *The Problemes of Aristotle* (Edinburgh, 1595), E2r–v; and (although in this case it was a white child who was born to black parents) *An Æthiopian Historie written in Greeke by Heliodorus,* trans. Thomas Underdowne (London, 1569), 53. Indeed, stories about this unusual phenomenon—and the social drama that it could produce—continued to trickle into English culture through the end of the seventeenth century; see, for example, John Mocquet, *Travels and Voyages into Africa, Asia, and America . . . ,* trans. Nathaniel Pullen (London, 1696), 227–229.

39. Boyle, *Experiments and Considerations Touching Colours,* 163. The best treatment of these issues is in Cristina Malcolmson, *Studies of Skin Color in the Early Royal Society* (Burlington, VT, 2013), 29–91.

40. John Josselyn, *An Account of Two Voyages to New-England* (London, 1674), 187.

In a passage similar to this one in the work of Josselyn, the traveler John Ovington maintained, in the course of his narrative of a voyage to Suratt, that "something must be added besides the Sun's Heat" in order to explain "the Complexion of the *Negroes.*" However, Ovington was only able to repeat the standard conventions of the time: on the one hand, that their blood was black and, on the other hand, that they had a third, middle layer of skin that could have "caus'd the Blackness." John Ovington, *A Voyage to Suratt, in the Year 1689* (London, 1696), 492.

41. On this subject, see, for example, Lorraine Daston and Katharine Park, *Wonders and the Order of Nature, 1150–1750* (New York, 1998); and Lorraine Daston, "Marvelous Facts and Miraculous Evidence in Early Modern Europe," in *Wonders, Marvels, and Monsters in Early Modern Culture,* ed. Peter G. Platt (Newark, DE, 1999), 76–104.

42. Browne, *Pseudodoxia Epidemica,* bk. 6, ch. 10: 323; and Best, *True Discourse of the Late Voyages of Discoverie,* 31.

43. "The seconde vyage to Guinea," in Martyr, *Decades of the Newe Worlde,* trans. Eden, 359v. About the requirement that peoples whose lands stood in the same relation to the Equator be affected by the sun in a similar manner, no less an authority than Ptolemy had written that "Reason herself asserts that all animals, and all plants likewise, have a similarity under the same kind of climate or under similar weather conditions, that is, when under the same parallels, or when situated at the same distance from either pole." *The Geography of Claudius Ptolemy,* trans. and ed. Edward Luther Stevenson (New York, 1932), 31–32. See also, for example, *Geography of Strabo,* trans. Jones, vol. 8, bk. 17, ch. 3, sect. 23: 209.

44. Bartholomaeus, *Batman uppon Bartholome,* trans. Trevisa and rev. and supp. Batman, 251r. The major modern source from which this chapter of the book was drawn was Leo Africanus, but the passage cited in this paragraph was taken in large part from the brief description of Africa that appeared in the Ortelius atlas that came out in Latin in 1570 and in English in 1606. Here Ortelius referred to the opinion of Postel, who, Ortelius noted, "imputeth the originall of this blacknesse unto *Chams* curse. Against which opinion I have nothing to allege." Ortelius continued, "Let the trueth of the matter rest upon the authours credit." Although Bateman did not reproduce this passage and made no reference to the Curse of Ham, he did keep the phrase from Ortelius that said he aimed to find the "efficient cause" of blackness rather than, as Ortelius had done, to discuss "the originall of this blacknesse" as well. Like Bateman, Ortelius soon came to realize that he had been unable to produce this "efficient cause." And Ortelius concluded that he would leave such issues "to be considered by them, who do more curiously search into the secrets of nature." Abraham Ortelius, *The Theatre of the Whole World* (London, 1606), fol. 4.

45. Lopes, *Report of the Kingdome of Congo,* trans. Hartwell, 173, 19, and 173.

46. George Abbot, *A Briefe Description of the Whole Worlde,* 2nd ed. (London, 1605; orig. pub. 1599), R2r. The remark from Abbot that the native peoples of America

were all "of a reasonable faire complexion" reflected a common perception in the early-modern period, since as Alden Vaughan has shown, "not until the middle of the eighteenth century did most Anglo-Americans view Indians as significantly different in color from themselves." Alden T. Vaughan, "From White Man to Redskin: Changing Anglo-American Perceptions of the American Indian," in Vaughan, *Roots of American Racism,* 3–33, 4.

47. Peter Heylyn, *Microcosmus, or A Little Description of the Great World* (Oxford, 1621), 382 and 403. In addition to the writers noted here, a number of authors discussed above cited the complexion of the peoples of America as evidence against the classical belief that the sun was the cause of black skin. See, for example, Best, *True Discourse of the Late Voyages of Discoverie,* 28; Browne, *Pseudodoxia Epidemica,* bk. 6, ch. 10: 324–325; and Boyle, *Experiments and Considerations Touching Colours,* 154.

48. Peter Heylyn, *Cosmographie in Four Bookes* (London, 1652), bk. 4, pt. 2: 100.

It should be observed that, in spite of what he had to say about it in the passage quoted here, a small number of authors in the second half of the seventeenth century believed that Heylyn had accepted the view that the Curse of Ham had caused the blackness of the Africans. For example, Heylyn appears to have been the "late most learned Critick" whom Boyle said "would have the Blackness of *Negroes* an effect of *Noah's* Curse ratify'd by God's, upon *Cham.*" Boyle, *Experiments and Considerations Touching Colours,* 159. See also an anonymous letter to the editor that ran in a popular periodical named *The Athenian Mercury* around the end of the century. In response to a note from the editors that declared no skin color was "natural to any people whatever, 'tis the effect of the Climate," the author of the letter said he would "rather incline to the opinion of Dr. *Heylin,* who ascribes the *Blackness* of the *Negroes* to the curse upon the posterity of *Cham.*" See *The Athenian Oracle: Being an Entire Collection of All the Valuable Questions and Answers in the Old* Athenian Mercuries, 3 vols. (London, 1704), vol. 3: 380. (The editors' note is in *Athenian Mercury* 17, no. 9 [Apr. 30, 1695].) The letter is undated in this collection, but it surely appeared sometime after the editors' note was printed and before the *Athenian Mercury* stopped its print run in 1697.

49. Martyr, *Decades of the Newe Worlde,* trans. Eden, 310v–311r. Gómara closed this chapter with the hope that the recent discovery of the color of the Indians would "give further occasion to phylosophers to search the secreates of nature and complexions of men with the novelties of the newe worlde." Gómara's sense of admiration for the marvels that were disclosed in the course of the encounter with the New World reflects what Stephen Greenblatt has taken to be a characteristic mode of European response in the Renaissance: see Stephen Greenblatt, *Marvelous Possessions: The Wonder of the New World* (Chicago, 1991).

50. Purchas, *Pilgrimage,* 546.

51. Heylyn, *Cosmographie,* 19–20. The verses that Heylyn quoted here were from [du Bartas], *Bartas: His Devine Weekes and Workes,* trans. Sylvester, 456. In similar fashion, Heylyn explained in his *Microcosmus* that men who were "one by originall, are of diverse complexions of body, and conditions of mind, according to the diverse climats of the Earth." Heylyn, *Microcosmus,* 6.

52. [Isaac La Peyrère], *Men before Adam,* trans. Anonymous, 22.

Even as La Peyrère had of course implied the separate origins of African nations, he seems to have mentioned them only once in his published works, in a sentence in which he noted that the ancient records of the Ethiopians, in addition to those of the Chaldeans, Egyptians, and Scythians, looked to predate the period when Adam was supposed to have lived. [Isaac La Peyrère], *A Theological Systeme upon that Presupposition That Men Were Before Adam,* trans. Anonymous (1655), F1v ("The Proeme"). Nevertheless, a number of scholars have made claims to the effect that "La Peyrère saw the differences between whites and blacks as so fundamental that he could not think of them as descended from the same original pair of humans." William B. Cohen, *The French Encounter with Africans: White Response to Blacks, 1530–1880* (Bloomington, IN, 1980), 12. In addition, see Fryer, *Staying Power,* 144; and Sujata Iyengar, *Shades of Difference: Mythologies of Skin Color in Early Modern England* (Philadelphia, 2013), 222–223.

53. L.P., *Two Essays Sent in a Letter from Oxford to a Nobleman in London* (London, 1695), 2 (and see esp. 15–28). See, for example, Francis Lodwick, "A Supposal of the Manner of Creation," in *Francis Lodwick: On Language, Theology, and Utopia,* ed. Felicity Henderson and William Poole (Oxford, 2011), 252–257. On these topics, see William Poole, *The World Makers: Scientists of the Restoration and the Search for the Origins of the Earth* (Oxford, 2010), esp. 27–38.

54. Matthew Hale, *The Primitive Origination of Mankind, Considered and Examined According to the Light of Nature* (London, 1677), 200. For another work in this genre, see Edward Stillingfleet, *Origines Sacræ, or A Rational Account of the Grounds of Christian Faith* (London, 1662), esp. 533–576.

Even though rumors of atheism had followed Raleigh since the 1590s, and he was sometimes said to believe that the Indians were more ancient than Adam, his *History of the World* conformed to the orthodox chronology and principally marked an advance upon a number of earlier models in the extent to which it used ancient pagan sources in order to confirm and expand upon the historical account in Scripture. See Nicholas Popper, *Walter Ralegh's* History of the World *and the Historical Culture of the Late Renaissance* (Chicago, 2012).

55. Thomas Robinson, *The Anatomy of the Earth* (London, 1694), 3–4.

56. Boyle, *Experiments and Considerations Touching Colours,* 164.

57. Some of these lists of inquiries appeared in print: see Robert Boyle, "General Heads for a Natural History of a Countrey," *Philosophical Transactions* (London) 1, no. 11 (1666): 186–189; Abraham Hill, "Inquiries for Guiny," *Philosophical Transactions* (London) 2, no. 25 (1667): 472; and John Woodward, *Brief Instructions for Making Observations in All Parts of the World* (London, 1696), 8–10. For reference, see also Malcolmson, *Studies of Skin Color in the Early Royal Society,* 29–91.

58. Thomas Birch, *The History of the Royal Society of London for Improving of Natural Knowledge,* 4 vols. (London, [1756]-57), vol. 4: 141; and Thomas Burnet, *The Theory of the Earth* (London, 1684), 191.

The opinions that were endorsed here by Wren and Burnet were also expressed by the editors of the *Athenian Mercury* in 1695. In response to a letter from a reader that presented the same unwelcome idea that Robinson had not wished to entertain—that is, that "if Blackness be natural to the *Ethiopian,* and whiteness to the *Europian;* how can they derive their Original from one single person?"—the editors explained that no color was "natural to any people whatever, 'tis the effect of the Climate." Then, in order to demonstrate this point, the editors observed that "English people that go near the *Line* shall in two or three Generations, tho' they marry only with *English,* become Tawny and Black." The reader's letter to which this note was written as a response had denied that Englishmen who went to live near the Equator would become black over time and had instead sided with what it took to be Heylyn's position: that the blackness of the people in the Land of Negroes came from the Curse of Ham. This letter from the reader and the response from the editors are in the *Athenian Mercury* 17, no. 9 (Apr. 30, 1695).

59. For a learned discussion of early-modern beliefs about the location of Eden, see Philip C. Almond, *Adam and Eve in Seventeenth-Century Thought* (Cambridge, UK, 1999), 65–109. In spite of the common belief in this period that Paradise had been in Asia, and in particular that it had been somewhere in the Middle East, a number of authors concluded that it had instead been in Africa. It so happened that Samuel Purchas was one such author. Perhaps inspired by the classical tradition from Diodorus that held the eastern Ethiopians to have been the first men, Purchas said that "the Hill Amara," a remote mountain fastness within the former empire of Prester John, was in truth "the place of our Fore-fathers Paradise." Purchas, *Pilgrimage,* 565. Heylyn made sure to correct Purchas on this point, however, and so did Milton. See Heylyn, *Cosmographie,* bk. 4, pt. 1: 64; and Milton, *Paradise Lost,* bk. 4, lns. 280–282. Both authors held that Paradise had been in Mesopotamia. Milton referred to Eden as an "*Assyrian* Garden"—even if, in his description of it, he reproduced themes that he had in encountered in Purchas and Heylyn's

accounts of Amara. On this point, see Evert Mordecai Clark, "Milton's Abyssinian Paradise," *University of Texas Studies in English* 29 (1950): 129–150.

60. Best, *True Discourse of the Late Voyages of Discoverie,* 30; Browne, *Pseudodoxia Epidemica,* bk. 6, ch. 10: 328; and Boyle, *Experiments and Considerations Touching Colours,* 166.

61. Martyr, *Decades of the Newe Worlde,* trans. Eden, 311r; and Purchas, *Pilgrimage,* 546.

62. *The Holy Bible,* The Actes of the Apostles, ch. 17, ver. 26. For further discussion of the issues treated in this section of the chapter, see Margaret T. Hodgen, *Early Anthropology in the Sixteenth and Seventeenth Centuries* (Philadelphia, 1964); Paolo Rossi, *The Dark Abyss of Time: The History of the Earth and the History of Nations from Hooke to Vico,* trans. Lydia G. Cochrane (Chicago, 1984); Colin Kidd, *British Identities before Nationalism: Ethnicity and Nationhood in the Atlantic World, 1600–1800* (Cambridge, UK, 1999); Colin Kidd, *The Forging of Races: Race and Scripture in the Protestant Atlantic World, 1600–2000* (New York, 2006); David N. Livingstone, *Adam's Ancestors: Race, Religion, and the Politics of Human Origins* (Baltimore, 2008); Poole, *The World Makers*; Rhodri Lewis, *William Petty on the Order of Nature: An Unpublished Manuscript Treatise* (Tempe, AZ, 2012); Popper, *Walter Ralegh's* History of the World; and Justin E. H. Smith, *Nature, Human Nature, and Human Difference: Race in Early Modern Philosophy* (Princeton, NJ, 2015).

Moreover, the argument presented here is in agreement with the consensus of recent decades that early-modern science was carried on within the bounds of a broad religious framework. Perhaps the most sophisticated statements of this position are Ann Blair, *The Theater of Nature: Jean Bodin and Renaissance Science* (Princeton, NJ, 1997); and Peter Harrison, *The Bible, Protestantism, and the Rise of Natural Science* (Cambridge, UK, 1998).

63. Purchas, *Pilgrimage* (1626), 759. On the representation of blackness in early-modern English drama, see, for example, Elliot H. Tokson, *The Popular Image of the Black Man in English Drama, 1550–1688* (Boston, 1982); Anthony Gerald Barthelemy, *Black Face, Maligned Race: The Representation of Blacks in English Drama from Shakespeare to Southerne* (Baton Rouge, LA, 1987); Kim F. Hall, *Things of Darkness: Economies of Race and Gender in Early Modern England* (Ithaca, NY, 1995); and Virginia Mason Vaughan, *Performing Blackness on the English Stage, 1500–1800* (New York, 2005).

For three recent accounts that examine representations of blackness in early-modern English culture, and the complex relationship between such representations and what the authors aim to establish was the construction of "race" in this context, see Urvashi Chakravarty, *Fictions of Consent: Slavery, Servitude, and Free*

Service in Early Modern England (Philadelphia, 2022); Kimberly Anne Coles, *Bad Humor: Race and Religious Essentialism in Early Modern England* (Philadelphia, 2022); and Noémie Ndiaye, *Scripts of Blackness: Early Modern Performance Culture and the Making of Race* (Philadelphia, 2022).

64. Herodotus, *The Persian Wars,* trans. A. D. Godley, 4 vols. (Cambridge, MA, 1920–1925), vol. 2, bk. 3, sect. 114: 141; *The Holy Bible,* Song of Solomon, ch. 1, ver. 5; and Jonson, *The Queenes Masques. The first, of blacknesse,* in *Workes of Benjamin Jonson,* 895. On the reception of this verse from the Song of Songs in early-modern English culture, see Iyengar, *Shades of Difference,* 44–79.

65. Mrs. A. [Aphra] Behn, *Oroonoko: or, the Royal Slave* (London, 1688), 21; and Boyle, *Experiments and Considerations Touching Colours,* 160.

For remarks about the beauty of African peoples, which in each case was set in contrast with their color, see, for example, Nicolas Villault de Bellefond, *A Relation of the Coasts of Africk Called Guinee,* trans. Anonymous (London, 1670), 51; Ogilby, *Africa,* 318; R.B. [Nathaniel Crouch], *A View of the English Acquisitions in Guinea* (London, 1686) 6; and Jean-Joseph Le Maire, *The Voyages of Sieur Le Maire, to the Canary-Islands, Cape-Verde, Senegal, and Gambia,* trans. Anonymous (London, 1696), 91.

For similar remarks that appeared in travelers' accounts that were not available in translation but were well known to English observers, see "Wilhelm Johann Müller's Description of the Fetu Country, 1662–1669," trans. Adam Jones, in *German Sources for West African History, 1599–1669,* ed. Adam Jones (Wiesbaden, Germany, 1983), 134–259, 153; and "Relation du voyage fait sur les Costes d'Afrique," in Henri Justel, *Recueil de divers voyages faits en Afrique et en l'Amerique* (Paris, 1674), 16.

66. Boyle, *Experiments and Considerations Touching Colours,* 160; and Thomas Herbert, *Some Yeares Travels into Africa & Asia the Great,* 4th ed. (London, 1677), 16. See Jordan, *White over Black,* 24. For another reference from the travel literature of the seventeenth century to the "devilish" character of African peoples, see John Smith, *Advertisements For the unexperienced Planters of New-England, or any where. Or, The Path-way to experience to erect a Plantation* (London, 1631), 30. Smith's purpose here was to condemn the Spanish African slave trade and to advocate that, in contrast, the English settlers in America should rely upon the native peoples of America to cultivate the land for their benefit.

67. Purchas, *Pilgrimage,* 539; [Pieter de Marees], "A description and historicall declaration of the golden Kingdome of Guinea," trans. G. Artus Dantise, in Purchas, *Pilgrimes,* bk. 7, ch. 2, 2: 926–970, 943; and Purchas, *Pilgrimage* (1617), 854.

For travelers' reports from the western coast about the black images that the local people seemed to worship, see, for example, "The voyage made by the worshipful M. John Hawkins Esquire," in Hakluyt, *Principall Navigations* (1589), 523–543, 527; and "The strange adventures of Andrew Battell of Leigh in Essex," in Purchas, *Pilgrimes,* bk. 7, ch. 3, 2: 970–985, 980.

68. Heylyn, *Microcosmus,* 379 (see Heylyn, *Cosmographie,* bk. 4, pt. 2: 53). The source for this poem, which Heylyn did not cite, was Richard Zouche, *The Dove: or Passages of Cosmography* (London, 1613), C1r.

For reports from European observers about the depictions of black gods and white devils in Africa, see John Smith, *The True Travels, Adventures, and Observations of Captaine John Smith* (London, 1630), 38; Browne, *Pseudodoxia Epidemica,* bk. 6, ch. 10: 332; Bulwer, *Anthropometamorphosis,* 255; Samuel Clarke, *A Geographicall Description of All the Countries in the Known World* (London, 1657), 54; Boyle, *Experiments and Considerations Touching Colours,* 160; *The Golden Coast, Or A Description of Guinney* (London, 1665), 3; Richard Blome, *A Geographical Description of the Four Parts of the World* (London, 1670), pt. 2, 49; and Job Ludolphus, *A New History of Ethiopia,* trans. J. P. Gent (London, 1682), 72.

69. Thomas Phillips, "A Journal of a Voyage Made in the Hannibal of London, Ann. 1693, 1694," in *A Collection of Voyages and Travels,* 6 vols. (London, 1732), vol. 6: 171–239, 219.

70. Jordan, *White over Black,* xiv. See also, for example, James Walvin, *Black and White: The Negro and English Society, 1555–1945* (London, 1973); Dorothy Hammond and Alta Jablow, *The Myth of Africa* (New York, 1977); Peter Fryer, *Staying Power: The History of Black People in Britain* (London, 1984); Kim F. Hall, *Things of Darkness: Economies of Race and Gender in Early Modern England* (Ithaca, NY, 1995); Alden T. Vaughan and Virginia Mason Vaughan, "Before Othello: Elizabethan Representations of Sub-Saharan Africans," *WMQ* 54, no. 1 (Jan. 1997): 19–44; Virginia Mason Vaughan, *Performing Blackness on the English Stage, 1500–1800* (New York, 2005). A similar argument is made with respect to French materials in William B. Cohen, *The French Encounter with Africans: White Response to Blacks, 1530–1880* (Bloomington, IN, 1980); and Christopher L. Miller, *Blank Darkness: Africanist Discourse in French* (Chicago, 1985).

71. Jordan, *White over Black,* 42. The formulation that is paraphrased in the final sentence of this paragraph appears in Jordan, *White over Black,* 152, in the course of a chapter titled "The Dynamics of Interracial Sex."

72. Martyr, *Decades of the Newe Worlde,* trans. Eden, 310v; Jordan, *White over Black,* 19 and 20.

73. Democritus Junior [Robert Burton], *The Anatomy of Melancholy* (Oxford, 1621), pt. 2, sect. 2, memb. 3: 321.

EPILOGUE

1. The Roman legal tradition thus reflected a particular account of freedom, as well as an account of slavery. Freedom was the natural condition of humankind, but it was not the only legitimate condition. In the course of human affairs, the natural freedom of all persons could be altered in certain circumstances. The Roman tradition thus accommodated both clear convictions about a pristine state of human freedom and the extreme forms of domination that had emerged in modern life. In the early-modern theories of natural law and natural rights that unfolded in the context of the reception of Roman legal ideas, it was common to remark upon this distinctive conception of freedom. The influential scholar of the civil law Alberico Gentili noted in this vein that humans "were not created free by nature so absolutely that very many of us may not be made slaves." Alberico Gentili, *De iure belli libri tres,* ed. James Brown Scott, trans. John C. Rolfe, 2 vols. (London, 1933), vol. 2, bk. 3, ch. 9: 332. See also, for example, Hugo Grotius, *The Rights of War and Peace,* trans. John Morrice (London, 1738), bk. II, ch. XXII, pt. XI: 478; and Samuel Pufendorf, *Of the Law of Nature and Nations,* trans. Basil Kennett (Oxford, 1703), bk. VI, ch. III, pt. IX (labeled XI): 127.

2. The principle in Roman law that the children of female slaves inherited their status was consistent across the standard texts of the *Corpus Juris.* See, for example, *The Institutes of Gaius,* trans. W. M. Gordon and O. F. Robinson (Ithaca, NY, 1988), 63: I.82; *The Digest of Justinian,* trans. and ed. Alan Watson, 4 vols. (Philadelphia, 1985), vol. 1: I.5.5.1; and *Justinian's Institutes,* trans. Peter Birks and Grant McLeod (Ithaca, NY, 1987), 39: I.3.4.

It was also the case in Roman law that the offspring of domesticated animals became the property of their owners. But there was one prominent exception to this rule. If an animal was in the possession of the owner of a usufruct in the animal, then its offspring—who were referred to as its "fruits," or in Latin *fructus*—became the property of the owner of the usufruct. A question thus arose in the minds of the Roman jurists as to whether the children of slaves would also be treated in this manner. The jurists decided that they would not. After all, as Gaius explained in the *Digest,* the children of slaves were persons, and "it seemed absurd that a human being should count as fruits, since nature provided all fruits for man." *Digest of Justinian,* trans. and ed. Watson, vol. 2: XXII.1.28: and for a similar statement from Ulpian, see *Digest of Justinian,* trans. and ed. Watson, vol. 1: VII.1.68. That said, in the same manner as beasts of burden that were not held under a usufruct, the children of slaves became the property of their owners—a point of resemblance between slaves and beasts that was much remarked upon in early-modern English culture.

3. For treatments of these issues in standard studies of the common law, see, for example, *Bracton on the Laws and Customs of England,* trans. Samuel E. Thorne, 4 vols. (Cambridge, MA, 1968–1977), vol. 2: 30–31; Henry Swinburne, *A Briefe Treatise of Last Testaments and Willes* (London, 1590), pt. 2, §7: 43v–44v; and Edward Coke, *The First Part of the Institutes of the Lawes of England* (London, 1628), bk. 2, ch. 11, sect. 187: 123v.

4. "Act XII. Negro womens children to serve according to the condition of the mother," in William Waller Hening, *The Statutes at Large; Being a Collection of All the Laws of Virginia,* vol. 2 (New York, 1823), 170. For the most careful introduction to these issues, see Christopher Tomlins, *Freedom Bound: Law, Labor, and Civic Identity in Colonizing English America, 1580–1865* (New York, 2010), 401–508.

5. For their part, the Roman authors of the *Corpus Juris* never bothered to explain or defend the permanent and heritable character of slave status. The standard pattern of status inheritance under the law of nations was that it passed down from mothers to their children. Since slavery came into Roman law under the law of nations, the jurists accepted that slave status would pass down in this manner.

In early-modern European culture, the most careful attempts to think through the standard structure of Roman law were those that appeared in the classic theories of natural law and natural rights. But not even the authors of these theories devoted much attention to the reasons for which slave status was heritable over time. Both Grotius and Pufendorf cited the most common early-modern argument on this point, which noted that because slavery arose as an alternative to death for captives taken in war, the children of persons who had been enslaved would also owe their lives to their masters, who could have chosen to kill their parents. See for example Grotius, *Rights of War and Peace,* trans. Morrice, III.VII.I–V: 602–604; and Pufendorf, *Law of Nature and Nations,* trans. Kennett, VI.III.IX (labeled XI): 127. But both authors also expressed discomfort with this argument, which they believed was not authorized by natural law. Both wished to limit slave status as much as possible to those persons who had entered into some act or agreement that would warrant their enslavement, and of course children who were born into slavery had never done this. In turn, Locke, who denied that slavery could be inherited at all, can be seen to have exposed the weakness of arguments put forward in favor of this common custom in the Roman tradition. See John Locke, *Two Treatises of Government* (London, 1713), 2T §179: 326.

6. See, for example, *Barbot on Guinea: The Writings of Jean Barbot on West Africa, 1678–1712,* ed. P. E. H. Hair, Adam Jones, and Robin Law, 2 vols. (London, 1992), vol. 2: 549–550 and 639–640.

7. Thomas Phillips, "A Journal of a Voyage Made in the Hannibal of London, Ann. 1693, 1694," in *A Collection of Voyages and Travels,* 6 vols. (London, 1732), vol. 6: 171–239, 219.

8. See Hans Sloane, *A Voyage to the Islands Madera, Barbados, Nieves, S. Christophers and Jamaica, with the Natural History . . . of the Last of Those Islands* (London, 1707). For an excellent biographical account, which devotes particular attention to his time on Jamaica and its importance for his later career, see James Delbourgo, *Collecting the World: Hans Sloane and the Origins of the British Museum* (Cambridge, MA, 2017).

9. Sloane, *A Voyage to . . . Jamaica,* lvi; and George Sandys, *A Relation of a Journey begun An. Dom. 1610* (London, 1637; orig. pub. 1615), 136.

The sale of children into slavery on the western coast of Africa was also mentioned in another work from this period that Sloane would have known well: *The History of the Carriby-Islands,* trans. John Davies (London, 1666). This book was a translation from another account: César de Rochefort, *Histoire naturelle & morale des Iles Antilles de l'Amerique* (Rotterdam, 1658). Davies provided a subtle treatment of the sources of slavery for the Africans held as slaves in the European colonies in the Caribbean. He explained that some of these persons had been enslaved in Africa as "Prisoners in War." But then there were some other Africans whose parents had sold them to avoid starvation in times of famine. "When they are reduc'd to those exigencies," Davies remarked, "the Father makes no difficulty to sell his children for bread" (200–201).

10. Sloane, *A Voyage to . . . Jamaica,* lvii.

11. Sloane, *A Voyage to . . . Jamaica,* Preface (B2) and lvii.

12. Sloane, *A Voyage to . . . Jamaica,* lvii. For a similar description of the punishments inflicted upon the enslaved Africans on Jamaica, produced by another English visitor to the island around the same time when Sloane was there, see *Jamaica in 1687: The Taylor Manuscript at the National Library of Jamaica,* ed. David Buisseret (Kingston, Jamaica, 2008), 269–270.

That the enslaved Africans in the Caribbean colonies seemed to welcome death, believing that when they died they returned home, was a common theme in English accounts from this period. See also, for example, Richard Ligon, *A True & Exact History of the Island of Barbados* (London, 1657), 51; George Warren, *An Impartial Description of Surinam upon the Continent of Guiana in America* (London, 1667),

19–20; and *Jamaica in 1687: The Taylor Manuscript at the National Library of Jamaica*, ed. Buisseret, 272–273.

13. For the instructions from Charles II quoted in this paragraph, see *Calendar of State Papers, Colonial Series, 1574–1660,* ed. W. Noël Sainsbury (London, 1860), no. 59: 492–493. For similar demands from metropolitan officials, see also, for example, the discussions that surrounded the appointment of a new colonial governor for Barbados, Richard Dutton, in 1680: *Calendar of State Papers, Colonial Series, America and the West Indies, 1667–1680,* ed. W. Noël Sainsbury and J. W. Fortescue (London, 1896), no. 1484 (588) and no. 1522 (607–608); and *Calendar of State Papers, Colonial Series, America and the West Indies, 1681–1685,* ed. J. W. Fortescue (London, 1898), no. 59 (24–25).

14. See Katharine Gerbner, *Christian Slavery: Conversion and Race in the Protestant Atlantic World* (Philadelphia, 2018). See also Travis Glasson, *Mastering Christianity: Missionary Anglicanism and Slavery in the Atlantic World* (New York, 2012).

15. William Edmundson, *A Journal of the Life, Travels, Sufferings, and Labour of Love in the Work of the Ministry of . . . William Edmundson* (London, 1715), 53 and 75; "An Act to prevent the People Called Quakers, from bringing Negroes to their Meeting," in *Acts, Passed in the Island of Barbados,* ed. Richard Hall (London, 1764), no. 64 (97–98); and *Calendar of State Papers, Colonial Series, America and the West Indies, 1667–1680,* ed. Sainsbury and Fortescue, no. 1535 (611–612).

16. For learned treatments of these and related issues, see Gerbner, *Christian Slavery,* 13–30; and Keith Thomas, *In Pursuit of Civility: Manners and Civilization in Early Modern England* (Waltham, MA, 2018), 86–133 and 159–182.

17. For reference, see, in order: Francisco de Vitoria, "On the Law of War," in Francisco de Vitoria, *Political Writings,* trans. and ed. Anthony Pagden and Jeremy Lawrence (Cambridge, UK, 2010; orig. pub. 1991), 293–327; Gentili, *De iure belli,* trans. Rolfe, vol. 2, bk. 3, ch. 9: 328–335; Jean Bodin, *The Six Bookes of a Commonweale,* trans. Richard Knolles (London, 1606), bk. 1, ch. 5: 32–46; and Grotius, *Rights of War and Peace,* trans. Morrice, III.VII: 602–608. For discussions of slavery in learned studies of the customs of the peoples of the world, see, for example, Charles Molloy, *De Jure Maritimo et Navali: Or, A Treatise of Affaires Maritime, And of Commerce* (London, 1676), bk. 3, ch. 1: 385–394; and Pierre Charron, *Of Wisdom: Three Books,* trans. George Stanhope (London, 1697), bk. 1, ch. 48: 437–442.

18. For subtle overviews of these issues, see Michael Guasco, *Slaves and Englishmen: Human Bondage in the Early Modern Atlantic World* (Philadelphia, 2014), 195–226; and Rebecca Anne Goetz, *The Baptism of Early Virginia: How Christianity Created Race* (Baltimore, 2012), 86–111.

For a report on an English court case decided in 1677 that affirmed the property status of enslaved Africans "untill they become Christians; and thereby they are Infranchised," see *Butts and Penny,* in Joseph Keeble, *Reports in the Court of Kings Bench at Westminster,* 3 vols. (London, 1685), vol. 3: 785. This case is treated in an important article: Holly Brewer, "Creating a Common Law of Slavery for England and its New World Empire," *Law and History Review* 39, no. 4 (Nov. 2021): 765–834.

19. Ligon, *True & Exact History of the Island of Barbados,* 50.

20. "Act III. An act declaring that baptisme of slaves doth not exempt them from bondage," in William Waller Hening, *The Statutes at Large; Being a Collection of all the Laws of Virginia,* vol. 2 (New York, 1823), 260; and "The Fundamental Constitutions of Carolina," in *The Statutes at Large of South Carolina,* ed. Thomas Cooper (Columbia, SC, 1836), vol. 1: 43–56, 55. It should be noted that the 1664 proclamation of laws for the colonial province of the Duke of York, known as the Duke's Laws, made a statement similar to those that soon followed for Virginia and Carolina. It stated that the law would not "sett at liberty Any Negroe or Indian Servant who shall turne Christian after he shall have been bought by Any Person." This provision could seem to have left open the chance that "Any Negroe or Indian" who became Christian could not then be purchased as a slave in the future. "The Duke of York's Laws," in *The Statutes at Large of Pennsylvania in the Time of William Penn,* ed. Gail McKnight Beckman (New York, 1976), 71–110, 78. On these and other similar laws from the period, see Tomlins, *Freedom Bound,* 452–504.

21. "An Act For the better Ordering of Slaves," in *The Laws of Jamaica, Passed by the Assembly, and Confirmed by His Majesty in Council* (London, 1684), 140–148, 140; and "An Act for the better ordering of Slaves," in *The Statutes at Large of South Carolina,* ed. David J. McCord, vol. 7: 343–347, 343.

22. "An Act on Barbados," in Ruth Paley, Cristina Malcolmson, and Michael Hunter, "Parliament and Slavery," *Slavery and Abolition* 31, no. 2 (Jun. 2010): 257–281, doc. 3: 268–269.

23. Robert Boyle, *Experiments and Considerations Touching Colours* (London, 1664), 151–167 ("Experiment XI"), 165; and "An Act to remove certain discouragements & Hinderances of the Conversion of the Infidels," in Paley, Malcolmson, and Hunter, "Parliament and Slavery," doc. 4: 269–271. This act, like the previous one cited above and the next one that will be cited below, is held in the Boyle Papers in the Royal Society. For a nuanced and comprehensive assessment, see Michael Hunter, *Boyle: Between God and Science* (New Haven, CT, 2009).

24. "Proposals for the propagating of the Christian Religion and converting of Slaves, whether Negroes or Indians in the English Plantations," in Paley, Malcolmson, and Hunter, "Parliament and Slavery," doc. 5: 271; and "Proposalls for the propagating of the Christian Religion and Converting of Slaves whether Negroes or Indians in the English Plantations," in Peter N. Moore, "An Enslaver's Guide to Slavery Reform: William Dunlop's 1690 Proposals to Christianize Slaves in the British Atlantic," *Church History* 91 (2022): 264–285, 283–284, 284. In the version of this proposal that is held in the Boyle Papers in the Royal Society, the final quoted phrase has been altered to read "knowledg, Arts & Sciences."

25. In advance of their treatment of the African slave trade, the editors of the *Athenian Mercury* had addressed what they seem to have believed was a related topic. The final question that they had answered in the previous issue of the periodical was "*Whether Negroes shall rise so at the last Day?*" The editors at first took this to be a question about "Whether *White* or *Black* is the *better Colour?*" To this, they responded that neither was the better color: the Negroes, who preferred black to white, "no doubt on't are as much in the right on't as we." But then the editors shifted their tone. They noted that black was the color of night, while white was the color of day. They explained that the blackness of the Negro was an "accidental Imperfection" of his physical form, which he would not take with him into Heaven. Rather he would leave it behind and assume "a brighter and a better" color upon his ascent. That was the editors' final answer to the question they had received. It was one that drew upon a number of common themes in the complex discourse on blackness in early-modern English culture. In turn, once the editors had reached a resolution about the manner in which the Negroes would meet their eternal reward, they felt prepared to answer a question about the commerce that delivered some of them across the Atlantic as slaves—which was a topic that proved to turn precisely on the matter of their salvation. See *Athenian Mercury* 3, no. 29 (1691): q. 6.

26. *Athenian Mercury* 3, no. 30 (1691): q. 1.

27. Morgan Godwyn, *The Negro's & Indians Advocate, Suing for their Admission into the Church* (London, 1680), 26. In 1681, the colonial governor on Barbados presented a proposal to the assembly for the conversion of slaves to the Christian faith. The assembly delivered a response similar to those that Godwyn had received and had now made public in his 1680 pamphlet. The assembly refused to act upon the proposal, because, "as to the making the negroes Christians, their savage brutishness renders them wholly incapable." See *Calendar of State Papers, Colonial Series, America and the West Indies, 1681–1685,* ed. Fortescue, no. 59 (24–25).

In a detailed and sinuous narrative, Rebecca Anne Goetz has maintained that the planters in Virginia in this period also came to believe that the African and Indian persons in the colonial settlement were incapable of Christian conversion. The artful term that Goetz has applied to this belief is "hereditary heathenism." Goetz is correct in the claim that the radical difference between Anglo-Americans and Africans and Indians was most often articulated in terms of their relation to Christian religion. Religion, as she explains, was the central site for the construction of human difference in seventeenth-century English America. See Rebecca Anne Goetz, *The Baptism of Early Virginia: How Christianity Created Race* (Baltimore, 2012).

That said, there is in fact little evidence for the development of a doctrine of "hereditary heathenism" in seventeenth-century Virginia. It seems to be the case that ideas about human difference were developed in response to the prospect that African and Indian persons would become Christian—not in order to assert that these persons could never do so. Much of Goetz's evidence for her central claim about Virginia comes from sources more concerned with Barbados. Even here, efforts at conversion had advanced further than Godwyn was aware or perhaps prepared to admit. See Katharine Gerbner, *Christian Slavery: Conversion and Race in the Protestant Atlantic World* (Philadelphia, 2018).

28. Godwyn, *Negro's & Indians Advocate,* 61: see also 27–32 and 61–78.

29. Godwyn, *Negro's & Indians Advocate,* 3.

30. Godwyn, *Negro's & Indians Advocate,* 38 and 21. Godwyn was also well aware of reports, which dated to the time of the Bible, of the establishment of Christian religion in parts of Africa and in particular in Ethiopia. See Godwyn, *Negro's & Indians Advocate,* 55–59.

31. Godwyn, *Negro's & Indians Advocate,* 36.

32. Godwyn, *Negro's & Indians Advocate,* Preface (unpaginated). Godwyn developed this indictment of the culture of the slave colonies into a sermon that he delivered in churches throughout London. This sermon was printed as Morgan Godwyn, *Trade preferr'd before Religion, and Christ made to give place to Mammon* (London, 1685).

33. Godwyn, *Negro's & Indians Advocate,* 3. Godwyn returned at several points to the Spanish conquest of the Indies as a point of reference in his polemic; see, for example, 82 and 107. His reference to the Spanish position on the "Brutality of the *Americans*" is on 12.

34. Thomas Trapham, *A Discourse of the State of Health in the Island of Jamaica* (London, 1679), 113.

35. See Godwyn, *Negro's & Indians Advocate,* 41–61. Godwyn was also careful to note that even if the Africans on Barbados were the descendants of Ham, they were still the children of God and entitled to inclusion within the Christian fold. According to Godwyn, one more early-modern biblical interpretation that had been seized upon and turned to vicious effect on Barbados was Isaac La Peyrère's notorious proposal that there had been some men before Adam. The planters had asserted that the Africans they held as slaves must have descended from these "Pre-Adamites." Godwyn ridiculed and worked to refute this assertion as well; see 14–19.

36. Trapham, *Discourse of the State of Health in the Island of Jamaica,* 115–117.

The most probable printed source for Trapham's assertion that African peoples had had "unsutable communication" with beasts was Thomas Herbert, *Some Yeares Travels into Africa & Asia the Great,* 4th ed. (London, 1677). In the course of his account of the people who lived at the Cape of Good Hope, Herbert had said that these people were "thought to have unnatural mixture" and "beastly copulation or conjuncture" with apes (14). For his part, Godwyn also appeared to admit that in Africa there were "too frequent unnatural conjunctures" between the native peoples and "*Irrational* Creatures, such as the Ape and Drill, that do carry with them some resemblances of Men." Godwyn, *Negro's & Indians Advocate,* 12. As his source, Godwyn mentioned the recent narrative of the French traveler Jean-Baptiste Tavernier; see *The Six Voyages of John Baptista Tavernier,* trans. J.P. (London, 1677). In all likelihood, however, this was a mistake, and Godwyn's source was also Herbert, who had in addition mentioned the Spanish debates about the human status of the Americans that made such an impression upon Godwyn.

37. Thomas Tryon, who had worked as a tradesman on Barbados in the 1660s, does not seem to have found the Aristotelian idiom in use on the island. That said, as he assumed the voice of an enslaved African to complain of the cruelties of the plantation complex, Tryon did work to refute the planters' presumption that, "by some super-excellent or higher Dignity of Nature above us, you claim a Right to make us your Slaves and Vassals." Philotheos Physiologus [Thomas Tryon], *Friendly Advice to the Gentlemen-Planters of the East and West Indies* (London, 1684), 114.

38. *Athenian Mercury* 15, no. 18 (1694): q. 1.

39. Aristotle, *Politics,* in *The Complete Works of Aristotle: The Revised Oxford Translation,* ed. Jonathan Barnes, 2 vols. (Princeton, NJ, 2014), vol. 2, 1986–2129, 1990: 1254a23–24.

Acknowledgments

IN THE PAST DECADE, this book has become such a part of my life that anyone who has known me—family and friends, mentors and students, colleagues and bartenders around the world—has had a role in it. I hope that I have made clear to them all how much each has contributed to my life. I hope as well that each is able to see themselves reflected in this book. Thank you, all.

I owe a special debt to those scholars who showed me how to be a scholar: Richard Brodhead, Peter Euben, Michael Gillespie, Ruth Grant, Malachi Hacohen, Fredric Jameson, Michael Valdez Moses, Alexander Rosenberg, Joyce Chaplin, James Engell, James Kloppenberg, Jill Lepore, Russell Muirhead, Eric Nelson, Nancy Rosenblum, John Stauffer, Richard Tuck, and Cheryl Welch.

I owe a debt as well to those dozens and dozens of scholars—in truth, well over a hundred—who took the time to talk with me about their work or who read and commented upon parts of mine. In particular, I would like to thank those scholars who read and commented upon the full draft of this book in manuscript workshops that took place in 2022 and 2023: Susan McWilliams Barndt, Jeffrey Collins, Aaron Garrett, S. Sara Monoson, Paul Monod, Neil Roberts, Michael Zuckert, Lorraine Daston, Adom Getachew, Timothy Harrison, Fredrik Jonsson, Sankar Muthu, and Kenneth Warren.

This book was conceived and composed at four institutions: Duke University, Harvard University, Middlebury College, and The University of Chicago. Research on rare materials was done at the David M. Rubenstein Rare Book and Manuscript Library at Duke University; the Newberry Library in Chicago and the Hanna Holborn Gray Special Collections Research Center in the Joseph Regenstein Library at The University of Chicago; and Widener Library, Houghton Library, and the Harvard Map Collection at Harvard University. Above all, I would like to thank the expert librarians at Houghton Library and the Harvard Map Collection, who saw this book develop from start to finish. At a crucial point toward the end, a generous grant from the Institute for Humane Studies enabled me to complete the manuscript.

It is my sincere pleasure to thank Harvard University Press, where Editorial Director Sharmila Sen first put her faith in me and my work. I would like to thank the two anonymous reviewers for the Press, as well as the Syndics of the Press, for their careful attention to the manuscript. My editor, the inimitable Emily Silk, has been a true partner in the realization of our shared vision for this book. I cannot believe how fortunate I have been to work with her.

Like much of my life, my work on this book has been shaped by my sister, Clare, who at once showed me how to persevere and how to have fun. My brother, Adrian, showed me the same—and also how to dedicate a life to a craft. This book is dedicated to my mother and my father, both writers, who first taught me how to read and then how to live—and then how to write. In the final period of work, which was a difficult time in my life, I met Priyanka Sethy. It was the beginning of a beautiful friendship.

Index

Page numbers in italics refer to figures.